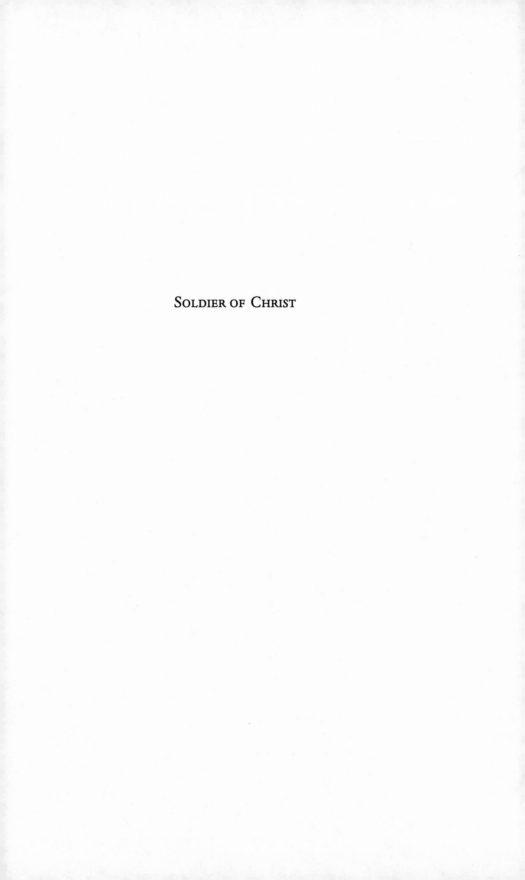

SOLDIER OF CHRIST

SOLDIER OF CHRIST

The Life of Pope Pius XII

ROBERT A. VENTRESCA

THE BELKNAP PRESS OF
HARVARD UNIVERSITY PRESS
Cambridge, Massachusetts, and London, England   2013

Printed in the United States of America

Library of Congress Cataloging-in-Publication Data

Ventresca, Robert.
Soldier of Christ : the life of Pope Pius XII / Robert A. Ventresca.
p.   cm.
Includes bibliographical references and index.
ISBN 978-0-674-04961-1 (alk. paper)
1. Pius XII, Pope, 1876–1958.   2. Popes—Biography.   I. Title.
BX1378.V46   2013
282.092—dc23
[B]   2012029809

Contents

SOLDIER OF CHRIST

Prologue

The Pius War

Miserere mei Deus secundum magnam misericordiam tuam: Have mercy on me, O God, in your great mercy.[1] With these words from the first verse of Psalm 51, Eugenio Pacelli, known to the world as Pope Pius XII, began his last will and testament.[2] It was scribbled on the back of a used envelope. Pacelli had a habit of saving and using scraps of paper for note taking, an idiosyncrasy that has contributed to the uncharitable caricature of the pope as an aloof eccentric.

By tradition, Psalm 51 is considered the "deathbed psalm"—recited as a form of confession when one is nearing death.[3] When he wrote his brief testament in 1956, two years before he died, Pacelli seemed resigned to the judgment of history, and of his God. He asked "with humility" for forgiveness from all whom he had offended, hurt, or scandalized "by word or by deed." He pleaded with those charged with caring for his mortal remains not to erect grand monuments to his memory. "It would be good enough if my poor mortal remains," he wrote, "are placed simply in a holy place, the more obscure the better." Beyond that, the usual Catholic prayers for the repose of his soul would suffice.

After his death in October 1958, things did not go quite as he had desired.

His tomb is plain—a simple white sarcophagus inscribed with his name and the traditional *labarum,* the monogram of Christ. It sits in a small side chapel just beneath Bernini's spiraling altar in St. Peter's Basilica, not far from the spot where, as tradition has it, Saint Peter himself was buried. Much more conspicuous is the imposing monument to Pacelli on the main floor of the basilica. Commissioned by some of the grateful cardinals he created during his pontificate, the massive bronze monument is the work of the Italian sculptor Francesco Messina.

Completed in 1964, Messina's *Pius XII* is, in a word, monumental. Mounted atop a marble pedestal, the larger-than-life figure of the pope is clad in a massive undulating cape that rises several feet to meet an outstretched hand poised, seemingly, to impart a blessing. The earnest, bespectacled face of Pacelli, with its characteristic angular features, is crowned by a towering bishop's miter, replete with intricate designs in a brilliant bronze gold finish. But it is the cape and outstretched hand that command attention. One source has it that the outstretched hand symbolizes the pope's ardent determination to put an end to the Second World War. Others believe that the pope's resolute gaze symbolizes his prophetic vision of the war's inevitably disastrous outcome.[4] Here is Eugenio Pacelli, soldier of Christ—a spiritual warrior stirring to resist the gathering forces of the enemies of Christ, which threatened from all sides.[5]

In fact, Pacelli's likeness is barely discernible, enveloped as it is by the weighty liturgical vestments that project an unmistakable sense of the power and dignity of the bishop of Rome. Messina's monument seems designed to inspire awe and admiration of the papacy as an institution, not to memorialize a dead pope. We have here not Eugenio Pacelli as he was in life but Pope Pius XII as his many admirers saw him or wanted him to be—a pope for all seasons.

The German playwright Rolf Hochhuth, in his controversial but highly influential drama about Pius XII's wartime activities, known in English as *The Deputy* (1963), also projected onto Pacelli his own assumptions of the papal office. In his stage notes, he advised actors cast to play Pius XII to remember "that his Holiness is much less a person than an institution: grand gestures, lively movements of his extraordinarily beautiful hands, and smiling, aristocratic coldness, together with the icy glint of his eyes behind the gold-rimmed glasses—these should suffice."[6]

Hochhuth's version of Pius XII contributed amply to what has become by far the most common perception of the wartime pope. In this account, Eugenio Pacelli is an ethereal figure who moves in a rarified, sheltered environment, far removed from the gritty daily reality of the millions of faithful whom he calls his flock. This Pacelli is the privileged son of an aristocratic Roman family whose titles were earned in the nineteenth century by dint of unyielding loyalty and service to the papacy. He is no ordinary parish priest. Intelligent, industrious, yet taciturn, Pacelli seems destined to wield influence. Prodigious academic abilities open the door to years of study in canon law, and then further study and practice in the art of papal diplomacy. So much time immersed in books and dusty archives, the argument goes, left Eugenio Pacelli with precious little pastoral experience, little meaningful contact with the ordinary faithful whose lives he would come to influence in profound if understated ways.

Pacelli's odd mannerisms and habits contributed to his reputation as someone painfully out of step with the world around him. Much will be made by future commentators of his habit of dining alone, his sole companion a pet bird perched atop his shoulder. Equally intriguing is the rumor that Pacelli issued orders to his gardener to refrain from facing the pope directly. Still other stories verged on the absurd: according to one account the pope decreed that his staff were to be on their knees when conversing with him by telephone.[7]

Whereas Messina's *Pius XII* wears the heavy cloak of spiritual leadership in opposing the approach of war, Hochhuth's pope wears the moral responsibilities of an institution that failed to defend the weak and powerless in the face of a ruthless and incorrigible enemy. The play's chief protagonist, the valiant young Jesuit Father Riccardo Fontana, who tries in vain to get the Vatican to issue an unequivocal public condemnation of Nazi brutalities, openly questions whether a pope such as Pacelli, who "stands so very high above the destinies of the world," can possibly comprehend the plight of the thousands of victims who crowd every corner of war-torn Europe, some of them under his very window. "The victims . . . ," Riccardo asks, "does [the pope] truly bring them to his mind? . . . Do you think he is *there,* that he has ever watched with his mind's eye—has ever seen the way they are deported from Paris . . . children under five snatched from their parents . . . eleven thousand Poles in mobile gas chambers—their cries, their prayers—and the laughing SS thugs."

Through Riccardo, Hochhuth delivers what has become for many the defining image of Pius XII during the Holocaust: "A deputy of Christ who sees these things and nonetheless permits reasons of state to seal his lips—who wastes even one day in thought, hesitates even for an hour to lift his anguished voice in one anathema to chill the blood of every last man on earth—that Pope is . . . a criminal."[8]

Hochhuth's Pius XII is indeed less a man than an institution. More to the point, the wartime pope is made to symbolize a deeply flawed institution that lacked the political foresight, spiritual integrity, and courage to confront publicly the Nazis' murderous treatment of the Jews. Here was a Vicar of Christ who opted for diplomatic caution and protocol in times that demanded the prophetic, even radical actions of a martyr.

In recent years, books with such provocative titles as *Hitler's Pope, A Moral Reckoning,* and *Fatal Silence* have solidified the image of Pius XII as, at best, timid and indecisive, and, at worst, uncharitable, anti-Semitic, and even sympathetic to Nazism. As the historian Frank J. Coppa observed, since the publication of *The Deputy,* scholarly research and public debate over the controversial role of Pius XII during the Holocaust have been "decidedly partisan," swinging from exaggerated suggestions of the wartime pope as complicit with Nazism, to hagiographic apologias of Pius XII as wartime saint. In a provocative response to Pacelli's critics, some commentators have suggested that Pius XII be considered a "Righteous Gentile" for, they say, his part in directing papal representatives and other Catholic institutions throughout Italy and Europe to rescue hundreds of thousands of Jews from certain death at the hands of the Nazis.[9]

In death, much more so than in life, Pius XII has become an intensely polarizing figure—to some, he is a venerable saint, and to others he is a damnable silent witness to unimaginable atrocities in the heart of Europe. The incessant partisanship of the so-called Pius War has consistently sacrificed historical interpretation for polemical and political purposes.[10] This pattern is evident even within the Catholic world, where, from the time of the Second Vatican Council in the mid-1960s, the figure of Pius XII has served as a lightning rod for both nostalgic conservatives and disgruntled liberals. For the former, Pius XII was the last truly magisterial pontiff; for the latter, he embodied everything that was wrong with the Catholic Church before the affable John XXIII (Roncalli), the "good pope," came to air out the static, stultifying atmosphere of the church before Vatican II. This elementary division was evident even at the time of the council when Pope Paul VI (Montini) officially began the process to bring beatification and perhaps eventually sainthood to both of his immediate predecessors. Recommending the causes of both Pius XII and John XXIII, Pope Paul VI reasoned, "will be in answer to the desire that has been expressed by innumerable voices in favor of each of these Popes. In this way, history will be assured the patrimony of their spiritual legacy."

Montini, who worked side-by-side with Pius XII throughout the tumultuous war years, was keen to craft an alternative narrative to the one taking shape in people's minds in the wake of Hochhuth's controversial play. Tellingly, two years before he formally opened the cause to have Pius XII made a saint, when he was still the cardinal archbishop of Milan, Montini wrote to the British Catholic periodical *The Tablet* to challenge Hochhuth's reading of a history Montini himself had lived. "History," the future Paul VI wrote, "will vindicate the conduct of Pius XII when confronted by the criminal excesses of the Nazi regime." For Montini, history would set the record straight; it was the only effective antidote to Hochhuth's version, which amounted to little more than the "artificial manipulation of facts to fit a preconceived idea."[11]

Despite Paul VI's belief that the path to sainthood for both popes would proceed "for no motive other than the cult of their holiness," it was clear even to outside observers that internal church politics would come into play. Referring to Pius XII, the *New York Times* reported that the "austere, distant and intellectual Pope has become the focus of conservative admiration." By contrast, his successor, John XXIII, who was described as "warmly human and simple," was said to be the "favorite" of the so-called progressives, if only because he had convened the Second Vatican Council, at which the "progressive" views seem to have prevailed.[12]

And so it has been, back and forth, for decades now. Despite occasional lulls in the Pius War, a dogged attachment to competing caricatures of Pius XII, to say nothing of the canonization cause, means that the war of words will persist, generating point and counterpoint *ad infinitum*. The tendency to see Pius XII as less a man than an institution has resulted in an abundant manipulation of facts—to borrow from Montini—arranged selectively to fit preconceived notions of what this pope did or did not do; what he said or did not say; what he could have or should have done. I leave it to the reader to decide whether history has vindicated Pius XII, whatever that means. It is to history, after all, that we must turn to find Eugenio Pacelli, the man, priest, diplomat, and pope.

The vast literature chronicling Pius XII's long and eventful pontificate has mostly centered on his seeming failure to speak out clearly and firmly during World War II to defend European Jews facing systematic persecution and murder by the Nazis. The claim that he turned his back on the Jews, and the riposte it provoked, gave life and sustenance to the "Pius War." Yet this war of words has done more harm than good to our understanding of this central figure of twentieth-century history. With very few exceptions, studies of Pius XII have offered a distorted or highly selective picture of the subject. We have become accustomed to reading interpretive leaps, which are grounded on counterfactual or normative claims about what the pope could have or should have done rather than a reasoned assessment of what he did or did not do—and why. This is to say nothing of the fact that, as understandable as it is, such a heavy focus on Pius XII's wartime record has obscured our view of the entire span of his active life in the service of the papacy. It is easy to forget that Pacelli's pontificate lasted for thirteen years after the end of World War II. We know comparatively little about the Cold War years and even less about Pius XII's prodigious teachings, which sought to address internal and external realities of Catholicism in rapidly changing times. However we might assess it, there can be no doubt that Eugenio Pacelli's pontificate left an indelible mark on the papacy and influenced the Catholic encounter with the modern world in ways we have scarcely begun to understand.

I

The Black Nobility and Papal Rome

When the future Pope Pius XII was ordained a priest at Easter, April 1899, he distributed ordination cards to family and friends that read simply: *Eugenio Pacelli, Roman*. It was a fitting way for the young Pacelli to describe himself, an expression of that quintessential pride and self-awareness characteristic of one born and raised in the Eternal City. But there was more to it than civic pride. After all, Eugenio Pacelli hailed from a new generation of the so-called black nobility, a class of Roman society distinguished by its loyalty and service to the Holy See. Eugenio's father and brother were both lawyers associated with the Vatican. His grandfather, the patriarch Marcantonio Pacelli, served the papacy in the tumultuous years of Italian Unification, when anticlericalism ran rampant in Rome, and earned for the Pacelli family honorific titles and a privileged place in the papal court, in gratitude for his unwavering loyalty even after the forcible capture of Rome by the young Italian state spelled the end of papal temporal sovereignty.

The capture of Rome and the struggles that ensued between church and state—which historians have dubbed the Roman question—left an indelible mark on Eugenio Pacelli. In those years, life in the Eternal City seemed an eternal squabble, and worse. The city was the scene of sometimes violent confrontation between anticlerical elements and papal defenders. When Pius IX died in 1878, he could not be buried in the Church of San Lorenzo Outside-the-Walls as he had hoped. Officials feared vehement protests from extreme anticlerical forces. When Pius IX's remains finally were moved to the San Lorenzo church in 1881, a mob of protesters tried to seize the coffin and dump it in the Tiber River. They were stopped at the last minute by local authorities, amid the invocations of the *Our Father* and *Hail Mary* by loyal papists and the cries of the anticlericals shouting, "Death to the pope! Death to the priests! Throw that filthy carcass into the river!"[1]

It was impossible to grow up in the Pacelli household and not be profoundly influenced by such an atmosphere. The fall of the last papal state and the loss of papal temporal power presented a serious challenge to the Pacelli family, and to all the black nobility, to say nothing of the papacy itself. Loss of the territorial independence of the pope caused the gravest concern. Experience had taught the Vatican that territorial sovereignty was vital to defending the pope's claims of spiritual sovereignty over the universal church. As Pius IX said to the French ambassador in 1871, "All that I want is a small corner of the earth where I am master . . . so long as I do not have this little corner of earth, I shall not be able to exercise in their fullness my spiritual functions."[2]

Pius IX's dream was not realized until 1929, with the establishment of Vatican City, whose creation was due in no small measure to the skillful negotiations of Francesco Pacelli, brother to the future Pius XII. At the time, Eugenio was a papal representative in Germany, soon to be called back to assume the office of the Vatican's secretary of state. Ever since he was a young boy playing in the narrow cobbled streets of central Rome, all of his personal, academic, and pastoral experiences prepared him for the lifelong task of defending that "small corner of the earth" where the pope was master and the church had concrete rights to protect its spiritual autonomy within the modern secular state.

Eugenio Pacelli, Roman

Eugenio was the third of four children born to Filippo Pacelli and Virginia Graziosi, arriving late in the evening of March 2, 1876. The family apartment was in the Palazzo Pediconi, a simple but dignified seventeenth-century edifice at the edge of the Ponte district of Rome's historic city center. The quarter is named for its proximity to the Ponte Sant'Angelo, the iconic bridge that connects Castel Sant'Angelo and St. Peter's to the southern and eastern part of central Rome. The Pacellis' neighborhood, an area known for centuries as Monte Giordano, is steeped in history and immortalized in the works of writers and artists. It was here that in the fourteenth century the Roman nobleman Giordano Orsini constructed a massive, fortress-like structure that dominated access to the only major thoroughfare leading to St. Peter's. The elevation that bears Orsini's name came to enjoy some fame by the Middle Ages because its height afforded a unique view of the basilica across the Tiber. From this location streams of pilgrims from across Europe caught their very first glimpse of the church constructed to mark the spot where, according to tradition, the Apostle Peter, the first pope, was crucified and buried.[3] The place also marked the intersection of one of the great cultural fault lines of Western civilization between the city's ancient Jewish community and its powerful Christian majority. Local memory recalls how in centuries past the popes would greet Rome's chief rabbi on Monte Giordano to publicly upbraid the Jews for their spiritual blindness and "hard-heartedness" in failing to recognize Jesus as the Messiah.

Eugenio spent almost all his life—except for the years as papal representative in Germany in the 1920s—living and working within a short walking distance from where he was born, just across the river from St. Peter's. In 1880, his family moved from the Pediconi building to their own apartment in the nearby Palazzo Rossini in Via della Vetrina. The family's new home was just a few minutes from the Palazzo Pediconi, which allowed for frequent visits with Eugenio's grandfather, Marcantonio.[4] According to family lore, the Pacellis preferred to live on the upper floors of the palazzo, to keep from being disturbed by the considerable noise emanating from the narrow paths of the street below. The location may have reflected, too, the family's modest economic means, since the lower levels of the Roman *palazzi* of the day were reserved for the traditional aristocracy and those of considerable economic means.[5] In later years, Eugenio nostalgically recalled how easily he mastered those stairs to the family's apartments: "I could jump two or three steps at once, because I had long legs." It did not escape the young Eugenio, a sensitive child, that his aged grandfather did not have such an easy time of it.[6]

The neighborhoods, or *rioni*, of Pacelli's youth were a dense maze of apartment buildings, offices, shops, and churches whose majesty and style are easily lost amid the semblance of uniformity, as well as the twists and turns of so many narrow and winding streets. These busy *rioni* stood at the crossroads of Rome, connecting the heart of the ancient city with the Vatican—a bridge between two universal and imperial impulses, secular and sacred, that have long animated the city's identity.

The *rioni* were monuments to a city that lived with one foot in the past and one in the present, one eye on this world and another on the world to come. In these streets, one finds the occasional artifact of the ancient world crowded out by the *palazzi* of the Renaissance, built at a time when the area was a center of banking and commerce. They share pride of place with the imposing churches of the Counter Reformation, conspicuous expressions of the combative Catholic resolve to overpower the Protestant reformers, places like the Church of Santa Maria in Valicella, known more commonly as the Chiesa Nuova, built at the start of the 1600s by the famed architect Borromini. The Oratorio dei Filippini (Congregation of the Oratory of Saint Philip Neri), where young Eugenio and his brother Francesco participated in a Catholic youth group for many years, is located next to the church. Here the newly ordained Eugenio Pacelli would receive his first pastoral assignments, a few steps from where he was born. A short distance away stands the Church of Santa Maria dell'Anima, popularly known as the Church of the German Nation, established to care for the pastoral needs of the city's German community. The church's sixteenth-century façade has among its many ornaments a biblical inscription from Isaiah 32:17: *opus iustitiae pax,* the work of righteousness is peace. Eugenio Pacelli would make this his papal motto.[7]

Eugenio's parents hailed from large Roman families with close ties to the city. Filippo Pacelli was so highly regarded in papal circles that he was eventually named dean of the Consistorial College, a prestigious body of twelve lawyers referred to as consistorial advocates. With rare expertise in both church and civil law, these lawyers were central to the internal legal processes of church governance. The future pope's cousin, Ernesto, was a high-ranking official of Vatican finance, and served as president of the influential Banco di Roma from 1903 to 1916.[8] Eugenio's older brother Francesco, his closest and perhaps only true confidant, was a Vatican lawyer who oversaw the negotiations between the Vatican and Mussolini's Italy to establish Vatican City in 1929.

Although the Pacellis have long been associated with the Roman nobility, theirs were essentially honorific titles, a gesture of papal gratitude for the elder Pacelli's loyalty to the pope during the 1848 revolutions. When republican rebels, led by Giuseppe Mazzini, chased Pius IX out of Rome, the pope fled to Gaeta. Marcantonio followed him into exile and was rewarded when the pope returned to Rome after 1850 to resume control of a restored papal state.

Of much greater consequence than honorific titles was Pius IX's decision to appoint Marcantonio Pacelli as deputy interior minister of the papal government, a position he held until the fall of papal Rome in 1870. Marcantonio was now privy to the inner workings of the papal government, including legal, security, and economic matters. He was also named as one of the ten-member censure committee that was established after the restoration of papal temporal power to rule on the future of papal bureaucrats who had served in the administration of the Roman Republic, as well as to deal with revolutionaries associated with Mazzini's boisterous but short-lived experiment in governing Rome without the pope.[9]

With Marcantonio's appointment to a prominent position in the restored papal government, the Pacellis had arrived. They were now members of a privileged club, an exclusive class that counted among its members the old Roman noble families like the Borghese, Barberini, Ruspoli, and Torlonia. Many of the new nobility were seen by the older Roman families as provincial *parvenus*. In a characteristically derisive tone, the old Roman patricians could be heard to ask the new title-bearers, "Have you any lamps and churches in your villages?" It was a pointed reminder of the modest rural origins of men such as Marcantonio Pacelli.[10]

In practical terms the Pacellis enjoyed what is best described as a middle-class status and existence. But like the old Roman aristocracy, the black nobility, represented by the pope's Noble Guards and other new title-bearers, stuck together. Their children attended the same schools; they worshipped in the same churches. Having obtained a position in one of the offices of the papal government, these solidly middle-class families were able to offer their children the promise of professional mobility and security in the service of the Holy See.[11] The status of the entire Pacelli clan for generations owed much to Marcantonio Pacelli's loyalty to the pope.

The restored papal court in which the elder Pacelli served after 1850 was governed by the charismatic but combative Pius IX, who was growing increasingly intolerant of the liberal reforms he had championed early in his papacy. The pope was also decidedly cool to the idea of Italian Unification; although as an Italian he openly sympathized with the movement, Unification threatened the vital interests of the French and Austrians, whose political and military support Pius IX needed to defend his territories and avoid a replay of the Gaeta experience.[12]

Pius IX's hardened attitude toward the cause of political and social reform of the papal states was accompanied by a deepening aversion to liberal ideas and to modern society as it was evolving in the late nineteenth century.[13] The pope who was known to be affable, warm, and accessible could also be illiberal, intolerant, and impetuous. He seemed constantly at war with the expanding Italian state, which had its eyes fixed on Rome as the future capital of a fully united Italy. It did not help that, with the advance of Unification under the leadership of Piedmont, territories that formerly belonged to the papal states were annexed, and then subjected to the same kind of vigorous secularizing measures known in Piedmont. In its more energetic form, secularization included the state's demand for a say in the nomination of bishops and even parish priests, a direct assault on the authority of the pope.[14]

This was a difficult time for the pope, who watched his territorial dominion being whittled away by an overpowering political and military movement. By the late 1860s, all that remained of the papal states was the area surrounding Rome itself, known as the "Patrimony of St. Peter's," whose defenses were buttressed by French troops. When the Franco-Prussian War erupted and the French troops were pulled out to attend to French defenses, the stage was set for the last, climactic act in the long, often bloody road to Italian Unification. For Pius IX, the capture of Rome by the Italian government in September 1870 and the attendant loss of papal territorial sovereignty were the last straws. The pope greeted the culminating moment of the *Risorgimento* with a characteristic blend of bombast and affected resignation, declaring himself a "prisoner of the Vatican" and refusing to leave. A correspondent for the *New York Times* who witnessed the fall of Rome wrote, "The Pope is still in the Vatican, surrounded by his friends, all evidently in a state of bewilderment. Their old plans are upset, and they are puzzled to know what to do next."[15]

Pius IX was not one to go quietly. Although he had resigned himself to the annexation of Rome, he refused to grant the king the blessing he sincerely desired. The king, like all of Italy, waited in vain for a papal blessing on the new state. Thus began what the Jesuit historian Robert Graham called the "second phase" of the Roman question, a protracted tussle between the Vatican and the Italian state over the political and legal status of the pope and the Holy See, which now found itself on sovereign Italian territory. Pius IX's anxiety over the future of the papacy was grounded in an awareness of the past. After all, the history of the institution had been punctuated by frequent, often violent conflict between popes and secular rulers over the territorial and political manifestations of papal independence.[16] Moreover, the Holy See believed that the pope's temporal power flowed from the will of God, as an indispensable basis of the pope's spiritual authority. Take away territorial or temporal sovereignty, and full spiritual independence could not truly be guaranteed.

In the febrile context of nineteenth-century European politics, practical considerations were at play. The popes could very well draw out fine distinctions in church law and convention to assert that the Holy See had juridical standing in its international relations, with accompanying rights and privileges vis-à-vis civil authorities. But Pius IX and his successors wanted more, believing that even a small measure of absolute territorial sovereignty would solidify papal claims of complete independence from outside interference.[17] Deprived of his territory, Pius IX went into a self-imposed exile in the confines of the Vatican, refusing ever again to leave the area between St. Peter's Basilica and the adjacent apostolic palace. Not until 1929, when Mussolini ruled Italy, would the Holy See receive from the Italian state assurances of "absolute and visible independence" as well as an "indisputable sovereignty" grounded in the newly created Vatican City.[18]

Together with the increased intensity and pace of secularizing campaigns among various European governments from the late 1870s onward, the loss of Rome left the Holy See feeling defeated and greatly diminished.[19] By this point, the long pontificate of Pius IX was drawing to a close. When the pope died in February 1878, he was almost eighty-six years old and had occupied the Chair of St. Peter longer than any pope in history. The British historian Owen Chadwick observed that when he died, Pius IX was "the most hated man" among some Romans, "but only some." For other Romans, and in much of the Catholic world, Pius IX was "almost at once a possible candidate for sainthood." His successor, Leo XIII, also governed for a very long time over a church facing unprecedented challenges.[20] An early biography of Eugenio Pacelli reached the obvious conclusion that both pontificates left an indelible mark on him: the former defined by the forcible capture of Rome and the loss of papal temporal sovereignty; the latter by its determined efforts to find ways to engage with a modern world that rejected the papacy's claim to temporal power but also questioned the most elementary tenets of Christianity itself.

After 1870 the Holy See faced serious difficulties in its dealings with European states, especially the most Catholic among them: Italy, France, Belgium, and Austria.[21] The year 1877 was pivotal. Across Europe, left-wing governments came to power, a portent of growing anticlericalism. In France, elections in 1877 resulted in a republican anticlerical government that had as one of its key objectives a revision of the 1801 Concordat with the Holy See. Some politicians even talked about scrapping the document altogether. A protracted diplomatic tussle ensued between successive French governments and the Vatican, culminating in the breaking of diplomatic relations in 1904. A year later, the Concordat—a legacy of the Napoleonic era—was repudiated officially.[22]

The pattern of church-state relations in Italy was distinct since even the most anticlerical politicians understood that the papacy and the Holy See were inextricably tied to Italian life. Rome especially was bound by history and tradition to be home to the spiritual leader of the universal Roman Catholic Church. Accordingly, the leading figures of Italian politics in these years expected some kind of accommodation; they hoped that the Holy See would come to accept annexation as a *fait accompli* and recognize the set of laws that the Italian parliament enacted in May 1871 (the Law of Guarantees) to define the legal and territorial status of the pope and the terms of church-state relations generally. But Pius IX refused to compromise. What sense was there in accepting, among other things, a salary from the very state whose legitimacy the pope continued to contest?[23]

City of God, City of Man:
The Pacellis after the Fall of Papal Rome

So it was that the Roman question remained unresolved for decades as the Italian state took its first steps. In practice, church-state relations were less envenomed than appearances suggested at the time, and there emerged a practical *modus vivendi* that allowed the church to enjoy a privileged place in

Italian life.[24] The culture of the Italian church into which Eugenio Pacelli was raised exhibited a paradoxical mix of humiliation and pride, of resignation and resolve. It was at one and the same time defeated, yet still alive, and even renewed. Above all, it was pragmatic in seeking a workable accommodation with the state, notwithstanding continued resentment of the state's very existence.

In the years after Unification, the neighborhood where Eugenio Pacelli grew up underwent profound physical, social, and cultural transformations while remaining grounded in a storied past. Rome's transition from heart of the papal states to capital of a would-be European power brought about rapid and far-reaching changes. The old city was difficult to recognize.[25] By 1872, the Italian government had legislated suppression of religious houses and the sale of church properties in Rome, mirroring a similar pattern under Unification in other parts of Italy. Virtually all the churches and religious houses of Rome—including seminaries, convents, and monasteries—were seized by the state; many were converted into government offices. Even historical papal properties in the city fell into government hands. Papal palaces such as the Villa Madama became the Italian Senate, whereas the Montecitorio palace was adapted to house the Italian Chamber of Deputies.

Befitting the ambitions of the young state, new and grandiose structures went up just as older, more modest buildings came down. The *rioni* of Eugenio Pacelli's youth were indelibly marked by the state's ambitions to transform Rome from provincial backwater to major European capital. In the 1880s, after repeated flooding devastated the neighborhoods on the Tiber's banks, massive concrete walls were erected. This massive public works project, though necessary, effectively destroyed much of the charm of the *rioni,* cutting off direct access to the river and removing the buildings that towered above the river banks. In the place of these charming *palazzi* was a modern city street that snaked along the old river at the height of the newly erected walls. In the 1880s, construction began on the Corso Vittorio Emanuele, an ambitious project to build a major thoroughfare connecting the old city center to the area around St. Peter's. The Ponte Umberto, a bridge completed near the close of the nineteenth century, joined the new Corso to the Vatican area across the Tiber. Both the bridge and the new street carried the name of Savoy monarchs, a concrete reminder of the power shift under way in Italian life.

The transformations were more than physical. Signs of change were everywhere. One contemporary observer spoke of a "moral revolution" that accompanied the fall of papal Rome: "The pyramid," he quipped, "has been inverted." As a correspondent for the *New York Times* put it in 1876, the pope's "monopoly" over power was "broken," ending one of the last vestiges of absolutism in Western Europe. The laity, previously assigned a supporting role to prelates in the affairs of the papal government, now called the shots; some of the more ambitious among them even presumed to tell the Holy See how it should manage its internal affairs. For the most part, the old Roman families survived, and many assumed administrative positions in the Italian government. Yet their particular claim to govern the political and social life of the city waned in the face of Unification. By and large, the men who had made Italy and helped to facilitate the capture of Rome were from the North or other parts of the peninsula. Unfamiliar with Rome, they were often disparaging of its provincialism and its crowded, dirty streets, not to mention its loud and unruly inhabitants. The traditional Roman families continued to think of themselves as an exclusive bunch, but the locus of power was shifting to national legislatures and thus to a national political class.[26]

The Pacelli family lived these years like most everyone else in the Eternal City: with one foot in the past and one in the present. Loyalty to the papacy and even nostalgia for the return of papal Rome coexisted with the practical necessity of getting on in the new Rome, capital of a unified Italy, a new player with grandiose ambitions on the world stage. The Pacellis had little choice but to make arrangements to guarantee their future in uncertain times.

This is not to say that the Pacellis were wholly unaffected by the forcible annexation of Rome. They were as defiant as other families of the black nobility, and as defensive of the pope's claims to territorial independence as the indispensable condition of his spiritual sovereignty. But there were some obvious realities to face after 1870. As lay persons, the Pacellis could continue to perform important functions within the church, but they would continue to play a secondary role to prelates, a situation that was exacerbated when the administrative business of running a papal government ended. It was doubtful whether the Holy See, with its material resources seriously reduced in the wake of Unification, could continue to provide lay employees with the kind of modest but comfortable income to which the Pacellis had grown accustomed.

Some sources have suggested that after the fall of papal Rome in 1870, the

Pacellis faced difficult financial times.[27] They were not especially wealthy, and no doubt the end of the papal state gave them cause to worry about their professional and economic future. The fall of the papal state meant, for instance, that Marcantonio Pacelli's position as deputy interior minister ceased to exist, although he continued to serve as an editor of the Vatican newspaper *L'Osservatore Romano,* an influential publication that was Pacelli's brainchild, first published in 1861. Sources suggest that the elder Pacelli was offered a position in the Italian government after 1870, an offer he declined as a gesture of continued loyalty to the pope. Still other sources suggest that Eugenio Pacelli's father, Filippo, continued to work as a lawyer with the Holy See while also working in the secular government as a civil lawyer and even city councilor.

The family appears to have managed its affairs quite well after 1870, enjoying a lifestyle much more privileged than that of most ordinary Romans, including some of the traditional aristocracy, who had fallen on hard times after Unification. They lived in a spacious, well-kept apartment, albeit one they rented, that was well appointed with antique furniture, some works of art, valuable porcelain, and a rich library. It was the library that Eugenio treasured the most.[28] The Pacellis were comfortable enough financially to be able to offer some limited assistance to the poor, a common practice among the well-to-do Roman families of the time; indeed, as elsewhere in Europe and the Americas, such almsgiving was seen not only as a Christian duty but as a way of demonstrating middle-class respectability. Other signs of middle-class status and material means included season tickets to the opera and frequent visits to the theater and open-air musical concerts. The Pacelli children were schooled in various European languages, notably French and German.[29] From a very young age, Eugenio demonstrated an affinity for classical music, playing the violin and piano. Even as a boy, he preferred the German composers: Wagner, Beethoven, and Bach.[30] On Sundays, the family often rented a carriage to spend the day in the pastoral Roman countryside or at the sea resort of Ostia. Summer holidays were spent between the beach and the modest country estate of a relative at Onano, Marcantonio Pacelli's home town. There was the occasional trip to Tuscany, but Onano was clearly the vacation retreat of choice. Here, Eugenio and his siblings indulged in their favorite pastimes: horseback riding and long country walks. It was to Onano that Eugenio came as an adolescent to recover from repeated bouts of illness that kept him out of school for months at a time.

In many respects, the Pacellis were a typical family. There was a great deal of affection among the Pacelli siblings, and between the children and their parents, albeit conditioned by a degree of formality that reflected the family's aristocratic pretensions. The Pacelli children addressed their parents with *lei,* a form of address usually reserved for formal occasions. The Pacelli children were expected to kiss their parents' hands before heading off to bed each night. Eugenio was especially close to his older brother Francesco, and after becoming the cardinal secretary of state in 1929, he lived for a year with Francesco and his family. His nephews, Carlo, Marcantonio, and Giulio, came to know him well in those years and witnessed firsthand the self-discipline and spartan lifestyle that became defining characteristics of his pontificate. They knew their uncle to be a hardworking and devoted priest, rising early in the morning to celebrate Mass, and staying up well into the night reading and preparing material for his work in the Secretariat of State. Yet they recall him as affable as well as prayerful; while Eugenio Pacelli was not one to dote on the children, he did seem to take a genuine interest in their lives, asking constantly about their studies and recounting stories from his own childhood.

After becoming pope, Pacelli met with family members infrequently—perhaps once or twice a year, and usually very briefly. But the strong sense of family loyalty remained, especially with his nephews. When Giulio was married, he asked Pius XII to offer a blessing. The pope obliged, insisting, however, that the ceremony be conducted in his private chapel and with only immediate family members present—Eugenio Pacelli always worried about the appearance of nepotism. As a wedding gift, he gave the couple a ring that his mother, Virginia, had given him when he was named a bishop in 1917. He told Giulio and his wife: "I am giving you this because it is an object that comes from the Pacelli family, and I want it to remain in the family."[31] In 1934, Giulio and his brother Marcantonio accompanied their uncle, by then cardinal secretary of state, to a large international Catholic gathering in Buenos Aires. Later, when Pacelli was pope, Francesco's oldest son, Carlo—who, like his father, was a leading figure in the Vatican City administration—became one of Pius XII's closest, albeit informal, advisors. Together with Count Enrico Galeazzi, also an influential Vatican City administrator with close personal and business ties to prominent American Catholics such as Cardinal Spellman and Joseph P. Kennedy, Carlo Pacelli met with the pope on almost a daily basis for much of Pius XII's pontificate. As Pius XII lay dying at Castel Gandolfo in October 1958, all three of Francesco's sons were at his side to the end.

Carlo recalled that, in one of his last moments of lucidity, when the pope saw his nephew standing at his bedside, he asked, "What are you doing here? Go to work!"[32]

When he was a schoolboy, roughly thirteen years old, Eugenio Pacelli was asked to describe himself in a school assignment. In a short essay titled *"Il mio ritratto,"* or "My Portrait," the future pope offered a disarmingly honest assessment of his physical and intellectual development. He described a budding adolescent of average height, rather thin, with a pale face set against otherwise dark features. Then there was that "aquiline" nose, with its pronounced bridge and curve, especially evident when viewed in profile—that quintessential eagle-like Roman nose, fitting for Eugenio Pacelli, Roman. The future pope offered a more generous assessment of his moral character and intellectual capacities. Nature had endowed him with certain intellectual gifts, so that, together with hard work and ambition, the young Pacelli felt he could accomplish many things. Here was a young man who enjoyed attending classes and was happy to read well into the night, as was his wont. He confessed to a great love of music and the works of classical antiquity. As to his vices, impatience and quickness to anger were foremost among them. An "instinctive generosity" of spirit made it easy for Eugenio to forgive those who offended him.[33]

More so than his siblings, Eugenio exhibited the qualities of his mother: reserved, taciturn but affable, deeply sensitive, introspective, and devoutly Catholic. The last trait was characteristic of the whole family. Signs of the family's intense devotion to the Blessed Virgin Mary were evident in the fact that each of the children was given "Maria" as a middle name, and in the fact that the family recited the rosary each evening before dinner. This intense Marian devotion stayed with Eugenio Pacelli all his life, culminating in the controversial proclamation of the Dogma of the Assumption of Mary. The intensity of young Eugenio's devotion was pronounced—he would spend hours alone in the chapel of the Madonna della Strada (Our Lady of the Way), a side chapel in the imposing Jesuit church Chiesa della Gesù in central Rome. Eugenio's mother was struck by her younger son's attachment to this particular Marian chapel, whose origins date back to Saint Ignatius of Loyola.

One day she asked, "Eugenio, what do you do in the chapel all that time?" To which the young Pacelli responded, "I pray, mother: I tell the Madonna everything."[34]

If Eugenio possessed his mother's reserve and piety, he also exhibited his father's legal mind and probity, a keen attention to detail, a carefulness and deliberation in thought and in speech. These are all traits for which Eugenio would later be praised, or assailed, as papal diplomat and pope. Those who worked closely with Pacelli in later years and who were favorably inclined to judge his actions as diplomat and pope acknowledged that he could demonstrate steely decisiveness, clear-minded reasoning, and moral certitude, but this was always mixed with a reflective, even hesitant temperament. He was able to see all sides of an argument and to assess and reassess ideas and opinions, even at the cost of decisive action.[35]

A devout and attentive mother gave Eugenio Pacelli and his siblings a solid grounding in orthodox Catholic belief and practice well before they began their formal schooling. Pius XII's younger sister Elisabetta recalled in particular the time and effort her mother devoted to preparing Eugenio and Francesco for their First Communion in 1886. Eugenio's exposure to a sound Catholic formation at home was buttressed by an early education in religious schools, first in a preschool run by the Sisters of Divine Providence in Piazza Fiametta, and then in a private elementary school at the Arco dei Ginnasi run by Professor Giuseppe Marchi. An early biographer of Pius XII wrote that Professor Marchi was known to rant in front of his pupils about the "hardheartedness of the Jews." The biographer goes on to remark, "There was a good deal to be said in favor of Signore Marchi; he knew that the impressions gained by small children are never lost."[36] A later biographer, John Cornwell, tried to make something out of Marchi's supposed influence, inferring that his rants against the Jews left an indelible mark on the young Pacelli.[37] Eugenio would have been about seven or eight years old at the time—an impressionable age, to be sure, but hardly formative for a boy who would go on to take university degrees in philosophy, theology, and canon law.

Far more significant to Pacelli's intellectual and spiritual development was the influence of Father Giuseppe Lais, a priest from the Oratory of Saint Philip Neri and vice-director of the Vatican Observatory.[38] From the Chiesa Nuova, not far from the Pacelli family home, Father Lais ran the renowned Collegio Vallicelliano, which functioned as a kind of youth group dedicated to catechesis and the spiritual life of the parish boys who, like Eugenio, were to become altar servers at Mass. The future Pius XII was about eight years old when his father decided to send him and Francesco to the college. Lais's work with the youth of central Rome was part of a wider grassroots initiative by many religious orders after the fall of papal Rome. In view of the state's seizure of church property and the suppression of religious orders, the priests were anxious about the spiritual health and intellectual formation of Catholic youths growing up in a secular and overtly anticlerical environment.[39] Father Lais was remembered by the Pacelli family as a kindly figure, greatly admired by the young people with whom he worked, not to mention their families. Among the many activities Father Lais organized were educational trips to visit the catacombs of the early Christians—that labyrinth of narrow passageways beneath the city that housed the tombs of the early Christians. Along with the other boys on these trips, Eugenio and Francesco learned to transcribe the inscriptions, words, and symbols that marked the clandestine life of the persecuted church in pre-Christian Rome.[40]

That his contact with the priests of the Oratory left an indelible impression on Pacelli is evident from his repeated public testimonials to the formative influence of priests like Father Lais and Giulio Castelli. Not long after being elected pope, in fact, Pacelli spoke publicly in favor of the beatification of Father Castelli, recalling this "tall and graceful figure" who acted always with humility and dignity. The newly elected Pius XII said that he hoped personally to be able one day to declare Father Castelli a saint. A few years later, when Rome itself was under siege from German and Allied troops, Pacelli recalled his childhood devotion to Saint Philip Neri, known as the Apostle of Rome, and invoked the saint's intercession to deliver the Eternal City from the horrors of war.[41]

Father Lais was a frequent visitor to the Pacelli home, evidence of the trust and respect he enjoyed among families like the Pacellis. The daily presence of the priests of the Oratory in the lives of the Pacelli boys in particular reflected the family's commitment to seeing that their sons received proper religious and spiritual guidance. Father Lais was especially impressed by young Eugenio's piety and devotion in assisting as altar boy at Mass. Eugenio's sister Elisabetta recalled that as a boy Eugenio would pretend to celebrate Mass, mimicking the gestures and incantations of the priest—his family even purchased vestments to lend an air of authenticity to this harmless diversion. Cardinal Marchetti-Selvaggiani, one of Pacelli's longtime advocates, who knew Pius XII since youth, recalled in later years that "even as a boy, he knew how to pray and to love God better than any of us."[42] Pacelli's sister recalled how, enthralled by the heroic accounts of the lives and martyrdom of Christian missionaries, the young Eugenio declared, "I also want to be a martyr! But without nails."[43]

In 1885, at the age of nine, Eugenio Pacelli was enrolled in secondary school at the Liceo-Ginnasio Ennio Quirino Visconti. The Visconti was housed in the historic Collegio Romano, an institute founded by Saint Ignatius of Loyola and the Jesuits in the mid-1500s to give seminarians a solid educational and cultural foundation. The Roman College counted some of the most formidable minds of the Counter-Reformation Church as both students and teachers, including Cardinal Roberto Bellarmino, Cardinal Pietro Pallavicino Sforza, and Saint Luigi Gonzaga. It was still in Jesuit hands in 1870 when the school passed to the newly unified Italian state, which proceeded to transform the storied college into a premier state school. By the time Eugenio Pacelli attended in the mid-1880s, all obvious traces of clerical influence over the curriculum were gone, replaced by a rigorous standard classical education, in an atmosphere rent with anticlericalism. Such were the times. Years later, when Eugenio was pope and was informed that students from the nearby Visconti school were coming to pay their respects to one of their most illustrious alumni, he quipped, "Now they come for an audience with the pope, but at one time, there were anticlericals and masons at that school."[44]

It is somewhat surprising that as devout Catholics and convinced papists, the Pacellis sent their son to be educated in such an environment. Perhaps they recognized that although the pope could choose to remain the proverbial prisoner of the Vatican, lay Catholics had to find a way to inhabit both worlds—to be loyal to the claims of papal Rome while learning how to survive and succeed in a secular, anticlerical environment. Maybe the Pacellis, mindful of the widespread sentiment against the surviving trappings of papal Rome, wanted to make sure that their children did not suffer socially and professionally for the family's open fidelity to the pope. Besides, there were few serious alternatives to the public school system, and the Visconti school was arguably the best public school in the city. Sending their son to an excellent state school was surely one way of helping him on his way.[45]

The Pacelli family's well-known papal connections did not inhibit Eugenio's academic progress. Many excellent teachers at the school recognized the young Pacelli's academic abilities, his diligence, and his maturity. Even those who were known to hold liberal and nationalist views created an atmosphere in which the young Pacelli felt free to express his thoughts, including his unpopular ideas on religion, history, and literature. His teachers recognized Eugenio as an exceptional student who completed his grammar school studies with distinction, including a gold medal in history. A former teacher described Eugenio as "serious, studious, and intellectually outstanding."[46] The future pope was off to an auspicious start. Pacelli remained an outstanding student through his university studies. He was always at or near the top of his class. In his final year of high school, in fact, he was exempt from final exams because of his excellent performance throughout the academic term.[47]

Such demonstrable academic excellence and a real enthusiasm for learning distinguished Pacelli from his peers. These qualities certainly helped to get him noticed in Vatican circles once his studies were complete. It also helped to have the Pacelli name. Unlike the seminarians he studied with in Rome, many of whom came from poor peasant families with no access to a high-quality education, Eugenio Pacelli enjoyed a privileged classical preparation of the kind that state schools such as the Visconti offered in those days. That meant a solid grounding in Italian, Latin and Greek, history and geography, mathematics, physics, chemistry, and philosophy and ethics. The young Pacelli had a particular affinity for the study of the classical languages and for history, but above all for poetry and literature. As an adult, he came to be known and respected for his sharp analytical skills, evidence of the legal mind and training, in keeping with the family tradition. The adolescent Eugenio Pacelli, though, was drawn to literature and poetry. He was barely a teenager when he began to compose his own poetry.

Pacelli was well versed in the works of Dante Alighieri and could quote from memory parts of *The Divine Comedy*. Dante occupies a singular place in Italian culture and national history. He was a great Christian poet, of course, and *The Divine Comedy* is a great allegory of the Judeo-Christian understanding of history, both sacred and secular. But this masterwork by a true genius of the late Middle Ages is also an innovative and unparalleled monument to the vernacular Italian language that Dante more than anyone helped to consolidate in a diverse and divided nation. In post-Unification Italy, which was eager to forge a national consciousness to buttress political unification, the curriculum of the day had a decidedly nationalist orientation. This may explain Eugenio Pacelli's affinity for the great figures of Italian literature, whose works his teachers encouraged students to read and internalize, not just for the love of the great works but for love of country. For the great figures of Italian literature, though, love of country could not be divorced from Italy's profound and rich Christian traditions, a fusion of patriotism and piety that appealed to the young Pacelli's sensibilities. If Pacelli was enamored of German composers in music, his tastes in literature and poetry were almost exclusively Italian: the names of Dante, Machiavelli, Petrarch, Leopardi, and Manzoni emerge from his high school notes as particular favorites. Vittorio Alfieri and Ugo Foscolo were also important influences on the young Pacelli's literary tastes and on his evolving ideas about the nation-state, which tended toward the romantic rather than the political or liberal variants of nationalism. Whether these influences were felt in Pacelli's thought and action as papal diplomat and pope is difficult to determine. It is clear, at any rate, that the histrionics of Mussolini and Hitler, or, worse yet, the pseudo-scientific theories of racial purity their followers proffered, were of a different ilk from the plaintive yearning for liberation and freedom Pacelli would have discerned in the romantic nationalism of eighteenth- and nineteenth-century Italian literature.

That Pacelli was an idealistic and introspective adolescent is clear from some of his earliest writing. In keeping with the *Zeitgeist* of his generation, the future Pius XII was quite taken with heroic deeds, with the great men of history, and with the power of ideas to drive human history forward. One of his essay titles expressed it aptly, if verbosely: "History, Describing Enduring and Heroic Deeds through Which Higher Ideals Are Achieved, Is Not Only Wisdom But Also Poetry of Life." The essay begins with a telling description of Pacelli's emerging conception of human history: "I would define the life of men and peoples as a struggle, more or less miserable, more or less disgraceful, but a struggle; continuous and non-stop struggle, which is directed towards the achievement of certain ideals." The essay goes on to discuss great figures of history who fought for freedom and justice. It cites in particular Gregory VII, who defended the freedom of the church and the divine right of peoples to enjoy political freedom. It cites too the twelfth-century struggle of northern Italian cities for freedom from the Germanic emperor Barbarossa. Here, again, Pacelli fused piety and patriotism, seeing church history and Italian history as interwoven parts of a complex but integrated whole. The struggle to protect the church from persecution at the hands of hostile world rulers could not be divorced from the struggle of oppressed peoples for freedom and what later generations would call self-determination.

His was a selective reading of history, to be sure, but in some senses the seeds of Pacelli's political philosophy were being sown. He may not yet have had the intellectual tools or the formal training in theology, history, or philosophy to express it precisely, but already the future Pius XII was grappling with a doctrine of church-state relations that saw the church and civil society as distinct and autonomous but also inextricably linked. There was no desire to return to the confessional state of old in which church and state were fused, no trace of a desire to restore the papal states of his grandfather's generation. It is a telling sign of his intellectual independence, perhaps, that Pacelli found the late fifteenth-century Florentine priest and civic leader Savonarola so admirable. The religious and political reformer, branded a heretic by the papacy and executed, struck the young Pacelli as an idealist who was struggling above all for political freedom and freedom of individual conscience. In a high school essay Pacelli even described Savonarola as a "protector of civil rights" and idealized the kind of state that exists to serve its people, not the other way around.[48]

One of the more pervasive images of Pius XII is that of a reclusive figure, someone far more comfortable in the solitude of his study than in active ministry. This is a distorted caricature, though grounded in some truth. The powerful American prelate and future cardinal Francis Spellman, one of Pacelli's closest friends and confidants from the 1920s, once quipped that while the future Pius XII was a good, loyal, and generous friend, he always maintained a "certain reverential distance, which could not be described in words."[49] As an adolescent, Pacelli exhibited a proclivity for solitude, prayer, and study; his great love of books nurtured a growing conviction that only divine ideals are ultimately real and true. Human relationships seemed somehow less important, even fraught with difficulties. In one high school essay titled "A Good Book Is Your Best Friend," Pacelli observed that it was better to spend one's time with an "ethically worthy" book than with friends who did nothing but "corrupt" one's innocence. Pacelli was about thirteen years old at the time. In the various papers that have survived from his adolescent years, he makes reference to a handful of friends. Some biographers, eager to acquit Pius XII of the charge of anti-Semitism, point to the interesting fact that one of the close friends he had as a teenager was Guido Mendes, who came from a Jewish family. By all accounts, the two were typical mates of that age group, spending time together at school and visiting each other's homes. When racial policies were enacted against Italy's Jews after 1938, then Cardinal Secretary of State Pacelli helped Mendes and his family leave Italy for Switzerland. They stayed there until 1939 before making their way to Palestine, thus avoiding the fate of so many of Italy's small but ancient Jewish communities.[50]

Aside from a few passing references to childhood friends, the future Pius XII was detached from his immediate social surroundings as an adolescent. He sought very much to fulfill the Christian admonition to be in the world but not of it. His principal spiritual guide was the rigorous devotional manifesto *The Imitation of Christ* by the medieval German monk Thomas à Kempis. The surviving essays from his adolescence are littered with references to the book. Pacelli could quote entire passages by heart. For centuries, it has been one of the most cherished and widely read books of the Christian world, severe and ascetical in its prescriptions for a contemplative life of self-denial lived in the imitation of Christ, for love of God. True to its monastic spirit, the book counsels the way of Christ by teaching "contempt for the world, and all its vanities." Pride, greed, the seeking of riches, coveting of honors, even the "empty learning" of academics—it was all vanity, and it would all pass. "'Vanity of vanities, and all is vanity' except to love God and serve him alone," Kempis declared, invoking Scripture. "And this is supreme wisdom—to despise the world, and draw daily nearer the kingdom of heaven." In order to imitate Christ and win the kingdom of heaven, Kempis advised readers to cultivate a pure heart, simplicity of mind, prudence in action, deliberation, and self-control in speech. He warned especially of "the danger of superfluity of words" and against "vain and worldly learning." The book's ascetic prescriptions for spiritual devotion and its uncompromising distaste for "earthly things" fitted well with Eugenio Pacelli's temperament. Although he was to reach the heights of power within the church and find himself courting and being courted by monarchs, presidents, and diplomats, Eugenio Pacelli always projected the aura of a mystic, one who was detached from worldly concerns.

A tall and slender frame, a thin, angular face with a prominent Roman nose, piercing eyes framed by steel-rim spectacles, a studious, taciturn look that was softened by the occasional boyish smile—this is how the world would come to know Eugenio Pacelli, through personal traits that gave life to legends and caricatures. His reputation for being severe, restrained, and aloof was at odds with how Pacelli interacted with guests to the apostolic palace, both before and after becoming pope. A correspondent for the *New York Times* who interviewed Pacelli weeks before he was elected pope in 1939 observed that in person, Eugenio Pacelli was more animated and more expressive than photographs suggested. Expecting to find Pacelli "austere and cold," the reporter was pleasantly surprised to find him "smiling, warm and vivacious."[51]

In other respects, though, the caricature could fit the man. Pacelli had a reputation for great propriety and formality, strict punctuality, various idiosyncrasies and minor compulsions, and immense personal discipline, both physical and intellectual. He was restrained and measured in his speech and fastidious in keeping to his routine. Writing of the new pope, *Time* magazine noted that Pacelli "does not smoke, eats sparingly, drinks little wine." He exercised regularly but otherwise prayed and worked constantly, allowing himself a few diversions, usually a walk around the Vatican grounds or perhaps a car ride to Castel Gandolfo, the papal summer residence just outside Rome. Those who were able to observe him close up could attest to certain idiosyncrasies that suggested some harmless compulsive tendencies. When the Kennedy family visited Pacelli in the days after he was formally installed as pope, Joseph P. Kennedy caught a glimpse of one of the odd behaviors. As the pope knelt to pray after Mass, Kennedy saw him reach into his pocket to remove a small object, which he glanced at and then put back, before returning to fervent silent prayer. After a short time, the pope once again reached into his pocket and, as Kennedy recalled, "went through [the] same performance as before. When Kennedy realized that the object of the pope's attention was a watch, it struck him as slightly odd. "It looked funny to be using this kind of watch," he recorded in his journal, "and also to be timing your prayers." Galeazzi explained to Kennedy that Pius XII "always uses exactly the same time to the minute every day."[52] In her memoirs, Mother Pascalina Lehnert, Pacelli's housekeeper for some forty years, recalled the pope's "exacting precision" in all things: he was "punctual for Holy Mass, punctual in his work and in his meetings, punctual at dinner, punctual with his daily walk." While he was empathetic and understanding with members of his staff, Mother Pascalina said, he insisted on precision and punctuality. It would have been against his nature to think of wasting any time.[53]

Already in his adolescence Eugenio Pacelli exhibited the patterns of behavior that later critics would deride as characteristic of a pope who was ill-equipped to deal with the mammoth political challenges of the twentieth century. On a few occasions during his studies, Pacelli was withdrawn from school for reasons that have been vaguely ascribed to rapid physical development, a delicate stomach, and anxiety. The first time was during the academic year 1890–91, just as Pacelli was set to begin senior-level studies at the Visconti. Again in 1895, a year into his studies for the priesthood, Pacelli withdrew from classes for reasons related to stomach ailments and apparent anxiety. Pacelli's parents sent their son to Onano for an extended period of time, to recuperate with family in the country.[54]

Pacelli's physical ailments were most likely caused by emotional or psychological stresses associated with the rigors of study, exacerbated by his intense work habits and drive to succeed. There is also some evidence that the emotional stresses in question were the result of a kind of spiritual crisis Pacelli experienced near the start of his high school studies. Two surviving entries from what appears to be Pacelli's diary or journal, written in August 1891, record the overwrought musings of a sensitive and devout adolescent experiencing, perhaps for the first time, doubts about his faith. The diary entries are preceded by a curious but revealing marker: a single blank sheet on which Pacelli sketched a design of a fish and anchor, heavily laden with Christian symbolism. The rudimentary sketch was accompanied by a phrase written in Greek, Latin, and Italian that read: *Know thyself.* The adolescent Pacelli was by his own admission following an ancient maxim—*Nosce te ipsum*—undertaking a deliberate exercise in self-discovery. He describes the human heart as a "mystery" and a "bottomless abyss," the depths of which only God can see. Repeated references to modern psychological terminology suggest some familiarity with this emergent field of study. It was precisely this encounter with new ideas and different ways of thinking that shattered the youthful certitude of the young Pacelli. In its place came a pervasive sense of doubt: doubt in previously held beliefs, practices, and received faith traditions; doubts even about the very existence of God. Speaking in the third person, as was his wont in these writings of his youth, Pacelli paints a picture of someone formerly content and assured in his faith. But, Pacelli wrote in August 1891, "What if God doesn't exist?" It was enough to drive the doubting believer to despair, even to the point of welcoming death or wishing he were never born. This rather dire entry ends with a prayerful invocation: "But Lord, enlighten him!"[55] It seems likely that these were little more than the melodramatic musings of a young man struggling earnestly through a spiritual crisis but fumbling with expression, making the crisis seem worse than it actually was. It is conceivable, too, that the adolescent Pacelli, like most youth, experienced periods of doubt and wondered seriously about the meaning and value of life.

Whatever the sincerity or depths of this apparent spiritual crisis, it culminated in a fortuitous decision. Sometime in the summer of 1894, just after graduating from secondary school, Eugenio Pacelli abruptly announced to his family that he wanted to study for the priesthood. A ten-day retreat in the Spiritual Exercises of Saint Ignatius Loyola helped to solidify his decision. There was nothing particularly unusual about his choice—Pacelli was certainly not the first or the last Catholic boy to think about becoming a priest. Nor did his family appear to influence him one way or another, although, here again, being raised in a devoutly Catholic family would have made a vocation to the priesthood perfectly plausible, even praiseworthy.[56]

Pacelli's parents seem to have been content to facilitate their son's call to the priesthood. By the fall of that year, Pacelli had entered the seminary at the historic Collegio Capranica and had also begun to study philosophy at the Gregorian Pontifical University. Pacelli distinguished himself at once for his academic abilities, earning top marks, praise from his instructors, the respect of his classmates, and even some academic awards.[57] Despite his academic successes, Pacelli found the rigors of seminary life and intense study almost too much to take. The social and intellectual demands of the seminary were challenging, characterized by a strict discipline and daily routine of prayer and study. Students awoke before sunrise for Mass, with the rest of the day punctuated by study and prayer. Meals were taken in common but consumed in silence.[58] The curriculum and social regimen of seminary life were designed to form a specific kind of cleric: a young priest imbued with the ideals of piety, self-sacrifice, detachment from the materialism of the world, and constant prayer and work.

Eugenio Pacelli's time at the Capranica was short-lived. After just one year of study there, a recurrent bout of the problems that had afflicted him during his time at the Visconti forced him to withdraw from the seminary. Eventually, his parents managed to get Eugenio a rare dispensation to continue studying for the priesthood as a day student, living at home rather than in nearby Capranica seminary, which was within easy walking distance of the Pacelli apartment. From his philosophy studies at the Capranica, Pacelli continued on to study theology at the storied Apollinare pontifical university, while also registering for courses at Rome's state university. Pacelli's university education thus mirrored a pattern seen from his childhood: a blend of personal and familial piety, formal religious instruction and spiritual direction, together with immersion in the secular, often anticlerical and antireligious atmosphere of the state-run university.

What kind of priest, then, did Pacelli become by virtue of the education he received in Roman seminaries at the close of the nineteenth century? Born and raised in Rome, educated in Rome's schools and seminaries, he was the quintessential Roman priest. Pacelli's clerical training was grounded firmly in a model laid down by Pius IX in the wake of the tumultuous revolutionary events of the mid-nineteenth century. Pius IX intended to create a seminary in Rome to train some of the brightest young priests from around the papal states. Eventually, the Seminario Pio, which he founded in 1853, came to occupy the Apollinare building, sharing its space with the much older Seminario Romano. What Pius IX wanted, and needed, was a clergy that was far better trained than was the case by the middle part of the nineteenth century, especially in the areas of canon and civil law. With the territorial and political status of the Vatican increasingly threatened by the avaricious ambitions of Europe's secular states, the embattled Pius IX needed a clergy trained for battle—of the pen, if not of the sword.

Pius IX bequeathed to the Roman seminaries a rigorous course of study and a deep, abiding fidelity to the papal cause. Both the Seminario Romano and the Seminario Pio distinguished themselves for their excellent instruction in Hebrew, which was taught to stimulate a more scientific study of sacred Scripture. The first two years of preparation for the priesthood were grounded in the study of philosophy: logics and metaphysics; ethics, natural law, and the natural sciences. Then it was on to four years of theology: biblical studies, Hebrew, moral and dogmatic theology, and church history. After the theology degree, graduates could pursue another degree in canon and civil law. This further study was highly specialized, and admission to the program highly competitive: it was reserved only for the most accomplished students of the Roman seminaries. Eugenio Pacelli made the grade easily. He was even tapped to become a professor of canon law. His superiors, however, had plans for the young Pacelli far removed from the sheltered, tranquil walls of academe.

If the structure of seminary training bore Pius IX's masterly imprint, the atmosphere of these schools when Eugenio Pacelli studied there owed much to the pioneering pontificate of Pope Leo XIII.[59] When Gioacchino Pecci became Pope Leo XIII in 1878, Eugenio Pacelli was just two years old. By the time Leo XIII died in 1903, Pacelli had been a priest for four years and was already working in the Congregation for Extraordinary Ecclesiastical Affairs. A young man in his mid-twenties by the time Leo XIII died, Pacelli had already completed degrees in philosophy, theology, and canon law and was fluent in German, French, and English. It is a telling indication of the spiritual and intellectual debt that Eugenio Pacelli owed to Leo XIII that in his first papal encyclical, *Summi Pontificatus,* issued in October 1939, Pius XII invoked the anniversary of Leo XIII's consecration of the world to the Sacred Heart of Jesus. This was in 1899, the year Pacelli was ordained a priest. For the newly elected pope, it was a providential sign that the first year of his pontificate should be associated with the memory of the first year of his priesthood and, more important, with the memory of Leo XIII, whom Pacelli praised as a pontiff "so sure in his diagnosis of the open and hidden needs and sores of his day." With another European war looming, and mindful of the pressing need for him now to diagnose the many "needs and sores" of his own time, Pius XII resolved to follow Leo XIII's lead.[60]

Thanks in large part to Leo XIII's spirited engagement with the modern world, Pacelli's clerical preparation came during the most intellectually vibrant and turbulent era in Catholic thought since the Reformation. Various schools of thought competed for the attention of young seminarians and for official approval in papal circles. At one extreme were those who continued to defend the letter and spirit of Pius IX's pontificate, punctuated by the claims of papal infallibility, the Syllabus of Errors—in short, asserting orthodoxy in matters of faith, and papal supremacy over both doctrinal and organizational matters related to church governance. At the other extreme were rumblings of what came to be known as the "modernist crisis," later to be denounced as heresy and expunged from the Roman seminaries under Pius X—whom Pacelli was to declare a saint in 1954. Heavily influenced by French, German, and English currents of thought, the modernists who taught in the Roman seminaries pushed the envelope of critical, scientific research on some of the most fundamental beliefs of orthodox Catholicism-Christianity. These included, among other questions, whether Moses was the actual author of the Pentateuch, the first five books of the Bible. More generally, they pushed against a literalist interpretation of Scripture. They demanded, above all, fidelity to the methods and insights of the critical-historical method of biblical scholarship, even if these ran counter to the "infallible" teaching of the church. Pushed to its extreme, modernism flirted with ideas that questioned the very divinity of Jesus. Between the two extremes of strict orthodoxy and modernism was a kind of middle way—a moderate current of thought that was open to new ideas associated with the critical-historical study of Scripture, while remaining faithful to settled doctrine and, most important, to papal authority for the final word on such matters.[61]

When Pacelli was studying for the priesthood, these competing schools of thought subsisted under the general revival then under way in Catholic seminaries and universities of the teaching of the philosophy of Saint Thomas Aquinas, or Thomism.[62] This revival was largely the work of Pope Leo XIII, who wanted to effect a major reorientation of Catholic theological and philosophical thought by offering the philosophy of Thomas Aquinas as a coherent, rational framework for reconciling faith and reason in modern times.

In a sense, Leo XIII engaged with modernity by proposing instead of imposing Catholic principles.[63] He was more interested in establishing working relationships with secular states than in fighting old battles from previous eras. He had to serve as the spiritual head of an increasingly global faith community, without the benefit of legal-juridical status in international law as a sovereign head of state, the first pope in centuries to face such a situation.[64] Leo XIII was as convinced as his predecessor that modern philosophies like liberalism and Marxism were essentially wrong-headed and bound to lead society astray. By recapturing the "wisdom of St. Thomas" and by making the "right use of philosophy," Leo felt that Catholics could find a way of dealing with the great intellectual challenge of the day: to reconcile faith and reason.[65]

Thanks to papal patronage, Thomism flourished in Catholic thought in the late nineteenth and early twentieth century. The revival of Thomism was evident in Catholic universities around the world, in particular in the faculties of theology and philosophy in the Roman seminaries and pontifical universities.[66] The Roman Thomists were criticized as being men of limited intellectual abilities with scant appreciation of historical processes or of modern philosophy; they were said to be intransigent and intolerant, more concerned with the appearance of passing on approved interpretations of Aquinas's teaching than with adhering to the Angelic Doctor's own venerable methods.[67]

These concerns reached into the heart of the classrooms and libraries where Eugenio Pacelli studied in the 1880s and 1890s. Most of the students sincerely seem to have been dreaming of a restoration of the papal state and the installation anew of the "pope-king" venerated in the streets of Rome with shouts of popular acclamation.[68] Leo XIII might have hoped that it was possible to keep one foot in the past and another in the present by proposing the thought of a medieval genius as antidote for the ills of modern society. But for many of the more committed Thomists, including prominent clergymen, the project to restore the philosophy of Aquinas assumed a wider cultural and political significance; the aim was to restore not just the philosophy of a cherished medieval mind but also the papal state as chief guardian against the ills of modernity.[69] The tussle between the Thomists and their liberal, reform-minded critics was more than a mere academic squabble; there were fundamental differences at work that reached far beyond matters of Scripture, theology, and philosophy, touching upon basic questions about the political and social order of modern times.[70]

Where did Eugenio Pacelli fit into all of this? It is difficult to say with certainty, since he left no spiritual testament and kept no diary or journal recording his time studying in the Roman schools. The few pieces of evidence that speak to this time in Pacelli's clerical formation suggest that he occupied a middle ground among the various competing schools of thought. Among Pacelli's professors at the Apollinare, three were critical to the future pope's formation: Father Riccardo Tabarelli, Monsignor Tito Martinetti, and Monsignor Francesco Faberj. Tabarelli and Faberj in particular reflected the basic divide between the Roman Thomists on the one hand, and the more liberal-minded anti-Scholastics on the other. Tabarelli was a deeply committed

Thomist. He was the very representative of the Thomistic revival that reached the height of its influence just around the time Pacelli was studying for the priesthood. Interestingly, Pacelli once served as a teaching assistant to Tabarelli for an exam taken by Angelo Roncalli, the man who succeeded Pius XII as Pope John XXIII. That Pacelli had a certain admiration for Tabarelli is evident in a remark he made in 1903 to Cardinal Francesco di Paola Casetta. Recalling his days in Tabarelli's classroom, Pacelli decried the fact that too many of the seminarians felt entitled to challenge Tabarelli's sound Thomistic critiques of modern theories.[71]

As a seminarian Eugenio Pacelli was not afraid to be associated with the same liberal, reform-minded currents that would come to be denounced as modernist heresies by Pius X a few years after Pacelli was ordained. We know, for instance, that Pacelli was close to Father Taberj, who was in many respects the antithesis of Tabarelli. Indeed, Faberj eventually was accused of spreading "modernist" heresies in his classes. Despite the fact that Faberj fell out of favor in Roman circles, Eugenio Pacelli kept in touch with his teacher, referring to him affectionately as "il mio ex maestro," that is, "my old teacher." When he was papal representative in Bavaria after the First World War, Pacelli wrote to Faberj to recall the "great ideal of our lives," which was the overriding commitment to work "for the good of the church and souls." For Pacelli, these were the very ideals that his dedicated professors, men like Faberj, instilled in young seminarians.[72]

The documentary record for this time in Pacelli's life is scarce, but the available sources indicate that, for a time at least, Pacelli was attracted to the ideas that later came to be denounced as modernist heresies. His association with Faberj is the first clue. It was Faberj who introduced Pacelli to Friedrich von Hügel, a wealthy nobleman and independent scholar based in England with close ties to leading modernists like George Tyrrel and Alfred Loisy. An Italian by birth, with German and Scottish roots, von Hügel was a devout Catholic who, while managing to avoid excommunication, always flirted with an official reproach for his open modernist sympathies. In the early 1890s, he and his family spent their winters in Rome to escape the cold and damp of England. It was during one of these visits that he came to enjoy the confidence and company of a group of young liberal-minded seminarians associated with Faberj, including Eugenio Pacelli, whom he first met in January 1896. Von Hügel and Pacelli continued to meet regularly for months afterward, enjoying friendly and lively conversations on a host of matters, including the burning issues in biblical studies.[73] In February 1896, together with Faberj and Pacelli, von Hügel attended a meeting of the Società degli Studi Biblici, a Bible study group founded by some of Faberj's students to foster a scientific, critical-historical study of Scripture. As a seminarian, Pacelli also attended Sunday lessons on church history offered by the French abbé Louis Marie Olivier Duchesne, then a distinguished professor of ecclesiastical history. Like Faberj and so many others who taught in the Roman seminaries in the late nineteenth century, Duchesne was eventually caught up in the anti-modernist wave, and his works ended up on the Index of prohibited books.[74] It is clear, at the very least, that Eugenio Pacelli's clerical training included exposure to cutting-edge research and liberal-minded professors who skirted and sometimes crossed the limits of orthodoxy.

In the end, though, there may be some truth to the suggestion that Pacelli's encounter with the modernist crisis heightened a well-developed ability to say the right thing to the right people, at the right time, and better yet, to know when not to say anything at all. By the close of 1896, scarcely a year after von Hügel first met Pacelli, the baron detected how the changing winds of acceptable scholarly debate in Rome altered the course of young seminarians like Eugenio Pacelli. When he returned to Rome in November 1896, von Hügel noted that already men like Duschesne had fallen out of favor in papal circles, and clergy like Cardinal Parocchi were being pulled away from their increasingly "liberal" tendencies. A hardening of the orthodox line that came from on high inevitably affected the mood in the scholarly circles in which men like Duchesne and Faberj moved. As von Hügel wrote from Rome in December 1896, "I see myself, by numberless unequivocal signs—and for that matter the Abbé Duchesne and Don Faberj tell me the matter is quite certain—that the situation has grown worse, narrowed, darkened since I left at the end of April."[75] Especially disheartening for the baron was the change in the young Pacelli. As he noted in his diary, "Eugenio Pacelli came to me; first sight of him this time; thought I noticed a change in his mind."[76] It seems that von Hügel was thinking of Pacelli when he wrote to Alfred Loisy of the signs of a changed atmosphere in Rome: "A young priest whom I found quite open in the spring, I find quite closed in the autumn."[77] According to some reports, von Hügel and Pacelli met a few more times that winter, but infrequently, and usually in the company of others. It is unclear whether the two kept in touch after the winter of 1896–97; some students of von Hügel suggest that the relationship effectively ended after 1897, while others point to continued, albeit infrequent, contacts between the baron and Pacelli in the years just before the First World War.[78]

With so many changes brought about by the fall of papal Rome in 1870, it is difficult to say whether there was anything typical about Pacelli's clerical training in the closing decades of the nineteenth century. For some observers, the fall of the last papal state and the effective end of the pope's territorial sovereignty were a sign that times were changing; whereas previously, the Roman priest had been trained to think and act more as a bureaucrat or administrator of the organizational life of the church, after 1870, the emphasis shifted to the pastoral dimension of the humble parish priest: the dispensation of the sacraments; direct daily contact with parishioners; charity for the poor; comfort to the sick and the dying. The model Roman priest was a pastor first and foremost. The study of doctrine was not so much a secondary pursuit as it was a buttress to charity—doctrine in the service of good works.[79]

Inevitably, though, studying and living in the shadow of the *cupolone*—the giant dome of St. Peter's, as the Romans put it—some Roman priests would invariably be attracted to a career in the governance of the church, whether it be work in the Roman Curia, the administration of dioceses and parishes, or in the skillful art of papal diplomacy. The *cupolone* projected an unmistakable air of the power and majesty of papal power: a symbol of the triumph of a once persecuted Christian minority over one of the world's greatest empires. Everything about papal Rome spoke of power. One can easily imagine the impression the Eternal City made on the young seminarians who came from across Italy to study for the priesthood, many of them from poor and humble origins. One seminarian called this phenomenon the "magical effect of Rome." How far removed these adolescents were from their small towns and villages, here at the very center of the Catholic world, partaking in regal papal rituals and processions, with proud, incredulous parents looking on at their humble contribution to this grand spectacle.[80]

For Eugenio Pacelli—who at his ordination had described himself pointedly as a Roman—the grand spectacle of papal Rome, even in its faded glory, was all he had ever known. Like other clerics of his generation who emerged from the papal seminaries in Rome, Pacelli tended toward pragmatism, moderation, and accommodation. The Roman priests mostly preferred working within existing frameworks and entities; they generally were suspicious of untested theories and grandiose utopias.[81] In this sense, Pacelli embodied what we might call the Roman paradox: on the one hand, being at the center of church governance, he exhibited at times a certain myopia that kept him from grasping fully realities beyond the shadow of St. Peter's dome; on the other hand, being at the heart of church governance afforded the future Pius XII a unique perspective, a sense of the universality and global reach of the Roman church and of its capacity for survival and adaptation while remaining true to its founding claims.

If Eugenio Pacelli did fit the model of the *prete romano,* it was because, unlike many priests who came from outside Rome or Italy, he accepted and defended the claims of papal supremacy and saw the pope's survival in Rome as providential and historical proof of Rome's "universal mission."[82] And like the other men in his family, Eugenio Pacelli would spend a lifetime working to fulfill Rome's universal, and eternal, mission.

2

The Diplomat's Vocation

Eugenio Pacelli always insisted that all he ever wanted was to work as an ordinary parish priest among the ordinary people of an ordinary parish. He said he dreamed of dispensing sacraments to the faithful—celebrating Mass, hearing confessions, offering religious instruction to young people and charitable works to the poor of his childhood neighborhood.

In the early days of his priesthood, Pacelli's wishes were realized when his first pastoral assignment was to the Chiesa Nuova, where he had spent so much time as a young boy. Yet it was obvious soon enough that Eugenio Pacelli was destined for another kind of pastoral assignment, one that concerned itself with saving souls through different means than those at the disposal of the average parish priest. At a time when the Holy See was working to build a formidable diplomatic corps to handle its often testy relationship with the European powers, Eugenio Pacelli was a highly attractive candidate. The Pacelli name certainly did not hurt, but quite apart from personal connections, the young Pacelli had the kind of talent and skill needed by Vatican diplomacy in a time of transition. He was known to be intelligent yet modest, with demonstrated competence in languages. Pacelli also had a reputation for being diligent and self-disciplined. If ever there was an ideal candidate for the new face of Vatican diplomacy at the beginning of the twentieth century, it was Eugenio Pacelli.

From the very beginning of his career there was something exceptional about the man who would become Pope Pius XII. While the other members of his cohort were ordained together in 1899 at the Church of Saint John in Lateran, one of Rome's oldest and most important basilicas, Eugenio Pacelli and his family celebrated his ordination in a private ceremony in the chapel of one of Pacelli's influential patrons, the Monsignor Francesco di Paola Cassetta. The family worried that Eugenio would not have the physical stamina needed to endure the longer public ceremony. Of course, Pacelli had known little of the communal experience of seminary life, so a private ordination was a fitting bookend to his clerical training.

Surrounded by family and friends, the newly ordained Pacelli celebrated his first Mass in the Church of Santa Maria Maggiore at the altar of the Madonna Salus Populi Romana—a devotion site venerated by Romans for centuries to invoke Marian protection over the Eternal City. It was a fitting beginning to Pacelli's life as a priest, given his family's long history of Marian devotion and his later role in promoting the cult of the Virgin Mary. Some might say that Pius XII was obsessed with Mary. Whether it was reverent veneration or obsession, or both, Pacelli's Marian devotion was one of the great constants of his spiritual life.[1]

As befitted a family with one foot in papal Rome and one foot in the city's secular affairs, Pacelli's first public function drew a number of high-ranking clerics as well as members of the city's political class, including Ernesto Nathan, a member of one of Rome's prominent Jewish families, grand master of the Masons, and future mayor of Rome. The Vatican newspaper, L'Osservatore Romano, remarked that the presence of the city's secular elite reflected the high esteem in which the Pacelli family was held.[2] Eugenio's father was conspicuously absent from the event, due to illness. Eugenio made sure to bring him Communion the next day.[3]

The exceptional arrangements made for Eugenio Pacelli's ordination and the attention it drew were in keeping with Pacelli's clerical training to this point. Within months of his ordination, while he diligently carried out his pastoral duties in parish life, Pacelli's superiors tapped the young priest for doctoral studies in canon and civil law, anticipating an eventual career as a scholar and university lecturer or possibly a papal diplomat. By the fall of

1899, Pacelli was enrolled at the leading pontifical universities in the city, where he studied church and civil law. Pacelli excelled in his studies, completing degrees in canon and civil law in 1902 and graduating *summa cum laude*. In 1904, he received a doctorate in canon law, making him part of a small and select group of church law experts.

Eugenio Pacelli's academic prowess combined with the respected family name and the strong backing of highly placed clerics made him a well-known figure in papal circles, especially in the offices of the secretary of state. Little wonder, then, that he caught the eye of Pietro Gasparri, the newly named secretary of the Sacred Congregation for Extraordinary Ecclesiastical Affairs.[4] The Congregation, which operated under the authority of the secretary of state, was a relatively new office in the government of the church, established in the wake of the French Revolution, to help the Holy See deal more effectively with secular states. The Congregation specialized in negotiating concordats—the formal agreements similar to treaties that regulated church-state relations. This was a matter of concern both to the Vatican as an international entity and to domestic churches that sought a working relationship with national governments. Whereas the Secretariat of State proper dealt directly with foreign governments, sending and receiving diplomats and dispatches, the work of the Congregation for Extraordinary Ecclesiastical Affairs was essentially consultative and internal—providing research and analysis of various matters arising from the church's relations with civil governments, and making recommendations to the pope on a given course of action in the Vatican's dealings with civil authorities.[5]

Pietro Gasparri was one of the most influential secretaries in the Congregation's history, and he was a seminal influence on Eugenio Pacelli's career. When he first met Pacelli in 1901, Gasparri was a rising star of Vatican diplomacy. He eventually served as cardinal secretary of state for two popes: Benedict XV and Pius XI, from 1914 until he retired in 1930, ceding the way to Pacelli.[6] The story goes that Pacelli was at home one evening early in 1901 accompanying his sisters on the piano, when Gasparri stopped by to ask the young priest to join the Congregation. Pacelli tried to deflect the offer, insisting that he was not fit for such work. A dejected Pacelli reportedly said, "But I had hoped to spend my life as a shepherd of souls."[7] Gasparri would not be dissuaded. He had heard from Pacelli's professors that Eugenio was an exceptionally talented student.[8] In a relatively small field of qualified candidates, Eugenio Pacelli immediately became someone to watch.

So in February 1901 Eugenio Pacelli joined the growing ranks of the Vatican's Secretariat of State as an *apprendista,* a junior functionary with the promise of eventual promotion. It was an exciting time to be joining the select ranks of the world's oldest diplomatic tradition. Papal diplomacy was being transformed—modestly expanding in size but, more important, growing in professionalism, which better equipped the Holy See to deal with civil governments.[9] In the decade or so before the First World War, the Vatican was building a network of well-educated, well-trained career diplomats. These men were to be drawn from the ranks of accomplished and promising young prelates, men such as Eugenio Pacelli, who were hand-picked from the top ranks of the pontifical universities for specialized diplomatic training at the storied Pontifical Academy of Noble Ecclesiastics. Arguably the greatest innovation was the establishment of a genuine meritocracy: one rose through the ranks by dint of effort and as a reward for achievement.[10]

Eugenio Pacelli found himself working quietly behind the scenes earning a reputation for his competence and his discretion. In early October 1903, Pius X promoted him to the position of *minutante* in the Congregation for Extraordinary Ecclesiastical Affairs. For someone with Pacelli's qualifications, the job of *minutante* did not have much to recommend it, except for the promise of advancement in the ranks of papal diplomacy. In the organizational structure of the Secretariat, the *minutante* occupied a kind of middle ground in importance and influence—between the secretary and his undersecretary at the executive level, and functionaries such as attachés, archivists, and typists at the opposite end.[11] The entire office operated under the jurisdiction of the cardinal secretary of state, who has been described as the civil equivalent to a prime minister or a foreign minister.[12]

Despite its radical transformation in those years, the papal diplomatic service remained a decidedly small world, in more ways than one.[13] On the eve of the war, scarcely more than two dozen individuals worked in the entire Secretariat, and roughly half of them, including Pacelli, worked in the sections that dealt with the Vatican's foreign relations. All but one of these functionaries was a priest, and virtually all were Italian, especially in the high-ranking posts of secretary and undersecretary. While progression through the ranks tended to come only after several years of administrative experience within the Secretariat, comparatively few of the men who staffed the Secretariat of State—even in the high-ranking positions—had very much experience in foreign affairs. By contrast, the foreign offices of civil governments were increasingly demanding international experience by the turn of the century.[14]

Eugenio Pacelli found himself at the nerve center of one of the Vatican's most powerful offices, working diligently, though inconspicuously, on some of the most consequential projects to emerge from that office under Gasparri's tutelage.[15] Gasparri later recalled that the relatively inexperienced Pacelli was one of the most competent members of his staff, "in whom I had particular confidence."[16] When Gasparri traveled to his home town of Ussita (Macerata) to complete one of the most pressing projects that crossed his desk in those years, he took Pacelli along. They worked long hours. Gasparri was impressed by Pacelli's work ethic and by his fortitude, despite his rather slight and at times sickly appearance. Gasparri remarked that Pacelli was at once "so gentle, so refined . . . yet at the same time very strong, very bold."[17]

Pacelli's work with Gasparri set the stage for their collaboration on a monumental project—entrusted to Gasparri by Pius X in 1904—of codifying canon law. This was a major component of the centralization of papal authority, bringing into one place the mass of church laws accumulated over the centuries. Pacelli performed the largely clerical tasks of the *minutante*, coordinating correspondence with the experts, drafting letters, memoranda, and summary reports. It was painstaking work requiring patience, careful attention to detail, and many hours of solitary work, which fitted well with Pacelli's training and temperament.[18] The project took almost thirteen years to complete, but its legacy was considerable.[19] Pacelli's direct influence on the project was fairly minor—more clerical than substantive. His primary function was to gather and organize material to supplement the hefty deliberations being conducted by seasoned experts.

But on at least one point of substance, the experts listened seriously to what the young Pacelli had to say since he did hold advanced degrees in theology and canon law.[20] In 1912, Pacelli published a highly technical treatise on the "personality and territoriality" of laws, especially in church law. Drawing upon the authoritative work of Saint Thomas Aquinas, whose philosophy reigned supreme in those days, Pacelli argued that church laws and decrees had a personality and autonomy of their own. He challenged the tradition that canon laws emanating from a specific bishop did not apply to his subjects outside the territorial jurisdiction in question. Despite what centuries of church law and tradition had said, Pacelli reasoned that a local bishop's authority over his priests, say, could extend beyond the strict territorial limits of his immediate jurisdiction.[21]

Coming as it did on the tail end of the antimodernist crusade, Pacelli's work reflected his obvious concern with two basic principles of church governance: the authority of the bishop and hierarchy, and the defense of orthodoxy in doctrine and practice. And so, Pacelli reasoned, if a bishop decreed that the priests of his diocese ought not to read certain unorthodox works lest they harm their own faith—or that, in order to avoid causing scandal among the lay faithful, the priests of his diocese should avoid attending public events—such decrees would apply to those priests even if they traveled beyond the territorial limits of their diocese.[22] The experts working to reform and codify the whole body of canon law gave some serious consideration to Pacelli's thesis, to the point of experimenting with revised wording that would have turned the existing doctrine on its head. In the end, the canonist experts decided to affirm the status quo, but the fact that they saw fit to consult the young priest showed that Eugenio Pacelli's star already was on the rise.

Pacelli did continue with some pastoral work, hearing confessions at the Chiesa Nuova, teaching catechism to the children of the parish, and providing spiritual direction to groups of young female religious and lay women. A few tempting offers came his way to teach at the university level; there was even vague talk of an offer to teach at the Catholic University of America in Washington, D.C. In the end, though, Pacelli settled on teaching one of the foundational courses in diplomacy at the papal diplomatic academy.[23] This was close to his home and his work, and required the least commitment in terms of teaching hours and preparation. It was also a quiet recognition that his work in the Secretariat of State demanded most of Pacelli's time and attention, and was of great interest to him.[24] One of Pacelli's former students at the diplomatic academy, Anton Maria Bettanini, who went on to teach at the University of Padua, recalled how Pacelli's academic expertise, combined with his practical experience working daily in the Secretariat, resulted in an applied approach to teaching papal diplomacy, weaving together history and theory with reflection on contemporary realities. Without revealing sensitive information, Pacelli incorporated real-world scenarios into classroom discussions, taken from the many files that crossed his desk at the Secretariat. Students were struck by Monsignor Pacelli's conviction that, through study and thought, and with a "lively faith and tranquil conscience," this new generation of papal diplomats had to prepare themselves for "bitter struggles to defend the rights of God and his church."[25]

For his dutiful service in the middling ranks of the Secretariat, Pacelli eventually was rewarded with promotions to executive positions within the office. In March 1911 he was named undersecretary for the reorganized Congregation for Extraordinary Ecclesiastical Affairs, replacing the polarizing Monsignor Umberto Benigni, who had been his direct superior since 1906. This was a time marked by the reactionary atmosphere of the antimodernist crusade led by Benigni. In 1912, Pacelli was named to be a *consultore,* or advisor, to the Sacred Congregation of the Holy Office, infamous in history and memory for its association with the dreaded Inquisition. That his skills and expertise were being called upon to deal with such hefty matters as the Holy See's relations with civil governments and internal doctrinal orthodoxy is a clear sign that Pacelli enjoyed the confidence—some would even say the favor—of Pius X and his inner circle.[26]

The Papacy at War, 1914–1918

The year 1914 was a turning point in Eugenio Pacelli's career. It began with a major promotion when Pacelli was named secretary of the Congregation for Extraordinary Affairs, the post vacated by Gasparri (later in the year, Gasparri was named secretary of state to the newly elected Pope Benedict XV). Eugenio Pacelli's time had come. What until then had been largely an administrative and consultative role gave way to a leadership position in the upper ranks of the Vatican's Foreign Office. Pacelli's first major assignment was to oversee the negotiations of a formal agreement between the Holy See and Serbia, a country at the center of the spiraling crisis that shortly would spark the First World War. Here, finally, was a major foreign affairs initiative for the Holy See in which Eugenio Pacelli played a direct role.[27]

Although Pacelli's laborious efforts to conclude an agreement with Serbia were overshadowed by the fast-moving events of the summer of 1914, his demonstrated ability to complete this major assignment on terms favorable to the Holy See made Pacelli the ideal candidate for the most important papal missions of the First World War. Within a few weeks of the outbreak of war, Pius X was dead, and by early September the papal conclave had elected one of Pacelli's former colleagues from the Secretariat of State, Giacomo Della Chiesa, then archbishop of Bologna. That Pacelli enjoyed the special confidence of the newly elected Benedict XV was clear when the pope entrusted him with two important peace initiatives during the war, preferring him over more seasoned diplomats.[28]

Pacelli's first major assignment came in January 1915, when the pope sent him to Vienna to meet with the Austrian emperor, Franz Joseph. The aim was to urge the Catholic ruler to use his influence to keep Italy out of the war by agreeing to Italian territorial demands for control over Italian-speaking areas of the vast and diverse Austro-Hungarian Empire.[29] The second peace initiative was a much more involved affair that saw Pacelli engaged in protracted discussions to sell Benedict's ill-fated peace proposal of 1917 to the Central Powers, and especially to Kaiser Wilhelm II of Germany. In both initiatives, Pacelli's objective was to convince the combatant powers that it was in the best interests of all parties to prevent the spread of the conflict and to work toward a lasting peace settlement. In the end, both missions, like Benedict's wider peace efforts, were in vain. But they are significant insofar as they constituted Pacelli's first real foray into the practical side of papal diplomacy, and this in a time of war—a kind of baptism by fire for a future pope whose leadership would be tested early on by an even more destructive global conflict. Here was an opportunity for all the years of Pacelli's academic study of papal diplomacy and administrative work at a staff desk in the Secretariat of State to meet the world of *realpolitik*. Pacelli would have to come to terms with the tension between theory and practice, between ideal and real, including a sober assessment of the limits of a wartime papacy. These were all lessons that Pacelli carried with him when, in the opening months of his own pontificate in 1939, Europe stood at the precipice of yet another conflagration.

By the time of his second major assignment, in 1917, in this case to meet with German leaders to gauge the prospects of a formal papal peace initiative, Pacelli had reached yet another important milestone in his diplomatic career, having been named papal nuncio to the all-important post in Munich,

Bavaria. Bavaria was the heart of Catholic Germany and had enjoyed formal diplomatic relations with the Holy See since the late eighteenth century. Even after German Unification, a papal nuncio remained in Munich as papal representative to the Bavarian kingdom, but no such representation was to be found in Berlin until the mid-1920s. Pacelli had been rumored to be a favorite for the job in 1916, but several factors had militated against the promotion, including, it seems, his relative lack of experience in the field. Instead, the post went to a seasoned papal diplomat, Monsignor Giuseppe Aversa, who arrived in Munich in December 1916. When Aversa died unexpectedly in early 1917 from surgical complications, Eugenio Pacelli was formally named apostolic nuncio to Bavaria.[30] In an unusual move, Benedict XV personally presided over the ceremony consecrating Pacelli as the titular archbishop of Sardis, an honorific title granted to mark Pacelli's promotion as nuncio. The event took place on May 13, 1917, the day many Catholics believe the Blessed Virgin Mary first appeared at Fatima, Portugal. It was a fitting coincidence—believers might call it a providential sign—given the future pope's special devotion to Our Lady of Fatima in his anticommunist crusade during the early Cold War.[31] Like his priestly ordination, Pacelli's consecration as archbishop and his promotion as nuncio were no understated affair. Leading officials of the Curia, including Merry del Val (the Vatican's secretary of state from 1903 to 1914) and Gasparri, were present, as were members of the Pacelli family, including his mother. His father, Filippo, had died a few months earlier, in late November 1916, from complications related to the Spanish flu epidemic.[32] In a telling sign of the Pacelli family's special standing in the papal court, the pope invited Eugenio, his mother, and his brother Francesco for brunch. The next day, the rest of the Pacelli clan was invited to a private audience with Benedict XV.[33]

Here was yet another major milestone in Pacelli's ascent through the ranks of the papal diplomatic service—an appointment to one of the most influential papal representations anywhere. It was a decisive turning point in Pacelli's career. Within a week of his appointment, Eugenio Pacelli left Rome for Germany, where he remained virtually uninterrupted until 1929.[34] The newly minted nuncio traveled to Munich in style, in a specially outfitted car of the Italian state railway, thanks to the generous assistance of Baron Carlo Monti, an Italian government chargé d'affaires to the Holy See.[35] Pacelli arrived in Munich on May 25, 1917, and several days later presented his credentials to King Ludwig III. The new nuncio was well received by Munich's Catholic power elite and also by its ordinary citizens. Soon after his arrival, in words eerily similar to his many wartime addresses as pope, Pacelli spoke to the residents of Munich of the need "in this grave hour . . . to reconstruct human society on the solid ground of Christian justice," and expressed the hope of reaching a "lasting peace . . . based solely on the solid bases of Christian law." In an era without parallel in human history, Pacelli said, the pope had entrusted to him the "mission to contribute to this work of peace" and also to lessen the "painful consequences of war."[36]

This was a critical time in the war. The year 1917 brought with it momentous developments, including the intervention of the United States and whirlwind revolutionary events in Russia that in the span of a few short months toppled one of the world's oldest monarchies, leading to the collapse of Russian politics and society.[37] It seemed a propitious time for the Vatican to put its much-vaunted impartiality to good use. The plan was to sound out the Germans to see whether the papal peace proposal was even viable before circulating a formal proposal to all the belligerent powers.[38] With little diplomatic experience under his belt, Eugenio Pacelli was thus engaged in a high-level, high-stakes diplomatic initiative that included meetings with Kaiser Wilhelm II and the leaders of the German government.

Pacelli's mission began well enough. He met first with German Chancellor Theobald Bethmann-Hollweg. Theirs was by all accounts a cordial encounter, couched in the usual diplomatic protocol and accompanying pleasantries. Pacelli was able to present the terms of Benedict XV's draft proposal, the so-called seven points that were to form the basis for an eventual peace settlement.[39] With a tinge of naïve optimism, Pacelli concluded from Bethmann-Hollweg's reaction that the pope's peace proposal stood a real chance to succeed. The new nuncio managed to secure from the German chancellor verbal assurances that Germany was indeed ready to negotiate seriously for peace. Bethmann-Hollweg assured Pacelli that the Germans were open to a reduction in armaments and to the idea of an international organization that would monitor relations among countries and help to avoid future conflicts. The Germans were even ready to talk about territorial concessions to France in the hotly contested areas of Alsace and Lorraine. Pacelli was so confident after his meeting with Bethmann-Hollweg that he told German Foreign Minister Karl Helfferich that, for the first time since the war began, there was a real chance for peace.[40]

His optimism was short-lived. Pacelli's meeting with Kaiser Wilhelm a few days later (June 29, 1917) at Bad Kreuznach brought with it a sobering dose of reality, despite the kaiser's favorable impression of the nuncio.[41] "Pacelli is a distinguished, likable man," he wrote, "of high intelligence and excellent manners, the perfect pattern of an eminent prelate of the Catholic Church." They conversed informally in French, the traditional language of diplomacy; although Pacelli had a good comprehension of German, he could not yet speak the language fluently.[42] For all the diplomatic niceties, it was a decidedly strange meeting characterized by the kaiser's long, rambling, and incomprehensible statements. Pacelli found the kaiser's manner odd, suggesting in his reports to the Vatican that perhaps Wilhelm was exhibiting the effects of three long years of war, making it difficult to conduct a meaningful conversation.[43] Pacelli managed to share with the German leader the pope's letter, in which Benedict XV suggested that, for the sake of peace, Germany might have to renounce some of its original objectives in prosecuting the war. In addition, Pacelli asked the kaiser to do everything in his power to stop the deportation of Belgian workers and others from German-occupied territories. While the kaiser defended the legality of these deportations, he agreed to consider the request in light of Pacelli's reasoning that, in the long run, ending the practice would work in Germany's favor by helping to repair its tattered image.[44]

In the end, the discussions of the summer of 1917 went nowhere. Benedict XV's peace plan was effectively dead in the water. Despite some promising starts made by Pacelli in his first meeting with the German chancellor, the German military high command was in no mood for the concessions Bethmann-Hollweg had seemed ready to accept earlier that summer. But Bethmann-Hollweg's days as chancellor were numbered. When Hindenburg and Ludendorff were named to the Supreme Command of the Army, it signaled a decisive shift toward an increased influence of the German army over the country's political establishment, and even over the kaiser.[45]

Writing to Gasparri in September 1917, Pacelli complained about the propensity of the German leaders to complicate matters, "drowning in a sea of useless words and inopportune statements," thereby neutering potential support for Benedict's peace plan.[46] Pacelli's reports to the Vatican reveal a sound grasp of the German situation at the time—impressive for someone who had been in the country for just a few months and who was still mastering the language. In trying to account for the German government's slow response to Benedict's peace proposal, Pacelli noted, among other factors, the considerable diversity of opinion among German political and military leaders. Public opinion, too, was divided, to say nothing of continued optimism in military circles that the war could yet be won, or at least ended on favorable terms. In Pacelli's mind, German optimism stood in the way of a quick end to the war. As he wrote to Gasparri at the end of September 1917, "without question the cause of peace in Germany has suffered a setback recently. It has always been that way here: when things are going badly, they are ready to accept any settlement; but if the horizon clears up even just a little, they abandon themselves to the craziest illusions and make unreasonable demands against the real interests of the country."[47]

Pacelli as Nuncio: Between Munich and Berlin

His tenure in Germany nurtured Pacelli's conviction that he knew the German reality as well as anyone in Vatican circles. It was in Munich that Pacelli formed a small group of friends and advisors who constituted a formidable, and deeply influential, inner circle to surround him for the rest of his life. It was in Munich that Pacelli first met one of his closest advisors, the Jesuit Robert Leiber. Father Leiber was fond of telling anyone in the nuncio's office whose work was hastily done or incomplete that he should go to work for just a month with Pacelli; he would change his ways soon enough. For his part, Pacelli knew he could count on Leiber to work effectively and discreetly, building an impressive library collection and procuring relevant information and analyses to help orient Pacelli in his dealings with civil authorities.[48] In Munich Pacelli also met and befriended Monsignor Ludwig Kaas, the future Center party chairman who became Pacelli's chief confidant on German matters in the 1930s.

The Bavarian sisters from the religious order Holy Cross of Menzingen ran Pacelli's household from the time he was nuncio in Munich through the years of his pontificate. Foremost among them was the headstrong Sister Pascalina Lehnert, often referred to as Mother Pascalina, who was in charge of the household. Lehnert and Pacelli first met sometime toward the end of March 1918 when Lehnert and a fellow sister were sent to Munich as house-keepers for the new papal nuncio. Lehnert served as Pacelli's housekeeper for forty years, following him to Rome in 1930 when he was named secretary of state and continuing as head of the papal household from 1939 until Pius XII's death in 1958. As Lehnert recalled, there was a moment of hesitation when she first met the future pope, not because there was anything awkward or imperious about his manner, but because of the "profound respect" he inspired. She was struck by his soft and gentle manner of speaking, and by the precision and care with which he attended to his daily tasks, from celebrating Mass in his private chapel to addressing the diplomatic matters that crossed the desk of a papal representative amid the febrile political atmosphere of postwar Germany.[49] Having studied German, she noted, he had a good grasp of the language, though it was painfully obvious from his frequent mistakes that the nuncio had had little practical experience in conversational German. Eager to master a language he admired and now hoped to use in the course of his diplomatic work, Pacelli dove into further study and asked Lehnert and the other sisters to speak to him only in German and to correct any mistakes he made.[50]

From the early days in Munich when some people questioned the propriety of such a prominent female presence in the residence of the papal representative, to the latter years of Pacelli's pontificate, when it was said that Lehnert would try to prevent cardinals she disliked from seeing the pope, Mother Pascalina was a constant source of gossip. She was undoubtedly an opinionated and domineering figure. She managed to antagonize many people who suspected that she was trying to exert inordinate influence over Pacelli, even on his decisions on ecclesiastical appointments. Inevitably there was gossip about the true nature of the close relationship between Pacelli and his housekeeper. One story suggests that in the late 1920s, after Pacelli and his staff had moved to the nuncio's offices in Berlin, some curial officials in Rome, principally Francesco Borgoncini Duca, grew suspicious of Lehnert's place in the nuncio's residence and sent a secret emissary to investigate the matter. It is not clear whether he was acting of his own accord or under the direction of a higher-ranking member of the Curia. Pacelli knew nothing of the investigation, although word eventually reached him through his good friend Giuseppe Pizzardo.[51] Lehnert also antagonized Pacelli's younger sister, who felt the German religious and her staff had usurped the familial role of caring for Pacelli when he returned to Rome in 1930 to assume the office of secretary of state.

Through his Munich associates Pacelli came to know and love the Swiss retreat of Stella Maris in Rorschach, on Lake Constance, which remained a regular vacation spot for him until he became pope. It was to this tranquil Swiss refuge that he retired when the stress of his diplomatic work aggravated the anxiety and digestive ailments that had troubled him since he was a boy. He was joined there for weeks on end at least once a year by his household, including the sisters whose religious order ran a school there. Other close friends who visited included Michael Faulhaber, the archbishop and soon to be cardinal from Munich; Monsignor Francis Spellman, future cardinal and leading member of the American hierarchy; and Monsignor Kaas, whose good humor was known to make the otherwise reserved Pacelli laugh heartily.[52]

Pacelli's attachment to Munich and to Bavaria was profound. And Munich's unique Catholic culture in turn had a deep and lasting influence on Pacelli's evolving political philosophy, especially as it concerned German affairs.[53] It is commonplace to assume that Bavarian Catholicism was uniformly conservative and papist, with a fiercely independent streak vis-à-vis the rest of largely Protestant Germany. This it undoubtedly was, especially in the rural parts of the region and among the Bavarian aristocracy and high clergy. The situation was different in Munich, though, where the majority Catholic population was more socially and politically diverse, contributing to a more liberal, reform-minded, and nationalist orientation. This made many Munich Catholics more comfortable than rural, conservative Catholics were with Bavaria's place in the wider German polity. It rendered Munich Catholicism more flexible and porous, lacking somewhat the doctrinal purity and unity of Catholicism in other parts of Germany.[54]

Perhaps no member of Munich's Catholic community exerted a greater influence on Pacelli than Michael Faulhaber. The close friendship formed between the two men in those years in Munich developed into a relationship of mutual trust and admiration whose influence was felt at decisive moments for more than two decades. According to Faulhaber's sister Katherine, the cardinal considered Pius XII one of his "best friends."[55] Theirs was a friendship grounded in a shared vision for German Catholicism. As a relative newcomer to the German political scene, Pacelli relied heavily on Faulhaber for his reading of German affairs and his assessment of the Nazi phenomenon.

Pacelli was not expected to stay in Munich very long, nor was he expected to get too deeply involved in the hopelessly complicated Bavarian political scene. His mission was clear and limited: to finalize a formal agreement between the traditionally Catholic state of Bavaria and the Holy See. This was considered an easy first step for nuncio Pacelli, preparing the way for the more arduous task of negotiating a formal agreement between the Holy See and the German federal state. This latter plan was a longstanding objective of papal diplomacy, a move that was helped along by the formal establishment of a papal embassy in Berlin by the summer of 1920.[56] In fact, it was widely expected in diplomatic circles that Pacelli would be transferred to the new Berlin embassy, a move vigorously opposed by the Bavarian bishops and also by Pacelli himself, who was worried that a premature transfer from Munich to Berlin could jeopardize the successful completion of the agreement between the Vatican and Bavaria. Pacelli also worried that opening a papal embassy in the German capital would heighten sensitivities among Protestant conservatives. All this confirmed him in his resolve to delay a move to Berlin for as long as possible, even though his superiors made it clear that his time in Munich, however productive, was to be temporary.[57] In the end, the decision was not his to make, though he did manage to convince the Vatican to allow him to continue living in Munich until 1925. He moved to Berlin only after the agreement with Bavaria was finalized in 1924.

In the wake of German defeat in the First World War, Pacelli found himself living amid the uncertainties that arise when one political order is dying and others struggle to be born. From his unique vantage point as papal ambassador, Eugenio Pacelli watched it all unfold: Germany's defeat; the fall of the Bavarian monarchy and, eventually, of Kaiser Wilhelm II of the Hohenzollern dynasty; the establishment of the Weimar Republic and the signing of the reviled armistice; and the rapid rise of Bolshevik-style revolutionary movements, which culminated in two short-lived Soviet regimes in the Bavarian capital. All this Eugenio Pacelli witnessed firsthand and reported in considerable detail to Gasparri and his staff at the Vatican.[58] As Pacelli's reports confirm, there was a very real fear that the entire German federal empire would collapse, threatened from within by movements in such places as Bavaria for greater autonomy or outright independence from Berlin. Even before it was formally swept away by revolutionary fervor, the Kingdom of Bavaria had tried to negotiate a separate peace deal with the Allied powers in early November 1918. The revolutionary movement led by Kurt Eisner of the Independent Social Democratic Party (USDP) seized on this opening to take Munich's workers and soldiers from the city's garrison into the streets in a massive protest against the Wittelsbach dynasty that had governed Bavaria for centuries.

Virtually overnight, the Bavarian monarchy collapsed, with Eisner declaring Bavaria a democratic Socialist republic. It was a sign of things to come.[59] Before long, massive street protests in Berlin signaled the beginning of the end of Wilhelmine Germany. But it was in Munich where the revolutionary dynamic lasted the longest, spawning successive waves of radicalism, which in turn sparked a series of counter-revolutionary reactions that were to grow in size and efficacy in the coming years. Here, in this atmosphere of revolutionary and counter-revolutionary excess, the seeds of Nazism were sown and, a short time later, Hitler's political career began.[60]

Pacelli wrote to Gasparri that an organized revolutionary minority had managed successfully to exploit the sufferings and privations of the ordinary masses and also of war-weary soldiers, who otherwise might have been expected to quiet the disorder. To Pacelli's mind, the recent success of the Bolsheviks in Russia—what he called the "Russian example"—had stoked the revolutionary agitation in Munich, to the great surprise of Bavaria's ruling classes. Pacelli wrote of an "indescribable" scene following the violent revolutionary agitation, detailing the utter collapse of the armed forces and of mass desertions of soldiers to the revolutionary cause. His reports told, too, of physical damage, even "devastation" and looting, and of the seizure and occupation of the city's infrastructure, including the train station, the telegraph office, and eventually the Landtag, the Bavarian state legislature.

Pacelli reserved his harshest criticism for the revolutionary cadres that had caused the trouble in the first place, especially the movement's leader, Kurt Eisner. Eisner, he observed, embodied the revolutionary movement in Bavaria—an atheist, a radical Socialist, a tireless propagandist with intimate ties to the Russian nihilists, a rabble-rouser imprisoned frequently for political crimes. What is more, Pacelli told his superiors, Eisner was a "Galician Jew." Pacelli concluded that Eisner was "the banner, the program, the soul of the revolution that . . . threatens Bavaria's religious, political, and social life." It was no secret that Eisner and his followers were deeply anticlerical. Pacelli told Gasparri that according to reports, at the first secret meeting of the revolutionary government, Eisner announced that the time had come "to be finished with those priests."[61] Some high-ranking prelates in Munich took Eisner's threat as more than overblown rhetoric and urged Pacelli to leave Munich for a time for the safety of Switzerland. According to some sources, this advice came from Faulhaber. At any event, Pacelli heeded the warning and made his way to the Swiss retreat at Rorschach.

Controversy swirled in papal circles in the wake of Pacelli's decision to leave Munich. The purpose of the move may have been to avoid the uncomfortable prospect of the Eisner government's asking to establish formal relations with the Vatican through Pacelli's office. Faulhaber warned that such a development, especially if the Holy See accepted the gesture, would cause consternation among the bishops and the Catholic faithful of all Bavaria. Pacelli's superiors at the Vatican purportedly were troubled by his flight amid such uncertainty. Pacelli had to explain to Gasparri that he left on the sound advice of the trusted archbishop Faulhaber, who was also worried about Pacelli's fragile physical and emotional state.[62] Pacelli was not without his insecurities, and he worried at times how his actions were being judged by his superiors. In a letter sent to his brother Francesco in December 1919, he was at pains to explain that his concerns about the revolutionary threats facing Munich in the months after the signing of the Treaty of Versailles had nothing to do with fear for his personal safety.[63] After all, even before the revolutionary fervor had subsided, Pacelli and his staff had returned to Munich and faced down a direct armed threat against persons and property of the papal embassy in April 1919 in the wake of the confusion that followed Eisner's assassination in February 1919 by Count Anton Arco-Valley, an army officer and a Catholic.[64] In a reputed show of calm, Pacelli stood down the armed threat when Munich radicals pointed a gun at his chest—an act of bravery that became the stuff of legend among Pacelli's inner circle for years afterward.[65]

Pacelli's description of Kurt Eisner as a "Galician Jew" reflected the influence on the nuncio of Munich's conservative newspapers and of his contacts with members of the city's social and political establishment, who were eager to discredit Eisner and his Bolshevik-style putsch. Eisner's critics exploited a deep-seated anti-Jewish sentiment that conflated revolutionary politics of the extreme Left with areligious and antireligious Jews while at the same time trying to depict Eisner as an outsider—not a *real* Bavarian.[66] It was no secret that many of the leaders of Bavaria's revolutionary movement were of Jewish descent. For those already prone to see the connection, it was a logical step to view Bolsheviks and Jews as indistinguishable. In his reports to the Vatican, Pacelli often referred to the Jewish origins of revolutionary leaders, branding them as immoral foreigners. Writing to Gasparri in April 1919, for instance, he described Max Levien, leader of the Munich Communists and head of the temporary revolutionary central council, as a "young man, also Russian and Jewish, of about thirty or thirty-five years of age. Pale, dirty, with expressionless eyes, and a hoarse and vulgar voice: a truly repugnant type, yet with an intelligent and sly face." Pacelli also painted a stark picture of the condition of the new government's head office, formerly the residence of Bavaria's royal family, as now being in chaos, overrun by workers and soldiers, crammed with an "army of employees," including many young women of dubious character—and all of them, men and women, "Jews . . . in all the offices with provocative airs and shady smiles." The leader of the group of women was Levien's lover, whom Pacelli described as "a young divorced Russian Jewess, who acts like the boss."[67] Pacelli clearly had adopted the prevailing cultural biases of his Munich circles, tinged with the reactionary ethnic nationalism of conservative Bavarians who saw Munich's revolutionary period as a scourge brought on by foreign Jews.

When Kurt Eisner was assassinated in February by Arco-Vally, Pacelli feared that the murder would spark a wave of anticlerical, anti-Catholic fervor among angry revolutionaries. He wrote to Gasparri warning of a pending "war against the clergy."[68] Pacelli described Munich as a city both paralyzed and in tumult. With government offices and businesses closed and public transportation ground to a halt, the city's historic churches were being made to sound their bells to summon city residents to street rallies. Red flags fluttered everywhere. At night, the streets were filled with the sound of gunshots as soldiers patrolled the city. It was impossible to say what was going to happen next. "One prepares possibly for days of blood and terror for poor Bavaria," wrote Pacelli. "May God spare her from such ruin!"[69]

Pacelli's prayers for Bavaria were answered. By early summer, the revolutionary fire that had engulfed the city for months sputtered out, giving way to an unstable but vibrant parliamentary system for the region—but not before one last ugly outburst of violence in late April and early May 1919. In an attempt to regain control of the city and put an end to the dreams of a Red Munich, counter-revolutionary groups, led by the notorious Freikorps, unleashed a campaign of repression—including mass executions—against supporters of the revolutionary cause. The Communist and Socialist forces responded in kind by executing a number of hostages who were being held in a Munich high school in what nuncio Pacelli denounced as the "bestial hostage murder." The reprisal sent shock waves throughout Munich and piqued a reaction against the Communist factions of the ruling revolutionary Bavarian council. Pacelli is reported to have said that the hostage murder warranted a severe response. In fact, the response was swift and severe—the Freikorps thus committed a good many excesses of their own, roaming the streets like thugs, brandishing weapons, sexually assaulting women, and conducting summary executions.[70]

The brief but violent revolutionary period that began in November 1918 made a profound impression on Pacelli, offering formative lessons on the nature of German politics and society. From the time he first visited Germany to promote the pope's peace proposal, to the volatile early months of the postwar period, Pacelli's thinking about the German situation came to be informed by a set of basic assumptions that remained with him for the rest of his career. The central tenet of Pacelli's evolving geopolitical worldview was based on a core belief—that the political stability and territorial integrity of Germany were essential to stop the spread of Bolshevism from the East and to counter the influence of an excessive secularism from the West.[71] Pacelli's commitment to Germany's political stability translated into very decided views about the terms of the peace settlement that was imposed on Germans by the Treaty of Versailles; about the role of Catholic parties in the political system; and about the dangers of political extremism in German life, whether it came from the revolutionary Left or the authoritarian, nationalist Right.

Pacelli had concluded quickly that there was a clear connection between the social and economic effects of the war and the growth of extremist political parties, especially of the revolutionary Left. Even before the decisive events of early May 1919, Pacelli wrote to Gasparri to convey his sense that a total Bolshevik takeover of Germany might yet be averted if the devastating effects of the war on the German people could be ameliorated. Everything depended on the outcome of the ongoing peace negotiations with the Allied powers. If the terms of the settlement proved to be "balanced," there was a chance for long-term peace and stability in Germany and by extension all of Europe. If, however, the terms imposed harsh dictates on the German people, it would be next to impossible to avert a Bolshevik "triumph" in all of Germany since even the parties of law and order would have neither the strength nor the will to hold back an angry and desperate populace.

According to one of Pacelli's contacts in the German diplomatic corps, someone whom the nuncio described as a "moderate," any punitive measures of the eventual peace treaty would make conditions "intolerable" and reduce Germany to "slavery," such that the German people would come to prefer Bolshevism to the democratic alternatives. Pacelli even had it from his contacts that the Russian Bolsheviks might consider an invasion of German territory to help their German comrades and thus move closer to the realization of a worldwide revolution. Pacelli painted a frightening scenario of a Bolshevik bloc, extending from Russia to Hungary to Germany, constituting an unstoppable "formidable danger" to France and Italy. Reporting this scenario to Gasparri, Pacelli prayed, "May God inspire moderation in the statesmen gathered now at the Paris Peace conference, to spare Europe from another scourge even worse than this war just ended!"[72]

Having come to Germany in 1917 to talk peace, Pacelli wanted nothing more than to see the Paris Peace Conference succeed at laying the foundations of a lasting peace settlement. Yet like so many of its critics, Pacelli did not see much hope for a lasting peace in the Versailles treaty signed in June 1919. He realized that the perception of the treaty as excessively harsh and punitive mattered as much as the reality, and was destined to inflame popular anger, sending more and more ordinary Germans to the extremes of the political spectrum. There was even the vague fear of what Pacelli called "national Bolshevism"—a rumored alliance between the revolutionary Left and radical nationalists to "break the chains of Versailles," as Pacelli put it.[73] There were fears about the practical consequences of the treaty's clauses, such as the reduction of the size and strength of the German army which might hinder the German state's capacity to deal with Communist insurgents.[74] There was something prophetic in Pacelli's assessment that the unpopular settlement would skew domestic German politics in such a way as to expose the so-called peace of Versailles as an "international absurdity" and a fleeting moment.[75]

Not that Pacelli shared the vehement opposition to Versailles of the staunch nationalists. Months before the treaty was signed, even before the war ended technically with the armistice of November 1918, the Vatican and Pacelli had shown a willingness to support a peace settlement promoted by the German Catholic politician Matthias Erzberger that entailed some major concessions on Germany's part. As leader of the Catholic party, Erzberger dealt with the papal nuncio frequently after Pacelli arrived in 1917. For much of the war, Erzberger, like most German Catholics, had been keen to prove his loyalty to the Wilhelmine state through an aggressively nationalistic and militaristic support for the continued German war effort. By the time he came to know Pacelli, Erzberger had changed his mind about the direction of the war and was leading a spirited crusade for a negotiated peace settlement. In fact, it was Erzberger who led the debate in the German parliament in the summer of 1917 which precipitated the crisis that brought down the Bethmann-Hollweg government and then saw the Reichstag pass a resolution favoring a negotiated peace settlement that included important concessions. Erzberger went on to play a central role in the move toward the Weimar system of parliamentary politics, and was a member of the delegation that signed the reviled armistice that ended the war in November 1918. For his association with the armistice, his championing of the Versailles settlement, and later his support for the Socialist government of Freidrich Ebert, Erzberger was despised by ardent nationalists and militarists, including many of the more conservative Catholics. Little wonder that the Catholic leader was eventually forced from office, and then assassinated by "nationalist fanatics."[76]

Pacelli had more than the political future to worry about. He decried the state of moral depravity spawned by the revolutionary atmosphere of the time. In one report from early 1919, he wrote disdainfully of the surreal quality of Munich society, in which hunger, deprivation, and revolutionary violence mingled with a penchant for dancing and socializing: "Here they do nothing other than dance, night and day, in private homes and in public places. The newspapers are filled with advertisements of dancing classes . . . of cafes and clubs for dancing. . . . Just like the decadence of the Roman Empire: *panem et circenses* [bread and circuses]."[77] All this, while Socialists in the provisional government in Munich talked openly about a future constitutional ban on religious instruction in schools. As a result, Pacelli and the Vatican felt there was an urgent need to negotiate a formal agreement that would protect some basic rights and privileges for Catholics, above all in the area of education.

Pacelli's fear of the spread of Bolshevism led to his approval of the Bavarian Civil Guards, a well-armed paramilitary force of several hundred thousand men drawn mainly from the middle classes but well funded and armed, thanks to Bavaria's political and social establishment.[78] At a time when the German Workers' Party, the future Nazi Party, was a small, obscure movement on the extreme right of Bavarian politics, the Civil Guard was probably the largest group at the core of a vast "counter-revolutionary network," with ties to other self-proclaimed civilian defense forces beyond Bavaria.[79] It is not clear whether Pacelli fully appreciated the militantly antidemocratic nature of the Civil Guard or of the group's ties to some decidedly unsavory paramilitary organizations that were ready and willing to cow and kill those whom they called "enemies of the Reich."[80]

The meteoric rise of the Civil Guards as an armed force—three hundred thousand strong—sounded alarms in Berlin and in other capitals of Europe and led to calls for the group to be disbanded. When word spread that the Civil Guards were to be suppressed by the German central government, several influential Bavarian Catholics approached the papal embassy in Munich, asking for the Vatican to intervene to prevent the move. Pacelli was receptive to their plea, since the Civil Guards were widely believed to be the only real defense against the Bolshevik threat.[81]

The extent to which Pacelli genuinely believed the Civil Guards were indispensable is revealed in a letter to his brother Francesco. Writing from Munich in December 1919, Pacelli told his brother that, in view of the restrictive terms of the Versailles settlement, the Civil Guards were the only reason the Communists had been held at bay so far. He had it from various authoritative sources, he said, that if the pressure to disband the group succeeded, Bolshevism would inevitably return to Bavaria, especially in Munich, and this time would be more firmly established. In a telling sign of some difficulties between himself and Gasparri's office, Pacelli said that having already been accused of being too easily frightened—presumably a reference to his flight from Munich in November 1918—he was more reluctant to write to the Vatican expressing his fears about the consequence of disbanding the Civil Guards. He was therefore asking Francesco to make discreet inquiries with Gasparri so that he had clear instructions about what to do in the event of future dangers. "My life has already been threatened once," he wrote, "and I don't know whether I'd survive a second time, but *I am ready for anything*, so long as someone tells me clearly and without qualifications what is expected of me in case of a threat." He worried that his superiors in the Vatican did not seem to take the threat all that seriously, assuming that the German people were naturally inclined to prefer political stability. This might be the case, Pacelli acknowledged, but the Allied powers would then have to provide the Germans with the means—presumably, the armed forces—needed to defend against the "numerous and powerful revolutionary elements." The nuncio trusted that Francesco would know best how to convey the sense of urgency about a situation that was causing him such anxiety and aggravating his frail health.[82]

The campaign to save the Civil Guards failed. The group was formally disbanded in June 1921, making room for other radical authoritarian nationalist groups, including Hitler's National Socialist German Workers' Party (NSDAP), to enter Bavaria's and Germany's political life.[83] Pacelli may have refrained from offering unqualified public support for the Weimar Republic or for the Socialist-dominated government of Friedrich Ebert, but he did demonstrate a consistent aversion to the extremist tendencies that threatened Germany's political stability from within.[84] A revealing insight into Pacelli's understanding of German politics comes from his report to Gasparri on the results of the federal election of June 1920. Pacelli described the vote as having "a special importance," as the first election after the formal proclamation of the Weimar Republic and the establishment of a Constituent Assembly to write a new constitution. He surmised that the big winners of the election were the extremist parties—both Right and Left—at the expense of the centrist parties. The latter included the Catholic Center Party, which saw a portion of its conservative Catholic support flow to the more hard-line German nationalist parties such as the *Deutsche-National-Volkspartei*. Pacelli attributed the victory of the more radical parties to several factors. For one, it was evident that the experiment in coalition government—which included Socialists, democrats, and some Catholics from the Center Party—was failing, since it pleased none of its key constituencies: workers, peasants, or members of the middle class. Pacelli also singled out the Versailles treaty as a major cause of the increasingly radical nationalism in German political life at the beginning of the Weimar era. "The rebirth of nationalism," he reasoned, "was almost fatal after that peace settlement which was accepted only by force and against the will of the conservative parties and others. The reaction spawned by the conditions dictated at Versailles, some of which are seen as too harsh while others altogether untenable have pushed a good part of the middle class toward those parties that previously were among the more energetic advocates of Germany's war policy."[85]

As for the Catholic Center Party, Pacelli suggested that its commitment to coalition government with Socialist and liberal parties had cost it the support of a good part of the Catholic middle class. The lingering hostility toward Matthias Erzberger did not help either, which explained, to Pacelli's mind, the gains of the Bavarian People's Party, that group of conservative Bavarian Catholics who broke with the Center Party to militate more aggressively for Bavarian autonomy. Pacelli warned that without the solid social bases upon which to build a workable majority government, the future portended more and more elections, resulting in continued political instability or, worse yet, "a lively class struggle which could lead to civil war."[86]

Pacelli's worries about Germany's political future proved to be prophetic. The perpetual political and social crises of the early 1920s opened the door for Hitler's nascent NSDAP to make its first serious foray onto the political scene. Pacelli wrote to Gasparri with a pithy report on the Beer Hall Putsch of November 1923—the ill-fated Nazi attempt to seize power in Munich and then all of Germany.[87] He reported calmly how on the night of November 8, Hitler and his armed cohorts had seized the Bavarian governor Gustav von Kahr and other ministers gathered in a Bavarian beer hall, and had proclaimed a new German national government with General Erich von Ludendorff as head of the army. Pacelli did not seem especially worried about the attempted coup, telling Gasparri that order would be reestablished shortly, though probably not without bloodshed.[88] It is not clear whether he thought the Nazi putsch was bound to fail, though it was clear that with the German army poised to march on Munich to deal with the situation, violence might ensue. But just as quickly as the Nazi coup had started, it ended. Pacelli reported to Gasparri that Hitler had been stopped and order restored.[89] What exactly he thought of Hitler and National Socialism at this early stage of the movement's political life is not clear from the records at hand; at the very least, he did not care to expound on his assessment of Hitler and the NSDAP in his uncharacteristically brief reports back to the Vatican. But he did recognize the "anti-Catholic" nature of the radical authoritarian nationalism espoused by the extreme Right, as witnessed in the rhetorical attacks leveled against Cardinal Faulhaber, archbishop of Munich, who had publicly criticized radical nationalist attacks on Jews.[90] The lesson Pacelli took away from the abortive Beer Hall Putsch, which confirmed him in a view first formulated in 1917, was of the inherent dangers of an inflated, aggressive nationalism. As he wrote to Gasparri in May 1924, nationalism might be "the most dangerous heresy of our time."[91]

By the time he arrived to take up permanent residence in the German capital in 1925, Pacelli's reputation had preceded him, increasing not only his profile in German power circles but also the profile of Vatican diplomacy more generally, despite continued German opposition to the idea of a formal agreement between the Holy See and the Reich. In less than a decade, Eugenio Pacelli had gone from being a relative unknown in the ranks of the papal diplomatic service to one of the Vatican's best known and most widely respected representatives abroad, rubbing elbows with the influential political, military, and diplomatic officials present in Berlin. Although his heart was to stay in Munich, Pacelli soon discovered that Berlin was a world all its own. It was, after all, the nerve center of German political and social life, a vibrant city brimming with activity. It was in Berlin that Pacelli came to frequent circles where he met leading German conservatives and leading Catholics—men such as Franz von Papen, a future chancellor of Germany and one of the central players in Hitler's rise to power in 1933. In fact, it was Papen who helped to initiate Pacelli into the conservative and Catholic circles of the capital, hosting him every so often at the prestigious Guards Cavalry Club. Papen later recalled that Pacelli was probably the first "Prince of the Church" ever to be invited to the club, together with other prelates, including the future bishop Clemens August Graf von Galen, who came to be mythologized in later years as the "Lion of Münster" for his open criticism of Nazi euthanasia policies and the regime's attacks against Catholic interests, and whom Pacelli made a cardinal after the war.[92]

Pacelli's attempt to formalize relations between the Holy See and the German federal government was made all the more challenging by the political instability of the Weimar system. Nor did it help the prospects of an agreement with the Vatican that the Catholic Center Party was an integral component of each coalition government, several of which were led by Center Party leaders, including devout and engaged Catholics like Wilhelm Marx, chancellor on two separate occasions in the 1920s. Any hopes that having a Catholic as chancellor would facilitate the successful completion of a formal agreement between the Holy See and the German Reich were quickly dashed. Pacelli realized as much in the early years of the Weimar Republic in his many meetings with Marx. As Pacelli noted in one report to Gasparri from December 1923, on several occasions he had asked the chancellor whether now was an opportune moment to bring about a rapid negotiation of a concordat between the Holy See and the Reich. The soon-to-be-ratified agreement with Bavaria provided a sound template, Pacelli reasoned. Chancellor Marx, however, remained noncommittal. By the end of 1923, Marx seemed quite certain that a concordat was not likely to be reached, given that the current government was soon to fall. Clearly frustrated, Pacelli wrote to Gasparri that the "good but timid" chancellor did not seem to appreciate fully that in the near future, Germany's federal politics would be even more polarized between extremes of both the Right and the Left, between Protestant nationalists on the one hand and Communists on the other. This made it all the less likely that an agreement favorable to the church could be reached.[93] In the end, of course, Pacelli was right; only in the summer of 1933—after Hitler signaled his intense desire to reach speedily an agreement with the Holy See, and with the Center Party on the verge of self-destruction—was the controversial *Reichskonkordat* finally signed, to the quiet satisfaction of Eugenio Pacelli, now ensconced as cardinal secretary of state—the Vatican's second most powerful figure.

Pacelli's dealings with the state of Prussia proved especially challenging and demanded most of the nuncio's time and effort. There was considerable resistance among the Prussians to the idea of a formal agreement with the Holy See. The one major incentive for the Prussians to reach such an agreement was to do so before the Vatican concluded a concordat with the German Reich itself. For this reason, the Prussian state pursued an agreement along the lines of the deal between the Holy See and Bavaria, thus protecting Prussian interests in advance of an eventual concordat between the Vatican and the German republic. The agreement between the Holy See and Prussia was finalized in July 1929. Although much vaunted, the Vatican's agreement with Prussia was a limited success. It was probably the very best that could have been hoped for given the fierce opposition Pacelli faced.[94]

Not long after successful treaty negotiations with Prussia were completed, Eugenio Pacelli learned that he was to be made a cardinal. There was more: he was tapped by Pius XI to replace Gasparri as the Vatican's secretary of state. In a private note the pope explained to Pacelli the reasons for his choice: "It is your spirit of piety and prayer that led me to this decision," Pius XI wrote, invoking Pacelli's impressive record as a papal representative in Germany. In this regard, the pope wrote, Pacelli proved that he knows "how to employ the many gifts God has given you for His glory and in the service of the Church."[95]

Before returning to Rome, a resigned yet anxious Pacelli sought refuge and a brief respite at Rorschach. He wrote to his brother as if he were genuinely surprised by a decision that had seemed all but inevitable for months. "I am so distraught and I don't know where to begin," he told Francesco, with so much to do in so little time before leaving Berlin for good. Pacelli worried that he did not even have the proper vestments for his new post, let alone lodgings or furniture. "I could never have imagined such a point-blank blow," he wrote. "May God's will be done."[96]

In early December 1929, Pacelli took leave of Berlin and Germany. German officials organized a grand send-off at the city's Kroll Opera, where President Hindenburg thanked Pacelli on behalf of the German people for his incessant efforts to promote peace and a harmonious relationship between the Holy See and Germany. The major German dailies offered laudatory assessments of Pacelli's legacy, a testament of the extent to which he had succeeded in winning over or at least placating a good part of the anti-Catholic movement that had greeted him upon his arrival in the German capital. Thousands gathered at the Anhalter train station to say good-bye to a man whose past, present, and future were indelibly marked by his German experience. The German Jesuit Friedrich Muckermann surmised that Pacelli's tenure as nuncio in Germany was unprecedented—never before had a papal representative been so well known and so widely admired, even by non-Catholics. It is said that by the time he left Germany, Pacelli was more popular than even the German bishops and cardinals.[97] As he prepared to leave Berlin in late 1929, Pacelli invoked the memory of the peace proposal that first brought him to Germany, trusting that his time and his activity among the German people, especially Germany's Catholics, had not been in vain. With this, he offered one last prayer asking God's blessing on "the Catholics of the capital of the German Empire, on our brothers and sisters in faith in all the German territory, for the prosperity and the peaceful development of all the German fatherland."[98]

Those who had come to know Pacelli well during his time in Germany knew that he left Berlin with a heavy heart. Even in later years, some of his closest collaborators attested to Pacelli's fond memories of his tenure as nuncio and of his resolve to defend all that he saw as good and noble about the German people and culture. Monsignor Giovanni Battista Montini, the future Pope Paul VI who would serve as undersecretary of state to Pius XII, reportedly said that "the Holy Father left his heart in Germany." The former bishop of Speyer, Isidor Markus Emanuel, reasoned that Pacelli showed this enduring attachment to Germany during the "darkest hours" after the collapse of Nazism. Eugenio Pacelli was, put simply, "the first and for a long while the only one who defended our people who were banished before the whole world."[99]

Render unto Caesar: Cardinal Secretary of State

Eugenio Pacelli returned to Rome to assume the second most powerful position in the Catholic Church at a time when the Vatican boasted a newfound stature in international affairs. In the late 1920s, while Pacelli was busy dealing with the German states, his brother Francesco was guiding the Vatican to a historic agreement with Mussolini's government that created Vatican City, thereby restoring territorial sovereignty to the papacy. The 1929 *Conciliazione,* usually referred to as the Lateran Pacts, formally guaranteed the Holy See "absolute and visible independence and an indisputable sovereignty." In effect, the pope was once again a *bona fide* sovereign head of state, and Vatican City was sovereign territory. The agreements affirmed that Roman Catholicism was the "only state religion" in Italy and expanded religious instruction in all of Italy's ostensibly public schools. In return, Mussolini extracted from the Vatican a formal promise to remain "outside the temporal rivalries between other states" while reserving the church's solemn right "to use its moral and spiritual powers."[100] What this meant in practice was not entirely clear at the time, as subsequent conflicts between the Vatican and the Mussolini government would reveal.[101] At the very least, though, Mussolini could be assured that the pope would tread carefully in his public dealings with the Fascist state, especially in the area of international affairs.

Scarcely had the ink dried when the Vatican and Mussolini's government began to clash over the practical application of the formal agreement. The disagreement was especially intense over the question of youth: to be specific, the Mussolini regime's aim to expand the Fascist Party's reach over Italian youth, which necessarily meant challenging the autonomy and influence of popular Catholic youth organizations.[102] Tensions reached a high point by 1931, when Mussolini ordered the dissolution of Catholic youth organizations, prompting Pius XI to respond with the biting encyclical *Non Abbiamo Bisogno* (June 1931) criticizing the Fascist regime for its hostile treatment of the lay organizations of Italian Catholic Action and Catholic Youth, and condemning not the Fascist Party per se so much as Fascist ideas and activities that were deemed to be "irreconcilable with the Catholic name and profession." This included, most gravely from the pope's perspective, the drift toward "Statolatry," that is, "a real pagan worship of the State" that was held to contradict the "supernatural rights" of the church.[103]

Having spent most of the preceding decade in Germany, Pacelli at first seemed out of his depth when it came to working with the Italians. Senior members of his staff had been dealing with Mussolini's government for years, and it was natural that they would take the lead on Italian affairs while Pacelli was still settling into his new post.[104] The new cardinal secretary of state was being eclipsed from above, as it were, by an energetic and combative Pope Pius XI, and from below by his subordinates, especially his friend Giuseppe Pizzardo, who pursued an openly confrontational line with the Mussolini regime through the crisis of 1931. The British ambassador to the Italian government wrote to the Foreign Office regretting Gasparri's departure. It was widely known that Pacelli preferred a more conciliatory approach than his predecessor. The Italian Foreign Ministry hoped that his appointment would improve Vatican-Italian relations. The Italian ambassador in Berlin, Count Luigi Aldrovandi, wrote glowingly of Pacelli's considerable accomplishments as nuncio in Germany and of his good working relationship with the Italian embassy. According to Aldrovandi, Pacelli on more than one occasion had expressed his "admiration" for Mussolini and his government.[105]

As much as they admired him, Italian diplomats, like their British coun-

terparts and other observers, sensed that Pacelli lacked the gravitas to mitigate the headstrong approach of Pius XI and other hardliners.[106] The British
chargé d'affaires at the Vatican, G. Ogilvie Forbes, wrote to the Foreign Office in his report for 1930 that throughout the year, Pius XI had exhibited
"great energy, personally controlling the conduct of affairs even of lesser importance, so much so that his Secretary of State [Pacelli] was in practice reduced to the position of a clerk."[107] The French cardinal Alfred Baudrillart felt
that Pacelli was a fairly marginal player in the papal court, despite his imposing formal title. Baudrillart wrote in his diary that Pacelli was "rather sickly
and not very influential," and he identified two men—Pizzardo and Alfredo
Ottaviani—as Pius XI's closest and most trusted confidants.[108] Baudrillart even
hinted at some evidence of poor judgment on the part of the new secretary
of state that had hurt his standing with the pope. Writing in April 1931, Baudrillart alluded to "a painful affair" when word reached Pius XI that an Italian
cardinal had blessed a Fascist banner. An angry and embarrassed pope is reported to have asked Pacelli, "Did you know about this?" To which the secretary of state responded, "Yes." The pope then asked whether Pacelli had approved the gesture. Pacelli once again said, "Yes," adding, "I told you, Holy
Father, that I would be incapable of carrying out the functions of the secretary of state."[109]

Whatever the story's accuracy, Baudrillart's account confirms the perception in certain circles that Eugenio Pacelli was not firmly in command of his
new job. Even a few years into the post, in fact, rumors spread that Pacelli
was asking the pope to find a new secretary of state.[110] It was no secret that
Pacelli himself had hoped fervently to be passed over for the position, claiming, perhaps with some false modesty, that he had neither the temperament,
nor the skills, nor the inclination to be secretary of state. Some scholars have
opined that Eugenio Pacelli was selected by Pius XI precisely because he was
considerably younger and much less experienced than Cardinal Gasparri, and
so could be relied upon to "do his master's bidding."[111] The more plausible
explanation for Pacelli's promotion was that Pius XI saw him as the man most
qualified for the job, possessing an unparalleled combination of intellectual
ability, work ethic, and, after a decade in Germany, practical diplomatic experience on some of the Vatican's most challenging files. Pacelli's superiors
and colleagues were unanimous in their praise of the future pope's talents
and above all his seemingly endless capacity for work. Domenico Tardini re-

called that Pacelli would spend hours working, often without pause, "reading, thinking, and taking notes." Pacelli could read with "extraordinary speed," Tardini said, and yet he had powerful comprehension skills that allowed him to grasp quickly the essential points of a given issue.[112] Even Cardinal Baudrillart knew not to underestimate the future Pope Pius XII. Baudrillart judged Pacelli "very clever" but also "secretive," which kept everyone guessing about his true political aims and intentions.[113]

From his unique vantage point at the British legation, British Envoy Francis d'Arcy Osborne reported to the Foreign Office that while Pacelli was someone of "great piety, intelligence and unusual personal charm," he was bound to be overshadowed by the man he served. Given what Osborne described as the "forceful personality" of Pius XI, the cardinal secretary of state would have "less say in the determination of policy" than his predecessors.[114] There is no doubt that Ratti was a headstrong and voluble character. But Osborne, like the other diplomats at the papal court, seriously underestimated Pacelli's own capacity for independent thought and action. They also underestimated how much Ratti trusted and counted on Pacelli, and the extent to which the future Pius XII translated this trust into serious influence over papal diplomacy. In fact, Pacelli did not shy away from hinting at a divergence of opinion with the pope. This may explain why several of his interlocutors perceived Pacelli to be more amenable to accommodation, and less openly confrontational, than his superior. This was especially true of Pacelli's dealings with Italian officials with whom he met most frequently—evidence of the unique relationship between the Vatican and Mussolini's Italy, which boosted Pacelli's working assumption that the Holy See could exercise more direct influence over Italy than over any other major power.

In short, Eugenio Pacelli found his gravitas soon enough. Under the auspices of the Congregation for Extraordinary Ecclesiastical Affairs, which he led deftly, Pacelli oversaw the inexorable growth in the influence of the Vatican's political and diplomatic offices. In this he was assisted by a small but growing staff of talented clerical administrators. Their numbers were small but their influence considerable. When Pius XI was elected pope in 1922, the Congregation counted a grand total of seven full-time staff members; by 1939, on the eve of Pacelli's election as pope, the number had risen to twelve.[115] More important than its overall numbers was the increasing weight the Congregation carried in church affairs, especially in the Curia. While the cardinals and experts attached to other Congregations might be consulted on various doctrinal matters—as happened in the mid-1930s, for instance, when the Holy Office was consulted about a possible papal condemnation of nationalism and racism—final decisions increasingly were taken by the pope in consultation with Pacelli and his staff.[116] In effect, the political-diplomatic office of the Holy See played the decisive role in papal decision-making on a range of issues through the 1930s, especially on church-state relations. The effect was not only to inflate the power and influence of Pacelli's office but also to centralize decision-making in the pope's hands. So it was that the most meaningful deliberations and important decisions about the degenerating situation in Germany and Spain in the late 1930s took place in Pacelli's office. In practical terms, this meant that the pope and Pacelli were acting with considerable latitude in the Holy See's dealings with powerful foreign governments.[117]

Pacelli had a clear understanding of his new role and a vision for papal diplomacy. The personal notes he kept of his daily meetings with the pope and with the diplomatic corps reveal that from the beginning Pacelli was very much engaged in the day-to-day operations of the Vatican's diplomatic service. While Pacelli could appear hesitant and uncertain in his meetings with foreign diplomats, in reality he was exceedingly well prepared and displayed acumen both in articulating papal policy and in assessing the political and diplomatic situation of the day. That he was dutiful, even obedient, in his work for the pope was clear enough to everyone. It was said that if Pius XI had declared some small inanimate object to be an elephant, Pacelli would have agreed readily.[118] Pacelli's daily meetings with the pope were usually lengthy and detailed, covering a wide range of issues. The pope would express his thoughts on various matters and issue directives, which Pacelli then had to translate into concrete measures and transmit to the small but far-reaching network of papal diplomats around the world. He met frequently with ambassadors of all the major European powers and heard from papal diplomats from across the world.

This gave the cardinal secretary of state a unique vantage point. In the course of an ordinary workday, Pacelli would meet with the pope to discuss papal responses to a given situation; then it was off to meetings with various ambassadors, each of whom sought to influence the Vatican in ways that were favorable to their respective governments. The ambassadors and other diplomatic officials provided Pacelli with important insights into the domestic situation of the various countries, including those beyond Europe. The Vatican was being drawn into ongoing tensions over the question of Palestine and the implications of Zionism for the region. In February 1934, Pacelli met with Emir Chekif Arslan, who asked the Vatican to intervene with the British government to help stem the flow of Jewish immigrants into Palestine. A month later, in agreeing that the pope ought not to meet with the Zionist leader Chaim Weizmann, Pacelli noted the papal response in his diary, "Zionism is their business. . . . We cannot side with the Arabs because they conquered the Holy Land. Nor can we side with the Zionists. We have no other choice but to stay out of this."[119]

Pacelli, Germany, and the Rise of Nazism

With the rise of Hitler and the National Socialists to power in 1933, German affairs moved to center stage of Vatican diplomacy. Pacelli, the resident expert on Germany, worked directly on the most consequential files. When the German bishop Johannes Neuhausler, an auxiliary bishop of Munich, thanked Pacelli in the mid-1930s for all he was doing on behalf of persecuted German Catholics, Pacelli replied, "Yes, yes, Germany gives me more work and more worries than the rest of the world."[120]

Already by the time Pacelli had returned to Rome in 1930, the German situation was showing signs of increased political and social instability evident in the rising electoral fortunes of the extremist parties—the Communists and the National Socialists—partly as a result of the economic crisis of 1929. The atmosphere bore an eerie similarity to the volatile period in 1918 when revolutionary and counter-revolutionary forces had been poised to plunge Germany into civil war. Having lived this experience firsthand, Pacelli knew all too well how quickly Germany's unstable and ineffective parliamentary system, which had been a defect of the Weimar Republic since its inception, could feed the rise of extremism. Pacelli also knew the grave dangers that such an atmosphere posed to the interests of German Catholics and the German church. His many German friends and acquaintances, prelates and lay people in whom he placed a great deal of trust, kept him apprised of the evolving situation. The most frequent correspondents included his old friend Cardinal Faulhaber, and lay men such as Baron Theodor von Cramer-Klett, a scion of Bavaria's Catholic aristocracy.[121]

Such men enjoyed Pacelli's confidence partly because they tended to affirm his long-standing conviction that political instability exposed all of Germany to the threat of Bolshevism. Because of this fear, some of his correspondents recommended overt Catholic political collaboration with the parties of the Right, including the rapidly expanding NSDAP, Hitler's National Socialist Party. At the same time, it was hard to ignore the obvious disdain that Catholics such as Cramer-Klett had for the aggressive parties of the extreme Right.[122]

Pacelli's response to the crisis bore heavily the imprint of two distinct influences from his time as nuncio. One was that of the more conservative German bishops, especially Cardinals Faulhaber of Munich and Bertram of Breslau, neither of whom had any reason to favor Hitler and the Nazis.[123] At the same time, because of his long-standing relationship with many of Germany's traditional conservatives, including Catholics such as Franz von Papen, Pacelli concluded that there might be sufficient grounds to make common cause with the "new right" on the basis of a few shared objectives that were politically authoritarian and socially conservative.[124]

These assumptions crystallized into actual policy around the contentious question of the role of German Catholicism, and especially of the Catholic political parties—principally the Center Party—in the crisis atmosphere of the last years of the Weimar Republic. On the eve of Hitler's rise to power, Catholics represented a robust minority of about one-third of the German population.[125] The church hierarchy was led by a core of intelligent, capable, and generally very cautious cardinals and bishops. Some of them were brilliant theologians and gifted teachers in their own right. Arguably, the most powerful were Cardinal Adolf Bertram of Breslau, who led the influential Fulda Episcopal Conference, the main organization of German Catholic bishops; Cardinal Michael Faulhaber of Munich, who chaired Bavaria's Munich-Freising bishops' conference; and Cardinal Joseph Schulte of Cologne. In addition a coterie of younger German clergymen went on to make a name for themselves as leaders of the German church, including Clemens von Galen of Münster and Konrad von Preysing of Berlin.[126]

By September 1930, Hitler's NSDAP had become the second largest party in the German Reichstag, a force to be reckoned with in any future government. This worried the German Catholic hierarchy. In their letters to Pacelli —both before and immediately after Hitler's appointment as chancellor—the papal nuncios in Berlin and Munich, Cesare Orsenigo and Alberto Vassallo di Torregrossa, respectively, sounded notes of concern about the danger that some Catholic voters would migrate to the NSDAP.[127] Pacelli and his staff shared this concern, as did the German bishops. This helps to explain why the German Catholic hierarchy was so determined to denounce certain Nazi doctrines, such as the racial theories espoused by Alfred Rosenberg, editor of the Nazi paper *Völkischer Beobachter* and author of *The Myth of the Twentieth Century* (1930), a book that provoked the ire of Pacelli and his circle of advisors.

Yet doctrinal clarity did not translate readily into political resolve. Part of the problem for prelates such as Pacelli and Faulhaber was that they were steeped in a political theology that expressed no particular preference for any one form of government. If anything, by virtue of their clerical training and personal histories, they were more likely to prefer traditional authoritarian systems over liberal democratic forms of governance.[128] In the absence of theological and philosophical commitment to the kind of liberal democratic principles that undergirded the Weimar system, the German church hierarchy, like the Holy See itself, found itself unable to respond in clear, unequivocal ways to the growing extremism of German political life.[129] Things were rendered all the more difficult in that the Nazis, for all their radicalism and un-Christian racial theories, could still be seen as a lesser evil—a way out of chronic political instability or, worse yet, German Bolshevism.[130]

Nowhere was this more evident than in the hierarchy's attitude toward Germany's Catholic political parties, especially the Center Party, which was a constant electoral force in German politics in the interwar era. It was joined in the 1920s by the Catholic party from southern Germany, the more conservative Bavarian People's Party. Because of its centrist inclinations, the Center Party proved especially amenable to the system of coalition governments that defined the Weimar system, meaning that its members participated in almost every government of the Weimar era.[131]

As he had done in the early 1920s, Pacelli watched closely to see what role the Center Party intended to play in the drama playing itself out in national politics. And, as in those years, he still had reservations about the Center Party's propensity to collaborate with the moderate parties of the Left when it was politically expedient to do so. The man to watch at the start of the 1930s was the Center Party leader Heinrich Brüning, a decorated war veteran, who served as chancellor from 1930 to 1932—one of the last leaders of the ill-fated

Weimar system. Brüning was tapped to lead a coalition government by the German military establishment, represented by General Kurt von Schleicher, who saw him as the obvious choice to head a cabinet that could rise above the partisanship of party politics and govern the country with a strong hand, backed by the power of the presidential emergency decree.[132] But the military's enthusiasm quickly evaporated as Brüning stubbornly pushed an unpopular fiscal reform agenda and then called elections for September 1930—in the middle of a severe economic crisis—hoping to win a mandate for a moderate right-of-center nationalist bloc. Instead, the radical parties scored historic gains, as millions of voters flocked to either the German Communist Party (the KPD) or Hitler's NSDAP. Any hope for a more stable and durable Reichstag governed from a moderate center quickly faded. With just under 5 million votes, the Communist Party claimed 77 seats, thereby increasing significantly their parliamentary presence. The stridently anti-Communist NSDAP, though, fared even better. Hitler's party, which had garnered slightly more than 800,000 votes and a paltry 12 seats in the German parliament in 1928, now could count well over 6 million votes and 107 National Socialist deputies in the Reichstag. Though it would take him a few years yet to get there, Hitler was well on his way to national power.[133]

Brüning managed to stay in power until May 1932, but to do so he had to rely on the parliamentary support of the Social Democratic Party. This did not sit well with important factions of Brüning's constituency, including the Vatican. Pacelli knew from the regular nuncio reports that although the Nazis were making impressive electoral gains across Germany through 1931–1932, the Catholic parties were more than holding their own at the local and national level.[134] This gave the Catholic parties strategic political significance. With their electoral strength essentially intact, especially in Bavaria and Prussia, they remained indispensable to governing at both the state and the federal levels.

From the reports he received from private citizens as well as leading prelates, Pacelli realized that he and the Vatican had to come to terms with the newfound political prominence of Hitler's National Socialists. Talk soon turned to a subject that would have been unthinkable a year earlier—the possibility of a coalition government between the Catholic parties and the NSDAP.[135] In correspondence with Pacelli in the year or so before Hitler's appointment as chancellor, the papal representatives in Berlin and Munich flirted openly with the idea of Catholic collaboration with the Nazis, though they acknowledged that this would demand major concessions on the part of Hitler's party. These included the demand that the NSDAP renounce its revolutionary goals; that it accept the Christian basis of an eventual government; and that it respect the Weimar constitution, as well as the various agreements already in place between the Holy See and several German states. From Berlin, Orsenigo wrote to Pacelli hoping that the Center Party's participation in government in largely Protestant Prussia would translate into a robust political defense of everything from Catholic schools to the sanctity of marriage and to laws against abortion.[136]

Given the nature of Nazism and Hitler's political will, such expectations were hopelessly naïve. Leading German Catholic politicians such as Brüning and Dr. Heinrich Held, head of the Bavarian People's Party, knew as much, and they let the Vatican know.[137] It is said that when one colleague suggested inviting the NSDAP into the cabinet after Hitler's electoral success in September 1930, Brüning responded angrily, "No, never, under no circumstances. The National Socialist movement is a symptom of the fever of the German people that will soon disappear again."[138]

Most members of the Center Party supported this view, with the notable exception of Franz von Papen, who eventually played the pivotal role in orchestrating Hitler's appointment as chancellor in January 1933. Like Brüning, the Center Party remained firmly oriented against collaboration with the radical Right in parliament and was increasingly eager to expand the state's power to combat the belligerence of Nazi organizations on the street. In a diary entry from April 1931, Josef Goebbels, the future Nazi propaganda minister, described Brüning as "our most dangerous enemy."[139] Just as Brüning's resolve against the Nazis deepened, the Vatican, including Cardinal Pacelli, was warming to the idea of a strategic alliance between the German Catholic parties and the NSDAP. Pacelli had always been nervous about Chancellor Brüning's constant reliance on the Social Democrats for political survival, and many German Catholics felt the same way, including the Center Party chairman Monsignor Ludwig Kaas, a longtime confidant of Pacelli from his days as nuncio in Germany. Kaas traveled to Rome to meet with Pacelli in 1931 and returned to inform Brüning of the Vatican's growing support for the idea of some kind of political collaboration with Hitler.[140] That August, Brüning himself went to Rome and heard Pacelli say as much directly.[141] In later years, Brüning recalled the meeting as cordial but tense, characterized by a sharp disagreement over two issues in particular: talk of a treaty between the Holy See and the German federal state, which Pacelli had long hoped to achieve; and the prospect of Nazi participation in a cabinet with the Center Party.

As Brüning interpreted it, Pacelli seemed to think that the two questions were inseparable. Presumably, a new, more stable government composed of the Center Party working together with the Nazis would hasten the successful conclusion of negotiations between the Vatican and the German state. In his memoirs, Brüning offered a harsh indictment of Cardinal Pacelli's reading of the German situation: "Even though Monsignor Pacelli had spent thirteen years straight in Germany, he never understood the fundamental features of German politics, or the special place of the Center Party." Brüning correctly identified a basic difference in philosophy between the career papal diplomat and the veteran lay politician. Cardinal Pacelli, Brüning concluded, was deeply "entrenched in the system of concordats" and saw these formal treaties as the surest way to defend Catholic interests in a given state. Like other politically active Catholics, Brüning believed that Catholic interests were best preserved and promoted in the political arena "by the power of lay Catholic politicians."[142] Perhaps more damning was Brüning's conclusion that Cardinal Pacelli simply "misunderstood" the true nature of Nazism.

Pacelli's long-standing unease over Catholic collaboration with the Social Democrats was well known, as was his fear of Socialist inroads in politics. Even some foreign observers felt that the Vatican's response to the meteoric electoral rise of the Nazis, and in particular the reluctance to condemn Nazism outright, was conditioned by the overriding fear of Bolshevism.[143] In a telling sign of papal interest in the party's political potential, Pacelli noted of his discussion with Pius XI in early March 1933 that "Hitler is the first statesman to speak publicly against the Bolsheviks. Up until now, the pope has been alone in this."[144]

Brüning, as he told Pacelli, believed that a Catholic alliance with Social Democrats was preferable to flirting politically with Hitler. "The Social Democrats in Germany were not religious," Brüning recalled, "but they were tolerant while, to my mind, the Nazis were neither religious nor tolerant."[145] After his difficult conversation with Pacelli, Brüning was surprised to hear the pope applauding the "courageous" German bishops for their "unequivocal" criticism of the "errors of national socialism." Whatever the Vatican actually thought about the situation, Brüning commented to someone at dinner that evening that he hoped the Vatican would "have better success dealing with Hitler and Hugenberg than with the Catholic Brüning."[146]

Brüning never forgave Pacelli for what he saw as a betrayal of the German Catholic political tradition and Brüning's leadership in particular at a decisive point in the life of the fragile Weimar system. For years afterward, he never missed a chance to express his disdain for Pacelli's stance on the Nazis. The American Catholic historian John Tracy Ellis, who studied briefly with Brüning when the ex-chancellor was teaching at Harvard, recalled that Brüning was critical generally of the church's "mistaken policies" but that he singled out Pacelli for particular blame. It was said that the former German chancellor in his lectures "never missed an opportunity at Harvard . . . to give a good slam against Pius XII." Bothered by this open criticism of Pacelli, a student approached Brüning after class one day to complain that such searing criticisms were hurtful to the church. Brüning was unapologetic. He claimed to have sent "documentary evidence" to the Vatican to convince the pope and his staff that Nazism posed a dire threat to the church. But, he stated, the documents never reached Pius XI; he claimed that "they had been withheld by Pacelli." In effect, Brüning blamed Pacelli for skewing the Vatican's response to the German political crisis in favor of Hitler at the expense of German political Catholicism.[147]

If true, such claims would amount to a damning indictment of Pacelli's approach to German politics on the eve of the Nazi rise to power. It is difficult, though, to substantiate Brüning's charge. It is unlikely that Pacelli would have had the temerity to keep such reports from reaching the pope's desk.[148] Pacelli conceivably could have filtered the information he relayed to Pius XI, especially since Pacelli and Brüning were increasingly at odds about how best to respond to the rising electoral fortunes and political significance of the Hitler movement. Whatever reservations Pacelli may have harbored about the true nature of the NSDAP, his characteristic pragmatism won the day, hence his openness to the idea of a strategic political or parliamentary alliance between the Catholic parties and the parties of the Right, including the sizable NSDAP. Such an alliance not only promised a way out of continued instability and the perpetual Socialist threat but also bolstered the likelihood of speedy negotiations to ratify an agreement between the Vatican and the German central government.

This cherished goal of Pacelli's diplomacy inched closer to realization in the months following Brüning's resignation as chancellor in late May 1932. Brüning's resignation signaled a decisive shift toward the Right, with the German political and military establishment acknowledging that Hitler and the NSDAP could no longer be ignored. That the Catholic parties remained essential to governing was evidenced by the fact that Brüning was replaced with Franz von Papen, another prominent albeit more conservative member of the Center Party. Papen was at odds with his own party in favoring a strategic alliance with the Nazis, but he enjoyed the backing of President Hindenburg and the military establishment, and evidently could count on a sympathetic ear from the Vatican. Reports to Cardinal Pacelli from the papal representatives in Germany now spoke much more openly about the possibility of a coalition between the Catholic parties and Hitler's NSDAP.[149]

The assumption that Hitler could somehow be tamed easily and his power thus harnessed for other people's political goals was one of the great miscalculations of history, culminating in Hitler's appointment as chancellor in late January 1933.[150] Pacelli greeted Hitler's accession with ambivalence and a healthy dose of caution. Meeting with the French ambassador within days of Hitler's rise to power, Pacelli expressed anxiety over what a Hitler government might do in the field of church-state relations, noting that in the past the National Socialists had tended to oppose treaties between German states and the Holy See. Pacelli went on to say, "Hitler is a brilliant agitator, but it is not yet clear whether he is a statesman: besides, his party includes people of the most varied tendencies." He also expressed concern that the new government might resort to an "act of violence" to achieve its chief territorial objectives.[151]

Despite this caution, Pacelli made negotiations of a treaty with Germany a top priority. His mind was eased by a conversation with the German ambassador to the Vatican a few weeks after Hitler became chancellor. As recorded in Pacelli's personal notes, he received "the fullest assurances that the current government will do nothing against the Catholic Church, nor upset its relations with the Holy See." The German diplomat pointed out that Hitler had been raised a Catholic and that many leading figures of his government were serious Catholics. Pacelli received similar assurances from the Italian ambassador in a meeting that same day. Mussolini was said to have counseled Hitler to hold firm against his political opponents but not move in any way against the churches.[152]

These assurances seem to have satisfied the Vatican enough to encourage the German Catholic parties to engage with Hitler in discussions that ultimately produced the much-desired treaty. Pacelli, ever the pragmatist, believed that the Vatican had no choice but to deal with the Hitler government constructively, just as it would with governments of other political stripes. He even welcomed a suggestion made by Italian diplomats in March 1933 that Hitler visit the Vatican if he came to Rome to meet with Mussolini. Pacelli told the Italians that he should have no problem arranging such a meeting. Since the führer was the leader of a legal government, he said, it would be "natural that, if he were to come to Rome, he should visit the pope."[153]

Monsignor Ludwig Kaas was the indispensable conduit between the Vatican and the German Catholic political parties in the months following Hitler's rise to power. As newly appointed chairman of the Center Party, Kaas enjoyed a unique position with a foot in two complicated worlds—the Roman Curia and German parliamentary politics. A certain degree of mystery still shrouds Pacelli's influence over Kaas and, in turn, Kaas's dealings with the Hitler government in the spring of 1933. On balance, the evidence suggests that after the national elections of March 1933, which saw the Nazis fall just short of a clear majority in parliament, Kaas, with Pacelli's support, resolved to seek some kind of working arrangement with the Hitler government and its coalition partners.[154] On March 6, 1933, the day after the election, Kaas met with Vice-Chancellor Papen, and it seems safe to assume—although the evidence is inconclusive—that they discussed the possibility of the Center Party's support in parliament for the Nazi's Enabling Act, which would allow Hitler to rule by emergency decree in exchange for his commitment to negotiate a treaty with the Vatican.[155] Before long, Kaas resigned as chairman of the Center Party and made his way to Rome, where he worked closely with Pacelli to negotiate the agreement. It was signed in July 1933—to the immense satisfaction of Cardinal Pacelli and Chancellor Hitler.[156]

Recalling this pivotal period in the early life of the Hitler regime, Heinrich Brüning spared little in his criticism of both Kaas and Pacelli. In his unpublished memoirs, he accused both men of being so eager to finalize a treaty with the German government that they muted what should have been a moral caution to German Catholics about the true nature of Hitler and the Nazis. Cardinal Pacelli, wrote Brüning, was prepared to sacrifice everything, it seemed, for the sake of a formal diplomatic relationship between the Holy See and the German government; Pacelli's faith in the "system of concordats led him and the Vatican to despise democracy and the parliamentary system." Both Pacelli and Kaas believed that "rigid governments, rigid centralization, and rigid treaties" were needed to introduce "an era of stable order, an era of peace and quiet."[157] Hence their readiness to make a Faustian deal with Hitler, offering Center Party votes for the Enabling Act in exchange for the promise of speedy treaty negotiations.

Brüning's criticism of Pacelli is overstated, but his description does provide an essentially accurate explanation of why the Center Party voted to support Hitler's Enabling Act, thereby handing Hitler the two-thirds majority needed to give his government the legislative instrument of authoritarian rule. Even before the vote, Hitler told his cabinet that he needed Center Party support to pass the bill and could get it only if the government reached an agreement with the Holy See. Hitler had always admired Mussolini's decision to make peace with the Vatican in 1929, considering it a feat of great political acumen on the part of Il Duce. In July 1933, with the concordat all but in place, Hitler told his cabinet that a treaty with the Vatican had been a central goal of his since becoming chancellor.[158]

What little resistance there remained among Center Party parliamentarians to the Enabling Act dissipated, leading even Brüning and like-minded Catholic politicians such as Joseph Wirth to fall into line and vote with the Hitler government. Only the Social Democrats voted against the measure.[159] Germany's Catholic political tradition, by contrast, strengthened Hitler's hand, perhaps unwittingly, out of a mixed sense of patriotic responsibility, a self-appointed duty to protect Catholic interests, political opportunism, and resignation. The absence of meaningful public ecclesiastical support did not help.

Scarcely a day had passed after the Enabling Act was approved than Monsignor Kaas left for Rome to help steer the negotiations that would lead in a few months to the signing of the *Reichskonkordat*. Events moved quickly from there as Vatican and German officials worked to produce a draft agreement.

Papen arrived in Rome on the eve of Holy Week, a hectic time at the Vatican amid preparations for Easter, the most important celebration in the church's calendar. Papen was insistent, though, hoping to return to Berlin with a draft agreement by Easter Monday. Pacelli and Kaas obliged, working with him late into the night to hammer out a draft. Father Ivo Zeiger, a German Jesuit who worked with Pacelli and Kaas on the draft, described it as "hurried work" that Pacelli shepherded with resolve and self-assuredness.[160]

Around the same time, Nazi minister Hermann Göring met with Orsenigo to discuss what the Vatican might do to encourage the German bishops to reverse their public condemnation of the Nazi movement.[161] It seems clear now that Pius XI and Pacelli felt that in view of the changed political circumstances, and with "new assurances" coming from Hitler's government that it would preserve and promote the rights and interest of the church in Germany, a "modification" of the bishops' condemnation might indeed be in order. In deference to the authority of the German bishops, the Vatican deemed it "neither necessary nor opportune" for the pope to intervene directly. Instead, at the pope's behest, Pacelli told the papal nuncios in Berlin and Munich to encourage the German bishops to rethink their public stance on Nazism. As Pacelli recorded in his journal, "Tell the nuncios not to wait for the bishops to come to them; that they should take the initiative."[162]

With this subtle but unmistakable signal from the Vatican, the German bishops issued a formal declaration renouncing their earlier condemnation. It was not that the bishops had suddenly jettisoned their suspicions of Hitler or changed their minds about the yawning doctrinal gap between Catholicism and National Socialism.[163] But they recognized the reality of Hitler's consolidation of power and realized that they should act quickly to protect the German church from insidious outside influences, including Nazism. Hence their official statement saying, in effect, that since Hitler had guaranteed the interests and autonomy of the church, Catholics could dispense with earlier "bans and warnings" about the Hitler movement. It was not an explicit endorsement of the Nazis, of course, but it was an implicit recognition of the legitimacy of the Hitler government. And it was just what Hitler wanted, and needed.

While the Vatican saw this as a step in the right direction, destined to hasten successful treaty negotiations, leading German Catholic politicians thought otherwise. Despite their recent parliamentary support for the Enabling Act, they were worried that the bishops' statement would weaken the voice of political Catholicism. In the end, neither the German bishops nor the Vatican mustered the resolve to provide the Center Party with the kind of public political support it needed to survive very long as Hitler moved ever closer to forging a one-party state.[164]

Without public ecclesiastical support, and lacking internal cohesion and sense of purpose, the Center Party did not have much of a future in German political life. From the time Hitler became chancellor, there had been an inverse relationship between the Vatican's diplomacy vis-à-vis the German government and the flagging fortunes of the Center Party. While Kaas traveled between Berlin and Rome, working closely with Pacelli to prepare the draft of an agreement to propose to Hitler, the Center Party slumped further into internal division and fatalistic resignation. Although Kaas was no longer party chairman, he continued to push the logic that the Center Party needed to provide a constructive political cover to the diplomatic negotiations taking place between the Vatican and Hitler. He even began to speak openly of the benefits to the church of dealing with Fascist states, pointing to the Lateran Accords between Mussolini's government and the Holy See as a model for church-state relations.[165] In this he found common cause with Pacelli, who, like most Vatican officials, had always been suspicious of the Catholic political experiment, whether in Italy or in Germany. Sir Robert Clive of the British legation at the Vatican reached this conclusion after discussions with members of Pacelli's office. Clive reported to London that the Holy See was "far more interested in the mass of Catholic voters in Germany than in the Deputies who had represented the [Center] party in the Reichstag." The Holy See also doubted it was possible to re-create the Center Party as a political force, he wrote, and it was frankly "not greatly interested in the question."[166]

Brüning, who had succeeded Kaas as party chairman in May, contested Kaas's vision for the party's future, insisting that it should continue to offer a robust opposition to counterbalance Hitler's growing power. Disagreeing with Kaas also meant disagreeing with the Vatican, and in particular Cardinal Pacelli, who, Brüning was convinced, continued to work at cross purposes with the German Catholic political tradition. In fact, in his negotiations with the Hitler government, Pacelli was showing more resolve than Brüning realized. For instance, when Hitler insisted that any treaty contain an explicit ban on clergy in politics—a stipulation of the Lateran treaties—Pacelli held firm to the view that such exclusion made sense only in countries where Catholics were in an overwhelming majority. In short, Cardinal Pacelli was willing to defend a continued overt Catholic presence in German political life.

Papen realized that even Monsignor Kaas, for all his eagerness to help forge an agreement between the Vatican and the German government, would have a difficult time urging the Holy See to agree to an explicit ban on clergy in German politics.[167] But the Vatican did give way in the end; Papen noted in a report sent to Hitler in early July 1933 that Article 32 of the final draft of the concordat "brings the solution which you have wished, Chancellor, whereby the Holy See issues regulations excluding membership and activity in political parties for all members [of the clergy] . . . and people belonging to Orders." Papen informed Hitler of an additional protocol contained in the final text of the treaty whereby the Vatican and the German government agreed to certain "general principles" to regulate the treatment of Catholic clergy "in case Germany should reintroduce general military service." Papen shrewdly noted that the actual content of the regulation mattered less than the fact that here, in the very early months of the Nazi government, the Vatican "is already reaching a treaty agreement with us for the event of general military service. I hope that this agreement will therefore be pleasing to you. It must, of course, be treated as secret."[168]

As the secret protocol suggests, Hitler's government had exceeded its own expectations—a telling sign of the political disparities between the Vatican and the Hitler state. At a Nazi cabinet meeting to discuss the draft of the concordat, Papen defended the "noteworthy provisions" of the agreement, which included "elimination of the clergy from politics and the introduction of an oath of loyalty for the bishops and a prayer for the State." For his part, Hitler brooked no serious debate on the agreement. He urged his cabinet to see "only the great success" in an agreement that would give the Reich "an area of confidence . . . which was particularly significant in the urgent fight against international Jews." Among the notable achievements of the concordat, Hitler singled out the dissolution of the Center Party, which he believed was made possible only after the Vatican "had ordered the permanent exclusion of the priests from party politics." It was, Hitler told his cabinet, a remarkable achievement to have reached a *modus vivendi* with the Vatican much sooner than he could have imagined when he became chancellor.[169]

From the start, Heinrich Brüning interpreted the treaty negotiations as a sign of things to come, intimating to the British ambassador in Berlin, Sir Horace Rumbold, that the Catholic party was poised to dissolve itself since Pacelli was "hostile" to its existence in its current form. Brüning sounded a prophetic note when he predicted in June 1933 that the dissolution of the Center Party would mean that "Hitler will have achieved what he calls 'totality.'"[170]

It is unlikely that Pacelli would have been so explicit. In fact, he reacted defensively when in mid-July 1933 word spread in Catholic circles in Holland that the Vatican had, in effect, sacrificed the Catholic parties for the sake of reaching a deal with the Nazi state. As he wrote to Lorenzo Schioppa, the papal nuncio at The Hague, the Center Party and the Bavarian People's Party had dissolved themselves entirely "of their own accord and completely independently of the Holy See." Pacelli rejected out of hand the charge that the parties were dissolved at the Vatican's instigation as a precondition for successful ratification of the *Reichskonkordat*. They had "dissolved themselves spontaneously, without even informing the Holy See," he asserted, insisting that the Vatican had no responsibility whatsoever in the demise of Germany's Catholic parties.[171]

In Pacelli's version of events, it was the dissolution of the Catholic parties and the inevitability of a German government dominated by Hitler and the Nazis that made the successful negotiation of a treaty all the more urgent. In view of the new reality of German politics, Pacelli told Schioppa, the Vatican had little choice but to do what it could to preserve the rights of German Catholicism, with its twenty million faithful in one of the most important states in the world. In its approach to the Hitler government, Pacelli reasoned, the Vatican took its lead from the German bishops, who agreed that a treaty was "the last hope" for the church in Germany and the only way to avert state-sponsored anti-Catholicism that would be even worse than the *Kulturkampf* of Bismarck's time.[172] For many months after the *Reichskonkordat* was formally ratified, Pacelli continued to insist that at no time had the Vatican demanded or even welcomed the dissolution of the Catholic parties. In a meeting with former Center Party politician Hermann-Josef Schmitt in February 1934, Pacelli expressed his astonishment that the Catholic parties had dissolved themselves so suddenly in the summer of 1933, reasoning that it had all come about much too prematurely. He claimed to know nothing of Kaas's apparent communications with Center Party leaders, in which the former party chairman, by then deeply engrossed in discussions with the Hitler government, gave the impression that the party's dissolution was a *fait accompli*. The story goes that in the first few days of July, Kaas telephoned Center politician Joseph Joos and asked in a surprised tone, "Have you people not yet disbanded?" Pacelli always maintained that he knew nothing of the call, just as he continued to assert that the future of the Catholic parties had played absolutely no role in the treaty negotiations through the summer of 1933.[173]

Abandoned by most of their erstwhile allies, with no support from the German bishops or the Vatican, the Bavarian People's Party and the Center Party willingly dissolved themselves in the first week of July 1933.[174] While it may be technically true that the disbanding of the German Catholic parties ultimately came from within, the absence of meaningful ecclesiastical support made the outcome all the more likely. Pacelli, taking his lead from Monsignor Kaas and the German bishops, was resigned to the fact that Hitler was moving toward a one-party state. When word reached him of increasing harassment of Catholics, especially the clergy, Pacelli was even more convinced that a quick ratification of a treaty with the Hitler government was the surest way to defend the German Catholic Church, its schools and associations, to say nothing of its bishops, clergy, and religious orders.[175] Tellingly, the two German officials charged formally with the task of negotiating with Pacelli —Vice-Chancellor Papen and Ambassador Diego von Bergen—were fully aware of Pacelli's anxiety over the immediate future of the church in Germany. When they met with Pacelli in late June and early July 1933, Papen and Bergen found him "visibly influenced" by reports from various sources of a systematic campaign against German Catholic interests, including "the arrest and maltreatment" of German clergy.[176]

Although he must have been quietly satisfied with the eventual ratification of the agreement with the German state in September 1933, Pacelli knew that Hitler could not be trusted to fulfill the commitments undertaken in the treaty. He said as much to the British chargé d'affaires, adding that the Vatican harbored no great love for the Hitler regime. Even in the weeks following the end of treaty talks, the British representative Sir Robert Clive reported to the Foreign Office that Cardinal Pacelli openly "deplored the anti-Semitism of the German government, their treatment of political opponents and the reign of terror to which they had subjected the whole nation." Moreover,

Pacelli explained that the Vatican had agreed to the treaty in the first place purely as a defensive measure, as a lesser evil between reaching an agreement with the Nazi state and, as Clive interpreted Pacelli's view of the alternative, "the virtual elimination of the Catholic Church in the Reich." And even when signs emerged later in 1933 that the Nazi Party had no intention of fulfilling its treaty commitments, Cardinal Pacelli insisted that the present treaty was better than none at all; at any rate, whatever "excesses" the Germans committed, the world would know that "they were in the wrong and that the Church had nothing with which to reproach herself."[177]

In both public and private, Pacelli continued to maintain that the Vatican's signing of the agreement was in no way tantamount to Vatican endorsement of the Hitler state or radical Nazi policies, domestic or foreign. In a meeting with the Austrian ambassador in July 1933, Pacelli had assured him that the Vatican had no stomach for Nazi talk of annexing Austria. Pacelli was worried about news that Austrian Chancellor Engelbert Dollfuss had begun to prepare a critique of the *Reichskonkordat* on the grounds that the agreement hurt his government's ability to defend Austrian autonomy against Nazi aggression. Mindful of the need to control his image for posterity, Pacelli had asked the Austrian ambassador to expunge any trace of Dollfuss's critique from the archives.[178]

On balance, the Vatican's response to Hitler's rise to power in 1933, like that of the German church more generally, produced mixed results, reflecting the contradictory interests at play at a critical moment of the interwar period. On the one hand, as secretary of state and the Vatican expert on German affairs, Pacelli was one of the leading exponents of an approach that hastened the evacuation of political Catholicism from German life precisely at a time when Hitler and the NSDAP were working to exploit legal, parliamentary instruments to pave the way for a one-party state and dictatorship.[179] Pacelli's approach reflected a sincere desire to defend the ability of the German church, and the Holy See behind it, to preserve the autonomy and doctrinal integrity of German Catholicism in the face of various modern heresies—godless Communism, pagan nationalism, and secularism. On the other hand, if the Vatican's apparent acquiescence to the political ambitions of Hitler so soon into his tenure as chancellor meant the silencing of political Catholicism and the stifling of potential Catholic opposition to Nazi designs for total control of state apparatus, the *Reichskonkordat* constituted a potentially important instrument to contest successive Nazi attempts to control or suffocate altogether the life of the German church.

It was in the political sphere that Hitler's machinations revealed both the potential and ultimately the limits of Pacelli's diplomacy vis-à-vis the evolving Nazi dictatorship. When Germans went to the polls in November 1933 in the first national election of what was now a one-party state, the German Catholic hierarchy and the Vatican continued to defend a principled Catholic opposition to Nazi sterilization laws. Even though the newly minted treaty expressly prohibited overt clerical involvement in politics, Pacelli insisted, with the pope's backing, of course, that in the pending election campaign, German clergy were "free to act according to conscience," in a manner consistent with church doctrine.[180] Presumably, this meant that Catholic laity, long an important demographic in German electoral politics, also had the right and the duty to act according to conscience and in a manner consistent with church doctrine. Yet the dilemma remained—how to defend Catholic doctrine without an effective political voice in electoral politics? Pacelli and the Vatican expected German Catholics to be free to preach, teach, and print in open opposition to certain Nazi policies. In the end, though, the laws were made in parliament, not in the pulpit or in the classroom or in the newsroom. The absence of any meaningful Catholic electoral opposition to the Nazis, coupled with a monopoly on legislative and bureaucratic power, revealed the extent to which Hitler's strategy for dealing with the church was paying the führer rich dividends. By contrast, the benefits to the church of the vaunted diplomatic entente with the German state were neither clear nor certain.

3

Conflict and Compromise

The German question dominated Pacelli's tenure as cardinal secretary of state, just as it would dominate and in some respects define his pontificate. Even before the treaty with the German Reich was ratified formally in September 1933, Pacelli had learned to doubt the sincerity of Nazi promises. Despite the apparent success of negotiations, Pacelli immediately was confronting German officials with what he called "disquieting reports" about Nazi intimidation and coercion against German Catholics. He was concerned not only about certain technicalities deliberately left unresolved during the last phases of negotiations that summer, but also about a fundamental divergence between the Vatican and the Hitler government on "essential points." More than anything else, Pacelli feared that in practice the agreement with the Germans had "been applied in a manner detrimental to the Catholic interests and contrary to the intention of the Holy See."[1]

It was a most inauspicious beginning to an arrangement that was meant to promote amicable relations between the Vatican and Hitler's regime. Pacelli later was to regret not having clarified the "essential points" before signing the agreement. The Holy See even hinted that it was prepared to walk away from the treaty if questions about its practical application were not resolved before formal ratification. The threat proved to be as idle as it was vague. The stage thus was set for a long season of protracted discussions and intense disagreement between Cardinal Pacelli and German officials over violations of the agreement negotiated so eagerly by both parties in the spring and summer of 1933. Pacelli quickly emerged in diplomatic circles as one of the most forceful critics of what he called an all-out Nazi assault aimed at destroying the Catholic faith altogether.[2] Yet when Pope Pius XI himself began to question the logic of continued diplomatic relations between the Vatican and the Hitler government, Pacelli defended the concordat as the single most important defense of Catholic interests in the Hitler state—a conviction from which the future pope never wavered, despite an abundance of evidence to the contrary. He was either unwilling or perhaps simply incapable of envisioning alternative means of engaging with Hitler. This was evidence either of a resolute character and prudential judgment, or, conversely, of a fateful inability to admit mistakes and to learn from them.

Among the disturbing reports reaching Pacelli's desk in 1933 were stories of Hitler's attempt to suppress the publication of Catholic newspapers that expressed opinions consistent with Catholic doctrine on such issues as eugenics and sterilization, sometimes in direct opposition to specific Nazi policies. Pacelli wanted to dispel any suggestion that the Vatican wanted to constrain or silence altogether Catholicism in German public life, so he pressed the Germans to guarantee the freedom of Catholic newspapers to "proclaim and defend Catholic principles publicly." Pacelli also told the Germans of his concern for Catholic organizations that faced intimidation and in some cases outright suppression. Nowhere was the pressure on Catholic associational life felt more than among Catholic youth groups, which were trying to resist government directives aimed at privileging membership in the Hitler Youth. Faced with the choice of joining the Hitler Youth or remaining in their Catholic organizations, many Catholic youths, the Vatican feared, might join the Hitler Youth "for professional and economic reasons."[3]

Although undoubtedly sincere in their concern, Pacelli and the Vatican were not prepared to push the issue to the point of actually jeopardizing the agreement. Meanwhile, Pacelli was calmed by German assurances that the Vatican's objections were duly noted and that upon formal ratification, the two sides would engage in a "friendly exchange of views" to resolve outstanding issues.[4] But the exchange of views was strained from the beginning.

When Pacelli met in September 1933 with the German chargé d'affaires, Eugen Klee, for the formal exchange of the ratification documents, the cardinal handed Klee a supplement to the "Short Note" outlining three points of concern: the question of Catholic groups, the status of the Catholic press, and the Nazi government's dismissal from government posts of Catholic employees, including those of Jewish descent. Klee responded that the third issue was not strictly speaking related to the concordat. Pacelli conceded the point, but asked for the rationale behind the dismissal of Catholics. Saying he was doing so at the expressed wish of Pope Pius XI, Pacelli submitted a written request for the reinstatement of Catholic employees who opposed Nazism either because they held different political views or for "reasons of conscience." The Vatican also demanded "the same treatment" for Catholics of Jewish descent as was afforded Catholics of so-called Aryan descent.

Klee bristled and replied that this was "not possible, since the Jewish question was not a religious but a race problem." To this, Pacelli said that the pope's "religious and humanitarian" beliefs compelled him to speak on behalf of these Catholics from Jewish backgrounds—whether they were converts from Judaism or had Jewish ancestors.[5]

Having allowed himself a brief respite at his favored Swiss getaway at Rorschach, Pacelli returned to Rome in mid-October 1933 to find Pope Pius XI increasingly agitated by repeated German violations of the agreement, to the point where the irascible pontiff seemed ready to go public with his objections. The pope instructed Pacelli to express in no uncertain terms the depths of his anger over the German government's treatment of Catholics. Pacelli was told to underscore that Pius XI was on the verge of a very spirited public condemnation of German behavior. In discussions with German diplomats, Pacelli emphasized the evolving view in papal circles that the Vatican had held its tongue for too long, in the face of too many blatant, unjustified excesses against German Catholics. Summarizing Pacelli's account of the pope's state of mind, the German ambassador to the Holy See, Diego von Bergen, told Berlin that Pius XI had come to believe that "the dignity of the Holy See requires that he emerge from the reserve which has heretofore been incomprehensible to the faithful." In fact, Bergen had it from Pacelli directly that a formal note of public protest was drafted and ready to be pronounced at an upcoming meeting between the pope and the cardinals. When Bergen warned Pacelli against any such public reprimand, Pacelli replied that the pope was "deeply annoyed" and would be hard to dissuade. But Pacelli said he would try, and he was successful. Pius XI's address to the cardinals contained no overt political commentary. Not for the first time, Pacelli had exerted a moderating influence on an increasingly combative Pope Pius XI, who was growing ever more concerned about the appearance of Vatican indifference to the plight of persecuted German Catholics and others.[6]

This, then, became the hallmark of Eugenio Pacelli's dealings with the Hitler state—pivoting constantly between private albeit formal and often biting criticism of the Reich for its violations of the concordat, and the urge to avoid a public repudiation if not a formal break in relations with the German government. To some extent, German recalcitrance may have been emboldened by the quiet assurance that the Hitler government could count on Pacelli to stay the hand of an increasingly impatient Pope Pius XI. As early as October 1933, Bergen wrote reassuringly that Pacelli had a "realistic attitude" and was working to dissuade the pope from making any kind of public gesture to denounce Nazi tactics against German Catholics. It helped that Pacelli was seeking advice from Monsignor Kaas, who, Bergen apparently told Berlin, was working hard "to counteract the opposition trying to block the path of the new Germany." At least Bergen said as much, perhaps as a strategy to convince skeptical German authorities to trust Catholic compatriots.[7]

When Hitler's government sent Dr. Rudolf Buttmann of the Interior Ministry to the Vatican to begin negotiations on a number of pressing issues left unresolved by the concordat, Pacelli used the occasion to launch the first volley in what would become a war of words between the Vatican and the Hitler state.[8] In addition to reiterating earlier complaints about the coercion and suppression of Catholic organizations, Pacelli voiced grave concern about the pervasive influence of Nazi racial theories in schools and other institutions, including hospitals. Referring specifically to Alfred Rosenberg's *Myth of the Twentieth Century*, Pacelli put the problem plainly: "Since there are substantial differences between certain national-socialist principles and Catholic doctrine, to impose such teaching is in open violation of article one of the Reich Concordat." Pacelli decried the "anguish of conscience" that Catholics experienced over Nazi sterilization laws and insisted that the German government respect the right of Catholics to abstain from practices that violated church teaching and individual conscience. He concluded with a thinly veiled threat to go public with the Vatican's concerns about continued German violations of the concordat. Unless the government's assurances to respect the treaty were soon translated into action, Pacelli warned, the Vatican would have no choice but to publicize its complaints. He added that the Hitler government should not misinterpret the public silence of the "supreme Authority of the Church" to mean immunity from judgment for the many "offenses against justice and against the freedom of the Church and its followers in Germany."[9]

German diplomats took Pacelli's threat seriously but pressed the Vatican to desist, offering the usual verbal assurances of their government's sincere intention to address the contentious issues. But instead of taking action to remedy the Vatican's grievances, the government resorted to rhetorical devices, invoking a common cause against a shared enemy, Communism, while assuring the Vatican that the Reich had no interesting in launching another *Kulturkampf* against German Catholics.[10]

For all his characteristic restraint, Pacelli protested that words were no longer enough—the Vatican, together with German Catholics, demanded concrete action to address the long list of complaints. As he wrote in his personal notes after a meeting with Pius XI in December 1933, "One cannot trust in the loyalty of Germany's rulers."[11] He was especially worried about the obvious ambition of the Hitler state to exert a monopoly over the education of German Catholic youth, and he denounced as illegal the activities of various branches of government that were coercing young Catholics into joining the Hitler Youth. With uncharacteristic sarcasm, Pacelli said he was perplexed that the German government repeatedly gave assurances of its desire to resolve these grievances and respect the concordat yet continued to allow serious treaty violations to continue. Pacelli also voiced his frustration at an emerging pattern in the Vatican's dealings with the Hitler government: when complaints were lodged with high-ranking government officials, they blamed overly zealous lower-level officials or untamed party members at the grassroots. When complaints were directed to the latter, the response invariably came back that everything had been approved by or even ordered directly from Berlin.[12] Clearly, the Germans were playing games to avoid confronting treaty violations.

Alarming reports about the status of Catholics in Germany continued to cross Pacelli's desk, with mounting evidence that the persecution of Catholics was intensifying.[13] In addition to the reports from the papal diplomats in

Berlin and Munich, there were letters from private individuals, addressed to the Secretariat of State or to the pope himself, expressing concern over the security and freedom of individual Catholics as well as Catholic newspapers and associations. From Berlin, nuncio Orsenigo wrote of a concerted "campaign against Catholics," recounting a now familiar litany of violations of the letter and spirit of the concordat, as well as new Nazi threats to ban the publication of diocesan bulletins that reprinted articles from the Vatican newspaper, *L'Osservatore Romano*. From Munich, the nuncio Alberto Vasallo di Torregrossa wrote to tell Pacelli about the arrest in August 1935 of the Bavarian Catholic aristocrat Baron Cramer-Klett, one of Pacelli's long-standing acquaintances from his days as nuncio in Germany. In a private letter, Pacelli told Cramer-Klett that his loyalty to the Holy See had surely been a factor in the baron's harsh treatment by Nazi authorities.[14]

Meeting with Dr. Buttmann in June 1935, Pacelli offered a sharply worded critique of the National Socialist press, which, he said, was attacking the church regularly with an "intemperance" that was unheard of even in Marxist circles. Buttmann tried to explain it away as the lingering effect of tensions between the NSDAP and the Center Party. Pacelli was having none of it. "Where is the Center Party?" he asked pointedly, adding that hardly anyone in Germany spoke of the party anymore, even less of its revival. Buttmann countered that while the party was no longer in parliament, the "Center spirit"—the *Zentrumgeist,* as he put it—remained. In fact, the Germans were convinced, or so they told Pacelli, that the Center Party was still alive and active in German politics, but by means of underground cells, and that the party's head offices were now in Rome. Pacelli dismissed the suggestion out of hand, pointing out that in signing the 1933 treaty, the church had hoped for a period of mutual trust and respect between church and state, which could have been achieved but for the "anti-Catholic attitude" of the Hitler government.[15] It was as close as Pacelli would ever come to acknowledging that the 1933 treaty was negotiated at the expense of German political Catholicism.

In January 1936 Pacelli sent German Ambassador Diego von Bergen a long and detailed protest of ongoing Nazi violations of the 1933 agreement.[16] The letter captures perfectly the substance and style of Pacelli's mode of engagement with the Nazi state at the time. It was a forceful denunciation of Nazi tactics against Catholic interests, especially the attempt to use the law and the courts as a cover to whip up anti-Catholic, anticlerical sentiment; it was also a detailed exposition of the prevailing political theology that informed papal diplomacy—a statement of how the church understood its relationship with the state, and above all a defense of the church's right to speak freely on matters related to Catholic doctrine. It illustrates Pacelli's capacity to stand up to the Hitler government but also shows the futility of a diplomatic protest without teeth. It was, in short, a paper tiger whose moral consistency meant little to a Nazi state that was moving inexorably to a redefinition of what was ethical, legal, and thus permissible in the political realm.

Despite such protests, the attacks on Catholics continued. In March 1935, the German government ordered the arrest of priests and nuns who were accused of having directed funds outside Germany without the required authorization, in violation of German law and ostensibly against the economic interests of the Reich.[17] The arrests were accompanied by a Gestapo search and seizure of religious houses—a sweep so brutal and so arbitrary, Pacelli wrote, that it caused serious physical harm to the accused, and in some cases death. In this matter, Pacelli concluded, the German government had violated its own norms of due process and the most basic precepts of justice. Moreover, the Nazi propaganda machine was using the arrests and trials to stir up anti-Catholic sentiment, a further offense to the norms of civility, and to the church itself.

Pacelli impressed on Hitler's representatives at the Vatican that the Holy See took its commitment to the Reich Concordat of 1933 so seriously that it would not tolerate any action by Catholic clergy that might be seen to violate any terms of the agreement. This, he said, was a sure measure of the extent to which the Vatican saw the maintenance of good relations with the German government "a precious gift and worthy of protection." But the Vatican had studied the charges against the accused priests and ruled that the case against them was flimsy—"deficient" was the exact word Pacelli used. The state's case against the German clergy was so flawed that it was hard to believe he even had to respond by means of a formal diplomatic exchange.

Pacelli knew that the Hitler government chafed at the Vatican's continued characterization of the Nazi treatment of German Catholics as a new *Kulturkampf,* but he continued to press the point. There was not a diocese, he argued, perhaps not even a parish, in all the Reich that had not witnessed some form of assault on church officials or organizations: "The Catholic press has been destroyed and forced through unseemly measures to cede its editorial rights; Catholic journalists are subject to an odious censorship which protects attacks against the church but gags its defense; the bishops' pastoral letters are sequestered or banned from circulation," Pacelli wrote. He went on to say that "Catholic priests lie in prisons and concentration camps because in exercising their ministry they defended the principles of Christian doctrine and the Christian conception of life . . . innumerable numbers of Catholic employees have been deprived of their jobs, and of their livelihood." In the face of such clear instances of anti-Catholicism, how could the Hitler government still insist that the bishops and clergy were free to continue with their pastoral activities?

The Nazis justified such behavior on the grounds that some elements of the German Catholic Church, bishops and clergy in particular, were mixing themselves in politics, to the point of promoting a new kind of "political Catholicism." The Nazis claimed that this activity violated the concordat and, more seriously, stood in the way of the National Socialist program for national regeneration. Pacelli dismissed the claim, suggesting that the government's true intention was not simply to prevent the resurgence of earlier traditions of German political Catholicism but to contain "those types of activities which are an essential part of the church's mission, which it cannot renounce." Pacelli insisted that the church had no interest in or authority to interfere with that which was Caesar's; even less did the church presume to express a particular preference for any form of government. "The Church fulfills its mission in monarchies or republics," wrote Pacelli, "in democratic states or so-called authoritarian states. The task which she has been assigned by her supranational mission and the experience she has acquired in two thousand years of work keeps her from giving excessive weight to questions . . . about the different forms states have assumed in the course of their development."[18] In short, the church could tolerate any form of government so long as it was intent on preserving and promoting notions of the common good that were consistent with the principles of Christianity. In this regard, for all their rhetorical paeans to the Christian roots of German culture, the Nazis were skirting the line of a political order grounded in Christian ethics. In both its principles and its policies, Pacelli warned, National Socialism was heading down a road guaranteed to exacerbate tensions with the church. For instance, the Nazi pretense to promote so-called positive Christianity was deeply problematic from the Vatican's standpoint. Pacelli said that if the Nazis understood the term to mean recognition of the divinity of Christ and of his teachings, with all that this entailed for the public sphere, the Vatican and all German Catholics would approve. But the words and actions of Hitler's government more often than not proved to be "diametrically opposed" to the precepts of Christianity.

At the heart of the conflict between the Hitler government and German Catholicism were matters of conscience. Pacelli reiterated his belief that the continued travails in church-state relations reflected the pernicious influence of a dogged anti-Catholic, anticlerical faction within the Nazi Party, typified by the likes of Alfred Rosenberg, who was excoriated by the German bishops and the Vatican for his anti-Christian, neo-pagan, racialist doctrines. The way forward, Cardinal Pacelli insisted, was to "liberate" the Nazi Party from the "anticlerical and anti-Christian rubbish" that, he believed, was the work of a small handful of individuals.[19]

German diplomats at the Vatican appreciated Pacelli's penchant for moderation and his ability to temper the increasingly abrupt and combative tone of Pius XI. After meeting with the pope for a New Year's audience at the start of 1936, the German ambassador Bergen complained bitterly to Foreign Minister von Neurath of the "resentment against Germany among leading Vatican circles," referring specifically to the verbal dressing-down Pius XI delivered in the course of their meeting about the persecution of the German Catholic Church. Bergen complained to Pacelli of the substance and tone of the pope's veritable diatribe. Eager to calm the diplomatic waters, Pacelli managed to procure a written statement from the pope explaining in more precise and temperate terms the Vatican's concerns about the ongoing "persecutions, restrictions and obstructions" of the church in Germany. For Bergen, extracting this papal statement was a signature of Pacelli's diplomatic style. He wrote glowingly to Berlin of how "Cardinal Pacelli constantly strives to pacify and to exert a moderating influence on the Pope, who is difficult to manage and to influence." It is telling indeed of Pacelli's style that the more moderate papal criticism of Germany concluded with the forceful restatement of papal displeasure at continued actions against German Catholic interests. "We can only say that friends do not behave like this. We are, in truth, deeply grieved and gravely displeased," Pius XI wrote. The net effect of this minor diplomatic incident was that the German ambassador found himself urging his own government to avoid any further conflict with the church and to seek a "truce" and a "tolerable relationship with the Curia," in the interests of both the church and the German state.[20]

The hope for a genuinely amicable working relationship between the church and the Nazi state was still alive, or so Pacelli said. He may even have believed this. The fact that he still thought the Vatican could deal constructively with the Nazis reveals important insights into his temperament and his political judgment. Pacelli had more than enough evidence to confirm a view he had expressed in other settings, to some British and Italian officials, for instance, that Nazi promises meant precious little. Meeting with the Italian ambassador to the Vatican, Bonifacio Pignatti, in March 1936, Pacelli said repeatedly that for the Nazis "treaties were mere pieces of paper." There was no reason to believe anything Hitler's government said.[21] Clearly, Pacelli knew what he was talking about. After all, close to three years had passed since the signing of the Reich Concordat and things were obviously getting worse.

Why, then, did he insist on preserving the Vatican's formal diplomatic relationship with Nazi Germany? Was this the pragmatism of a career diplomat at work, reflecting a deeply seated conviction that, like it or not, the church had to deal with the Hitler government, even on unfavorable terms? Or was it a form of naiveté, a misjudgment of the true nature of National Socialism, and an underestimation of Hitler's capacity to manipulate his dealings with the Vatican for political gain? Perhaps it was a measure of the extent to which Pacelli's thinking about German affairs reflected the advice he sought from German prelates such as Monsignor Kaas and the Austrian prelate Alois Hudal, rector of the German national church in Rome—the Santa Maria dell'Anima—who would have reinforced Pacelli's own inclination to keep open the lines of communication with the Hitler government.[22]

Into the late 1930s, despite evidence of the increasing radicalism of Nazi domestic policies—sterilization laws, anti-Jewish measures including the Nuremberg Laws, and ongoing attacks against Catholic interests—Pacelli continued to believe that a genuine working relationship with Hitler's government was not only possible but essential. Some sources suggest that Pacelli placed an inordinate hope in Hitler himself, convinced for reasons that are not entirely clear that the führer was being unduly influenced by some radical fringes within the party elite. In response to a meeting in early November 1936 between Munich's Cardinal Faulhaber and Hitler, Pacelli agreed that Faulhaber had done well to express the church's continued grievances with the German government, especially with its vociferously anti-Catholic factions—what Faulhaber labeled *die Rosenberg-Stimmung*, the Rosenberg effect.[23] Still, Pacelli saw some signs of hope in Faulhaber's account of the meeting. As he wrote to Faulhaber, for all the outstanding grievances between church and state, Hitler's "personal attitude" suggested that everything was not as "hopeless" as it seemed.[24] The challenge, then, was to reinforce the seemingly moderate factions, associated with men like Göring, who, presumably, would help the führer to come to amicable terms with German Catholics and the Vatican.[25]

Pacelli's patience with the Germans doubtless reflected his deep emotional attachment to the German people. But a more important factor was his genuine concern for the survival of German Catholicism if its ties with the papacy were severed. Pius XI, Achille Ratti, was not so patient. Ratti had been elected pope in 1922, the same year Benito Mussolini came to power in Italy. Ratti and Pacelli had known each other for some time. Both men came from the professional papal diplomatic corps of the early twentieth century, but whereas Pacelli cut his diplomatic teeth in the heady climate of Weimar Germany, Ratti did so in Poland. As young papal diplomats, then, both men had witnessed firsthand the complex matrix of ideological, social, and economic factors that pushed much of Europe between revolution and reaction in the contentious years after the First World War. Ratti had long admired Pacelli's diplomatic abilities and sound judgment, and had tapped him to be his secretary of state in large measure because of Pacelli's intimate knowledge of German affairs.

Theirs was a unique relationship, characterized by mutual admiration, even genuine affection. Yet they were vastly different men in temperament. Ratti was a colorful character, emotive, outspoken, and argumentative. Pacelli was decidedly more reserved and introspective. The two were capable of open disagreement with each other, but nothing, it seems, seriously threatened their mutual respect and common sense of purpose. As Pacelli once told his housekeeper, Mother Pascalina, in all the years he served as Ratti's secretary of state, "I never said yes to the Holy Father when I meant no, and no when I meant yes."[26] The two men appreciated the complementary dynamic of their working relationship, and it has been suggested that Ratti felt he could speak more bluntly in public because he knew that Pacelli would serve as a moderating force and help to mediate any difficulties that arose.

For his part, Pacelli knew that his cautious and prudent manner found its necessary complement in Ratti's more forthright approach.[27]

Eugenio Pacelli no doubt had a moderating effect on the irascible Ratti, who was known in diplomatic circles to be quick to anger. Pacelli's influence was evident during the very first months of his tenure as secretary of state, when the Vatican found itself at odds with Mussolini's government over the status of Catholic youth organizations in Fascist Italy. It was also apparent in the Vatican's dealings with Nazi Germany in the late 1930s, when growing Nazi radicalism in domestic and foreign policy seemed to be pushing Pius XI to the edge of breaking off all diplomatic ties with the Hitler regime. Already by 1936, the Vatican was moving toward more public criticisms of Nazi behavior.[28] Following the Nazi remilitarization of the Rhineland, for instance, the Vatican newspaper *L'Osservatore Romano* published an article that spoke of the "moral duty to respect treaties." The article, which Pacelli's office certainly would have authorized if not penned, was intended to send a clear message to the Germans about the immorality of their violation of a key provision of the Versailles treaty.[29]

Pacelli and Vatican Interwar Diplomacy

In his dealings with foreign governments, Pacelli had to wear several hats at once. His oversight of Vatican interwar diplomacy in turbulent times rested on a complex matrix of distinct yet related interests and calculations, sometimes complementary but often conflicting. It was demanding work for a staff of limited size and means, and with limited practical influence on civil governments. It demanded a constant balancing act that took into account the needs and interests of the national churches while also reflecting the Holy See's standing as an actor in international affairs. Predictably, then, papal diplomacy of the 1930s produced mixed and often disappointing results from the perspective of the Vatican's own stated objectives. The future Pius XII thus confronted as secretary of state a dilemma similar to what he had experienced as a young diplomat in the First World War: the practical limits of papal influence on civil governments of various forms and ideological leanings.

Nowhere was Pacelli's balancing act, and its limited efficacy, more evident than at home, in the Holy See's complicated relationship with Mussolini's Italy. In his meetings with the Italian ambassadors to the Holy See—Cesare De

Vecchi and later Bonifacio Pignatti—Pacelli expressed repeatedly his hopes for a genuine détente in Italy's relations with the Vatican in the aftermath of the 1931 crisis over Catholic Action.[30] It is not that Pacelli was under any illusion about the true nature of Mussolini's attitude to the church. As he recorded in his personal notes, "Among the Fascists there are some good Catholics, but Mussolini is not one of them." In a similar vein, when the Italian ambassador met with Pacelli in April 1931 to say that Fascism was the "antithesis of Bolshevism," Pacelli was not shy about retorting that there were, in fact, some fundamental similarities between the two systems.[31] In his dealings with the Italians, then, Pacelli's clear desire to maintain good diplomatic relations did not cloud his judgment or fool him into thinking that Mussolini's Fascism was something other than what it was; indeed, from the very beginning of his direct dealings with the Fascists, Pacelli exhibited his characteristic ability to marry diplomatic engagement with a clear-minded resolve to insist that the Mussolini government respect the letter and the spirit of the 1929 agreements.[32] In effect, Pacelli was prepared to give Mussolini's government considerable latitude in pursuing its domestic and international objectives, so long as doing so did not impinge upon the church's free reign over its own affairs and Mussolini's policies avoided the radical and aggressive tone exhibited increasingly by the Hitler regime.

Italian officials realized early on that Pacelli would prove a formidable interlocutor and should not be underestimated. They were frustrated from the start in their attempts to get a good read on the man who would lead Vatican diplomacy for the foreseeable future. Pacelli's characteristic reserve impressed and frustrated Fascist informants in the Vatican, who complained that it was hard to obtain any good information on Pacelli because he was, as one of them put it, "as mute as a statue."[33]

Italy's imperial and racialist turn in the mid-1930s—expressed principally in its invasion of Ethiopia—tested the logic and the limits of the imperfect but mutually convenient accommodation achieved between the Vatican and the Mussolini regime after the 1929 *Conciliazione.*[34] The planned invasion of Ethiopia was evidence of Mussolini's goal of remaking Italy through imperial conquest.[35] His imperial design against a member state of the League of Nations, of course, sparked the most serious diplomatic crisis of the interwar era to that point. In so doing, it tested the mettle of papal diplomacy by laying bare the complicated nature of the Holy See's formal relationship with the Italian state. The radicalization of Mussolini's foreign policy agenda exposed some of the fundamental incompatibilities between Catholic doctrine and Fascist ideology. More to the point, Fascism's imperialist designs left the Holy See caught on the horns of a dilemma that was to a large extent of its own making. By virtue of its overriding commitment to preserve the 1929 agreement with Italy, the Holy See willingly limited its direct involvement in matters of state, which meant treading carefully in its response to Mussolini's aggression. The establishment of formal diplomatic relations with Italy may have won for the church critical spheres of autonomy in Italian life, and international standing for the Holy See, but it tied the hands of the pope and his men, principally Eugenio Pacelli, in political and diplomatic matters. To this extent, it curtailed the Holy See's capacity to act as a neutral mediator in the diplomatic crisis of 1935–1936 and revealed the tensions inherent in papal claims to lead a universal flock. In his annual political review for 1937 the British representative d'Arcy Osborne surmised that the papal reputation had perhaps "suffered severely" because of its perceived "tenderness" for the Mussolini regime. In the eyes of many, Catholics and non-Catholics alike, Osborne opined, the Holy See had perhaps paid too heavy a price for the Lateran Accords, a price measured by "the loss of spiritual and moral independence and of that universality in which the authority and tradition of the Church are grounded."[36] In a manner that foreshadowed the strident critique of the so-called silences of the papacy during World War Two, the Holy See's refusal in the mid-1930s to condemn in clear, unequivocal, and public ways Mussolini's invasion of Ethiopia left Pius XI and Pacelli especially open to charges of partiality, timidity, and moral failure in the face of an aggressive war of conquest that violated international norms and conventions.

Presented with Fascist foreign policy that was deemed to be the proper and exclusive purview of the state, the Holy See could or would say only so much to criticize the Mussolini regime, whether in public or in private. Consequently, as the diplomatic crisis worsened through the second half of 1935, leading to a Fascist invasion of Ethiopia in early October 1935, Pius XI vacillated between open confrontation of the Mussolini regime and appeasement. So it was that within the span of a few weeks in late August and early September 1935, Pius XI spoke publicly both to condemn aggressive wars of conquest and territorial expansion and to call for a peaceful resolution to the conflict over Ethiopia in a way that would recognize legitimate Italian interests.

Speaking in late August to a group of Catholic nurses, Pius XI warned against "an unjust war," calling it a "horrible" thing. This was arguably the strongest public denunciation that Pius XI ever delivered to warn against the threatened invasion.[37] Yet a few weeks later, while speaking to a group of Catholic war veterans, he went so far as to identify personally and publicly with what he described as "the needs of a great and good people." He was referring, of course, to Italians, with whom, by virtue of his background, the pope identified.[38]

The Janus-faced nature of Pius XI's statements on the threatened Italo-Ethiopian war was but the public expression of similarly conflicted impulses among his diplomatic staff. Privately, Pius XI continued to tell his diplomats to impress upon Italian officials that "this war in Abyssinia must not happen, for Abyssinia's sake and for Italy's."[39] Mussolini's pursuit of imperial conquest in the face of a diplomatic crisis pushed the pope to the brink of open confrontation with the Fascist government in the late summer and early fall of 1935. Pius XI was reported to have said that if the invasion of Ethiopia did proceed, then he would be compelled to "take a very serious step" that he had been contemplating for some time, which presumably meant a public rebuke of the Fascist regime if not the formal rupture of diplomatic ties.[40] In the end, though, despite initial signs that the seemingly combative Ratti was ready to go public with his condemnation of the planned invasion, nothing came of it. With Pacelli's constant encouragement Pius XI chose the way of continued diplomatic engagement with the Mussolini regime as the means to precise ends. It was not so much complicity with the Fascist imperial project that tempered the Vatican's response, though undoubtedly there was some excitement in papal circles at the prospect of exploiting Italian occupation in East Africa to further the work of Catholic missions. After all, as was true of the church's relationship with other European powers from the late nineteenth century onward, tense church-state relations at home could give way to constructive collaboration in the colonies, born of mutually beneficial political, economic, and sociocultural arrangements.[41]

More important, though, was the Vatican's rationale that diplomatic engagement with the Fascist regime was the means to a specific end: preservation not only of the church's autonomy within the Fascist state and society but also of the Vatican's presumed diplomatic influence with the Mussolini government. For Pacelli especially, this influence was essential to the success of any attempt on the part of Vatican diplomats to steer Mussolini's Italy away from closer alignment with Nazi Germany. When Mussolini's government reacted angrily against Pius XI's August 1935 speech warning about the consequences of a possible Italian invasion of Ethiopia, Pacelli distanced himself from the tone and substance of the pope's statement. Meeting with the Italian chargé d'affaires Giuseppe Talamo Atenolfi, Pacelli explained that the pope had spoken publicly in this manner from a profound sense of pastoral duty, and thus addressed universal moral principles about the just causes for military action. Pacelli knew that Italian officials appreciated his efforts to temper the pope's public address on the matter. Pignatti, the newly appointed Italian ambassador to the Holy See, reported to Mussolini in December 1935 that Pacelli could be counted on to "pour water into [Pius XI's] pacifist wine" —an obvious allusion to Pacelli's resolve to impress upon the pope the consequences to church-state relations in Italy of a public papal statement in favor of a negotiated settlement to the Italo-Ethiopian conflict.[42]

Of course, Pacelli's influence cut both ways, suggesting that juxtaposing papal intransigence with Pacelli's moderation was part of a deliberate strategy to preserve both the moral authority of the papal office and the practical efficacy of papal diplomacy. For instance, when the Italian government issued threats against the Vatican newspaper for a series of articles advocating a peaceful resolution to the Ethiopian crisis, Pacelli counseled restraint and patience. In this instance at least, the Italians listened. In moderating both the papal line and the Fascist response, Pacelli's style of diplomatic engagement worked, at least in the short term—even if the effect was simply to paper over obvious ideological divisions between church and regime that were to grow wider and deeper in the late 1930s.[43]

In his effort to be constructive rather than combative in dealing with the Mussolini government over the Ethiopian crisis, Pacelli hoped to win for papal diplomacy a significant public relations coup, namely, credit for having worked diplomatically behind the scenes toward a much-desired mediated settlement. Pacelli told the Italians that the pope hoped the Mussolini government would accept the concessions being offered by the British and French so that the Holy Father might announce a peaceful resolution to the conflict at an upcoming Consistory, the traditional meeting of the College of Cardinals. For its part, Mussolini's government cautioned Pacelli and the Vatican against any public statement that might be seen to hurt Italian interests in the current crisis. Pacelli assured them that no such statement was being planned. The papal representative to the Italian government, the Jesuit Father Pietro Tacchi Venturi, even met with Mussolini personally in mid-December to assure Il Duce that the pope would resist saying anything at all in the upcoming Consistory about the Italo-Ethiopian conflict.[44] Although the Vatican continued to lobby Mussolini to concede to some form of papal commentary on the conflict, it was unwilling to press very hard on the matter, lest doing so jeopardize its formal diplomatic arrangements with the Italian state.[45]

Not for the first or last time, the price to be paid for diplomatic engagement with Fascist Italy was to mute the church's public voice on the wisdom, to say nothing of the morality, of Mussolini's imperialist misadventures. The effect was to confine to secret diplomatic channels the Vatican's deep anxiety about the Ethiopian crisis, and to keep hidden from public view the Vatican's persistent efforts to lobby the major powers toward a quick and durable peace settlement.[46] So it was that the Italian ambassador could write to Mussolini that in his public addresses, the pope "spoke like a good Italian." In other instances Pignatti wrote to tell Mussolini that the Vatican was trying to achieve a "just" settlement that would favor Italy, and that papal nuncios in various countries were working effectively to promote the Italian cause among Catholics in those countries. Pignatti may have been overstating things for effect, knowing perhaps that Mussolini did not look kindly on the bearers of bad news. At any rate, the full extent of the Vatican's anxiety over Mussolini's territorial ambitions did not receive the kind of public airing the Italian leader's critics were hoping to hear from St. Peter's successor.[47]

Behind the scenes, Pacelli and his staff worked hard to maximize their presumed influence over Mussolini's government while keeping open lines of communication with the other powers by means of frequent and meaningful face-to-face meetings with British and French officials. Writing to the French ambassador from his holiday retreat in Switzerland at the start of October 1935, Pacelli, who was unaware at the time that the Italians had already begun their military campaign in Ethiopia, noted that every effort ought to be made to resolve the conflict peacefully, lest it spiral out of control and provoke "greater and more serious complications."[48] For papal diplomacy to be effective at all, it was imperative that Cardinal Pacelli facilitate good working relationships with France and Britain, whose responses to Mussolini's increasingly aggressive foreign policy plans put them on a collision course with Fascist Italy. Pacelli worked especially closely with the French ambassador François Charles-Roux; theirs was an amiable and effective working relationship that was solidified through frequent meetings at the Vatican and through the cardinal's highly publicized trips to France in the late 1930s. Charles-Roux saw in Pacelli an astute observer and quintessential diplomat. Although the French ambassador was at times frustrated by Pacelli's vague allusions to unspecified Vatican initiatives vis-à-vis the Mussolini government, Charles-Roux was confident that Pacelli and the Holy See saw the Fascist invasion as ill-advised and dangerous, making all the more unlikely one of Pacelli's admittedly vain diplomatic hopes: a rapprochement between Italy and France. This objective reflected a long-standing Vatican interest in the emergence of what one historian calls a "bloc of Catholic states" to maintain peace and stability on the European continent.[49]

The frequency of Charles-Roux's visits to Pacelli at the Vatican did not escape the watchful eye of suspicious Italian officials. At the height of the international crisis spawned by the Italian invasion of Ethiopia in the autumn of 1935, Charles-Roux's meetings with Pacelli convinced Italian diplomats that the Vatican was working in tandem with the French government toward a mediated settlement of the crisis.[50] The Italians grew even more suspicious about Pacelli's role in the opening months of 1936, when Pacelli and members of his staff started asking some blunt questions about Italy's capacity to continue fighting in Ethiopia. Ambassador Pignatti assumed that Pacelli and his advisors were working on information from an unnamed source close to the Mussolini government. In fact, Pacelli and his staff had reliable information from an "interlocutor" of the Vatican's financial expert Bernardino Nogara that Italy's finances were strained almost beyond capacity, which in turn exposed the Mussolini government to serious internal political threats. Nogara reported to the pope that Mussolini's calm public face masked Il Duce's "state of physical depression, or rather, fatalism."[51]

Such reports stiffened Pacelli's resolve to push the Mussolini government toward a negotiated settlement. Italian representatives bristled at Pacelli's intensified efforts in the early spring of 1936 to mediate between Italy and the other Western powers, but Pacelli persisted, fearing that growing international reaction to Italian aggression in Ethiopia would further isolate Italy and, worst of all, strain the country's relations with France and Britain to the breaking point.[52] The Vatican worried that such a rupture would only push

Mussolini's Italy toward a closer alliance with Hitler's Germany, with dire consequences for Italy and for all of Europe. Pacelli's distrust of the Hitler government, caused by years of persistent violations of the *Reichskonkordat* and intensified attacks on German Catholics, deepened with the German remilitarization of the Rhineland in March 1936. Unmoved by Hitler's assurances of peaceful intentions in the wake of remilitarization, but convinced also that the French did not want to go to war with Germany over this and other violations of the Versailles settlement, Pacelli redoubled his efforts to use papal diplomacy as the cornerstone of a strategy to counter German ambitions by means of an Italian détente with the other major powers. As Pacelli told Ambassador Charles-Roux, an "irreconcilable break" between Italy and Britain had to be avoided at all costs, lest there be "more serious consequences." While concerned about British intransigence vis-à-vis the lifting of sanctions against Italy, Pacelli understood how news that Mussolini's armies were using chemical weapons in Ethiopia, including poison gas, angered public opinion in England and made a quick resolution to the crisis that much more difficult.[53] The Vatican may have hoped for a quick resolution to the conflict, but the Italians were in no such rush; they certainly had no sincere inclination toward the Vatican's push for a negotiated settlement and compromise. And none was forthcoming: The invasion of Ethiopia was announced on October 2, and Italian troops were on the move the very next day.[54] Fascist Italy had marched off to war and begun the conquest of a Fascist Empire. Papal diplomacy had failed to achieve a primary objective. For Pius XI and even more for Secretary of State Pacelli, there was little to do but to come to terms with Fascist imperialism despite lingering anxiety about its moral and political wisdom.

As in his dealings with Fascist Italy, Pacelli's response to growing civil strife in Spain after 1935 reflected the complexity of balancing diplomatic commitments with civil governments on the one hand with the various doctrinal and pastoral duties expected of the Holy See on the other. The brutal campaign by Spanish Republican forces against Catholic clergy in the late 1930s appalled the Vatican. Yet, true to form, Pacelli counseled restraint and recognition of the duly constituted Spanish government. While moving the Vatican toward public support for the nationalist forces arrayed behind General Franco, Pacelli warned against the type of radical nationalism seen in Italy and Germany. In meeting with Marquis Antonio Magaz, whom Pacelli described as a "secret agent" sent to seek formal Vatican recognition of Franco's government at Burgos, the cardinal expressed his hope that the nationalists would not resort to violence and "pointless atrocities." As for talk of a "new Spain" among radical nationalists, Pacelli said that he hoped this would not translate into the kinds of problems the church faced in the new Germany.[55]

Pius XI was uncharacteristically hesitant about how best to respond to the situation in Spain. In a role reversal of sorts, it was Eugenio Pacelli who pressed for unequivocal public expressions of sympathy for Catholic Spain, and it was he who resolved almost immediately that the conflict in Spain needed to be understood in religious and cultural as well as geopolitical terms —as a struggle for the survival of Spain's Catholic heritage.[56] Evidence suggests that Pacelli played the decisive role in pushing Pius XI toward a clear public denunciation of anticlerical violence by Republican forces. The pope's first public reference to the civil war was a speech in September 1936 in which he praised the church's "persecuted children" in Spain for their heroic acts of "faith and martyrdom." The chief author of the speech was none other than the cardinal secretary of state.[57]

Pacelli confided his deep anxiety over events in Spain to the French ambassador, Charles-Roux, ever the trusted voice of a country that found itself in a difficult position on the Spanish question. Pacelli felt that events in Spain had reached a level of atrocity not seen in Europe since the Terror at the height of the French Revolution. Spanish refugees in Rome, he confided, told of churches and altars being sacked and destroyed, and of priests being summarily executed. Pacelli had seen in some French newspapers photographs of the skeletal remains of nuns taken from sepulchers and posed mockingly for public display. It was clear, he said, that Republican elements were aiming for "the barbarous destruction of religion" in a bastion of Catholic Europe. In the face of such violence, Pacelli believed, "the church cannot remain neutral." Hence his move to lodge a formal diplomatic complaint with the Spanish government, which, he reasoned, had armed "anarchist and subversive elements" and now did not have the means to control them.[58]

Pacelli realized that the French government found itself in a difficult position. With the Soviet Union, Fascist Italy, and Nazi Germany all meddling to significant degrees in the Spanish Civil War, France faced the prospect of a virtual encirclement by some form of authoritarian government, Fascist or Communist. Moreover, with its own domestic scene fractured by internal support for the Republican or nationalist causes in Spain, there was a very real danger that the French government would collapse, thus exposing France's democracy to instability and political extremism. If the government was not able to contain domestic pressure in support of the Spanish Republican cause, or, worse yet, if the French Communists seized power by legal or extralegal means, the effect would be twofold: the Soviets would gain a foothold in Western Europe from which to ignite their long-awaited "worldwide revolution," and Fascist Italy and Nazi Germany would move toward a closer diplomatic and military alliance. Paradoxically, while worrying about an entrenchment of the Hitler regime, Pacelli still feared a creeping Communist influence in Germany, where, he said, Hitler's war against religion would only serve to accelerate the rise of Bolshevism.[59]

Pacelli's handling of the Spanish Civil War exhibited the hallmark signs of his political philosophy and diplomatic style. He respected the formal terms of diplomatic engagement with the duly constituted Spanish government and continued to do so until the political situation in Spain warranted Vatican recognition of a new government. This occurred in the spring of 1939, by which time Pacelli had been installed as Pope Pius XII. It fell to the newly elected pope in April 1939 to formally welcome the victory of Franco's forces, thanking them "for the gift of peace and of victory, with which God has seen fit to crown the Christian heroism of your faith and love, demonstrated in so much selfless suffering."[60] Such a public affirmation of General Franco and his supporters had never crossed the lips of Pacelli's predecessor. But although Pacelli welcomed the victory of Franco's forces and the end of the bloody civil war, he was wary of the *Generalissimo*'s openness toward Hitler's Germany and his tolerance of certain racist tendencies that clearly were inconsistent with Spain's Catholic traditions.[61]

That France occupied a special place in Pacelli's diplomatic maneuvers in the mid-1930s, and in his vision for the future of Christian Europe, was evident during his visits there in 1935 and 1937. Ostensibly, these were spiritual missions—pilgrimages, as it were—to popular devotional sites at Lourdes, Lisieux, and Notre Dame de Paris. As always, though, contemporary political and social realities were never divorced from doctrinal and spiritual considerations. Cardinal Pacelli's French pilgrimages were a great public relations success. Thousands of people, from devout Catholics to curious onlookers, turned out to catch a glimpse of the Vatican's second-in-command, the man whom many already were saying would be pope some day. Speaking at Lourdes on his first visit in 1935, Pacelli sounded a pessimistic tone on the state of Catholicism in the contemporary world, which he took to be a symptom of the "deprivation and poverty of our time." The crisis of modernity was evident from within Catholicism and from without. Pacelli aimed a particular criticism at Left-leaning currents within the French Catholic world—"intellectuals" and "workers," he said, who had abandoned their faith for the materialist promises of godless ideologies; "[n]ot to mention those who lie in the shadows of paganism," he thundered, "or those whom heresy has separated and torn from Peter's boat, and finally those for whom disobedience has caused them to leave the church." Pacelli acknowledged that economic crisis and social dislocation were causing widespread poverty—worse than had been seen in a lifetime. By exploiting the genuine suffering of so many ordinary people, he reasoned, opportunistic agitators had managed to "attract the people, deceived by false promises, to the errors of Socialism and Communism"; worse yet, the masses had been deceived into an outright rejection not just of the Christian faith but of the divine altogether.[62]

It would be tempting to read into such an address a reflection of Pacelli's strident anti-Communism, which, it has long been assumed, clouded his judgment of Fascism in general and of Nazism in particular. It is true that while he made only veiled allusions to the dangers of "paganism"—which presumably was meant to refer to the radical ethnic nationalism of the Nazis and other Fascists—Pacelli chose to refer explicitly *only* to the errors and dangers of Socialism and Communism. The message would not have been lost on those French Catholics who favored Catholic rapprochement with the parties of the Left as part of a broad anti-Fascist coalition intended to defend the French Republic from the radical Right. Nor would the message have been lost on French Catholic intellectuals associated with Left-leaning Catholic journals such as the Dominican magazine *Sept,* which was suppressed by the Holy Office in August 1937.[63]

As with his attitude toward politically active German Catholics since the days of the Weimar Republic, Pacelli had profound misgivings about French Catholic collaboration with Socialist and Communist parties. This should not be taken to mean that Pacelli saw Fascism as a lesser evil than Communism or that he somehow approved of French Catholic support for the radical authoritarian nationalism that animated Fascism in Italy and Germany. A couple of days after specifically denouncing the errors of Socialism and Communism, Cardinal Pacelli spoke in clear and direct terms of the twin threat posed to Christian civilization by Marxist materialism and radical nationalism. With the Grotto at Lourdes as his backdrop, he decried how the masses were rallying "around the banner of social revolution," with its "false conception of the world and of life"; but he also deplored those who were "possessed by the superstition of race and of blood." Both philosophies, he noted, were fundamentally at odds with the Christian faith, and thus the church could *never* subscribe to such ideas.[64]

On Pacelli's second visit to France, in the summer of 1937, he gave highly publicized and well-attended speeches in Lisieux, at the inauguration of the Basilica of Saint Thérèse de l'Enfant Jesus (Thérèse of Lisieux), and at Notre Dame in Paris. As with his previous trip, Pacelli's purpose ostensibly was religious—there were no diplomatic meetings scheduled and no treaties to be signed. Yet with a Popular Front government in power in France, a visit by the Vatican's second most powerful personality carried obvious political significance. The symbolism was not lost on the German press, still smarting over the papal reproach of the Hitler regime just a few months earlier, when the Vatican had issued an encyclical criticizing Nazism, albeit indirectly. Some German observers complained that Pacelli had gone to France to impart his "blessing" on the Popular Front government while continuing to launch anathemas against the Third Reich.[65]

Pacelli used the occasion to defend France's Christian heritage and its Christian vocation in the face of multiple dangers posed by modern philosophies, echoing a message conveyed during his 1935 visit. Speaking at Notre Dame de Paris on July 13, 1937, he warned the French against falling prey to deceptively simple solutions to difficult social questions. Building on the refrain *Vigilate*—beware—which evoked Christ's warning to his disciples on the night of his betrayal and arrest, Pacelli expressed his deep concern over the loss of religious faith, which, he said, fundamentally betrayed France's spiritual heritage. His speech was also a stinging critique of the prevailing forms of capitalist economic organization—a restatement of classic Catholic social and economic principles. There were unmistakable corporatist undertones in the speech, which evoked Leo XIII's *Rerum Novarum,* the great papal teaching that underlay modern Catholic social philosophy. Pacelli decried capitalist exploitation with its complex, impersonal system of production that had rendered the individual superfluous and even sowed the seeds of a looming demographic crisis caused by declining birthrates. He condemned the way modern man, so eager to give machines the appearance of life, was "afraid to transmit his own life to others," leaving the cemeteries full and overflowing and the cribs empty.[66]

Cardinal Pacelli's trip to the United States in October and November 1936 was another public relations coup for the Vatican's chief diplomat. But it was also much more than that, since Pacelli was able to use the occasion to meet prominent American politicians, including President Franklin D. Roosevelt, to discuss the state of Vatican–U.S. relations and the possibility of a closer working relationship. The trip proved to be a seminal moment in Vatican-American relations and helped to pave the way for a strategic rapprochement between the Holy See and the American administration on the eve of the Second World War. It was also a sign of the Vatican's recognition of the growing size and influence of American Catholicism, above all of its mounting financial and political clout and its contributions to the Vatican coffers.[67]

The genesis of the trip remains shrouded in mystery, though it was clear enough at the time that it was more than a leisurely holiday. Pacelli and the Vatican said that it was a vacation, that instead of spending his holiday in Switzerland as usual, he had decided at the last minute to go to America because he had "a great longing to see the United States." Pacelli insisted that there was nothing at all "political" about the trip.[68] To underscore the personal nature of the trip, the Vatican announced that the cardinal would be staying in New York at the Long Island estate of Genevieve Brady, the widow of noted philanthropist and convert to Catholicism Nicholas F. Brady, and that he was traveling without other high-ranking officials from the Vatican.[69] The cardinal's principal traveling companion was the Vatican senior administrator Enrico Galeazzi, an Italian representative of the Knights of Columbus and a man with extensive connections to prominent American Catholics, notably Joseph P. Kennedy.

Despite the official denials, media commentators could hardly take seriously the claims of a purely personal visit to the United States from the second-highest-ranking prelate in the Roman Catholic hierarchy, the pope's right-hand man. Underscoring the extraordinary nature of the trip was the fact that it would make history, marking the first time that a papal secretary of state had ever visited the United States. *Time* magazine reported that "secular gossips" were working "overtime" to account for Pacelli's visit. Some speculated that he had been invited to collaborate with the American government in the church's "battle to the death against Communism."[70] Other rumors suggested that the pope had sent Pacelli to deal covertly with the troublesome anti-Semitic Father Charles E. Coughlin, who was using his radio broadcasts from just outside Detroit to push an increasingly shrill anti-Semitic agenda. It was also said that the cardinal was planning to meet with the president, a story that alarmed leading Catholics, who urged the Vatican to reconsider any such meeting in the middle of an election campaign, lest it create the appearance of Catholic support for the Democratic incumbent.[71]

A meeting between the American president and the Vatican's cardinal secretary of state did materialize, though informally, at the president's family residence in Hyde Park, New York. But it came only near the end of Pacelli's trip, in the first week of November, after Roosevelt had secured re-election. Thus both the president and the cardinal were able to avoid any charge of untoward papist influence in American presidential politics. Pacelli was coming off the heels of a cross-country tour that seemed to reinvigorate more than tax the sixty-year-old chief papal diplomat and future pope. Pacelli's American sojourn contrasted starkly with the slow pace and predictable routine of life at the papal court. After a few days of rest and relaxation at Mrs. Brady's Long Island estate, where he was fêted with an elegant reception attended by high society types, Pacelli made the rounds of northeastern cities, bastions of American Catholicism: Boston, New York, Washington, Baltimore, and Philadelphia. Everywhere he went Pacelli met with high-ranking American prelates, prominent American business and political leaders, and thousands of ordinary Catholics who turned out to catch a rare glimpse of the Vatican's second-most-powerful man. In the nation's capital, Pacelli spoke at a luncheon in his honor at the National Press Club, telling journalists that he was happy to be able to recognize publicly "the ideas and ideals of your press in reporting with accuracy events in all parts of the world." From there it was off to Mount Vernon, Virginia, where Pacelli laid a wreath at George

Washington's tomb, and then on to a thunderous reception by students and faculty at Georgetown University, where he received an honorary degree in canon and civil law.[72]

As if to avoid appearing to interfere with the presidential elections, Cardinal Pacelli embarked on a far-flung weeklong tour of the American Midwest and West Coast, which included a widely publicized "6,500-mile plane tour" that took the future Pius XII as far west as the Boulder Dam, all the way to San Francisco and Los Angeles. On his way back to the East Coast, the cardinal asked to be flown over Niagara Falls—the dam and the falls, Pacelli told reporters, were among the "highlights" of his trip. Pacelli marveled at the "grandeur of America by air," one newspaper reported. Other reports told of his whirlwind tour of "seven cities in seven days," which included memorable stops at the University of Notre Dame in South Bend, Indiana, where he received yet another honorary degree, one of several from top-ranking American Catholic universities. In Chicago Pacelli spent some time at the home of the influential Cardinal George Mundelein before heading back to New York for further honors at a widely attended gathering at Fordham University.[73] At Fordham, Pacelli received the honorary degree of doctor of laws before close to three thousand guests. His address was broadcast by radio across the United States and filmed for the newsreels. The Fordham speech was one of Pacelli's most impassioned and most forceful. The future Pius XII spoke at length of the "great need today of an education of the heart and of the will as well as of the mind and of the intellect; an education which develops the whole man, morally and intellectually, spiritually as well as scientifically, an education that rests upon the rock of truth and not upon the sand of materialism, a truly Christian education illumined by the light of faith."[74]

Such public events and his cross-country tour gave Cardinal Pacelli a first-hand look at the vibrant state of American Catholicism. But it was Pacelli's meeting with President Roosevelt over lunch at Hyde Park on November 6 that had the most consequential and most lasting impact on Vatican-American relations. The cardinal was accompanied by a small party that included Bishop Spellman, Joseph P. Kennedy, and Enrico Galeazzi. Just what Roosevelt and Pacelli discussed as they conversed privately by the fireplace in the living room at the Hyde Park estate that afternoon is not clear, since neither recorded the details. There were strict controls on media reporting of the luncheon. Afterward, Pacelli gave a very brief statement and answered a few reporters' questions as he left Hyde Park but said nothing of any substance. The cardinal limited himself to predictable expressions of gratitude, speaking only of the president's "truly American family" and saying how grateful he was to have had the chance to meet with them over lunch. When reporters tried to pry something more out of the Vatican's secretary of state, they were cut off abruptly by Bishop Spellman. The American prelate and longtime Pacelli confidant evidently knew well enough how to deal with persistent American media, more so than the cardinal, who, in the words of one newspaper, seemed "bewildered" by intense media questioning as he left Hyde Park.[75]

The time was not yet ripe for anything close to formal diplomatic relations—anti-Catholic sentiment and suspicion of papist influence ran deep, after all, in American life. Roosevelt knew that any such move would encounter stiff resistance from the American public, not to mention the U.S. Congress, which held the power to authorize formal diplomatic relations with foreign governments. Even so, during the next two years, he had informal talks with Cardinal Mundelein and Bishop Spellman to see whether some kind of formal arrangement might be made with the Vatican. In October 1937, at a lunch with Mundelein in Chicago, Roosevelt reportedly floated the idea of sending a "special envoy" to the Vatican, someone who would enjoy the rank of ambassador, without the official title.[76]

It would be another two years before Roosevelt's plan for a more prominent American presence at the Holy See was realized. By then, the Nazi conquest of Europe had begun and Pacelli had been sitting on the papal throne for more than half a year. But his brief visit with Roosevelt in November 1936 had made it all possible. In this respect, Pacelli's American tour was much more than a public relations triumph for Vatican diplomacy: it was a turning point in Vatican-American relations. If nothing else, it brought the two men closer together and helped to forge a cordial relationship; in their correspondence after Pacelli became pope, they frequently recalled fondly the 1936 luncheon and addressed each other in familiar, friendly terms. Pacelli's 1936 U.S. tour also increased the stature and influence of Cardinal Mundelein, Bishop Spellman, and Joseph P. Kennedy, all of whom were indispensable conduits between the Vatican and the Roosevelt administration at a critical time in global affairs. Pacelli's American "vacation" proved in the end to be not only a decisive strategic move of papal diplomacy but also something of a boon for

American Catholicism.[77] In particular, it helped to reinforce the idea of American Catholicism as a cultural, financial, and political power bloc both at home and in deeply traditional Vatican circles long accustomed to thinking of American ideals and values as modernist heresies.[78]

A closer relationship with the United States was especially important for the papacy in the closing months of 1937 because of the Vatican's worsening relations with the Hitler regime. As the reports of anti-Catholic attacks had increased earlier in the year, the Holy See's patience with the German government had worn thin. In January 1937 Pius XI summoned several high-ranking German prelates—Faulhaber, Betram, Schulte, Preysing, and Galen—to the Vatican to address the situation of the church in the Third Reich. The German prelates impressed upon the pope that the time was ripe for a forceful public papal critique of the continuing persecution of German Catholics. After some discussion of the form the protest should take, Vatican officials agreed that the most effective approach would be a papal encyclical—an open letter from the pope to the German bishops that would make an authoritative statement about the ongoing Nazi persecution of the German Catholic Church.[79] At last, the Holy See intended to make good on its word to publicize its disapproval of Nazi theories and policies. It would instruct German bishops to have the papal statement read from the pulpit of every German church on Palm Sunday, the week before Easter. The Vatican could thus be assured of a wide captive audience, even though the papal letter would have to be smuggled into Germany and then distributed secretly to parishes across the country.[80]

As secretary of state, Eugenio Pacelli oversaw the drafting of *Mit Brennender Sorge* (March 14, 1937), Pope Pius XI's encyclical "On the Church and the German Reich." It remains the strongest public papal confrontation of aspects of Nazism issued by the Vatican before the end of the Second World War. In a clear rejection of the Nazi doctrine of racial purity, *Mit Brennender Sorge* said that only "superficial minds could stumble into concepts of a national God, of a national religion; or attempt to lock within the frontiers of a single people, within the narrow limits of a single race, God, the Creator of the universe, King and Legislator of all nations before whose immensity they are 'as a drop of a bucket' (Isaiah xI, 15)."[81] To Pacelli goes the credit for what is arguably the most forceful and consequential paragraph: "Whoever exalts race, or the people, or the State, or a particular form of State, or the depositories of power, or any other fundamental value of the human community . . . whoever raises these notions above their standard value and divinizes them to an idolatrous level, distorts and perverts an order of the world planned and created by God; he is far from the true faith in God and from the concept of life which that faith upholds."[82] A measure of the significance Pacelli himself ascribed to this fundamental principle was evident many years later, when in June 1945, as Pius XII, he harked back to the encyclical to find a point of doctrinal consistency in his approach to the Nazi state. Pacelli recalled that the "fundamental incompatibility" of the Nazi state with Catholicism found its most forceful expression in this part of the encyclical.[83]

Members of Pacelli's inner circle, including Father Robert Leiber and Mother Pascalina, recalled in later years just how deeply immersed Pacelli had been in the process of writing the encyclical. With his characteristic attention to detail, he had read and reread every last word; he even made stylistic corrections of the German version, leaving the German members of his entourage impressed with his grasp of their mother tongue.[84] Pius XI reportedly told a group of German bishops visiting the Vatican a few days after the encyclical was issued, "Not one line leaves this office which [Pacelli] does not recognize."[85]

In the deliberations that produced the encyclical, Pacelli balanced the increasingly combative mood of Pius XI with the more restrained approach counseled by Faulhaber, who had long enjoyed Pacelli's trust on German matters. Pacelli made no apologies for having helped to stay Pius XI's hand in 1937 when Ratti was resolved to recall the papal nuncio from Berlin and break off diplomatic ties with the Hitler government. As Pacelli told the German cardinals at the Vatican, just days after he was elected pope, "Pius XI once was so disgusted by the events in Germany that he said, 'How can the Holy See continue to have a nuncio there? This goes against our honor.' I responded, 'Holy Father, what would we do otherwise? How would we maintain our ties to the Bishops?' He understood and calmed down." As he prepared to follow in the footsteps of his much-admired predecessor, Pacelli acknowledged the basic philosophical difference between the two men: whereas Pius XI had worried that world opinion would not understand how the Vatican could maintain diplomatic relations with a government that treated the church in such a way, Pacelli reasoned that "it is best that things remain as they are. If the government breaks off relations, fine—but it would not be wise for us to do so."[86]

Not that Cardinal Pacelli found Nazi behavior toward Catholic interests any less frustrating than did Pius XI. On the contrary, as the Vatican official with the closest and most frequent German contacts, he had all the more reason to be exasperated by the Hitler government's unwillingness to put an end to systematic persecution of German Catholics. Pacelli's frustration was obvious to other diplomats. The Italian ambassador Bonifacio Pignatti, who met with Pacelli on a weekly basis through the late 1930s, reported that the normally tight-lipped Pacelli let loose whenever talk turned to the German Reich. In one such meeting, Pacelli admitted that having spent some thirteen years in Germany he was inclined to look favorably upon any German government. It pained him, then, to learn that the word of German leaders meant nothing. Worse yet, the government's treatment of clergy accused of improprieties was "ferocious." Pignatti listened intently to Cardinal Pacelli, who, according to the ambassador, spoke excitedly and gesticulated wildly. As Pignatti put it, whenever Pacelli spoke of German affairs, he lost all control.[87]

Pacelli knew how to send clear if nonverbal signals of his anger toward the Nazis. When in June 1936 the Italian ambassador tried to arrange a meeting between Pacelli and Anton Mussert, the Dutch Nazi leader, Pacelli let it be known through Giuseppe Pizzardo that he was not likely to grant an interview to someone so closely associated with German National Socialism. Pignatti wrote to Count Galeazzo Ciano, the Italian foreign minister, to complain that Pacelli's anti-German campaign obviously was having its effect in the upper echelons of Vatican diplomacy. In the interests of maintaining a good working relationship with the Italians, Pacelli relented and met with Mussert. Their conversation must not have gone especially well. In recounting the meeting to the Italian ambassador, an animated Pacelli became so worked up that the veins on his neck were pulsating.[88]

The 1937 papal encyclical on the church and the German Reich has been praised as the "crowning" achievement of Pacelli's handling of the Vatican's relations with the Hitler state after the Reich Concordat of 1933.[89] Other historians have given most of the credit to Pius XI himself, arguing that the letter's undeniably defiant tone reflects Pius XI's determination to send a clear signal of papal disapproval to the Hitler government.[90] To be sure, the language in parts is surprisingly sharp and evocative. Referring implicitly but obviously to the Nazi persecution of Catholic institutions and associations since 1933, the encyclical spoke of "fixed responsibilities" and "intrigues" on the part of civil authorities whose aim from the start was "a war of extermination." But sending such a stark, unprecedented signal of disapproval was not tantamount to diplomatic rupture; nor was the encyclical intended as a political manifesto. To the contrary, the aim was to find ways of preserving and promoting the mutually beneficial accommodation worked out in 1933 but never fully actualized. That the encyclical intended to deliver an unqualified rebuke of certain aspects of Nazi ideology and practice is clear enough. Yet even here, the real target was not so much Nazi racial theory as it was the persistent violation of the letter and spirit of the 1933 concordat, of the Hitler government's incessant attempts to interfere with, curtail, or repress altogether the full and free expression of German Catholic life in its varied dimensions. To that end, the encyclical admonished not only the state but German Catholics as well: those who might, even under considerable duress, choose loyalty to the state over "faith in the church" or allow religious ideals to be "emptied of their content and distorted to profane use." Faith in the church, the encyclical reads, "cannot stand pure and true without the support of faith in the primacy of the bishop of Rome."[91] Yet Pius XI was not asking German Catholics to put faith in the church or in the pope above their fidelity to the state. It was the state, not the church, that was imposing such a stark and—the encyclical infers—false choice. This was said to be the case, for instance, with national youth organizations in which membership was obligatory even though, as the encyclical lamented, these organizations expressed "manifestations hostile to the church and Christianity." Sounding a hallmark diplomatic note, though, the encyclical offered assurances that the church had no intention of preventing young Germans from establishing what it called a "true ethnical community in a noble love of freedom and loyalty to their country." Rather, the pope was objecting to the "voluntary and systematic antagonism raised between national education and religious duty."[92] So there could be room after all for young Catholics in a *true* German ethnic community, so long as that ethnic community acknowledged Christ as King. Was this an indirect but pointed assault on the Nazis' totalitarian aim to control every aspect of society and eventually to supplant Christianity with a heretical national religion? Or was this the expression of a naïve belief that Nazism might yet be tamed, might yet be made to coexist with Christianity and to acknowledge God as the Sovereign Master? Either way, the circumlocution characteristic of such papal pronouncements did not translate readily into doctrinal clarity, even less into political clarity for ordinary Catholics who daily grappled to reconcile fidelity to their faith with loyalty to the state and compliance with the law.[93]

The encyclical's careful attempt to defend doctrinal principles and religious freedom for German Catholics by means of a measured, diplomatic rebuke—evidenced by the absence of any explicit reference to National Socialism, Hitler, or the Nazi Party—was almost certainly due to Pacelli's influence. It was Pacelli who invited Cardinal Faulhaber to write the first draft, thereby guaranteeing a more restrained document than might otherwise have been the case.[94] From the start, Faulhaber urged that the encyclical should be careful in its tone and substance and should avoid any explicit reference to National Socialism or the Nazi Party.[95] Faulhaber's first version was short, pointed on doctrinal matters, and careful in its wording. It walked a tightrope of doctrinal clarity while avoiding an open confrontation with the Hitler regime.

In this regard, Faulhaber and Pacelli were in accord—doctrinal clarity need not translate into a diplomatic rupture with the German government; that would only harm the church's capacity to fulfill its spiritual mission. Pacelli's direct influence is felt most heavily in the first half of the document, where the emphasis was on the Reich Concordat of 1933 and the repeated good will shown by Catholic interests to respect the spirit and letter of the treaty. The second half of the encyclical, which dealt at length with the doctrinal incompatibility between Christianity and Nazism, was drawn almost entirely from Faulhaber's original.

The papal encyclical had an immediate effect. For many observers, including Catholics long frustrated by the Vatican's policy of engagement with the Hitler state, it was the papal word they had been waiting for—a glimmer of hope. The excommunicated Italian Catholic activist Romolo Murri, who disapproved bitterly of the Vatican's diplomatic relations with the Fascist states, wrote to his sister that the pope's message to the Germans was "superb." This was the way the church should "speak and act," Murri wrote, seeing in the encyclical "a great promise for the future." It was to be the start of

Murri's gradual return to the Catholic fold, which culminated in his rehabilitation by Pius XII in 1944.[96]

Hitler's government responded angrily and swiftly, ordering the Gestapo to confiscate as many copies of the pronouncement as possible and instructing the German representation at the Vatican to launch formal diplomatic complaints.[97] Nazi officials saw the letter as a provocation and as a violation of the 1933 Reich Concordat, claiming that the encyclical had "the character of a political document." In a stern diplomatic note, the German government condemned the papal "attempt . . . to arouse the world against the New Germany" and denounced the secret circulation of the letter as proof that German church authorities knew of "the illegality of their procedure and the violation of their obligation as citizens." It complained that the papal statement about Germany "destroyed the effect of the papal encyclical against Communism . . . and dealt a dangerous blow to the defense front against the world menace of Bolshevism, so very desirable for the Catholic Church in particular." The Germans intimated that they might walk away altogether from the 1933 treaty, which Hitler had lauded as a master stroke of political genius.[98]

Ambassador Bergen at the Vatican told Pacelli that it was difficult to find the words to express the "uproar" caused in Germany by the papal statement. Bergen warned that there was talk in Berlin of taking serious measures in response. Even the French ambassador to Germany, François-Poncet, had it on good authority that the encyclical left Hitler's government "full of rage and wanting vengeance."[99] The Hitler government was so incensed by *Mit Brennender Sorge* that it ordered the resumption of legal proceedings against Catholic clergy on charges of financial and other improprieties.[100] Hitler's lingering anger may have been on display the year after the encyclical was pronounced when, during an official visit to Italy in May, he and his entourage studiously avoided visiting the pope.[101]

The antagonism was mutual. Although Italian officials approached the Holy See to discuss the possibility of a meeting between Hitler and Pius XI, the pope said he would do so only under certain conditions, one being that Hitler use his visit to Rome to denounce the persecution of German Catholics. Recognizing that the pope's conditions were unrealistic, Cardinal Pacelli, with characteristic pragmatism, believed that some good could come of a formal meeting between the Holy Father and the German leader.[102] In this instance, though, Pius XI won the day. When Hitler visited Rome, the pope actually left Vatican City for the papal residence at Castel Gandolfo. Commenting on the Nazi banners and flags throughout the Eternal City, he remarked that it was sad that Rome should be bedecked with a cross—the swastika—"which is not the Cross of Christ."[103]

Increased tension between the Vatican and the Hitler state was not the effect Pacelli had been hoping for when he worked so carefully to craft a statement intended to be firm yet conciliatory. Still, he was not prepared—let alone authorized—to concede anything of the Vatican's position in order to quell German anger at the papal letter.[104] In a lengthy note to Ambassador Bergen at the end of April 1937 in response to the German government's formal complaints over the encyclical, Pacelli held his ground on both doctrinal and tactical issues. While his reply left open the lines of communication, he gave no hint of appeasement nor any desire to placate or pacify the Nazi complaints. The cardinal said simply, "It is my duty to reject the unjust criticism" of the papal letter of March 1937. In a resolute and unapologetic tone, he dismissed as "erroneous" and "astonishing" the German government's characterization of the papal letter and its intention. He contested the description of the encyclical as a political document, stressing its unmistakable religious and doctrinal aim. While acknowledging that the Vatican appreciated "the formation of inherently sound and vigorous defensive political fronts against the danger of atheistic Bolshevism," he said that fear of Bolshevism could not blind the papal office to the fact that these errors had developed among anti-Bolshevist "political defensive fronts"—a thinly veiled allusion to Nazism. Fear of Bolshevism, in other words, ought never to induce the Holy See to turn a blind eye to its authority and thus responsibility on religious and spiritual concerns. In fact, Pacelli argued, nothing would strengthen the hand of Bolshevism more than the "erroneous belief" that the threat of "atheistic Communism" could be defeated only by "external power," thereby denying "spiritual powers" their "rightful place" in the struggle against godless Communism.

Turning from more general statements of principle, Pacelli addressed the German complaint that the encyclical violated the spirit and the letter of the concordat with the German government. He was incredulous, he wrote, to hear the Germans complain of such violations after so many years of constant pressure by the Vatican to get the Germans to respect the terms and conditions of the 1933 treaty. In a meeting with Bergen to discuss the furor caused by the encyclical, Pacelli said, "No one wants religious peace more than we do." But the Vatican's patience with the German government had worn thin. In effect, he said, German intransigence had forced the pope's hand. After all, since 1933, the Vatican had been warning that continued German violations of the *Reichskonkordat* and escalating persecution of the German Church were bound to lead to a public papal statement: "They have had three years of patience. But finally this public manifestation just had to be made."[105]

Cardinal Pacelli did acknowledge that the Hitler state had effectively removed the threat of German Communism, but he was not willing to concede that National Socialism could take the credit. He also pushed back against the German government's insistence that it had shown a "great spirit of cooperation . . . in word and deed" toward the Catholic Church in the very favorable terms of the 1933 treaty. These terms, Pacelli pointed out, were neither unprecedented nor especially favorable, since the Nazi government had reduced its promised payments to the church and enacted other financial measures that effectively damaged the financial standing of parishes and church institutions. And where the Germans accused the Vatican of taking the side of "liberalist parliamentary democracy" against the "New Germany," he responded with the conventional statement of Vatican impartiality, reiterating that the Holy See "has friendly, correct or at least tolerable relations with states of one or another constitutional form and orientation." Pacelli held out the hope that this might yet be true with regard to the German state, but it all depended on the extent to which Hitler's government acknowledged what *Mit Brennender Sorge* upheld, namely, the "principle that the organic law of every state is subject to the law of God." Pacelli concluded by dismissing the German government's claim that the encyclical constituted a serious breach of the 1933 treaty. "A more amazing reversal . . . of all the basic concepts of contract law than that attempted here," Pacelli wrote, "is hard to imagine." Still, he left the door open to a better working relationship between the Vatican and the Hitler state: he hoped for "the release of the leadership of the State, and of the movement sustaining the State, from the ever tightening embrace and the increasing penetration of the ideological and anti-Christian currents which draw their strength from the struggle against the Church."[106]

Pacelli had occasion to repeat this message often in the months after the papal letter was issued. In September 1937, in the wake of the annual Nazi

Party rally at Nuremberg, Pius XI instructed the cardinal to write and have published in the pages of the Vatican's newspaper a pointed reminder of the Nazis' continued transgressions of their obligations and promises related to the church in Germany.[107] As if front-page coverage in the Vatican's official newspaper were not enough, Pacelli instructed papal representatives around the world to have his article translated and distributed to bishops and clergy, and published in national newspapers. The papal representative in Washington, Amleto Cicognani, had copies sent to various ambassadors in Washington, as well as to American Secretary of State Cordell Hull.[108] From Vienna came word that various newspapers there, secular and Catholic, had also seen fit to publish the editorial. One Catholic paper even ran a special edition to publicize the piece.[109]

The widespread diffusion of Pacelli's unsigned but authoritative editorial was a remarkable demonstration of the church's capillary presence around the globe and of the potential for papal communication through the mass media. The article was a forthright rendering of the private complaints Pacelli had been registering with German officials for years. He intoned against the ongoing "hidden and open struggle against the Church in Germany and against the rights guaranteed to her in a solemn concordat." The article singled out the troubling "penetration" of "neo-paganism" into the Nazi movement, epitomized in the racialist theories of Rosenberg's *Myth of the Twentieth Century.* As for the claims made at the recent Nuremberg Congress that the Nazi revolution "had not taken a hat from even one churchman"—an obvious allusion to the anticlerical violence associated with the Spanish Civil War—Pacelli warned that what happened to the church in Spain had its precedent in anticlerical and antireligious literature such as that written by Rosenberg.[110]

Further evidence of the Vatican's increasing boldness in dealing with the Hitler regime emerged in May 1937, when Cardinal George Mundelein of Chicago publicly criticized the regime's spurious legal proceedings against religious orders. Speaking to a group of priests at a diocesan retreat, Mundelein asked, "How is it that a nation of 60,000,000 people, intelligent people, will submit in fear and servitude to an alien, an Austrian paper-hanger, and a poor one at that."[111] The Germans were so incensed by Mundelein's comments that Ambassador von Bergen at the Vatican was instructed to lodge a formal complaint with Pacelli's office.[112] The Vatican used the occasion to offer both public praise of Mundelein and to reiterate in private its continued disapproval of the Hitler government's apparent unwillingness or inability to rein in anti-Catholic excesses. In his private meetings with von Bergen, Pacelli agreed that parts of Mundelein's speech were not particularly constructive, especially the personal insults directed at Hitler, but he explained that Mundelein was speaking not on behalf of the Holy See but as a free citizen acting within the rights afforded him by the Constitution of his own country.

More important, though, was the fact that Pacelli refused to consider any kind of public rebuke of Cardinal Mundelein and used the meetings with the German ambassador to reiterate that the German government was not doing enough to address anti-Catholic actions despite repeated diplomatic promises to respect the terms of the 1933 Reich Concordat. In his private meetings with Pius XI and other members of the Secretariat, Pacelli reasoned that to criticize Mundelein in public would be seen as an "act of weakness" on the part of the Vatican. Worse yet, it would do nothing but "make the National Socialist leaders even more arrogant, including Hitler, who in his self-delusion thinks that the entire world should bow before him."[113]

The Mundelein incident prompted a rare joint session of the leading cardinals of the Curia in June 1937. Under discussion was the "fierce persecution" of the Catholic Church by the Nazi government in the wake of the 1937 papal letter, followed a few months later by Cardinal Mundelein's blunt assessment of the Nazi leader. A sign of just how seriously the Vatican's relations with the German government had deteriorated can be seen from the fact that this was one of the few times in his long pontificate that Pius XI chose to be present at such a meeting and to direct it. The cardinals stood firmly behind Pacelli, dismissing the fuss over Mundelein's speech as the proverbial tempest in a teapot, while the pope commended Pacelli's masterly application of papal policy.[114]

The year 1937 was a turning point in the Vatican's relations with the Hitler government. Since 1933, when the ink on the Reich Concordat was barely dry, the Vatican had been threatening to go public with its criticism of the German government's violations of its treaty obligations and especially for its persecution of German Catholics. In the years that followed, Pacelli had consistently voiced the Vatican's disapproval of the German government's anti-Catholic policies, expressing his objections formally to German representatives and confidentially to fellow diplomats. Commenting on the Spanish

Republicans, for example, he told some Italian officials that the "reds" were doing immediately and violently in Spain—burning churches and killing priests—what in Germany was being done "more slowly but gradually and systematically, with a war of destruction against the Church and Christianity itself."[115] This was arguably the most explicit language Pacelli ever used to denounce Nazi persecution of the German Church. That the normally restrained and evasive Pacelli would say such things to diplomats from Italy and France underscores both the depth of his anger and the seriousness of his resolve to get the Hitler government to comply with the terms of the 1933 agreement, in which Pacelli had invested so much of his time, energy, and expectations.

To his brother cardinals in the Curia, Pacelli used similarly direct language to decry the situation of the church in Germany. In a joint session of curial cardinals in June 1937, called to discuss possible Vatican recognition of the victory of Franco's nationalist forces in the Spanish Civil War, Pacelli urged caution and restraint, however much he may have hoped for a defeat of the anticlerical Republicans in Spain. Pacelli worried above all that quick Vatican recognition of the nationalist side would appear to the world as if the Holy See were joining the "Fascist bloc made up of Italy and Germany (with Japan not far behind)." Besides, Pacelli continued, did it make sense for the Vatican to be seen joining sides with Nazi Germany, the very regime that "persecutes the church"? Even if the Vatican did not intend it, joining publicly a bloc of pro-Franco Fascist states would, Pacelli warned, "make it seem that the Holy See were in agreement with a group that wants to destroy religion. Even among Franco's followers there are those who have a tendency to divinize Hitler."[116]

For the Vatican, and especially for Pacelli, the ball was in Hitler's court. In a meeting with the Spanish ambassador in 1938 to discuss Spain's relationship with Nazi Germany, Pacelli insisted that the Vatican had "nothing against Germany and the German people, which it loves." Nor did the Vatican have anything against the current government per se; the Vatican was only concerned about the "religious situation" in Germany, and with "the salvation of souls currently exposed to grave dangers."[117] Though the Nazis had for years consistently and systematically refused to play by the rules, Pacelli hoped that there was truth to Hitler's claim that he wanted to make "peace" with the church. When word reached the Vatican in December 1937 through Munich's

Cardinal Faulhaber that Hitler had approached the auxiliary bishop of Augsburg, Franz Eberle, ostensibly carrying an olive branch, Pacelli was receptive but characteristically cautious. As always, he pointed to the 1933 concordat as the sole basis for continued talks between the Holy See and the Hitler government.[118] Not for the first or last time, Pacelli's hopes of meaningful talks with the Hitler government proved to be in vain.

As it was, on the eve of his election as pope, Cardinal Pacelli knew that the Vatican's relations with the Hitler government were at an all-time low. Whereas Bishop Hudal continued to press for an accommodation between the church and the Hitler state, the German bishops themselves let Pacelli know that the situation was at an impasse. Meeting in Rome in late October 1938 with high-ranking German prelates, including Cardinals Bertram and Schulte, Pacelli was told in no uncertain terms that the situation was too dire at the moment to conceive of some kind of accommodation. Both Bertram and Schulte believed that there was "nothing to do" at present; Schulte went further in detailing the growing radicalization of the Nazi hierarchy, and of Hitler himself. Schulte told Pacelli that it was clear the Nazis sought the "destruction of the church," and so the approach adopted by the German bishops and the Vatican to this point had been the wisest course of action. The Vatican's options were limited, the German bishops insisted. True, there were signs of growing discontent among the population with Hitler's foreign policies around the time of the Munich Crisis. In the end, though, the bishops reasoned that Hitler's diplomatic successes allowed the Nazis to emerge from the crisis stronger than ever, and more fanatical.[119]

An air of frustration and anxiety hung over papal circles, mixed with a growing sense of futility. In a private letter to the U.S. ambassador to Great Britain, Joseph P. Kennedy, Pacelli acknowledged the anxiety with which the Vatican was watching the radicalization of Nazi domestic and foreign policy, including Hitler's long-threatened annexation of Austria. Pacelli wanted to assure his American friend that the Vatican had no intention of giving its assent to the move for the sake of making peace with the German Reich. This was clear enough from the Vatican's immediate repudiation of statements made by the Austrian bishops opening the door to a formal recognition of *Anschluss*. What Pacelli hoped for above all, he told Kennedy, was the realization of the "plan that we had thought of while in America," an obvious allusion to the establishment of closer ties with the Roosevelt administration. "It would make the world think over the ever increasing necessity in the present troubles of keeping in touch with the Supreme Moral Powers of the world, which at times feel powerless and isolated in their daily struggle against all sorts of political excesses from the Bolsheviks and the new pagans arising amongst the young 'Arian' generations."[120]

The bellwether of this growing fanaticism was, as always, the Nazi treatment of Jews. While Pacelli and German church leaders were worried about the fate of German Catholics, their concern about the "religious situation" in the Nazi state stopped short of an explicit acknowledgment that the persecution of one religious minority, German Jews, had reached intolerable levels in a purportedly civilized society proud of its Christian heritage. After years of informal and formal measures meant to marginalize Jews, stripping them of rights and freedoms, social standing and property, Nazi anti-Semitism took a decisive, brutal turn in November 1938 with the infamous events of *Kristallnacht,* when Jewish businesses and places of worship—in the thousands— were vandalized, looted, or destroyed altogether. Some one hundred Jews were killed, while hundreds more were injured, and close to thirty thousand innocent Jews were arrested and imprisoned in concentration camps.[121] The gas chambers of Nazi-occupied Europe were still some years from being built, but the events of November 1938 foreshadowed what was to come. Pacelli learned of the riots from nuncio Orsenigo in Berlin, who described the mob violence in detail and had the distinct impression that the initiative had come from "very high up" in the Nazi hierarchy. Orsenigo told of new ordinances intended to isolate Jews even further, barring them from businesses, public schools, theaters, and cinemas. A final indignity was that the Jews themselves were being made to pay a fine of one billion *Reichsmarks* for having provoked the violence in the first place.[122] Orsenigo was equally disturbed by subsequent developments, including the move to nullify marriages between so-called Aryans and Jews. These included marriages in which a Jewish spouse had converted to Catholicism, a blatant intrusion by the Nazi state into church affairs.[123]

The Vatican archives contain no record of Pacelli's response to Orsenigo's alarming reports. It is safe to assume that Pacelli, like Pope Pius XI himself, was disturbed by the depressingly familiar news that the Nazis were employing such brutish tactics while using the cover of legality to intrude into areas that were the proper purview of the church. In the realm of practical action,

Pacelli and the Vatican used their moral suasion to mobilize a marginally successful rescue effort. Following the lead of clergymen like Cardinal Innitzer of Austria and Cardinal Hinsley of Westminster, and with Pius XI's blessing, Pacelli's office showed considerably more resolve than other foreign governments, including the prospering democracies of North America, to help facilitate the migration from Germany of some 200,000 "non-Aryan Catholics." Working through bishops from around the world, Pacelli encouraged the establishment of committees to assist the emigrants with concrete material and moral aid, and also to press their governments to ease entry requirements in order to maximize the rescue and assistance efforts.[124]

Yet there was no formal, public Vatican response to the anti-Jewish riots of November 1938. Nor was there any such response by other churches, the press, and foreign governments everywhere. It fell to Cardinal Arthur Hinsley, the Catholic archbishop of Westminster, to prod Pacelli and Pius XI to consider making some sort of public statement condemning such brutal acts of violence—a paternal word of comfort and support from the Vicar of Christ on behalf of the thousands who were suffering persecution on the basis of "religion or race," as Hinsley put it. Hinsley implored Pacelli to consider having the pope make such a statement, which Hinsley characterized as "an authentic word of the Holy Father" to declare before the world "that in Christ discrimination of race does not exist." Hinsley was convinced that such a statement, in addition to helping the persecuted, would garner newfound respect for the Vatican, especially in the Anglo-American world.[125]

Pacelli's response to Hinsley's suggestion was characteristically evasive. On the one hand, he encouraged Hinsley to make a statement on behalf of those who were suffering unfairly, and even to speak on the pope's behalf. On the other hand, he never explicitly mentioned the persecution of Jews, let alone the horrific events of *Kristallnacht*. Nor was it likely that the pope himself would speak out directly on behalf of persecuted Jews, including the nearly 100,000 so-called non-Aryan Christians—Jewish converts to Catholicism. Pacelli explained that Pius XI was dealing with some health problems and that an overwhelming number of other tasks demanded his attention; hence the decision not to offer a public comment from the Vatican about the worsening situation of Jews in the Third Reich.[126] In other words, the pope was too sick and too busy to offer a public statement condemning one of the most violent anti-Jewish episodes in modern memory.

Eugenio Pacelli, who was just months away from becoming Pope Pius XII, was not indifferent to the plight of the persecuted Jews. But could he articulate a meaningful *political* response to Nazi violations of the norms of civility and morality? In addition to providing emigrants with aid, there were other signs that Pacelli understood the dire situation of Germany's dwindling Jewish communities. Just weeks after *Kristallnacht,* he delivered a moving speech in the Roman Church of San Giacomo, to commemorate the 200th anniversary of the canonization of Saint Vincent de Paul. Pacelli evoked the imagery of the children of Israel forced into exile, and likened the spiritual travails of the great Catholic saint to the "anguished lamentations" of the Jewish people in exile in Babylon.[127] It was a moving tribute, no doubt, to the great saint and to biblical Israel. As a spiritual exercise, it had much to recommend it. But it was a decidedly tepid political response to the escalating excesses of the Hitler state. Even after years of tussling unsuccessfully to get Hitler to respect the terms of the lauded 1933 treaty, Eugenio Pacelli was still struggling, seemingly in vain, to find an effective political response to increasing Nazi radicalism.

Eugenio Pacelli, c. 1883. The young Eugenio is said to have been reserved, introspective, and deeply sensitive. By all accounts, Pacelli family life was stable, happy, and materially comfortable with the aristocratic airs befitting a family with a nominal noble title. (Getty Images)

Eugenio Cardinal Pacelli as the Vatican's secretary of state. He served in this role from 1930 until his election as pope in 1939. (Bundesarchiv, Bild 183-2011-0209-500/photo: o.Ang)

Monsignor Eugenio Pacelli as papal nuncio in Germany, 1919. (Budesarchiv, Bild 183-S46735/photo: o.Ang)

Nuncio Pacelli at the Opel company headquarters in Rüsselheim, Germany, October 1928. He is being presented with the gift of a title to a Pullmann limousine. (Bundesarchiv, Bild 102-06728/photo: Georg Pahl)

Nuncio Pacelli in procession, October 1925. This photograph was taken while German press reports were suggesting that he would soon leave Berlin for Rome in order to be made a cardinal. In fact, Pacelli remained in Germany for almost five more years. (Bundesarchiv, Bild 102-01953/photo: Georg Pahl)

The signing of the *Reichskonkordat* between the Holy See and the German Reich, Rome, July 20, 1933. (left to right): Monsignor Ludwig Kaas, Franz von Papen, Giuseppe Pizzardo, Eugenio Pacelli, Alfredo Ottaviani, and Dr. Rudolf Buttmann of the Reich Interior Ministry. Although negotiations concluded rapidly—and successfully—to the satisfaction of both parties, unresolved issues and Vatican complaints of German violations of its terms marred the concordat from the start. (Bundesarchiv, Bild 183-R24391/photo: o.Ang)

Eugenio Cardinal Pacelli together with Patrick Cardinal Hayes, archbishop of New York, leaving St. Patrick's Cathedral in New York City, October 8, 1936. Pacelli's month-long American tour was historic, marking the first time a papal secretary of state had visited the United States. Although it was officially touted as a vacation, the trip included a private meeting between Pacelli and Franklin D. Roosevelt and helped to encourage closer Vatican–U.S. relations on the eve of World War Two. (Associated Press)

Eugenio Cardinal Pacelli during his historic trip to the United States in 1936. His good friend Francis Spellman, future archbishop and cardinal, is seen emerging from the plane. To avoid appearing to interfere in the presidential elections at the time, Pacelli took a widely publicized plane trip as far west as California. (San Diego Air & Space Museum)

The Kennedy family at the Vatican during the coronation of Pope Pius XII, March 12, 1939. (left to right, back row): Patricia, John F., Joseph P., Eunice, Rosemary. (left to right, front row): An unidentified Vatican guard, Kathleen, Robert F., Rose, Edward M., Jean, and another unidentified Vatican guard. President Franklin D. Roosevelt sent Joseph P. Kennedy, then ambassador to Great Britain, as his personal representative. (The John F. Kennedy Presidential Library and Museum, Boston/Fotografia Felici)

The newly elected Pope Pius XII with Spanish troops during a general audience at the Vatican, June 11, 1939. As secretary of state and as pope, Pius XII worried that General Francisco Franco's regime would drift toward closer ties with the Hitler regime. Even still, he greeted the 1939 victory of Franco's forces in the Spanish Civil War as a triumph for Catholic Spain. (Associated Press)

An anguished Pius XII praying with the people of a Roman neighborhood on October 15, 1943, as part of a tour of central Rome after an Allied air raid in August. (Associated Press)

Members of the Royal 22nd Regiment with Pope Pius XII in Rome, July 4, 1944. (Canada. Department of National Defence/Library and Archives Canada/PA-166069)

Lieutenant Paul E. Vincent and members of the Canadian Army with Pope Pius XII in Rome, December 20, 1944. (Canada. Department of National Defence/Library and Archives Canada/PA-166066)

Pope Pius XII with an old acquaintance, Joseph P. Kennedy, former U.S. ambassador to England, during an audience at the Vatican, June 22, 1955. (Associated Press)

Pope Pius XII with the Harlem Globetrotters at the papal summer residence of Castel Gandolfo, August 1, 1952. Eager to give the papacy a mass appeal, Pius XII met frequently with athletes and celebrities from around the world. (Associated Press)

Pius XII, who was very much at ease with modern appliances, using a typewriter. Although the photograph was staged, Pius XII was often at his desk well into the early-morning hours working on drafts of speeches and other papal pronouncements. (Fotografia Felici)

Pius XII giving gifts and imparting a blessing to school children during one of his daily walks. Despite the popular perception of Pacelli as an aloof intellectual—and perhaps to counter it—the pope often was depicted interacting directly and warmly with the laity. Some commentators suggest that staged photos such as this were intended to promote something of a personality cult around Pius XII. (Fotografia Felici)

Pius XII, wearing an elaborate tiara, being carried into St. Peter's Basilica in Rome on the *sedia gestatoria,* which was a portable throne used only for certain formal occasions, notably during papal coronations. The twelve *palafrenieri,* or footmen, who bear the throne are flanked by Swiss Guards. On either side of the *sedia* are two *flabella,* or fans, made of feathers. Such ancient vestiges of papal pomp and ceremony have largely been abandoned by the popes, starting with Paul VI. (Fotografia Felici)

Pius XII holding a goldfinch. A great lover of animals, especially birds, Pius XII purportedly almost always dined alone with his pet goldfinch Gretel as his sole companion. (Fotografia Felici)

A bronze monument to Pius XII from the main floor of St. Peter's Basilica in Rome. Commissioned by a group of cardinals who had been named by Pius XII, and unveiled by Pope Paul VI in 1964, it is the work of the Italian sculptor Francesco Messina. The pope's raised arm seems to be imparting a blessing, although some commentators surmise that it is intended to symbolize Pius XII's attempts to stop the war that was to define his pontificate. (Photo by Barry Berenson)

4

A Tremendous Responsibility

Pope Pius XI, who had done more than anyone else to advance Eugenio Pacelli's career, died in the early morning of February 10, 1939. Pacelli kept vigil, praying by the dying pope's bedside, in the final hours of what had been a long and painful illness. Pius XI and his secretary of state had had their differences over the years, especially in the preceding months as the pope's resolve to confront the Fascist dictators publicly clashed with Pacelli's worry about an all-out confrontation. Yet there could be no doubt of the genuine affection between the two men, the fruit of years of almost daily interaction and a shared sense of service. When Pius XI died, Pacelli bent over to kiss his forehead and his hands in a gesture that took some of the papal court by surprise, given Pacelli's reputation for emotional reserve. In keeping with prescribed ritual, Pacelli called out the pope's given name, *Achille*. When there was no response, a visibly shaken Pacelli declared, "The pope is truly dead."[1]

Pacelli took immediate control of the transitional period that followed, thus setting the stage, perhaps unwittingly, for his own succession to the papal throne. In part, his actions flowed logically from his responsibilities as *camerlengo*, the cardinal charged with the task of preparing the papal funeral and, more important, organizing the conclave to elect a new pope. The fact that the late pontiff had placed so much trust in Pacelli over the years gave the secretary of state unsurpassed influence over church governance during the period of *sede vacante,* that administrative limbo between the death of one pope and the election of another.

Pacelli worked deliberately to steer the transition in a direction that reflected his own view of the church's future, especially regarding its dealings with the major powers. One of his first decisions was to delay the start of the conclave to the beginning of March to allow cardinals from the Americas to attend. This included the U.S. cardinals—O'Connell of Boston, Dougherty of Philadelphia, Mundelein of Chicago—as well as cardinals from South America. The decision was not lost on expert Vatican watchers, who commented favorably on the fact that the whole College of Cardinals, including non-Europeans, would be assembled for the vote. It was a sure sign of the internationalization of church governance, which was one of Pius XI's most undervalued accomplishments. As pope, Pacelli would accelerate the trend.[2]

That Pacelli would play the dominant role during the transition was clear in the weeks before Pius XI's death, when an ailing but still combative pontiff resolved to make a definitive stand against Fascist policies. The pope hoped to live long enough to see the commemoration of the tenth anniversary of the Lateran Accords, the 1929 agreements between the Holy See and Mussolini's government. Pius XI had planned to convoke a meeting of Italian bishops for the occasion, and to use the gathering to offer a pointed critique of the current state of church-state relations both in Italy and in Germany. With his physical and intellectual capacities reduced, the pope relied more and more on his trusted secretary of state. Though Pacelli worried about the pope's drift toward more explicit public criticism of the Fascist regimes, he nevertheless dutifully helped to compose the speech, making just a few minor revisions but without altering the substance of the dying pope's forceful message.[3]

The speech, which was drafted as Pius XI lay dying, was strongly worded, its tone biting in its criticism of so-called pseudo-Catholics—a clear allusion to Catholics with Fascist sympathies.[4] Mussolini's government and the general public would have grasped the substance of this papal critique—if the address had ever been delivered. But the pope did not live to give the speech, which was scheduled for February 11, the day after he died. The timing gave rise to an improbable rumor that Pius XI's death had been hastened by one of his doctors, Francesco Saverio Petacci, the father of Mussolini's mistress. By dying when he did, Pius XI was prevented from delivering what would have been one of the most formidable public expressions of open opposition to Mussolini's policies in close to twenty years of Fascist rule.[5]

Pacelli's actions at the time contributed to the unsettled atmosphere. It was no secret that even though he had helped to draft the speech, he disagreed fundamentally with the pope's inclination to respond aggressively to Fascist policies. Because of the pope's sickness, the Vatican's relations with the Mussolini regime were in a holding pattern, but within hours of Pius XI's death, Pacelli was already sending out peace feelers to Italian officials. When the Italian foreign minister Ciano arrived at the Vatican to convey his government's condolences, Cardinal Pacelli took him into the Sistine Chapel to pay his last respects to the deceased pope. According to Ciano's diary, the cardinal used the occasion to speak of church-state relations in "conciliatory and hopeful terms."[6]

Some Vatican insiders were struck by Pacelli's markedly cordial reception of a high-ranking member of the Mussolini government. It was a sign of the well-known difference in style between the deceased pope and his secretary of state.[7] Pacelli's tone pleased Ciano, who had been growing increasingly worried that tension between the Vatican and the Mussolini government was driving diplomatic relations to a breaking point. Most troubling of all was the fact that Mussolini himself seemed to care less and less about what the Vatican said and did. As Ciano noted in his diary, news of the pope's death on February 10 scarcely made an impression on Mussolini, who was altogether "indifferent." Mussolini's reaction indicated a definite change in his attitude toward the Vatican.[8]

Despite this apparent detachment, Mussolini and members of his government were very interested in who would succeed Pius XI and in what direction the new pope would take the Vatican in its relationship with the Italian government. Rumors circulated soon after Pius XI died—Ciano said they came from American sources—that the late pope had left behind a written statement or testament of some kind. Mussolini was very keen to confirm whether this was true, and he was even more eager to see a copy of the docu-

ment. Given their level of interest in the story, Italian officials must have suspected that the document related to the speech Pius XI had planned to deliver
to mark the anniversary of the 1929 *Conciliazione.*[9]

If the rumored document really was the speech Pius XI had prepared on
his deathbed, the Italians need not have worried. Pacelli had already ordered
an immediate stop to the publication of the text of the address, which was all
but ready for wide distribution to the Italian bishops. One of Pacelli's trusted
colleagues, Domenico Tardini, recalled that within hours of Pius XI's death,
Pacelli demanded that any and all materials related to the preparation of the
pope's address be remanded to Pacelli's office; any copies or templates of the
speech that were with the publishers were to be destroyed immediately.[10]

What are we to make of Pacelli's role in suppressing what would have
been a historic speech by a dying pontiff, even more so if the speech had been
published posthumously? One possibility is that Cardinal Pacelli was simply
doing his job—fulfilling his task as the man in charge of the transition to keep
an absolute veil of privacy over the deceased pope's intellectual and material
property. Of course, it is also true that after becoming pope Pacelli was completely at liberty to do what he wished with his predecessor's speech, including making it public or at least known to the cardinals.[11] Pacelli said nothing
about the speech, ever. Tellingly, it was not published until 1959—just months
after Pacelli's own death. Pacelli also decided after becoming pope not to pursue publication of a papal statement that had been in preparation by his predecessor condemning explicitly Nazi racial thought and anti-Semitism in particular—the so-called hidden encyclical of Pius XI, which did not emerge until
many years later.[12] In both instances, Eugenio Pacelli showed himself very
much to be his own man, deftly steering a course for papal diplomacy consistent with his temperament and philosophy.

The Conclave

Pacelli's machinations in the days after Pius XI died enhanced his chances of
becoming pope, despite his stated eagerness to retire to the quiet life of a parish priest. For years, the cardinal secretary of state had been considered by
insiders and Vatican watchers as a likely *papabile,* a leading candidate to become pope. It was no secret that Pius XI had always considered Pacelli ideally
suited to be his successor. This explains his constant efforts, against Pacelli's

wishes, apparently, to advance Pacelli's career and to publicize what Pius XI saw as Pacelli's rare combination of intelligence, skill, and dedication. A secret dossier prepared for the Italian Foreign Ministry in the late 1930s by Monsignor Enrico Pucci, who acted occasionally as an informant for the Fascist police, surveyed the list of potential successors to Pius XI and concluded that Cardinal Pacelli was indeed an early favorite.[13] Not for nothing had Pius XI increased Pacelli's stature by sending him on those historic trips to Latin America, France, and the United States between 1934 and 1936. When a bedridden Pius XI met in January 1937 with three German cardinals, the pope heaped praise on his trusted secretary of state, making a deep impression on the leading German prelates who would eventually be called upon to elect a new pope.

It mattered little that Pacelli continually expressed his desire to be finished with papal diplomacy and curial affairs. Diplomats at the papal court realized Pacelli was not entirely happy in his role as cardinal secretary of state, let alone at the prospect of being considered a leading *papabile*. In a report from 1934, British officials at the Vatican confirmed that Pacelli's role as chief papal diplomat was "uncongenial to him" and that he really did "prefer work of a more pastoral kind."[14] This time around, with the stakes so much higher, it was said that Pacelli hoped all the more fervently to be passed over by the College of Cardinals so that he could live the quiet life of a parish priest. History was on his side: it was rare for a cardinal secretary of state to be elected pope; it had been more than a century since such a thing had happened.[15]

According to Pacelli's most intimate acquaintances, he was sincere when he said that he intended to leave Rome immediately after a new pope was elected. He ordered the sisters who ran his household to begin packing his apartment in the apostolic palace and to have their passports ready to travel to their favored Swiss retreat just as soon as a new pope was installed. His nephew Carlo Pacelli recalled seeing luggage and boxes packed and ready to go on the very day Pacelli was elected pope. Another nephew, Giulio Pacelli, insisted that his uncle neither expected nor wanted to be elected pope. Nor did he want the new pope, whoever it was, to keep him on as secretary of state, hence his plan to vacation in Switzerland immediately after the election.[16]

The election of a new pope came at a delicate moment in international affairs, and secular states around the world took an unprecedented interest in the papal election. It was widely believed that the major European governments, especially Italy and Germany, would try to exert pressure on the cardinals to choose a pope who was friendly to their interests. Vatican watchers told tales of intrigue and "behind-the-scene manoeuvres" to influence the voting. Reporters told of "prodigious whispering and bustling of emissaries around Cardinals' palaces," and of "secular diplomats" who had a "big stake" in dealing with the cardinals "as if they too were secular diplomats." Observers from the Anglo-American world reported that Italy and Germany were engaged in "some clumsy, public hinting" to pressure the cardinals to avoid selecting a pope who might alienate Mussolini and Hitler.[17] The cardinals were being warned openly by the Fascist and Nazi press about the consequences to church-state relations of electing a "political pope," a euphemistic way of advising against the selection of someone like Pius XI, who was seen by Fascist authorities as too prone to intervene in what were supposed to be purely political matters. One Fascist newspaper in Italy alleged that a Jewish-inspired anti-Fascist press was hoping for the selection of a pope who was "decidedly hostile to fascism . . . a political pope who will compromise the church and provoke a schism."[18]

Some elements of the German Catholic Church were said to welcome the election of a nonpolitical pope, in order to allow the German church "to make peace with the state." For many Nazi commentators, Cardinal Pacelli, having been Pius XI's closest advisor, could hardly be considered nonpolitical; for this reason, he was attacked by some Nazi publications such as the SS-controlled *Der Schwarze Korps*. To many Germans, Pacelli was the person largely responsible for what one reporter called the "anti-German trend" in relations between the Vatican and the Third Reich. The Nazi security agency concluded in a 1939 report that Pacelli had gained a reputation while secretary of state for attacking National Socialism.[19]

The major powers thought seriously of ways to influence the highly secretive conclave. French Foreign Minister Georges Bonnet told the British ambassador to Paris, Sir Eric Phipps, that the Western democracies should work together to help guarantee the election of a pope who would help to defend liberal democracy from the gathering threat of an aggressive authoritarianism. Bonnet thought Pacelli was the most logical choice in this regard. The British representative to the Vatican, D'Arcy Osborne, agreed. Pacelli was the favorite even of leading German and Italian diplomats, notably German Ambassador to the Holy See Diego von Bergen and Italian Foreign Minister Galeazzo Ciano.[20] Pacelli, it seems, was a *papabile* for all seasons.

Other German officials, especially in the rabidly anticlerical security service (SD), held firmly to the view that Pacelli was deeply anti-German and too overtly political to be acceptable. Far better from their perspective was someone like Cardinal Ildefonso Schuster of Milan, who was considered favorable to the Mussolini regime—or better yet Maurilio Fossati of Turin or Elia Dalla Costa of Florence. Dalla Costa in particular was seen as a "nonpolitical" candidate and thus unlikely to cause the Fascist dictatorships any real trouble. The height of Nazi intrigue surrounding the election came when a would-be Vatican insider approached Albert Hartl, the former priest now in charge of the SD intelligence network on the church, saying that for some three million marks, the Germans could help to secure the election of a pope favorable to the Third Reich. The SD relayed the offer all the way up to the führer, who was said to be intrigued by the prospect of buying the papal election. Hitler considered the idea seriously but was eventually dissuaded on the grounds that if word of the bribe leaked out, it would be a propaganda nightmare.[21]

Many of the reports of diplomats, intelligence officers, and spies attempting to influence the outcome of the voting were wildly inflated or downright fantastical, such as the story of the Nazis trying to bribe dozens of cardinals.[22] The Vatican understood that the pressure being brought to bear on the College of Cardinals was unprecedented. To guard against any outside attempt at manipulation, it created a special committee of a few cardinals to scrutinize the credentials of anyone asking for access to the conclave.[23] There was apparently one potential breach of the strict secrecy of the process, a planted dictaphone in the Sistine Chapel, but it was caught just before the balloting began.[24]

Even before the voting began formally in early March 1939, some cardinals were saying in hushed tones that Pacelli's victory on the first ballot was all but certain.[25] But his election was by no means a sure thing. There were several formidable candidates—all of them Italian—with a solid base of support among influential blocs of cardinals. Cardinal Luigi Maglione, for one, who would go on to become Pius XII's secretary of state, enjoyed the backing of the influential French cardinal Eugène Tisserant. Cardinal Dalla Costa of Florence was another contender, probably the most serious challenger to

Pacelli's candidacy, whose support was especially strong among a unified group of Italians in the College of Cardinals. Dalla Costa was seen as the quintessential nonpolitical candidate favored by a bloc of cardinals who thought the church ought to be led by a more strictly spiritual and pastoral pontiff, someone more like Pius X than Pius XI, and thus someone less likely to be combative in dealing with the authoritarian states. So although Pacelli enjoyed widespread support among the French and German cardinals, a distinctly curial, Italian faction was aligned against his election. Despite his many years working in the very heart of the Curia, Pacelli was *not* the choice of powerful insiders.[26]

The divisions were apparent in the voting: it took three votes for Pacelli to achieve the two-thirds majority he needed to be elected. The successful vote came just a day after the conclave began, in the early evening of March 2, 1939, which happened also to be Pacelli's sixty-third birthday. Most reliable accounts of the voting suggest that Pacelli won by at least forty-eight votes—just six more than the two-thirds majority needed. This suggests that a determined group of supporters refused to give up on Dalla Costa of Florence, at least not until the very end, when Pacelli's election was all but certain.[27] Pacelli's success was due largely to the solid support of non-Italian cardinals.[28]

Sitting next to him in the Sistine Chapel during the balloting was Cardinal Manuel Goncalves Cerejeira, the patriarch of Lisbon, who observed that at the start of voting, Pacelli was calm, seemingly lost in prayer and almost detached from the momentous event. Other firsthand accounts agree that Pacelli appeared perfectly serene at the start of voting, going about the normal routine of his day, including his daily walks and Rosary recitations. He was even permitted the special privilege of remaining in his own apartment in the apostolic palace during the conclave, since technically it was within the restricted area. In a fitting symmetry with the early years of his clerical training, Pacelli did not share in the communal experience—he took his meals alone during the conclave while all the other cardinals ate and deliberated together in cramped quarters.[29]

As Pacelli realized that he was the clear front-runner, his demeanor changed. Cardinal Goncalves Cerejeira noticed that Pacelli had begun to pray quietly but audibly, repeating *Domine Jesu, Miserere mei:* Lord Jesus, Have mercy on me. Cardinal Luigi Lavitrano, who sat on the other side of Pacelli, tried to encourage him, saying that his election was to be taken as a sign of God's favor, to which Pacelli retorted, "But it is also a tremendous responsibility."[30] Gone was the serene detachment of a few hours earlier. Gone, too, was Pacelli's celebrated composure. Just before voting began on the third and final ballot, a distracted Pacelli tripped and fell down a few steps—a minor fall that left him unharmed.[31]

When the final results were known, the ritual of certifying acceptance of the office began. Ceremonial officers walked the length of the Sistine Chapel, lowering the canopies over the chairs of each cardinal, to symbolize their submission to the newly elected pope. Only Pacelli's canopy was left standing. According to prescribed ritual, three cardinals stood directly in front of Pacelli and asked, *Acceptas ne electionem in summum pontaficem?*: Do you accept your election as Supreme Pontiff? Pacelli replied meekly that, though he believed himself to be wholly unworthy of such a high office, he accepted the election as God's will, and asked for prayers. Cardinal Gennaro Granito Pignatelli di Belmonte, dean of the Sacred College, then asked the customary question, *Quomodo vis vocari?*: How do you wish to be called? Pacelli answered, "I wish to be called Pius XII"—in appreciation for the years spent serving under pontiffs of that name, but especially the late Pius XI, who had shown the new pope particular affection.[32]

Although his election had been all but foretold, Pacelli seemed overwhelmed by the result, as if he suddenly realized the enormous responsibility that now rested on his shoulders. One of the cardinals sitting close to him said that Pacelli gave the impression of accepting his election as a kind of sacrificial lamb, to the point of being visibly shaken.[33] Those who knew him best were struck by the immediate change that came over him after he returned to his apartment that evening. Enrico Galeazzi was moved almost to pity by the appearance of the new pope, who already seemed to be bearing physically the burden of such a high honor—and the responsibility. A tired Pacelli sank into his chair and said, "Do you see what they've reduced me to?"[34] Mother Pascalina described him as a man transformed by the papal office. "It was no longer Cardinal Pacelli that was coming home," she said, "but Pope Pius XII." With tears in their eyes, Mother Pascalina and the other sisters of the household knelt to kiss his hand. With tears in his own eyes, Pacelli said, "Look at what they've done to me." It was difficult to tell whether these were tears of joy or sorrow, Mother Pascalina said.

Family and close friends soon arrived to pay homage to the new pope. Pacelli's longtime German confidant Cardinal Faulhaber stopped by late in the evening but was overcome by emotion and decided to return at a later time. Another of Pacelli's German confidants, Monsignor Ludwig Kaas, offered a friendly reminder that the former papal diplomat and secretary of state had always said he wanted a proper diocese of his own. "Are you happy now to have received such a large one?" Kaas asked, playfully. Still wrought with emotion, Pacelli replied, "not one this large."[35]

The Roman Pope

By the time Pacelli emerged from the central balcony of St. Peter's Basilica to greet the crowds and impart the traditional blessing, it was close to 6:30 P.M. Scarcely an hour had passed since he had accepted his election. At least fifty thousand people had crowded into St. Peter's Square to catch a glimpse of the new pope, who had the great distinction of being one of their own— the first Roman to be elected pope since the early 1700s.[36] Pius XII was well known to the people of Rome, but thanks to his years in the papal diplomatic corps and nearly a decade as secretary of state, he had a prominent international profile too, even beyond the strict confines of the diplomatic corps. Arguably the Germans knew him best. Pacelli was not quite a household name in Germany, but he was probably better known and more popular than leading German churchmen. He was well known elsewhere, especially in France, where he had traveled on a few occasions in the 1930s and addressed large audiences.

Pacelli's election meant that for the first time in history the papal office was occupied by someone who had traveled to the United States and had close ties to members of the American Catholic ecclesiastical hierarchy, as well as to influential American Catholics such as Joseph P. Kennedy. It was not lost on American commentators that the man soon to be sitting on the Chair of St. Peter had a few years earlier chatted informally with FDR over lunch at Hyde Park, and relaxed in the Kennedy family's sitting room when he visited their home in Bronxville, New York. Nor did it escape attention that Pacelli had expressed great admiration and "enthusiasm" for the United States. As he told the New York Times correspondent Anne O'Hare McCormick, he marveled at the geographical, intellectual, and spiritual expanse of

American life, and its capacity for the free expression of religious faith and practice.[37]

The Kennedy family's special connection to the new pope was evident when President Roosevelt sent Joseph P. Kennedy, then ambassador to Great Britain, to attend Pius XII's formal coronation at St. Peter's in March 1939. It was an unprecedented gesture and a measure of just how seriously Roosevelt intended to cultivate his administration's working relationship with the Vatican. The entire Kennedy clan traveled to Rome for the historic event, which culminated in Pacelli's first Pontifical Mass, celebrated on Sunday, March 12. Representatives from various civil governments were present, including delegates from Great Britain and a surprisingly large contingent of Italian officials. Among them was the Italian foreign minister Ciano. Even Mussolini's sons Bruno and Vittorio had managed to procure tickets for the ceremony. So great was the demand for tickets that the Italian ambassador to the Vatican, Pignatti, complained of a veritable "avalanche" of requests for tickets, which were impossible to honor.[38]

Ambassador Kennedy's papers record in great detail the pomp and circumstance that accompanied Pius XII's coronation. The day of the coronation was cold but clear. St. Peter's Square and the surrounding streets were packed with tens of thousands of people. Pius XII entered the basilica at about 8:45 A.M. to an exuberant crowd of close to 50,000 people chanting, "Long live the Pope!" During the Pontifical Mass, the Kennedys were seated just opposite the papal throne, and thus had a near "perfect view" of the ceremony. Ambassador Kennedy was both bemused and disturbed as Galeazzo Ciano, Mussolini's representative, gave the Fascist salute, "bowing and smiling" as he walked through the basilica. The elder Kennedy thought that Ciano looked and acted like a buffoon.[39] For his part, Ciano recorded in his diary that the new pope was as "solemn as a statue"; when he had met with the cardinal just a month before, Ciano said, Pacelli had been a man just like any other. Now, he noted that the former papal diplomat had been touched by the divine, elevated by the papal office.[40]

For the Kennedys there were even greater privileges to come. The day after his installation, Pius XII invited the ambassador and his family to a private audience in his old office at the apostolic palace. Ambassador Kennedy, together with Enrico Galeazzi, met privately with the pope first. Kennedy noted in his journal, "We went into the room and Genuflected [*sic*] and then to my amazement as he was sitting behind a table he got up and I went to meet him he advanced a few steps towards me. I knelt and kissed his ring and then stood up. He smiled, motioned me to sit down and then sat down himself. He told me how happy he was to see me. He recalled his first visit to the house and his picture taken with all the children surrounding him. How nice they all were and how he 'rejoiced' that the President had sent me to Rome."[41] With the diplomatic niceties exchanged, and after having recalled his "pleasant visit" with Roosevelt at Hyde Park, Pius XII turned to the business at hand—formal American recognition of the Vatican. Kennedy believed that the greatest obstacle was the apparent opposition of the American Catholic hierarchy—the American cardinals in particular—who feared that formal diplomatic relations between the United States and the Holy See would somehow lessen their power and influence both at home and in Vatican circles. Pius XII reassured the ambassador that the cardinals had nothing to worry about. Kennedy pledged to do what he could but asked whether the pope might have someone speak directly to the cardinals. It is not known how Pius XII reacted to this request. Kennedy recorded simply that the pope "was cheerful, most kind and showed a real affection for me." Just before inviting Rose and the children to join them, Galeazzi made what Kennedy took as an attempt to "put in a boost for his friend Bishop Spellman of Boston."[42] Galeazzi reminded the pope of Kennedy's Boston roots, and Kennedy took the hint and spoke glowingly about Spellman, whom Pacelli had known well since the 1920s. The pope described the American prelate as a "good man and a good friend." Such a recommendation bolstered Spellman's standing at home and in Rome, such that during Pius XII's pontificate, Spellman became arguably the most powerful man in the American Catholic hierarchy.

Two days later, the Kennedys were back at the Vatican for a rare privilege, probably arranged through Galeazzi: Teddy, aged seven, received his First Communion from Pius XII in the pope's private chapel at the Vatican. When in 1962 Teddy was running for his brother John's Massachusetts Senate seat, his doting mother recalled his First Communion in a television special; she claimed that it was the first time ever that an American Catholic had received such an honor. Teddy's journal for the day noted,

> We got there a little while before Mass, so we all prayed. Soon the
> Pope came in and he put on all his vestments right in the Chapel

in front of the Altar. Then he said Mass. He was all dressed in red and white. At Communion the Pope came down to your seat and gave us all Holy Communion. . . . After Mass, one of the three nuns who were there brought out a present for me on a plate and put it on a chair, and then she touched the Holy Father's arm and I guess he knew that she had gotten the present alright. So then he went over and got it and gave it to me. He made the sign of the Cross on my forehead and said, "Keep this for a souvenir and be good and pious during your life." It was a lovely silver Rosary and he blessed it right in front of us.

Writing in his journal, Ambassador Kennedy said that Pius XII was "awe-inspiring, majestic, kindness personified and with the humility of God." In a brief report to the European Affairs desk at the State Department, he wrote, "Besides being a most saintly man, he has an extensive knowledge of world conditions. He is not pro-one country or anti-another. He is just pro-Christian. If the world hasn't gone too far to be influenced by a great and good man, this is the man."[43] A few weeks later, Kennedy offered a more pointed assessment of the new pope's likely influence on the course of international affairs. Writing to Sumner Welles, the under-secretary of state, Kennedy reasoned that Pius XII "was far from having any political prejudices, except a subconscious prejudice that has arisen from his belief that the tendency of Nazism and Fascism is pro-pagan and, as pro-pagan, they strike at the roots of religion." Kennedy was sure that this pope had more influence in Italy than had any pope in the past century or so, though he was realistic about the practical limits of the Vatican's influence over the Mussolini regime: "I don't believe that it is very practical to imagine that the Pope could stop Mussolini from fighting a war which he had persuaded the people was for the glory of Italy." But, he insisted, the pope's influence "could be utilized for the cause of peace in ways under the surface rather than in a big gesture."[44]

Kennedy's enthusiasm for the new pope was by no means universal. At the time of his election, some cardinals complained that Pacelli was a "man of peace" at a time when the world needed a pope prepared to "do battle." He was too much the diplomat, too careful, to provide the kind of resolute leadership needed in a world threatened imminently by totalitarian repression and war. But his supporters reasoned that a skilled diplomat such as

Pacelli, with firsthand experience dealing with the warring states of Europe in World War One, was precisely what was needed in the heady climate of 1939. His detractors, and there were many, nurtured a nagging sense that Pacelli's "indecisive" and "hesitant" nature would translate into a less openly combative confrontation with the Fascist dictators who occupied power in the two countries Pacelli knew best, Italy and Germany. The French ambassador to the Holy See, Charles-Roux, who knew Pacelli as well as any diplomat at the papal court, reported back to the French Foreign Ministry that the impression of Pacelli as too indecisive and too cautious had convinced Cardinal Tisserant, the lone French cardinal in the Roman Curia, to oppose Pacelli's election in favor of Maglione. In his memoirs, Charles-Roux criticized Pacelli's tendency to want to appease and please, which he saw as a "permanent feature" of Pacelli's character.[45]

Ordinarily, this is what the faithful would expect in a clergyman, especially the would-be Vicar of Christ: humility, kindness, and servitude. Inevitably, though, the logic of *realpolitik* drove the assessments of Pacelli's character as he stood poised to assume the highest office in the Catholic Church. Hints of the tension between Pacelli's pastoral inclinations and the unsparing world of European power politics had been evident for years. For instance, an Austrian representative at the Vatican a few years earlier had praised Pacelli as a model priest with an "ascetical" disposition, but added that these qualities could constitute significant weaknesses in someone charged with leading papal diplomacy in treacherous times.[46]

Similar sentiments were expressed by Italian officials as they pondered the implications of Pacelli's election for their own government and for the Third Reich.[47] Ciano and other members of the Mussolini regime were pleased with Pacelli's election, and expected him to be more agreeable toward Mussolini's government than his predecessor had been. Ciano wrote in his diary that news of Pacelli's election "does not surprise me," recalling Pacelli's conciliatory tone at the time Pius XI died. According to Ciano, even an increasingly detached Mussolini was "pleased" with Pacelli's election.[48] The Fascist minister Giuseppe Bottai was also pleased, viewing the new pope as a "mystic," someone "who acts, who speaks with measure; someone who knows what he wants."[49]

It was understandable that observers would see Pacelli as someone with a record of appeasing if not favoring authoritarian regimes. There were hints of this tendency in his sympathy for Franco's cause in the Spanish Civil War, his constructive working relationship with Fascist Italy, and his continued pursuit of better relations with Hitler's regime despite years of diplomatic tension. In some circles Pacelli was clearly perceived as a "pro-Nazi pope," as the American diplomat William R. Castle noted in his diary during the 1939 conclave. For this reason, Castle concluded, Pacelli's election was bound to "really wreck the Church. And the Roman Church, whatever one thinks of it as an institution, is certainly a bulwark against most of the subversive influences in the world at present."[50]

Diplomats and journalists from the Western democracies especially welcomed Pacelli as an ally in the gathering threat to peace and stability. U.S. President Roosevelt sent a friendly note to the pope saying that the election gave him "true happiness." Evoking fond memories of their meeting at Hyde Park a few years before, FDR said simply, "I wish to take this occasion to send you a personal message of felicitation and good wishes."[51] Other American political and religious leaders similarly praised Pacelli's election as a positive sign in the gathering confrontation with totalitarian systems. American reaction also reflected the view that, having visited the United States a few years earlier, and with personal ties to leading American churchmen, the new pope had a particular understanding of and appreciation for the vitality of American society and the growing importance of Catholicism as a social and political force in American life. Monsignor Michael J. Ready, general secretary of the National Catholic Welfare Conference, the de facto conference of American Catholic bishops, noted that during the whirlwind 1936 tour, Pacelli had "demonstrated his liking for the American way of doing things." Non-Catholic religious leaders praised Pacelli's "progressive policies," his formidable intellectual and diplomatic preparation, and his "deep humanitarian sympathies."

Nowhere was praise for Pacelli greater than in American Jewish circles. The chairman of the American Committee for the Protection of Minorities declared, "Jews and all other religious and racial minorities throughout the world know that in the election of Cardinal Pacelli they have a friend." Rabbi Hyman Judah Schachtel of the West End Synagogue in New York City was quoted as saying, "The whole world can rejoice in the election of Cardinal Pacelli. The mantle of Elijah could fall on no more deserving an Elisha. He will continue the great humanitarian interests of his illustrious predecessor."[52]

The diplomat William Castle was quick to revise his thinking on the newly elected pope. As Castle noted in his diary, "Someone had told me that Pacelli would not do as he was very political and very pro-Nazi. The last, I am told, is quite contrary to the truth, and I am told also that he is a very spiritual man, a philosopher who will make a great Pope in these troublous [sic] times. I certainly hope that he is a stabilizing influence as was his predecessor and that he will keep the Church of Rome out of politics except as it must be there to protect the things in life which must be protected and are too often forgotten." Having concluded prematurely that Pacelli's election as pope would "wreck" the Catholic Church, Castle now expressed the hope that "the reign of Pius XII be long and happy and useful."[53]

Newspaper headlines from around the world greeted Pacelli's election as a sign of continued Vatican opposition to totalitarian regimes. The *New York Times* declared boldly, "Pius XII Not the Pope Totalitarians Desired," reasoning that Cardinal Pacelli was expected to continue the "virile policies" of his predecessor against racist and oppressive authoritarian systems. The journalist Edwin L. James argued that when electing a new pope, the cardinals had faced a simple choice: they could choose "a man of compromise and holiness," or they could elect "a man of holiness and virility." By choosing Pacelli, James concluded, the cardinals "made the second choice. They took the bolder and the braver choice and one which will command respect the world over."[54] The British press delivered a similar interpretation of Pacelli's election, praising the cardinals for having defied the "overt warnings" from the Fascist regimes against the election of a "political pope." Considered to be Pius XI's "right-hand man," Pacelli was expected to continue his predecessor's aggressive policies against totalitarianism.[55]

For their part, the Germans reacted with caution and uncharacteristic reserve to news of Pacelli's election. It was not immediately clear whether the new pope's intimate familiarity with German affairs was a good or a bad thing from the perspective of the Nazi state.[56] Behind the formulaic words of congratulations coming from Hitler and from German representatives to the Vatican was ambivalence about Pacelli's election. The Germans had good reason to conclude that in breaking with tradition and electing a sitting secretary of state, the cardinals wanted to send a strong signal of continuity with the tough line adopted by Pius XI in the last few years of his pontificate. True, German Catholics welcomed Pacelli's election, seeing it as validation that the cardinals saw fit to elect a pope with such long-standing and intimate knowledge of German affairs. It was also true that as secretary of state, Pacelli had helped to steer Vatican diplomacy away from open confrontation with the Hitler regime, despite years of repeated objections to Nazi treatment of the German church.[57]

Still, there were early signs from the new pope that, while he might adopt a more conciliatory line than his predecessor, he would be no less insistent that the Third Reich make good on its empty promises to respect the spirit and the letter of the 1933 concordat. This is to say nothing of the fact that Pacelli continued to express grave reservations, albeit privately, about the increasingly aggressive tone of Nazi foreign policy.[58] One commentator put it aptly when he observed, "Pius XII as a Pope is an unwritten page." It remained to be seen just what Pacelli's "reputation for astute diplomacy and keen political vision" meant for the Third Reich, and for the immediate course of international affairs in the volatile months ahead.[59]

Pope Pius XII and the "German Problem"

One thing was immediately clear following Pius XII's election as pope—his greatest priority was dealing with the Third Reich. The sense of urgency was evident when a few days after he was elected, even before he was formally installed as pope, Pius XII invited the German cardinals—as well as Cardinal Theodor Innitzer of Vienna—to meet with him at the Vatican. He told them plainly: "The German problem is for me most important. I will deal with it myself."[60] He was keen to discuss the status of the church in Germany and to strategize about future directions for papal diplomacy in the Vatican's dealings with the Third Reich. Word of the supposedly secret meeting leaked out, and soon the story of German cardinals' meeting furtively with the newly elected pope was front-page news around the world. Speculation about papal motivations was fueled when word spread that the new pope also planned to meet with the German ambassador to the Holy See, Diego von Bergen. The Germans, it appeared, enjoyed privileged access to the new pope.[61] Was this a sign of things to come?

His meetings with the German cardinals in particular set the course of Pius XII's policy toward the Hitler state for years to come.[62] In advance of the first meeting, scheduled for March 6, Cardinals Bertram and Faulhaber both drafted memoranda that summarized the dire condition of the church in Germany and urged the pope to consider ways of normalizing church-state relations. A détente with Hitler's Germany was the order of the day, according to the German prelates, because it was the only way to protect German Catholicism from a hostile, implacable state. Even though such reconciliation was unlikely to succeed, Faulhaber argued that the effort should be made and, more important, be seen to be made.[63] At a practical level, he urged that a lesson be learned from German reaction to the 1937 encyclical *Mit Brennender Sorge*. As he reminded the pope, the Hitler regime had been so angered by the papal statement that it very nearly broke off all diplomatic ties and intensified its persecution of German Catholics. The need was greater than ever for papal restraint and caution in dealing with the Nazis.

This piece of advice had particular resonance in the opening days of Pacelli's pontificate and affirmed the new pope's preference for behind-the-scenes diplomacy over grandiloquent speeches. One of the pressing issues Pius XII wanted to discuss with the German cardinals was the so-called *Rassenfrage*, the racial question. He needed to decide whether to address Nazi racial policies directly by means of a papal encyclical or whether an explicit public statement would further exacerbate church-state relations. Presumably the question was whether to finish the encyclical his predecessor was having prepared at the time he fell ill and died. It soon became clear that Pius XII had heeded Faulhaber's advice to learn from the Nazis' reaction to *Mit Brennender Sorge*. The new pope would make no public statement to denounce Nazi racial theories, nor would he issue a pointed papal denunciation of Nazi anti-Semitic laws and policies. Pius XII would decline even to issue a direct public criticism of the increasingly aggressive foreign policies of both the Hitler and the Mussolini regimes.[64]

Pius XII staked out a clear position in which the preservation of the church in Germany, including open lines of communication between the Vatican and the German bishops, was the top priority. Preserving German Catholicism, the pope reasoned, made a *modus vivendi* with the Hitler state indispensable. Even if attempts at détente failed, he told the cardinals, the world will have seen that "we did everything possible to live in peace with Germany." Clearly, it was imperative that the papacy resume serious diplomatic negotiations with the Hitler government. As he told the German prelates, "We want to see, to dare an attempt. If they [the Hitler government] want a fight, we are not afraid. But we want to see whether it is somehow possible to come to some kind of peace."[65] The list of complaints against the Third Reich was as long as ever, ranging from the closure of private Catholic schools, the attempt to place religious instruction under state supervision, hostile acts against Catholic properties and organizations, and acts of "sacrilegious vandalism" to intense anti-Catholic propaganda in the Nazi press.[66]

Where did the *Rassenfrage* fit on this list of grievances? Even though Nazi anti-Semitic policies had grown more radical and aggressive, to the point where many German Jews already were leaving the country, Pacelli continued to cling to the same principle that had dictated the Vatican's response to Nazi anti-Semitism from 1933—that while the persecution of Jews or any other group on religious or racial grounds was decidedly un-Christian, ultimately it was a *political* matter, the purview of the civil authorities, and therefore not something the church had any standing to address. Thus went the answer in 1939, as it had in 1938 in the wake of *Kristallnacht,* and as it had been as early as 1933, with the advent of the very first Nazi measures to marginalize Jews in German public life.

The pope's decision not to proceed with any formal papal condemnation of the racial politics of the Fascist regimes was a sign of things to come. The aggressive foreign policy of both Mussolini and Hitler tested Pius XII's resolve to resist what increasingly was being demanded of him from various quarters: an explicit public expression of papal disapproval with the radical turn of the dictators. As Europe and the world were drawn inexorably into another conflagration, Pius XII held his ground: the church would do what it could to avoid war and, once it came, to bring about a quick and equitable peace settlement. But it would not do so by sacrificing its cherished impartiality, or by sacrificing the tangible good that came from the Vatican's formal diplomatic relations with civil governments, even murderous ones.

Even his would-be admirers were frustrated early on by Pius XII's stubborn insistence on preserving the public appearance of papal neutrality. When in April 1939 President Roosevelt issued a direct appeal to Hitler and Mussolini floating the idea of an international peace conference to resolve the issues that threatened to plunge Europe into diplomatic crisis and war, he turned in vain to the newly elected pope for support.[67] The Vatican's new secretary of state, Cardinal Maglione, politely informed the Roosevelt administration that the pope did not think that any public demonstration of papal support for the initiative was feasible; he refused even to consider making a behind-the-scenes diplomatic feeler, citing the current delicate state of the Vatican's relations with the Hitler regime. As for the Italians, the pope had already authorized approaching the state to discuss peace, but to no avail. Pacelli and Maglione both knew from experience that when it came to Mussolini, there was little to be gained from papal invocations for peace.[68]

This early difference of opinion between Vatican and American officials foreshadowed what was to follow. The issue hinged on the reputed value of a public papal intervention. A disappointed Sumner Welles wrote to Monsignor Ready of the National Catholic Welfare Conference to express his regret that the pope would not publicly come out in open support of Roosevelt's modest but sincere peace overture: "We here cannot . . . help but believe that some public pronouncement by the Pope in support of the peace message would have the most beneficial effect throughout the world." The U.S. undersecretary of state continued to prod the American Catholic hierarchy to get Pius XII to change his mind, but his attempts were in vain.[69]

The "Silent" Pope

The first weeks of Pius XII's pontificate thus were ripe with fresh diplomatic challenges that tested papal neutrality. The most serious came from the Mussolini regime, the government over which Pacelli was presumed to have the greatest immediate influence. When the Italians invaded Albania in early April 1939, the pope faced a dilemma similar to that his predecessor had faced in 1935 with the invasion of Ethiopia—to speak or not to speak. Should Pius XII publicly condemn this violation of international norms that threatened the peace and stability of the region? The invasion was even more shocking to many Catholics in that it had been launched on Good Friday, one of the most solemn days on the church calendar.

How would the new pope balance the tension between avoiding direct papal intervention in Italian affairs as stipulated by the 1929 treaty and respecting the presumed moral imperative of the spiritual leader of Catholicism to denounce military aggression by a would-be Catholic nation on one of the holiest days of the year? Pius XII chose to avoid any explicit mention of the Fascist invasion of Albania. To be sure, he made a few pointed warnings about the dangers of war and offered the predictable invocations to peace among all peoples, but he did not directly acknowledge the invasion, nor give any word on how such action on the part of a Christian people ought to be judged.[70]

The pope's failure to address the matter directly at Easter did not go unnoticed. Barely a month into his pontificate, Pius XII already was being criticized for his public silence in the face of Fascist military aggression. The most searing criticism came from the Catholic world. The French Catholic intellectual Emmanuel Mounier, one of the most influential voices of the vocal Catholic Left in France, nurtured a long-standing distaste for Vatican diplomatic accommodation with authoritarian regimes. Still, for Mounier, as for many other observers, Catholics and otherwise, a line had been crossed with the invasion of Albania that demanded a resolute papal response. After all, Italy, "the most Catholic nation of Europe," was engaged in a brutal aggression against a smaller, unarmed state—and on Good Friday of all days, the most somber and sacred day in the Christian calendar, as Mounier wrote. Yet what was the pope's response? "Not a word from his mouth about this bloody Good Friday," Mounier lamented.[71]

Mounier realized that the pope was working behind the scenes and expressing his concern to Italian officials. But Mounier argued that this did not absolve Pius XII of the responsibility to use the full force and range of the papal office to invoke the moral authority of the church's teaching to condemn Fascist aggression. There was a world of difference, Mounier insisted, between Vatican diplomacy and church doctrine. The former might choose diplomatic caution, impartiality, even what Mounier called a "false docility." But docility, passivity, impartiality in political or diplomatic dealings, he said, were fundamentally at odds with the church's true nature and mission. For this reason, the pope's choice not to condemn Fascist aggression against Albania, which Mounier called the "scandal of silence," made a profound impression on thousands of the faithful, and beyond. Whether in the name of Albanian civilians soon to find themselves marching in step with the Fascist *passo romano,* or for the sake of the Spanish people, victims of those who presented themselves as having been blessed by the Holy Father as "soldiers of God," Mounier wrote, "we asked only for a few words. So that the Word also may bring life."[72] He appreciated that Pius XII was torn over whether to choose "negotiation or heroism." The pope would find thousands of people of goodwill ready to follow his spiritual leadership, Mounier promised, if only Pius XII would choose heroism.[73]

Pius XII found such calls for heroism over negotiation ill-conceived and unpersuasive. The experiences of the preceding decades spoke to him of the practical limits of papal diplomacy in times of crisis and war. In his first formal address to the Sacred College of Cardinals on June 2, 1939, Pius XII laid out the philosophy of papal engagement with civil society, which had been the guiding principle of the generation of papal diplomats from which he came. It was a supreme moral imperative for the papacy, and for the church as a whole, to work ceaselessly for peace and to offer its "maternal services" to avoid the use of force with all of its "incalculable material, spiritual, and moral consequences." To do so, however, the church must remain extraneous to competition among the civil powers. The church ought not to allow itself to advocate for or be persuaded by "special interests, or to become tangled up in territorial competitions among states, or to get dragged into the intricate conflicts which emerge therefrom."[74]

A more direct explanation of this rationale came from Cardinal Maglione in response to demands from French Ambassador Charles-Roux that Pius XII abandon vague talk of a great-power peace conference to avoid war, and move instead to a resolute, explicit papal statement of a "moral" nature. This was another way of saying that the pope ought to abandon the path of diplomatic caution and public impartiality and identify the Fascist dictators as the real threat to peace and stability in Europe. He ought to take sides in the gathering crisis by refusing to weigh German or Italian demands as morally equivalent to the position of Britain or France. Maglione resolutely defended the papal line: "When [Pius XII] speaks to governments and to peoples to promote peace, he cannot and he should not draw distinctions." Besides, Maglione insisted, the Vatican's support for the idea of a peace conference in the middle of 1939 had had the desired effect; above all, it had demonstrated that all sides genuinely wanted a peaceful resolution to the impasse that was threatening to spiral into armed conflict.[75]

The French ambassador remained unconvinced, in part because he simply refused to see peaceful motives behind German and Italian maneuvers. Charles-Roux was expressing a general sentiment that was taking hold in certain French circles, with echoes in diplomatic and political circles in other Western democracies: a nagging sense that Pius XII had veered decisively away from his predecessor in pursuing more conciliatory relations with the Hitler regime. Meeting with Valerio Valeri, the papal nuncio in Paris, Charles-Roux conveyed the sense in many French groups that the differences in attitude and approach between Pius XII and his predecessor were, in a word, "excessive." It was normal to expect some modest changes in temperament and method from one pontificate to another, but Pius XII's desire to placate the Germans, it seemed, had moved the Vatican to the point where it no longer saw fit to denounce the continued religious persecution in the Third Reich. Charles-Roux was unmoved by Valeri's defense that this might be because the pope's conciliatory approach had reduced religious persecution in the Nazi state; the evidence demonstrated otherwise. If the pope sincerely wanted to contribute to the cause of peace, the ambassador reasoned, there were two possible approaches: either by means of diplomatic initiatives behind the scenes or by affirming publicly basic moral and doctrinal principles to counter certain "theories in vogue" being perpetuated by the Fascist regimes. Charles-Roux was convinced that the latter approach was the wiser course of action.[76] After all, the diplomatic approach employed to date had failed to yield the desired results.

There was further grumbling in French circles about Pius XII's response to the crisis that threatened European peace in the spring and summer of 1939. By the summer, the Polish crisis emerged to test papal resolve to deal squarely with Hitler's territorial ambitions. For many French observers, Pius XII's response to this latest international outrage was woefully inadequate. Valeri wrote to tell the Vatican that some were even accusing Pius XII of demonstrating favoritism toward the authoritarian regimes.[77]

French authorities, like their British and American counterparts, appealed to the Vatican to at least make a statement defending certain fundamental principles. The French Dominican priest Martin Gillet wrote directly to Pius XII in late June 1939 to report on his conversation with French Foreign Minister Bonnet, saying that the French government now seemed to think that the pope's peace efforts would be most constructive if he were to defend the church's "doctrine of peace." It seems the French were thinking of an encyclical—a weighty papal document that would expound clearly on essential points of Catholic doctrine: to defend the dignity of the human person, for instance, and individual freedoms; and to denounce the "political and social heresies" that threatened those principles. A forceful, authoritative papal message of that sort, they believed, might actually impel the political leaders and military planners to shelve plans for aggressive territorial expansion.[78]

It may have been wishful thinking to believe that something as dense as a papal encyclical could single-handedly dissuade the Fascist dictators from their maniacal designs to remake Europe. That was not the point. The argument was simple enough: as Europe was drawn inexorably into a conflict by the German-Polish dispute over Danzig and the Polish Corridor, and with a German offensive against Poland all but certain, what remained to the pope but to exercise his moral authority to make a public statement placing responsibility for the crisis squarely on the Germans? Charles-Roux continued to prod the Vatican into action, reasoning that the time for papal impartiality had passed. Writing to Monsignor Domenico Tardini in August 1939, the French ambassador made yet another pitch for a public papal condemnation of Nazi aims. There could be no doubt, he said, where the responsibility lay if and when Europe fell again into war: Germany and Italy threatened peace and stability. Charles-Roux concluded that the aggressors thus assumed a preponderate "moral responsibility" that the Vatican itself could not ignore, adding that "the cause of peace" would be bolstered "if the pope were to speak with his singular authority," pointing out that if war broke out, the responsibility for it would rest with the countries seeking further territorial expansion.[79] The British agreed with this assessment and also pressed the Vatican to have the pope make a public statement confirming basic ethical principles. The British representative d'Arcy Osborne warned the Vatican that Hitler's real aim was not to gain control over Danzig or territorial access by means of a Polish Corridor. "I strongly suspect that Hitler is determined to destroy Poland," he told Tardini. If this were to happen, a profoundly Catholic country "will fall under German rule and the Catholic Church will suffer as she has in Austria."[80]

Pius XII was not oblivious to the gravity of the hour or to the pastoral imperative that demanded some public statement from one of the world's foremost spiritual leaders. It was in this capacity, as a spiritual leader rather than as a head of state, that he took to the airwaves on the evening of August 24, broadcasting a memorable appeal for peace via Vatican Radio. "The human family yet again faces a grave hour," the pope intoned, his voice heavy with anxiety.[81] Although the speech was moving in its own right, it was not the partisan peace appeal that Charles-Roux and others had wanted. On the same day that the pope issued his appeal, news broke of the Nazi-Soviet agreement, sending shockwaves through diplomatic and political circles. Poland's fate was sealed. Diplomatic officials rushed to the apostolic palace to make more desperate pleas for Pius XII to condemn any invasion of a Catholic country. The Polish ambassador, Casimir Papée, in particular asked the pope to condemn the impending invasion of his country. The message to the pope was clear: if the Nazis invaded Poland, the Holy See ought to pronounce its judgment of the immorality of such an act.[82]

While assuring the Poles that they enjoyed particular papal "affection," Pius XII still refused to be drawn into taking sides or appearing to take sides. Instead, he instructed his diplomats to urge the respective parties to continue negotiating, giving paramount consideration to the terrible costs of war. So desperate was he to find a peaceful resolution that the pope authorized his representative to speak directly with Mussolini to see whether there were grounds for a mediated settlement that would avoid war. Following Mussolini's lead, the Vatican suggested that the Poles make some modest concessions, perhaps over the city of Danzig, which might yet appease Hitler. But the pope refrained from formally endorsing any plan to resolve the crisis, reminding the Poles that armed conflict would cost them much more dearly.[83]

Soldier of Christ: Pius at War

Pius XII issued one last public appeal, just before war began. It was not the kind of direct and forceful statement that many hoped for. The pope still refused to single out one side as bearing particular responsibility for the situation. With a Nazi invasion of Poland imminent, the French ambassador Charles-Roux again urged the pope to issue a statement to "condemn explicitly" German behavior. Even after the war began in early September 1939, with the Nazi and then Soviet onslaught against Poland progressing rapidly, Charles-Roux would repeat that call with greater urgency. Writing to Tardini, the ambassador put it plainly: the public was "waiting for the Holy Father to say something to the effect that he was passing judgment on, and that he resented, this explosion of violence and cruelty."[84]

The official response in those first weeks of the war became the Vatican's standard line for the duration of the conflict: an explicit public condemnation was not necessary, since the pope had already spoken out clearly and repeatedly in the name of peace. In short, the church was doing what it could, and the facts would speak for themselves.[85] Among Pius XII's advisors, there was a palpable frustration that the pope's efforts to avert war, and now to mitigate its worst excesses, were not fully understood nor widely appreciated. Aside from the constant diplomatic efforts taking place behind the scenes, there were frequent occasions on which Pius XII had publicly decried what the coming of war would mean for Poland. But in his language Pius XII took great care to avoid spelling out in explicit terms that the moral responsibility for Poland's fate lay at the feet of the Third Reich. Instead, the pope confined his public utterances to formulaic appeals to universal peace and brotherhood and demands that the belligerents respect the rules of war, that civilians be sheltered from military operations, that the occupying armies respect "the life, property, honor, and religious sentiments" of local inhabitants, that prisoners of war be treated humanely and have access to the comforts of religion, and that the belligerent armies refrain from using poison gas or other forms of chemical warfare.[86] These were important statements of principle, to be sure, but they fell far short of the moral judgment of Nazi behavior that was being asked of the pope from various quarters.

Pius XII was not oblivious to the plight of the Poles, who found themselves under the heel of two repressive totalitarian systems—precisely the systems that Pacelli had spent years criticizing, though in carefully worded terms. Here, in the tragic position of a predominantly Catholic nation overrun and occupied by hostile forces, Pius XII found an apt demonstration of the consequences of a world order ruled by what he was to call the "changeable and ephemeral standards that depend only on the selfish interests of groups and individuals." In a concession to demands coming from the Poles for a papal word on their fate, Pius XII made special mention of Poland in his first encyclical, *Summi Pontificatus,* which was issued on October 20, 1939. As if to answer the growing chorus of critics, Pius XII asked, "Do We need to give assurance that Our paternal heart is close to all Our children in compassionate love, and especially to the afflicted, the oppressed, the persecuted?" Then, in referring to the nations that were being "swept into the tragic whirlpool of war," he singled out Poland: "The blood of countless human beings, even non-combatants raises a piteous dirge over a nation such as Our dear

Poland, which, for its fidelity to the Church, for its services in the defense of Christian civilization . . . has a right to the generous and brotherly sympathy of the world, while it awaits . . . the hour of resurrection in harmony with the principles of justice and true peace."[87] In his Christmas Eve address that year, Pius XII was even more outspoken, denouncing the "premeditated aggressions against a small, industrious and peaceful people." He deplored the "atrocities" and the "disregard for human dignity, liberty and life," saying that such acts "cry for the vengeance of God."[88]

With Nazi and Soviet armies brutally destroying a mutual enemy, the pope's explicit *cri de coeur* for Poland's fate showed that Pius XII was prepared to speak directly and resolutely when he felt it was warranted. Indeed, the spiritual head of Catholicism's praying for the hour of Poland's resurrection at a time when the country was overrun by foreign armies was arguably a powerful symbolic and practical gesture of papal solicitude for Poland's future. In his encyclical, Pius XII went even further. After years of public silence on Nazi anti-Jewish measures, Pius XII made a pointed statement affirming the "unity of human society" that flowed from "our common origin and by the equality of rational nature in all men, to whatever people they belong." The statement was inescapably a moral indictment of radically secular states "with unlimited authority" that substituted God's law with "standards stripped of the ethical content of Revelation on Sinai, standards in which the spirit of the Sermon on the Mount and of the Cross has no place." In light of so many errors in the life of individual nations and the international order, wrote the pope, was it any wonder that "the Soldiers of Christ," clergy and laity, were "incited and spurred on to a great vigilance, to a more determined resistance by the sight of the ever-increasing host of Christ's enemies?"[89]

The British representative D'Arcy Osborne wrote to London expressing his satisfaction with the encyclical. Although the Germans had not been named directly, Osborne surmised, it was clear to everyone that the pope meant to hold the Nazis accountable for the war and its dire consequences.[90] But was this enough? Was the dense, lengthy, and somewhat obtuse style of an encyclical, authoritative though it was, the best way of signaling papal disapproval? The encyclical certainly served well as a systematic exposition of doctrinal principle. But what value did it possess as a political or diplomatic tool to translate the fine points of doctrine into practical, effective resistance to the destructive policies of totalitarian regimes? Who were Christ's enemies: the Nazis, the Soviets, and the Fascists? Why not speak bluntly about the specific governments and specific policies that were threatening European peace and stability?

Predictably, Pius XII would not do so. He chose instead the course of diplomatic engagement. That meant attenuating in public the profound anger and anxiety experienced in papal circles over the start of war. Even though the years of diplomatic protest and thinly veiled critiques of Nazi policies had failed to achieve Pacelli's objectives in the Vatican's relations with the Hitler state, the operating principle of papal diplomacy remained constant: to avoid doing or saying anything in public that might provoke the Germans—or the Italians, for that matter—into ramping up policies that the church had for years been working to mitigate. This approach called for supreme rhetorical restraint, a careful measuring of every word and sentence so that papal disapproval was couched in ways that allowed for the preservation of the Vatican's formal diplomatic relations with the belligerent powers.

The pope hoped also that rhetorical restraint would avoid making matters worse for Catholics and other civilians on the ground. During his first Christmas address, in December 1939, Pius XII laid out the terms of what he called a "just and honorable" peace settlement, but he did so in such a way as to avoid offending the Fascist regimes. The pope was mindful of the fact that the Soviets, who had now invaded Finland as well as Poland, also were intent on territorial expansion. The result was a typically Pacellian amalgam of principle and pragmatism—the defense of the right of a nation to exist in language that could not be taken as a direct assault on Nazi and Fascist territorial ambitions yet subtly condemned the recent Soviet invasion of Finland.[91] "One nation's desire to live must never translate into a death sentence for another," he wrote. In an earlier draft of the speech, Pius XII had adopted the term *spazio vitale* in place of *vivere*—a literal allusion to the Italian Fascist territorial claim to "living space." Several months later, when he met with German Foreign Minister Joachim von Ribbentrop, Pius XII admitted that he had deliberately tempered both his first encyclical and the Christmas message in order to avoid offending any government, despite his "mission" "to speak the Truth."[92] How directly one spoke the truth was another matter altogether, hence Pius XII's veiled reference in the 1939 Christmas message to the plight of European Jews when he invoked the "Christian ideal" that in the name of "universal love" builds bridges toward those "who do not enjoy the benefit of belonging to our faith."[93]

Disappointment and frustration with persistent papal restraint were the price to pay for achieving Pius XII's main objectives: the maintenance of Vatican neutrality; the preservation of diplomatic relations with the belligerent states; and avoidance of greater harm to civilians on the ground. All of this, the pope believed sincerely, would in due course leave the Holy See in the unique position of being able to facilitate an effective peace settlement. It was a delicate balancing act, one that was sure to alienate and disappoint many people. Pius XII simply saw no practicable alternative.

The inevitability of alienating even his most ardent supporters was evident when Pius XII met with Ribbentrop at the Vatican in March 1940.[94] Not surprisingly, news that a high-ranking Nazi had been granted a private audience with the pope caused more than a few murmurings, especially among the Poles.[95] Questions already were being raised by the Western powers about Pius XII's purported impartiality. In the wake of his Christmas address and his public statements to the effect that the combatant powers ought to sacrifice their national interests for the sake of peace, the British government instructed d'Arcy Osborne to ask the pope for clarification. Was he in some way criticizing French and British war aims? The pope's response was a rather tepid assurance that it was not the Western powers he was criticizing but the Soviets, whose domestic policies obviously ran counter to the basic principles of Catholicism. As far as Germany was concerned, though, Pius XII defended the Vatican's ongoing diplomatic relationship with the Hitler government, despite what the newspapers characterized as "some points of difference" between the Holy See and the Nazi regime.[96]

In view of these nagging suspicions about Pius XII's impartiality, Ribbentrop's visit was sure to exacerbate tensions. In fact, the pope used the meeting to upbraid Ribbentrop and the Nazis for their actions, both at home and in occupied Poland, noting in particular that the German government consistently failed to fulfill its promises to respect standing treaties and norms. The pope was especially persistent in pointing out that despite repeated assurances to the contrary, the German government was in effect waging war on the church. But he reserved his most stinging criticism for the Nazis' military agreement with the Soviets and pressed Ribbentrop to allow a papal delegate to travel to German-occupied Poland to assess the situation on the ground.[97]

This exchange with Ribbentrop is an apt demonstration of Pius XII's political philosophy in action: having exercised restraint in his first encyclical and in his Christmas message—as he admitted to the German foreign minister—the pope now expected something in return: concrete action to address the countless acts of persecution against the German church and guarantees that the German occupation of Poland was being conducted according to prevailing legal and moral norms. Concurrently, also as part of his peace efforts, the pope was working to establish direct if informal relations with the Roosevelt administration, a long-standing ambition of both men. Given the political problem of getting the U.S. Congress to agree to formal diplomatic relations, Roosevelt and Pius XII agreed that the president would appoint Myron C. Taylor—who was chair of the Inter-Governmental Committee on Refugees—as his personal representative, an "extraordinary ambassador," to the Vatican. This arrangement would avoid the requirement of seeking congressional approval and could be presented to the American public as Roosevelt's commitment to resolving an escalating European crisis. According to Archbishop Spellman, selling the Taylor mission to the American public would be helped by the goodwill generated by Pacelli's "historic" and "fruitful" 1936 American tour.[98]

Although politicians and Protestant religious leaders in the United States were critical of the Taylor mission, it gave the Roosevelt administration unprecedented access to the Vatican and newfound gravitas in papal circles. FDR certainly thought he had a close ally in Pius XII. He spoke of the need for a "closer association between those in every part of the world—those in religion and those in government—who have a common purpose," and he looked ahead to the restoration of "world peace on a surer foundation," grounded on "common ideals." In response, Pius XII assured the Americans that Taylor was guaranteed access to the pope "at any time that he desired." The American representatives at the Vatican took heart from these assurances, though they worried about Pius XII's weak grasp of the English language; it was not clear that the pope always understood what American officials were saying.[99]

Aside from a few minor challenges, the tangible effects of this rapprochement between the Vatican and the Roosevelt administration were felt immediately. Meeting in March 1940 with Under-Secretary of State Sumner Welles, who was at the Vatican to present Myron C. Taylor to the pope, Pius XII said that from his recent discussion with Ribbentrop, it seemed clear that the Germans were determined to continue waging war for the foreseeable future. So it was premature to talk about a negotiated peace settlement. It was not too late, though, for the Roosevelt administration to use its considerable influence to try to "dissuade" Mussolini from entering the conflict on Hitler's side. In return, the Americans continued to urge the pope to use his privileged position with the Italians to do the same.[100]

Although both Pius XII and President Roosevelt entreated Mussolini personally to keep Italy from declaring war on the side of Germany, Mussolini promised nothing. Instead, he implied that Italy was likely to "enter the field of battle" to protect its "honor, interests, and . . . future."[101] It was all but certain now that the fighting would spread. The specter of escalating violence loomed larger when word reached the Vatican in early May 1940 that the Germans were poised to launch a massive offensive on the Western Front, an attack that likely would target Holland and Belgium. The information came from a trusted source, Josef Müller, a Munich lawyer with known anti-Nazi sympathies who had the ear of the pope's closest German advisors—Monsignor Kaas and the Jesuit priest Robert Leiber.[102] Müller had the pope's ear as well. The two had known each other from Pacelli's time as nuncio in Munich and had kept in touch over the years. Recalling his meeting with the pope in 1945 just after being released from a concentration camp, Müller said that Pius XII had embraced him, saying that it was as if he were welcoming back one of his own family members.[103]

In a striking departure from his usual caution and presumed neutrality, Pius XII was quick to pass along this information to those states now a target of Nazi aggression. The Vatican authorized the nuncio in Brussels, Archbishop Clemente Micara, to deliver personally a warning to King Leopold, while Pius XII himself met with the French ambassador Charles-Roux to pass on word of an imminent German attack in Western Europe. The British representative Osborne was similarly informed and relayed the warning to the Foreign Office, despite his own misgivings about the credibility of the threat.[104]

In the early morning of May 10, 1940, German forces launched a major offensive against Belgium, Holland, and Luxembourg, three neutral states. The invasion and fall of France followed. It took little more than a month for Hitler's armies to vanquish virtually all of Western Europe. As France was falling, Mussolini joined the war on Hitler's side. The Fascist domination of Europe was now a reality, a stunning failure of the diplomatic maneuvering of the preceding months and years. Having failed in its major diplomatic initiatives to contain the spread of war and keep the Italians from allying with Hitler, the Vatican was confronted anew with the demand that Pius XII condemn in the bluntest way possible such naked acts of military aggression.

Before the invasion of France, Charles-Roux had been pressing his government's case, saying that in view of the Nazi invasion of the neutral Low Countries, "the whole world was waiting for [Pius XII] to offer with his high authority a solemn condemnation to stigmatize this odious attack," which had been motivated by nothing other than German strategic interests, in clear violation of the norms of warfare. The French government stressed that for the pope's intervention to be effective, it needed to be "immediate"; there ought not to be any delay "between this abominable violation of law and morality and the Pope's protest denouncing it." The French reasoned that a public papal condemnation had to be expressed "in sufficiently strong and explicit terms" so as to influence Italian public opinion decisively against any planned Fascist military action.[105] British and American officials demanded the same. Lord Halifax wrote to the pope saying that it was time for a "public and formal condemnation of the German aggression by the Holy See, in the name of the Church and of civilization." The pope was uniquely placed, Halifax reasoned, to invoke the "authority of Christian morality" to condemn "criminal" German behavior.[106]

Pius XII moved swiftly to write directly to leaders in Belgium, Luxembourg, and Holland, expressing his "paternal affection" for the invaded countries, and offering prayers for the "reestablishment" of their "liberty and independence." The telegrams were displayed prominently on the front page of the Vatican's *L'Osservatore Romano*. Yet the pope fell short of including any forceful and, most important, explicit condemnation of the Nazi invasion. In fact, the tone and substance of the pope's telegrams to the three leaders were notably more restrained and carefully worded than the early drafts drawn up by Tardini, which had said that the Vatican "deplored the injustice and the evil" of the invasion, and that the pope was compelled to "raise His voice to deplore yet again such inequity and injustice." As sent, the pope's telegrams were more generically worded, evincing paternal anguish at the state of affairs and invoking divine intercession to restore "justice and liberty." Implicitly, the pope condemned the invasions, but he studiously avoided using language that would denounce the Nazi aggression specifically as immoral and unjust.[107]

Invariably, the pope's public response to the Nazi assault on northwestern Europe provoked disappointment and anger, though for vastly different reasons. The Mussolini government and the Fascist press saw the pope's telegrams as a frontal assault on their ally. In a few incidents, vendors selling the Vatican newspaper or those caught buying it were beaten. Copies of the paper were confiscated and kiosks destroyed. The situation was so serious that Cardinal Maglione lodged a formal complaint with the Italian government. A few months after the invasion, the Fascist Party journal *Regime fascista* recalled "that a telegram from the Pope goaded Belgium's Catholic king to have his people shed their blood for the sake of the Jews, the Freemasons and the bankers of the City."[108]

By contrast, diplomats from Western Europe thought the pope's messages of sympathy were not nearly specific enough or tough enough on the Fascist perpetrators of such unprovoked aggression and violence. From his temporary residence within Vatican City in the weeks after Mussolini's Italy formally entered the war on Hitler's side, a palpably frustrated D'Arcy Osborne wrote to Philip Nichols at the Foreign Office to complain that on the Vatican's response to Italian intervention in the war, Pius XII "has not uttered" a word. Osborne described the Holy See's attitude as one of "anxious inactivity," owing perhaps to its weakened position with the Italian government as compared with World War One—the product presumably of the 1929 Lateran Treaty, which appeared to have given the Mussolini government considerably more latitude in church-state relations than was previously the case.[109]

For their part Vatican officials began to grow tired of complaints coming from Western diplomats like Osborne, but especially from the French and Polish ambassadors, that the pope should put his criticism of the Nazis in blunter terms, leaving no room for doubt that the Vatican condemned the Nazi invasions as criminal acts. Monsignor Tardini assured the French ambassador Charles-Roux that the pope had indeed spoken with clarity, with dignity, and with great affection for invaded states. What more could the pope do? Tardini said that the pope's telegrams had accomplished precisely what Charles-Roux and others demanded. The French ambassador was persistent. It was one thing to express sympathy with those who were suffering the consequences of military aggression; it was another thing altogether to condemn explicitly the aggressor.[110]

Tardini's defense of the pope's position was no doubt sincere, but it was also somewhat self-serving. The pope and his advisors knew full well what was being asked of the pontiff by Western diplomats. They knew, too, that Mussolini was angry with the pope for speaking directly to the leaders of the invaded countries, seeing it as an attack against an ally and against Mussolini's own ambitions. Meeting with the outgoing Italian ambassador Dino Alfieri, Pius XII stressed that he had deliberately avoided saying anything that could be construed as offensive to the Germans or their allies. With the Italians intimating that the pope's response to the Nazi thrust westward would have serious consequences, an indignant Pius XII told Alfieri that he had every reason to condemn in even harsher terms the actions of German armies across Europe. The pope knew that people everywhere looked to him to say something, to demonstrate that he was not indifferent to suffering and injustice. Why, he asked Alfieri, was the Mussolini government surprised to hear him express sympathy for the plight of states that enjoyed friendly relations with the Vatican? Above all, he said, he expected from the Italians some recognition that he had held his tongue in order to avoid exacerbating the situation. Like him, the Italians knew the "horrible things" that were happening in Poland. As pope, he ought to offer "words of fire against such things," yet as he explained to Alfieri, he had refrained from doing so, knowing that if he spoke in harsher terms to condemn Nazi behavior, it would only make matters worse for those already suffering under the heel of occupation and war.[111] It was a frank admission—he could indeed be more forceful in his public statements, but he was choosing to temper his language to avoid doing more harm than good.

There was substance to the Vatican's insistence that Pius XII was doing everything within his power to bring about a quick and lasting peace settlement, above all to alleviate the suffering of innocent civilians. One of his boldest moves in this direction was also his most secretive, with Pius XII acting as an intermediary between anti-Hitler factions of the German military and British authorities. The aim was to get Hitler and the other Nazi leaders removed from power, thereby setting the stage for a quick negotiated peace settlement.[112]

The genesis of the plan dated back to September 1939, in the closing days of the Nazi rout of Poland, when anti-Nazi German intelligence officers devised a scheme to enlist the pope to sound out the British on possible terms for a negotiated peace settlement.[113] The officers singled out Josef Müller to serve as their conduit to the pope, knowing of the Munich lawyer's close working relationship with Pius XII and with some of his intimate associates such as Kaas and Leiber. Not only was Müller familiar with Catholic circles in Germany, but he had extensive business and legal connections that could be of some use. Pius XII and Müller never actually met during the period of the so-called Roman conversations; Father Leiber was the essential contact between the pope and Müller.[114] Acting ostensibly on official German intelligence business, Müller shuffled back and forth between Rome and Berlin for months in late 1939 and the first half of 1940. Müller would arrive in Rome with instructions from Hans Oster and Hans von Dohnanyi of the German intelligence service, both of whom were also active members of the resistance against Hitler. He also brought news from the German bishops, who wished to let Pius XII know of the latest Nazi attacks on the church. Müller and Leiber usually met at Leiber's office at the Gregorian University in Rome's historic quarter, though eventually, in order to avoid scrutiny, they met in the Jesuit church of San Bellarmino outside the city. Father Leiber then relayed Müller's information to the pope, who in turn met secretly with the British representative to the Vatican, d'Arcy Osborne.

What did Pius XII hope to achieve with such a high-risk initiative, one that was at odds with his stated preference for diplomatic means married to rhetorical restraint? According to Müller, the pope hoped the talks would achieve two objectives: first, to bring about a quick end to the war; and second, to restore Polish sovereignty and territorial integrity so that Poland could act as a "buffer state" between Germany and the Soviet Union.[115] After the war ended, the Vatican admitted publicly in its official newspaper that the pope had helped to facilitate the exchange of information between anti-Hitler elements of the German military and the Allies so that Germany might be "liberated from National Socialism."[116]

That the scheme came to naught does not lessen the significance of the pope's role in the plan. Here, after all, was the normally cautious Pius XII positioning himself and his office in the middle of a high-stakes gamble involving military secrets and strategies to undermine a government whose legitimacy the Vatican had recognized since it came to power in 1933. It was a risky move for the military men and diplomats involved on all sides, but, as historians David Alvarez and Robert Graham suggest, Pius XII arguably risked the most. His actions "compromised the traditional neutrality of the Vatican, and jeopardized his personal position as well as that of the papacy." The pope knew this; hence his care in keeping the scheme secret even from his principal advisors, notably Maglione, Tardini, and Montini.[117] Despite appearances, Pius XII evidently was capable of bold decisive leadership, and of subterfuge —more than even those close to him knew.

That Pius XII felt morally and strategically justified in facilitating discussions between elements of the German resistance and Allied intelligence belies the notion that he was incapable of resolute action. It also lays bare one of the basic assumptions that informed his response to the Third Reich—that a strong and unified German state freed from the Nazi mania was an indispensable bulwark in defense of Christian civilization against the Communist threat. If his affinity for the German language and culture conditioned Pius XII's response to Nazism, it caused him to see Nazism itself as the problem, not Germany in general. This is what led him to argue early on in the war against the notion that all Germans were responsible collectively for the Third Reich and its destructive policies.

The preservation of German Catholicism was inextricably connected to the pope's vision of a strong and united Germany freed from the Nazi scourge. The coming of war and the continued radicalization of Nazi policies at home and in the occupied territories accentuated Pius XII's long-standing fear for the fate of German Catholicism if its relationship to the Vatican somehow was sundered. To avoid this, the pope openly encouraged the German bishops to write to him frequently and directly during the war via the papal representation in Berlin. The bishops wrote in great numbers and with relatively little difficulty until the last year of the war. Their letters helped to keep the pope well informed about events in Germany, just as his correspondence from the nuncios and bishops in occupied territories offered Vatican diplomacy a unique perspective on the situation on the ground.[118]

Pius XII insisted that he had a spiritual imperative, a "duty of conscience," as he put it, to avail himself of every opportunity to achieve an "acceptable peace" between church and state. But he did not intend to advocate for "peace at all costs." As he explained to Cardinal Bertram near the end of 1940, any such peace would be "incompatible with the principles of the Faith and with the very nature of the Catholic Church."[119] To seek an accommodation with the Hitler state was not a form of appeasement. Rather, Pius XII thought of his approach as a principled and prudent course of action, consistent with the moral and administrative dictates of his office. In fact, he rejected outright any suggestion that the Vatican was neutral in the present conflict. As he explained in a letter to his old friend Cardinal Faulhaber of Munich, *neutrality* implied some measure of indifference; he preferred to think of his policy as one of *impartiality*. "For Us impartiality means judging things according to truth and justice," the pope told Faulhaber. "But when it comes to Our public statements, We have closely considered the situation of the church in the various countries to spare the Catholics living there from unnecessary difficulties."[120] Pius XII used his correspondence with the German bishops to acknowledge the difficult choices he faced by virtue of his office and the competing demands being made on the Vicar of Christ from the faithful throughout Europe and the world. The logic of allowing bishops and priests to act according to their own assessment of local circumstances was evident in 1940, when the Holy Office condemned the Nazi euthanasia program. Having asked the authoritative judicial office of the Curia to respond officially to the program, which was clearly at odds with Catholic doctrine, Pius XII left it to the discretion of bishops and pastors to take matters into their own hands. So when Bishop von Galen of Münster delivered his famous sermons in the summer of 1941 to denounce the gassing of mentally ill patients in area hospitals, Pius XII let it be known that he appreciated the courageous move. In a letter to Bishop Preysing, the pope said of von Galen's sermons, "They brought about in Us a consolation and a satisfaction which We have not experienced for a long time as We walk down a sorrowful path with the Catholics of Germany."[121]

The desire to avoid doing more harm than good, to avoid a greater evil, as Pius XII put it, had determined another defining feature of his wartime policy: to devolve to the local level—to bishops and even parish priests—decision-making about how best to respond to evolving conditions on the ground. Pius XII sought the opinion of his brother bishops to help him decide on the proper course of action as the war intensified. In April 1940, he wrote to Bishop Preysing to ask about German reaction to a Vatican Radio broadcast detailing the situation of the church in Germany. The pope explained that the broadcast had aired because "it was thought that complete silence on the part of the Holy See before the public might have resulted in German Catholics losing courage." Also, outside Germany "such a silence would have led to a misunderstanding, with people believing that everything was normal with the church in Germany, or in any case that things would improve." Yet the pope was right to worry about Nazi reaction to the broadcast. Word of reprisals reached him from Germany. As a result, the pope suspended the broadcasts "until We can safely evaluate their pros and cons."[122]

Pius XII and his advisors may also have been hedging their bets in case Hitler and the Nazis eventually won the war, thus setting the stage for a prolonged period of Nazi-Fascist domination over Europe. This was the impression that the American Harold H. Tittmann, a member of Myron Taylor's office, took from a candid conversation he had with the pope in 1941. Pius XII "frankly admitted" that relations between the Holy See and the German government were not good, and had not been for some time. As Tittmann noted, Pius XII realized that "things were going from bad to worse." Still, as pope and thus spiritual pastor to Catholics everywhere, irrespective of their form of government, he refused to sunder formal relations with the Hitler state. If, he said, Catholic members of the German military came to Rome and asked to meet with the pope in his pastoral capacity, then he must accede to their request. Tittmann discerned in the pope's rationale not so much an impulse toward neutrality as self-interested pragmatism. "I had come to the conclusion," Tittmann later recalled, "that the true reason for its [the Holy See's] noncommittal attitude stemmed not from this [neutrality] but rather from the conviction that as things were going then, a German victory in Europe was inevitable and that the Pope, responsible for the welfare of the Church, was obliged to shape his policies accordingly as best he could, always in the interest of the millions of Roman Catholics." Yet Tittmann was convinced that although he never said so directly, the pope and his advisors "deep down in their hearts" realized that "the only hope for the Church to avoid the neopaganism of the Germans and the atheistic communism of the Russians was an Anglo-Saxon victory."[123]

This assessment was echoed by a detailed American report prepared for the director of strategic services in early 1944 outlining the military implications of political conditions in Rome. In its section on the Vatican, the report stated that it was a "neutral State" and intended to keep it that way, hence its studious attempt not "to alienate Catholic groups in Axis or pro-Axis countries." The Vatican was also anxious to avoid doing anything that could give the Nazis "the diplomatic excuse to enter Church lands." For these reasons, said the report, the Vatican put on a diplomatic show of neutrality when in reality "the Church in Italy is actively pro-Allied." While there was no evidence that the Vatican itself was directly organizing or sponsoring overt resistance activity against the Axis powers, intelligence sources did detect covert and indirect ways in which the Holy See was helping the Allied cause in Italy. By maintaining at least the semblance of neutrality, the church was able to help "everyone from anarchists to monarchists"; this included Jews, former Fascist officials, anti-Fascist political figures—all of them, the report noted, "found haven and guidance in the church and convent network through North Italy." The report concluded that "the Vatican is a sure source of aid in the fight against the Germans."[124]

For Pius XII a top priority was still to preserve formal diplomatic relations with the Hitler government and to reduce the tension that had been building between the Vatican and the Third Reich during his predecessor's pontificate. It was clear from Pacelli's record as secretary of state that he had always seen diplomatic engagement with the German government as the best chance to improve conditions for persecuted German Catholics. He also saw it as essential that the pope and the German bishops do everything in their power to conserve open and secure lines of communication. If the alienation of the German episcopate from the Vatican was one of the long-standing objectives of the Hitler regime, then it was Pius XII's objective to thwart it, even to the point of tempering public criticism of the German government so as to avoid provoking counterproductive reprisals. As the pope wrote in May 1939 to Bishop von Preysing of Berlin, the German episcopate should continue to work toward an improvement in relations with the Hitler government, pressing the long-standing demands that the government recognize the terms of its 1933 agreement with the Holy See. It was imperative that the bishops do so, Pius XII urged, "without inciting useless conflicts." In a letter written a year later, after receiving word of an intensification of the Nazi persecution of Catholics, Pius XII told Preysing that he did not want to "impose useless sacrifices on German Catholics, who already are so oppressed for the sake of their faith."[125]

For the pope, a more forceful and explicit public criticism of the Nazis by the Vatican would only make matters worse for people on the ground, with no commensurate improvement in the situation. The operative philosophy in Pius XII's inner circle, therefore, remained rhetorical restraint and diplomatic mediation. As Domenic Tardini put it, history would someday show that the Vatican had done all it could for the cause of peace, that it had fulfilled its duty without compromising its dignity.[126] This was a view soon to be contested.

5

War and Holocaust

When in September 1939 the Nazis invaded Poland, subjecting Polish civilians, Jews, and Catholics to a brutal occupation regime, the world had waited in vain for Pius XII to issue an explicit statement condemning Nazi aggression. As weeks of Nazi occupation turned into months, and as the rest of Europe was drawn inexorably into yet another world war, the pope still refrained from issuing the public statement that was expected of him. Even Polish Catholics, who were early targets of Nazi military aggression, wondered why the pope refused to protest Nazi crimes, which included the murder of Polish priests and religious. The perception spread among many Poles that the pope, to whom so many pledged filial devotion, simply was indifferent to their plight.

For the remainder of the war, in fact, Pius XII kept the public waiting for an explicit public condemnation that never came. Not even when the Nazis occupied Rome and began a systematic roundup of Rome's ancient Jewish community in October 1943 did Pius XII issue a public protest. Just over 1,000 of the Roman Jews arrested in October 1943 were eventually transported to Auschwitz, and most were gassed within a week of arriving. All this, it was said, happened "under the Pope's very window," and yet still there was no public protest, no word to the effect that the pope condemned such obvious transgressions of God's law.[1]

But the pope was not *silent* during the war. Nor was he oblivious to the complaints that the Holy See was not doing enough or, rather, not saying enough to condemn Nazi actions. As we have seen, it was Pius XII's policy to leave it to bishops and pastors who were working at the local level to decide whether or not to protest. His rationale was that they were in a better position than he to judge "the danger of reprisals and of various forms of oppression." As he explained to Bishop von Preysing of Berlin, the aim was to avoid a greater evil—*ad majora mala vitanda*.[2] This single phrase expresses the reasoning behind Pius XII's refusal to speak out forcefully to condemn directly Nazism and its manifest crimes throughout Europe. The principle of avoiding greater evil was consistent with all of his diplomatic training and his cautious character. It may even have saved lives. Still, a nagging question remains: was this enough?

Pius XII and the Church in Occupied Europe

The outbreak of war heightened Pius XII's sensitivity to what he saw as the competing demands and expectations placed upon the pope. It was understandable that he should worry about the fate of German Catholics, but what of the Catholics in countries living under German occupation? "Times are hard" for the pope, Pius XII told one bishop in February 1941, with the Vatican finding itself in a "complex and perilous situation" that was without historical precedent. "Where the pope wants to cry out loud and strong," he explained, "it is expectation and silence that are unhappily often imposed upon him; where he would act and give assistance, it is patience and waiting."[3]

Nowhere was this logic tested more than in Poland, which was now under Nazi and Soviet occupation. Both occupying powers, in distinct but related ways, were bent on breaking the church's structure and spiritual influence. Before long the pope had to confront what he described as "terrible things" happening to civilians in Poland, including a systematic campaign of terror, intimidation, and violence.[4] In the first months of the Nazi occupation, before the Nazis had decided to use Poland as the epicenter of their extermination system, high-ranking Polish prelates wrote directly to Pius XII with shocking details of Hitler's war on Polish Catholicism, which they saw as the bedrock of Polish identity. Early reports told of the roundup of thousands of priests and other religious, male and female, who were arrested and imprisoned in concentration camps. Among them were several bishops, who, along with thousands of Catholic prelates, would perish in Nazi concentration camps during the war. One report on the situation in the Reichsgau-Wartheland estimated that of the 2,000 priests active in the region, upward of one-third had been killed and several hundred were in prison.[5] The leading Polish prelate, Cardinal August Hlond, sent Pius XII a series of detailed reports that added up to a clear indictment of the Nazi regime and its calculated campaign against Polish Catholicism. Hlond told the pope, "Hitlerism aims at the systematic and total destruction of the Catholic Church in the rich and fertile territories of Poland." Hitler's ultimate aim, he said, was to reduce the Poles "to the status of slaves, who shall serve and promote the prosperity of the 'superior race.'" With prophetic clarity, Hlond predicted that the Nazi occupation of Poland "will constitute one of the darkest pages in human history."[6]

The Nazis were not the only masters of a brutal occupation regime: in Soviet-occupied parts of Poland, as in Ukraine and the Baltic states, reports reached Pius XII of bishops being deported to prison camps, several of whom were imprisoned for the duration of the war and perished while still in Soviet hands after 1945.[7] Eyewitness accounts told of Soviet confiscation of Catholic property, the closure of Catholic schools and institutes, and an attempt to "corrupt" Catholic youth with atheism and immoral leisure activities such as dancing and music. One bishop decried the undeniable Soviet contempt for religion, while another wrote to the Vatican saying that there was no other way to explain the Soviet system than to speak of "a mass diabolical possession." He even asked the pope to authorize a wholesale exorcism of Soviet Russia. In a similar vein, another bishop wrote that Soviet troops "are fierce beasts animated by the spirit of the devil."[8]

Reports of this kind reached Pius XII's desk as early as late December 1939 and continued to arrive, though intermittently, as the war dragged on. They provided the pope and his advisors with some of the earliest and most graphic accounts of the true nature of Nazi and Soviet occupation. If the pope had had any inclination to view Nazism as a lesser evil than Soviet Communism, the news coming from Central and Eastern Europe would have dispelled such a notion. As Bishop Szeptyckyj of Lviv, Ukraine, wrote to Pius XII in August 1942, the initial relief in that area, where the Germans were first greeted as liberators for clearing out the Soviet occupiers, was short-lived. Now, as a result of its "regime of terror and corruption," the German occupation was unbearable. Everyone agreed that the Germans were at least as bad if not worse than the Bolsheviks. The Nazis were, put simply, "evil, almost diabolical." Szeptyckyj spoke of "the most horrible crimes" taking place on a daily basis, including execution, rape, and stealing. One group in particular was suffering the wrath of the occupying forces and their collaborators. "The Jews are the first victims," the bishop wrote, adding that he was certain that well over 200,000 of them had been killed in "our small country."[9] Written in August 1942, this is one of the earliest and clearest warnings—and from a Catholic bishop—that Jews were the first and primary target of Nazi brutality.[10]

This pattern was repeated throughout occupied Europe, with Catholic bishops on the ground sounding warning bells of the unfolding tragedy for Europe's Jews.[11] Pius XII appreciated that reports of such excesses warranted vigilant monitoring. In late 1939, he instructed his diplomatic staff to prepare a dossier with reports from Poland. He also instructed them to contact the Hitler government, demanding that the German Foreign Ministry investigate charges against German forces in parts of occupied Poland.[12] Although the Poles and others were frustrated by what they perceived to be a lack of papal engagement, in fact Pius XII was using the various tools at his disposal to at least spread information about German atrocities. For instance, he authorized Vatican Radio to broadcast news in several languages, including German, describing German practices in Poland.[13]

As expected, the German government reacted angrily to these broadcasts. It complained to the Vatican that they were full of inaccuracies and exaggerations and warned that they would damage relations with the Vatican if they continued. Always keen to improve relations with the German government, Pius XII agreed to suspend such broadcasts, albeit temporarily. There was a quiet expectation in his inner circle that the pope intended to resume the broadcasts soon enough.[14]

Pius XII and his advisors considered it possible that some of the claims being made about German behavior in parts of Poland were exaggerated. They therefore made discreet inquiries through former Italian diplomats in Poland to verify claims that the Germans were sterilizing Polish women and girls and transporting them to German brothels. Pius XII also wanted verification of rumors of the widespread rape of Polish women by German troops. The pope's close advisor Father Leiber confirmed years after the war that while the pope knew that the Germans were committing unspeakable atrocities in Poland, neither he nor the members of his immediate staff believed the stories of Polish girls being targeted in such a manner.[15]

Despite persistent diplomatic efforts to protest German occupation policies in Poland and elsewhere, there was a growing perception that the pope was not doing enough. As Cardinal Hlond put it, the filial devotion and affection Poles felt for the Holy Father were diminishing amid a sense that Pius XII had abandoned them in their time of need.[16] Writing directly to the pope in early December 1941 to decry in frank terms the Nazi aim of "extermination," which seemed destined to wipe out all traces of the church in Poland, Cardinal Hlond informed Pius XII of the many private letters crossing his desk asking ever more plaintively: "But does the Holy Father know?"[17] Hlond agreed that the perception of papal indifference was unfair and that anticlerical elements stood to gain by spreading rumors and half-truths about the pope's response to the situation. But even high-ranking churchmen stressed that whether fair or not, the perception that Pius XII had abandoned Catholic Poland to its fate was palpable. Arguably the most evocative complaint about perceived papal indifference came from the bishop of Wloclawek, Karol Radonski, who from exile in London wrote to Maglione in mid-September 1942 describing a list of abuses and saying that "the people, deprived of everything, die from hunger, and the pope remains silent as if he did not care for his sheep."[18]

Even the influential archbishop of Krakow, Adam Sapieha, wrote to the Vatican to warn of the widening sense of papal indifference to what he described as the "tragic" condition of the Polish people under occupation. "We live in terrible horror," Sapieha wrote, in fear of being deported and imprisoned in camps "from which but few leave alive." Sapieha realized that Pius XII knew of their plight, but increasingly, he said, ordinary Catholics were asking questions to which he and other church leaders had no answer. "You might say," Sapieha noted, that "the Catholic world awaits a defense of justice, even if this is not likely to change the German government's behaviour." Sapieha explained that resentment against the pope was growing among many ordinary Poles, who, in the face of ceaseless "violence and atrocities . . .

wish to hear a condemnation of these crimes."[19] In a similar vein, Cardinal Hlond advised that perhaps the time had come for an "explicit word" from the pope directed to the Poles, to answer the growing chorus of papal critics.[20] Outside clerical circles, too, diplomatic officials like Harold H. Tittmann, Myron Taylor's assistant, who were otherwise favorably disposed toward Pius XII, began to feel that the pope's refusal to condemn publicly and in direct terms Nazi atrocities was damaging the "moral prestige" of the papacy and undermining "faith both in the Church and in the Holy Father himself." Tittmann, like other colleagues in the diplomatic corps, had repeatedly warned the Vatican about this "danger," but to no avail.[21]

The Vatican was frustrated at the lack of appreciation for the pope's constant work on behalf of the persecuted Poles. After all, much effort was being expended on diplomatic approaches, albeit hidden from the view of ordinary Catholics.[22] In a letter to the Polish president in exile, Wladislas Raczkiewicz, in January 1943, Pius XII responded to the accusations that he had not done enough or said enough to condemn Nazi brutality. The pope's Christmas address, in which he had alluded in general terms to those who "solely because of their nation or their race, have been condemned to death or progressive extinction," had clearly not been enough to placate the ever-frustrated Poles. They expected more from the Vicar of Christ. In a letter to Pius XII in the weeks after the papal Christmas message, Raczkiewicz insisted gently but firmly that what the Poles and others wanted from the Holy Father was not so much "material or diplomatic help," since clearly there was only so much the pope could do in this regard. What the people wanted, Raczkiewicz said, was for "a voice to be raised to show clearly and plainly where the evil lies and to condemn those in the service of evil." The Poles in exile felt that a clear articulation of the principles of "divine law" might give those living under the heel of Nazi occupation "the strength to resist" and induce civilians everywhere to do as the Catholics of Warsaw had done, namely, "to protest, in the name of Christian principles, against the violence done to the Jews and against their murder, even though each word of their appeal might have brought down upon them the most dire suppression."[23]

The pope assured Raczkiewicz that he took every opportunity available to him to remind all the combatant powers that the logic of war ought never to trump basic values of humanity, decency, and justice. The problem is that no one had listened to him, and now it pained the pope to learn that the Polish people had not even been told of these many admonitions. The pope's own frustration with the perception of papal silence was clear on at least one occasion, when he reacted angrily to the nasty rumor being spread that he somehow was favorable to the Fascists and cared little for the fate of the Poles. In an audience with the Polish Order of the Sisters of Nazareth, Pius XII is reputed to have said, "Tell everybody the Pope loves Poland. He who says otherwise is lying." To the persistent Polish ambassador at the Vatican, Casimir Papée, who never missed an opportunity to ask for further papal intervention on behalf of the Poles, an exasperated Pius XII displayed an uncharacteristic flash of anger. As Papée recalled, "I remember when I came to see the Holy Father for . . . perhaps the tenth time, in 1944; he was angry. When he saw me as I entered the room . . . he raised both his arms in a gesture of exasperation. 'I have listened again and again to your representations about Our unhappy children in Poland,' he said. 'Must I be given the same story yet again?'" Undeterred, Papée promised to keep coming to implore the pope to do more on behalf of the Poles.[24]

When Bishop Radonski wrote with searing criticism of the papal silence, Secretary of State Maglione offered the usual explanation—the pope had chosen to temper his public statements in part to defer to local bishops who wanted to avoid exposing their flock to even more brutal reprisals.[25] To this Radonski replied:

> I wonder just which bishops have asked the Holy Father to remain silent, and I do not venture to judge whether their advice has been well chosen. According to Your Eminence, they did so out of fear of aggravating the persecution. But the facts prove that with the pope being silent, each day sees the persecution becoming crueler. Infants are now being snatched from their parents and deported as a group to Germany, and the mothers who try to defend them are immediately killed. When such crimes, which cry out to heaven for vengeance, are committed, the inexplicable silence of the supreme head of the church becomes for those who do not know its reason—and there are thousands of them—a cause for spiritual downfall.[26]

With the stroke of a pen, Bishop Radonski had encapsulated the sharpest Catholic criticism of Pius XII's wartime policy. For all the diplomatic maneuvers and behind-the-scenes complaints, the pope's refusal to condemn explicitly Nazi aggression—"the inexplicable silence of the supreme head of the church"—began to feel like a failure of moral leadership, a betrayal of the pastoral function of the papal office. The pope's diplomatic staff realized as much. In one of his characteristically lucid and frank internal memoranda, Domenico Tardini asked rhetorically whether the time had come for the Holy See to employ some "public act" to condemn and to protest the many injustices against the Poles. Tardini fell back on a tried and true justification for saying nothing—practical considerations counseled prudence. He reasoned that explicit public statements would play right into Nazi hands. The German government would surely exploit any papal condemnation to justify intensifying attacks on the church and to impede the Vatican's already hampered ability to deliver charitable aid at the local level.[27] This explanation was plausible, but it was not what those who were living under occupation wanted to hear. Although Catholics in Poland and beyond looked to the pope for something akin to a Sermon on the Mount—a bold, simple, but powerful exposition of the Christian message—they found the cerebral casuistry of an academic and the diplomatic propriety of a statesman.

The Church and the Jews

In his response to the Nazi persecution of Jews, from the 1930s onward, Pius XII revealed himself to be a man of his time, which is to say a man of limited vision with a correspondingly limited ability to perceive the precise nature of the Nazi war against the Jews. In this respect, he bore the unmistakable signs of a generation of clerics who had received their training in the late nineteenth and early twentieth century, when the church was reacting against the modern world, including the secular state. Part of this rejection of the modern state entailed an attack on Jews—the group that was seen to have gained the most from liberalism and secularization, at the church's expense.[28] Nonetheless, during the 1930s the Vatican and leading bishops in Europe had decried as incompatible with Catholic doctrine certain tenets of National Socialist ideology and practice. The 1937 encyclical *Mit Brennender Sorge,* which Pacelli helped to draft, was an unprecedented papal critique of Nazi divinization of race and state. It was followed in April 1938 by a pointed directive from the Sacred Congregation of Seminaries and Universities—sometimes referred to as the *Syllabus against Racism*—condemning certain "pernicious" and "false" racialist and statist ideas, such as notions of racial superiority-inferiority or pretensions of racial purity. For these and other pronouncements in the late 1930s, Pius XI and the Vatican garnered the gratitude of Jewish leaders everywhere. When Pius XI fell gravely ill in late 1938, Isaac Herzog, chief rabbi of the Holy Land, cabled Cardinal Pacelli to express wishes for the pope's "speedy recovery," conveying what Herzog described as the Jewish people's "deep appreciation" for Pius XI's "firm stand against anti-Semitism."[29] Expectations therefore ran high when Pacelli was elected pope in 1939 that he might build on the work of his predecessor in defending human rights. Herzog sent Pacelli his "sincere blessings" on his election and hoped that as pope, Pacelli would draw on the Vatican's recent experiences in dealing with Hitler to guide his leadership going forward. "I trust your noble and faithful belief in the highest human values," Herzog wrote, "revealed in your devotion during the days of the Nazi atrocities will guide you in your new and important position.[30] As the British representative D'Arcy Osborne reasoned, Pius XI's "courageous and uncompromising condemnation of racialism and neo-paganism" had "greatly enhanced" the "prestige and authority of the Papacy throughout the non-Catholic world." And so, he felt, Pacelli and the Vatican were better situated in 1939 to help the cause of peace than they had been during the First World War.[31]

Despite such important statements of principle, however, the papacy delivered no explicit condemnation of the singularly repressive and increasingly violent treatment meted out by the Nazis and the Italian Fascists to Jews. As we have seen, Catholic voices in all quarters decried the persecution of individual groups on the basis of "race" or "belief." In fact, as secretary of state and as pope, Pacelli was the author of authoritative statements condemning the cult of race or state as idolatry. Yet he made no explicit official condemnation—by name, that is—of the worsening violation of the civil rights of Jews from which flowed progressively violent anti-Semitism, first in Germany and then throughout Hitler's Europe.

Pacelli shared the conventional view that Jewish questions were not the primary concern of the church. As such, issues pertaining to the civil rights of Jews or to their economic and social status in Germany after 1933 could be categorized as political, not religious, matters.[32] This was not so much indifference to the plight of a persecuted minority as the church's desire to respect its formal agreements with civil governments, whether Mussolini's Italy or

Hitler's Germany. As the leading Vatican exponent on the concordats, Pius XII held that only if the policies of civil authorities impinged on the church's doctrinal prerogatives should the church speak out on political matters. It was one thing for the Vatican to denounce Nazi sterilization laws or the regime's attempt to compel Catholic physicians and nurses to participate in practices that were contrary to the precepts of their religion, just as it had been the church's prerogative to speak against the Fascist racial laws of 1938, which presumed to redefine the legal grounds of marriage according to racial principles inconsistent with Catholic teaching. It was quite another thing, however, to speak publicly in defense of the civil rights of Jews.

There is a common thread running throughout Pacelli's response to Nazi anti-Jewish measures: a qualified and restrained criticism of anti-Semitic "excesses," grounded in the Holy See's "universal mission" to show charity to all men, irrespective of religious or social distinction.[33] In years of diplomatic exchanges with German authorities to denounce various violations of the 1933 concordat, Pacelli never once mentioned the Nazi persecution of Jews, other than to condemn in general terms the racial theories proffered by the likes of Alfred Rosenberg. Evidently, the future Pius XII did not believe he had the authority, or the responsibility, to defend the civil rights of German Jews as vigorously as he defended German Catholics. The persecution of Jews was a concern for the Vatican on humanitarian, not political, grounds. The universal mission of charity to all humanity, it seemed, stopped short of the public square.

In this respect, Pacelli proved to be more of a follower than a leader, deferring to the conventional thinking of his generation and to the judgment of the German bishops whom he trusted most. Having failed to grasp the true nature of Hitler's repressive measures against the Jews, or feeling helpless to do anything about it, all the pope and his men could do when Nazi anti-Semitism grew so maniacally in the 1940s was to try to mitigate some of the worst excesses by means of the same combination of restraint, caution, and diplomatic negotiation. As word reached him from eyewitnesses that Jews were being slaughtered in the thousands, all a tearful Pius XII could muster were prayers and a few rather oblique allusions to the singular suffering of Europe's Jews. His insistence on maintaining the public face of impartiality undermined the political credibility of the papacy and, worse yet, left the institution vulnerable to the charge that it had failed the test of moral leadership at one of humanity's darkest hours.

The pope's rhetorical caution in wartime did not mean inaction, just as impartiality did not mean indifference. While studiously avoiding the explicit public condemnation being asked of him, Pius XII authorized papal representatives around the world to mobilize whatever resources they could muster to help those facing persecution and certain death because of race or creed. Perhaps the most celebrated case was the *Brasilienaktion*, which saw the pope interceding with the Brazilian government to allow the immigration of Jewish-Catholic families who were desperate to leave the Third Reich.[34] The Brazilian plan had its origins in the early weeks of Pius XII's pontificate, springing from Cardinal Faulhaber's request that the new pope intervene to help so-called non-Aryan Catholics. For the Nazis, of course, Jewish converts to Catholicism remained inescapably Jewish, a position that raised the ire of the Vatican as inconsistent with Catholic doctrine. Eager to shelter these Jewish converts from the hostility of the state and the resentment of the Jewish community, the Vatican encouraged the work of the German St. Raphael Society, a Catholic organization established in the nineteenth century to assist German Catholic emigrants. In the mid-1930s, the society established a Relief Committee for Non-Aryan Catholics, which was empowered with the administrative and material means to facilitate the migration of German Catholics of Jewish descent. In this work, it could count on a measure of Vatican financial support.[35]

At Pius XII's behest, the government of Brazilian strongman Getúlio Vargas was pressed to honor its commitment to provide some 3,000 entry visas to non-Aryan Catholics from Europe, mainly Germany. That it took close to one year for the pope's appeal to translate into action by the Vargas government underscored just how limited papal influence was over civil governments, even in predominantly Catholic countries such as Brazil. By March 1940, the Brazilians said that they were ready to release the visas, 2,000 of which were to be provided by Brazil's ambassador to Germany for distribution to non-Aryan Catholics who were still in Germany and who had been identified by the St. Raphael Society. The remaining 1,000 would be given to the Vatican to distribute to non-Aryan Catholics who had already left Germany to seek temporary refuge elsewhere in Europe.[36]

The Brazilian scheme worked only partially, to the Vatican's great disappointment. Pius XII and his advisors took some solace in knowing that by early 1941 the Vatican had managed to issue most of the 1,000 visas in its possession, with travel costs defrayed thanks to the financial generosity of a group of American donors.[37] But the 2,000 visas that were to have been distributed by the Brazilian ambassador to Germany never materialized. The pope's direct appeal to President Vargas was not enough to overcome the inertia and prejudice that lay behind the foot-dragging of Brazilian officials in Germany. They said they could not be sure that these non-Aryan Catholics were bona fide converts or whether conversion was a ploy for survival and escape. By November 1941, citing new emigration restrictions, the Brazilian authorities informed the Vatican that they were suspending the visa immigration scheme.[38] Appeals to other governments in Latin America to ease their entry requirements to make room for Jewish-Catholic families also fell on deaf ears.

The ultimate failure of direct papal intervention on behalf of just a small fraction of Jewish refugees—and baptized Catholics at that—illustrates Pius XII's limited capacity for effective action even by means of trusted diplomatic channels. This did not stop the Vatican from defending its approach and answering repeated calls for papal intervention with its standard if increasingly worn response. When a desperate Cardinal Innitzer of Vienna pleaded with the pope in early 1941 to do something on behalf of the thousands of Jews in Vienna, many of them converts, who faced imminent deportation, he was reminded firmly of all that the Vatican had done and would continue to do on behalf of Jews. Innitzer pointed out that Jewish converts were especially vulnerable since they often did not receive assistance, moral or material, from Jewish aid organizations. Pius XII sent the cardinal $2,000 to assist non-Aryan Catholics.[39] Innitzer was grateful, no doubt, but this was hardly the kind of bold and decisive action he expected. To be effective, the cardinal told the pope, assistance for the isolated Jewish Catholics of Vienna had to be "audacious and daring" and immediate. Might the Vatican intercede with the Spanish and Portuguese governments, for instance, both Catholic nations, to see whether they might allow baptized Jews to emigrate to one of their colonies? Speaking of the baptized Jews of Vienna, Innitzer noted that many of them were being deported to Poland, where they faced a "harsh fate with courage worthy of admiration, and they go to the uncertain fate of their exile with a Christian heroism that edifies the Jews of the Mosaic rite." The response to the cardinal's impassioned plea laid bare the Vatican's resignation: "there is nothing that can be done."[40]

What is clear from the record is that the pope and his staff knew two things for certain by the second half of 1941: the Nazis and their collaborators were perpetrating shocking atrocities against civilians, Jews in particular; and there was mounting anger and disappointment with the pope's refusal to issue an explicit condemnation of Nazi behavior. Month after month the reports continued to come in from a wide range of sources, telling of deportations in Germany, massacres in the Ukraine, and intensified persecution in Poland. Father Pirro Scavizzi, an Italian field hospital chaplain, began sending Pius XII and his advisors detailed reports in late 1941 that told of angry reaction in occupied Poland to the pope's apparent silence and inaction. Traveling with the Italian army through occupied central Europe, Father Scavizzi had a frontline view of Nazi occupation, which he related back to Pius XII and his closest advisors.[41]

In November 1941, Scavizzi passed along a letter that was addressed to Pius XII from a Dominican priest named Lycrakow. It was a far cry from the usual diplomatic niceties the pope was accustomed to—noting that constant talk of the Vatican's charitable work on behalf of suffering peoples was unconvincing. What people wanted and expected was to hear the pope taking sides, that is, offering a "clear, public, and decisive" ideological stance against Hitler's Germany. Until then, the Poles would continue to speak of the pope's "crime of silence."[42]

Father Scavizzi also was the source of the most detailed description to cross the pope's desk of what was happening to Jews in Nazi-occupied Poland. His reports coincided with inquires coming from the American delegation at the Vatican, asking for confirmation of rumors that told of the systematic murder of Jews in Poland.[43] The Vatican's initial response to the American inquiry was to confirm that there was some information to this effect, but that the Vatican had not been able to verify the accuracy or specific details of the story. In fact, as early as May 1942, the Vatican had received word from authoritative sources that the Nazi persecution of Jews was entering an unprecedented, unimaginable phase of complete annihilation. In a letter to Pius XII, Father Scavizzi told of Cardinal Innitzer's severe criticism of nuncio Orsenigo's "silence" and timidity in confronting German authorities about their intensified persecution of Jews. Scavizzi added that the Nazi anti-Jewish "struggle is implacable and getting worse all the time, with deportations and even mass executions. The massacre of Jews in the Ukraine is now complete. In Poland and Germany [the Nazis] also want to bring it to completion, with a system of mass murder."[44] A few months later, in September 1942, Count Malvezzi, a representative in Poland for Italy's Istituto per la Ricostruzione Industriale, a state-owned entity that provided financial backing to save faltering companies from bankruptcy, met with Monsignor Montini to report on two "grave" facts. The first was the Russian aerial bombardment of Polish cities; the second was the "systematic murder of Jews." According to Montini's notes of the meeting, Malvezzi indicated that the slaughter of Jews "has reached frightening proportions and detestable forms." Nazi aims truly were stunning: to liquidate by means of systematic mass murder the ghettoes filled with hundreds of thousands of Jews.[45]

In October 1943 Scavizzi sent a chilling report describing just how far the Nazis were prepared to go to achieve racial purity. "The elimination of Jews," he wrote, with "mass executions, is virtually totalitarian, without regard for children or nursing mothers. In any event for Jews—who are marked with a white bracelet—civil life is impossible. They cannot go to market, or to the store, or ride a streetcar . . . watch a show, visit the home of a non-Jew. . . . It is said that over two million Jews have been killed. . . . The Poles are being allowed to move into houses in the ghettoes, which daily are being emptied by the systematic murder of the Jews."[46]

In addition to his written reports, Father Scavizzi was able to meet secretly with Pius XII on at least two occasions during stopovers in Rome. Many years after the war, he claimed that when the pope listened to his account of the brutality of the Nazi occupation, Pius XII "cried like a child, and prayed like a saint." When Scavizzi informed the pope that some people were wondering whether Hitler and his Catholic followers should be excommunicated as a sign of papal disapproval, the pope stood there, "moved and shaken." He then raised his hands to the heavens and said, "Tell everyone you can that the Pope agonizes for them and with them. Tell them that more than once I thought of striking Nazism with excommunication, of denouncing to the civilized world the bestiality of the extermination of the Jews." But Pius XII insisted that trustworthy voices had advised him against speaking out too forcefully or explicitly, and thus risking even more brutal reprisals: "After many tears and much prayer, I decided that a protest from me would not have helped anyone, and would have provoked the most ferocious ire against the Jews, and multiplied the acts of cruelty, because they are defenceless." The pope acknowledged that a forceful public protest would have won him the admiration of the civilized world, but he maintained that it would have meant an even harsher fate for the Jews than that which they were already suffering.[47]

With overwhelming evidence that Jews were being killed systematically and en masse, Pius XII's rationale of avoiding a greater evil began to look like a serious error of judgment. Bishop Preysing was probably the most authoritative voice to challenge the logic of papal public restraint and the propriety of the Vatican's maintaining formal diplomatic relations with the murderous Hitler state. And if the Vatican was to preserve diplomatic ties with the Third Reich, Preysing wondered, was nuncio Orsenigo the right man to be representing the pope in Germany? Preysing saw Orsenigo as too cozy with the Hitler government and too resigned, even defeatist, to convey forcefully and effectively the church's growing concerns about the plight of civilians, especially Jews, in the ever-more repressive and exclusionary Hitler state.

Doubtless, Orsenigo was pessimistic in his reports to the Vatican about the prospect of pressuring the Nazis to change course in their sustained campaign against the Jews. In numerous missives over the span of several years, Orsenigo explained to the Vatican that the German government viewed the Jewish question as an "internal political matter." In one instance, he told Cardinal Maglione that the "situation of Jews here is beyond all friendly intervention." In October 1942, he wrote bluntly of the "impotence" of papal diplomacy on any question pertaining to the status of Jews. Some of his German contacts, Orsenigo said, were telling him not to bother bringing certain requests on behalf of German Jews to the government's attention since these approaches were being consistently rejected. In other words, nothing further could be done.[48]

That the Vatican accepted as essentially true and accurate the information attesting to the systematic deportation and murder of Jews in Central Europe is revealed by an internal memorandum prepared by the Vatican's Secretariat of State in early May 1943:

> The Jews. A dreadful situation. There were approximately four and a half million of them in Poland before the war; today the estimate is that not even a hundred thousand remain there, including those who have come from other countries under German occupation. In Warsaw a ghetto had been established which

contained six hundred and fifty thousand of them; today there would be twenty to twenty-five thousand. Some, naturally, have avoided being placed on the list of names. But there is no doubt that most have been liquidated. Nothing is known of the thousands and thousands of persons who month after month have been deported. The only possible explanation here is that they have died, especially considering the enterprising character of the Jew who, if alive, in one way or another makes himself known [se vive si fa vivo]. There are special death camps near Lublin (Treblinka) and Brest-Litovsk. It is said that by the hundreds they are shut up in chambers where they are gassed to death. Transported in tightly sealed cattle trucks with lime on their floors.[49]

Such jarring descriptions of what was happening sat uneasily with Pius XII's public restraint in not condemning explicitly the Nazi treatment of Jews. A few months earlier, in his Christmas address—a typically dense speech that was widely broadcast and reported around the world—the pope had referred to "the hundreds of thousands of persons who, without any fault on their part, sometimes only because of their nationality or race, have been consigned to death or to a slow decline."[50] Six months later, in his annual address to the College of Cardinals on June 2, 1943, Pius XII similarly spoke in veiled terms to victims who were "destined sometimes, even without guilt on their part, to exterminatory measures." The pope used the occasion to reiterate the rationale for his policy of restraint in his public pronouncements. "Every public allusion," Pius XII reasoned, "should be seriously considered and weighted in the very interest of those who suffer so as not to make their position even more difficult and more intolerable than previously even though inadvertently and unwillingly."

The 1942 Christmas broadcast in particular was interpreted by commentators around the world as an implicit criticism of the Third Reich. Media in the Allied countries, especially in the United States, tried to put a positive spin on the pope's Christmas address, helped along with official government talking points that aimed to inflate the anti-Axis emphases of the broadcast. The New York Times declared that Pius XII "assails the perils of 'Godless State,'" condemning implicitly "Marxist socialism" but also authoritarian governments "that disposed of individuals like a 'herd' of lifeless things."[51]

Privately, though, Allied authorities continued to express frustration that Pius XII was not as bold or direct as he could be in clearly condemning the Axis powers. For his part, Pius XII insisted that he was doing and saying as much as was prudent. Harold Tittmann wrote to Cordell Hull in early January 1943 to say that the pope had reacted defensively to his suggestion that the Christmas message did not go far enough, did not speak explicitly enough, to condemn Nazi atrocities. Pius XII sincerely believed that he had spoken "clearly enough to satisfy all those who had been insisting in the past that he utter some word of condemnation of Nazi atrocities," Tittmann said. The pope was "surprised" at the suggestion that everyone did not share this conviction. Pius XII insisted it was "plain to everyone" that his Christmas address referred directly to Poles and Jews. He told Tittmann that he had to avoid being too explicit when talking of Nazi atrocities since he could not do so directly without also speaking of Soviet behavior. The pope assumed that such direct reference to the Soviets "might not be wholly pleasing to the Allies." No doubt Pius XII was correct in this assumption, though his rationale for creating equivalence between Nazi and Soviet atrocities remained unspoken. In the end, Tittmann conceded that, on the whole, the pope's Christmas message was the best that could be hoped for in present circumstances.[52]

Frustration with Pius XII's refusal to be more explicit was laid bare in a special report prepared by the U.S. Office of Strategic Services (OSS) in January 1943. Looking for ways to exploit the Christmas broadcast for propaganda purposes, the report acknowledged that many observers had the impression that the present pope avoided "clear commitments in this war of ideologies." It was obvious that Pius XII was very careful not to appear to be "choosing sides." The key to understanding his complex public statement, said the report, was to think as the pope did, which was by means of "syllogism"—a form of reasoning that presumed the listener or reader could deduce the logical conclusion of an argument from a statement of basic propositions. For someone like Pius XII, steeped in Thomist philosophy and methods, it was almost second nature to think this way. And so, as American intelligence officials understood it, Pius XII's approach was to begin with the statement of general principles regarding, for instance, totalitarianism, and assume that "his listeners or readers" would apply it to the type of totalitarian regime with which they were concerned. Thus anyone who paid attention to the pope's Christmas address would find "the ideological guidance they need."

They would infer logically that when he referred to the thousands of innocents who were facing death or decline because of religion or race, he meant the persecuted Jews of Europe.

There was an obvious advantage for the Allies in spinning the pope's Christmas message in these terms. Theirs was an eminently plausible analysis of Pius XII's mode of reasoning. Still, there was no escaping the sense that such papal circumlocution in wartime was less constructive than more direct language would have been. In its confidential comment, the OSS report concluded that while Pius XII's critique of the Axis powers seemed to be sharpening, there was yet considerable room for even stronger, unequivocal language, reasoning that "there is still not the maximum of decided opposition to Nazism which could be expressed by a Pope." In short, Pius XII really could say more things more bluntly. His predecessor, the report lamented, had not been afraid to "call the different forms of totalitarianism by their names in several encyclicals and published declarations." Especially in times of crisis, Pius XI had "used sharp words." Pacelli was of a different ilk. By virtue of his training and his temperament, the report concluded, Pius XII's approach was "very different from that of the rather outspoken and abrupt personality of his predecessor."[53]

The pope's closest advisors readily conceded the point. Pius XI would have "spoken sharply, more forthrightly," said Pacelli's long-time advisor Father Leiber. But Leiber was not convinced of the virtue of such an approach. One word from the pope could "provoke an explosion," he said. For this reason, he held that the Jews themselves were "glad" that Pius XII had been cautious in his pronouncements.[54]

The pope's refusal to call by name the Nazi war against the Jews fed the growing perception that Pius XII was not doing everything in his power to condemn Nazi atrocities. Even the pope's long-time friend and confidant Archbishop Spellman reportedly worried that the pope's "authority suffered somewhat among the Catholics of North America" because of the impression that he was being "too lenient" toward the Axis powers.[55] It is commonly asserted that the accusation of papal silence during the Holocaust was an invention of the postwar era—first in Soviet propaganda, then in the contrived historical fiction of Hochhuth's play The Deputy. In fact, the criticism of Pius XII's reluctance to speak out against the Fascists stretches back to the early weeks of his pontificate.

It is true that the full extent of the Final Solution did not become clear until war's end. But as we have seen, the Vatican's own records demonstrate that early on in the war Pius XII and his advisors knew not only that the Nazis and their collaborators were perpetrating a sordid campaign to eliminate Jews but also that it was successful. In May 1943 a Redemptorist priest named Theo de Witte wrote to Pius XII from Amsterdam asking for direct papal intervention on behalf of the Jews of Holland, in particular Jewish converts facing imminent deportation. De Witte belonged to a clandestine Catholic network established to aid refugees, and he acknowledged what the Vatican had already done to help Jews.[56] But the circumstances demanded yet another papal intervention, he explained, and it had to be "valid and effective." Presumably, he knew what had happened the previous summer when the Dutch Catholic bishops had publicly denounced the deportation of Jews. The Nazis had responded with one of the more notorious reprisals of the war, using the bishops' intervention to justify the immediate deportation of Jewish converts.[57] With the Nazis preparing for another wave of deportations, this time of all Jews, converts or not, De Witte hoped that the Vatican might be able to prevent it by shaming the Nazis publicly, publicizing to the world the measures being taken against the Jews.[58]

Of course, recent experience in Holland contradicted De Witte's rationale. After all, the deportations of the previous year proved that the Nazis were not susceptible to public criticism from the Catholic Church. True, a strongly worded denunciation from the pope would carry an authority and have a global reach the Dutch bishops did not have. Yet Pius XII and his advisors were skeptical and resigned about their practical influence. Experience led them to conclude that doing something further to help Dutch Jews was "not that easy." Among the ideas bandied about, for instance, was to ask Portugal or Spain to harbor Dutch Jews for a time while arranging to have Jews immigrate to Latin America. The pope could make entreaties with the governments of Spain, Portugal, and Cuba, something the Vatican did do, at American urging, in 1944.[59] But as Vatican officials put it when responding to De Witte, "the governments of South America do not want to hear about the Jews."[60]

The Vatican's response to the call for papal intervention on behalf of Dutch Jews betrayed a sense of pragmatism and realism with distinct traces of resignation and defeatism. Even some Vatican insiders could appreciate the need for pragmatism, but they challenged the sense of resignation. They also worried aloud that the pope's public stance of impartiality, justifiable though it may be, was coming to be seen as a moral failure of epic proportions. In a remarkably frank criticism of the pope's policy of tempering his public statements to avoid provoking the belligerent powers, Monsignor Carlo Respighi, prefect of Pontifical Ceremonies, wrote to the Secretariat of State in May 1943 to say that people everywhere were "waiting for a strong and solemn word from the Holy Father in defense of humanity." It might be that the pope was working behind the scenes by means of diplomatic channels, Respighi admitted. Still, these initiatives did not seem to be working; nor did they receive any meaningful public attention. This explained why, as Respighi said, people were "not only surprised but also disgusted by papal silence and inaction." Public disgust did not bode well for the prestige of the papacy, the prefect worried, nor its future capacity for influence. Respighi's advice was simple: the pope ought to use the forum of the Consistory, a formal gathering of the cardinals, to speak in clear and direct terms, avoiding the tendency for grandiloquent but obtuse speeches. Respighi understood that the pope feared the practical consequences of an explicit public condemnation, that Pius XII wanted to avoid provoking the ire of belligerent powers and in so doing making matters worse for civilians on the ground. The problem, Respighi concluded, was that private initiatives and diplomatic maneuvers were having little obvious effect. "Those private letters to the bishops," he told Maglione, "have no particular worth." What people expected of the Holy See was a bold and courageous *public* show of decisive leadership. A forceful and clear papal statement might provoke a reaction from the offended governments, Respighi reasoned, but it would win for the Vatican and the pope "the appreciation of humanity."[61]

Other well-placed prelates in Roman circles, some of them with close ties to the pope's inner circle, expressed similar concerns about both the immediate and the long-term consequences to the moral prestige of the papacy. The American Jesuit Vincent A. McCormick, former rector of the Pontifical Gregorian University and a fixture at the Jesuit headquarters in Rome through the 1940s and 1950s, was among the most well-connected American prelates in Rome, with ties to the pope's personal secretary, Robert Leiber, and the American delegation at the Vatican. McCormick was dumbfounded and frustrated by the Holy See's policy of public caution and restraint. Writing in his diary in early December 1942, telling of growing fears that Italy soon would find itself in the crosshairs of the Axis-Allied confrontation, McCormick hoped the pope would make a public appearance or statement to help defuse the tension and fear. Without some kind of public papal gesture, the church risked leaving it to "George VI and Roosevelt to call for days of prayer. The moral, I was going to say religious leadership of the world is being asserted by non-Catholic countries." It did not escape McCormick's notice that when word reached the Vatican of possible Allied bombing of Italian cities, the pope's men were prepared to move "every power" to prevent this from happening. Privately, McCormick mused that the newfound papal resolve for direct action was too little, too late. "Alas, I fear the voice has lost its resonance for its too long silence," he wrote in December 1944. "I only pray that not too much harm may come to Church and souls thru [*sic*] policy of Holy See.[62] When the pope did speak publicly to condemn the worsening violence, as in the 1942 Christmas Eve address, McCormick felt that Pius XII still was being too obtuse, too academic. He told Robert Leiber as much, saying that the pope's speech was "much too heavy, ideas not clean-cut and obscurely expressed." In the secrecy of his diary McCormick added that Pius XII "should get away from German tutoring; have an Italian or a Frenchman prepare his text."[63]

Defensor Civitatis: Pius XII and Nazi-Occupied Rome

It did not escape the notice of those familiar with the papal court that Pius XII was eminently capable of decisive public action and pointed rhetoric when he judged it necessary. This was especially evident when the Italians joined the war in June 1940 on Hitler's side, after which time Pius XII and his advisors lobbied the belligerent powers, most of whom were represented at the Vatican, to avoid the aerial bombardment of Italian cities. The fate of Rome was especially close to the pope's heart, and the foreign diplomats residing in Vatican City were keenly aware of it. It even gave rise to the perception in certain Anglo-American circles of a double standard on the pope's part. Some churchmen agreed. In February 1943, upon reading a letter Pius XII sent to the cardinal archbishop of Palermo, Luigi Lavitrano, to offer papal prayers after Allied bombing of the area, Vincent A. McCormick, S.J., confided at length to his diary,

Holy See seems to manifest very keen interest in sufferings of civilian population when this population is Italian. They are fully
aware of what cruel sufferings have been inflicted on civil population in Slovenia, Croatia and Greece, and this by Italians—burning of whole towns, murder of innocent hostages in revenge, and
no letter of sympathy has been published as sent to Bishops in
those parts. I am finding it more and more difficult, really impossible to defend the neutrality of the present-day Vatican. Catho-
licity is very much compromised. Would that I were miles away
from here, in some place where I could forget it all![64]

McCormick's disappointment with the Holy See only deepened as Allied
bombers began inflicting serious damage over cities in northern Italy in late
1942 and early 1943. The papal response was swift and unequivocal. Pius XII
openly lamented the attack on Italian cities, repositories of the cultural heritage of Western civilization. The Vatican warned Allied representatives that
inflicting such suffering on Italian civilians was destined to inflame public
opinion and rally people behind the Nazi-Fascist war effort. Attacks against
Rome especially, the Allies were told, would likely turn worldwide Catholic
opinion against the Allied cause and also force the pope to issue a formal protest. The American and British representatives diplomatically reminded Pius
XII that he had refrained from issuing an explicit public condemnation of
the Axis attacks on London, Warsaw, even Pearl Harbor. To do so now that
bombs were falling on Italian cities, against what were deemed to be legitimate strategic military targets in a hostile state, could be interpreted to mean
that the pope favored the Axis powers, and effectively was doing Mussolini's
bidding.[65] Speaking as a Catholic priest with unmistakable sympathy for the
Allied cause, Vincent McCormick noted in his diary in mid-April 1943 his own
bitter disillusionment with Pius XII's response to the Allied air assault:

The Pope has written a letter again this year to Cardinal Maglione. . . . Referring at the beginning to the present deadly war he
laments almost bitterly the bombing of peaceful cities. Where
are these "peaceful" cities? Do military headquarters in a city de-
prive it of the characteristic "peaceful"? Are military ports "peaceful"? I do think that Christ would be more interested in lamenting

and condemning the violent deportation of 100,000s of innocent boys and girls from their homes into Germany to work for the avowed enemy of their country in circumstances most dangerous to their faith and morals. Of all this only silence![66]

The Allies knew, of course, that Pius XII and the Vatican had long opposed Italy's involvement in the war and had worked constantly for years to keep Mussolini from falling into Hitler's arms, all to no avail. By the second half of 1943, they were confident enough in their dealings with the Vatican to approach the pope and his staff about strategizing for a post-Mussolini Italian government, which was seen as the one obvious way to get Italy out of the war. While the pope wanted to avoid appearing to interfere with internal Italian affairs, he authorized papal diplomats to make entreaties with King Victor Emanuel III in June 1943, to discuss options for getting Italy out of the war and sparing Rome the horrors of aerial bombardment or direct occupation.[67]

In what was yet another blow to papal pretensions to influence governments with which the Vatican enjoyed excellent relations, Allied bombers descended on Rome the morning of July 19, dropping what one contemporary estimated was 1,000 tons of bombs on the Eternal City. American bombers targeted strategic military sites like the Roman rail lines, but among the physical casualties of war were the nearby historic Church of San Lorenzo Outside the Walls and the Verano cemetery. Harold Tittmann recalled a surreal scene as he watched with his family from the roof of the Santa Marta diplomatic residence sheltered within Vatican walls, as dark clouds of smoke billowed up from the direction of the San Lorenzo quarter. Tittmann described a "dark pall" hovering over Rome and the pervasive, acrid smell of smoke. His son recalled thinking, as smoke rose from the San Lorenzo neighborhood, that "it was Rome's turn to suffer the horrors of war."[68]

They were late in coming, but when they did, the horrors of war visited Rome in a brutal way.[69] For Pius XII, the first Roman-born pope in centuries, the Allied bombing of his city felt like an intensely personal attack. For the first time since Italy declared war in June 1940, he left the safe confines of Vatican City to make an emotional visit to the San Lorenzo district. It was one of the most memorable moments of his long pontificate and is etched in the popular memory of the city, memorialized in a statue of the pope that now stands in a courtyard directly in front of the old church. An anguished

Pius XII, in a dirtied white cassock, stands in the square with his arms outstretched in prayer, surrounded by a throng of devout residents. Together with his assistant Montini, the pope mingled for hours with residents of the badly damaged district, kneeling amid the rubble to pray for the victims of this and other aerial bombardments. Pius XII even offered a personal cash donation to the Capuchin monks of the district to be distributed to the neediest families.[70]

The Allied attack on Rome and the bombing of the San Lorenzo district strained the pope's otherwise excellent relations with British and American authorities. Although he refrained from issuing anything like a formal diplomatic protest against the bombing of Rome, Pius XII did find ways to publicize his deep disappointment with the action, which irritated Allied officials. In a letter featured prominently in the Vatican newspaper, the pope deplored the fact that despite his many requests to both belligerent powers, the attack on Rome was a "sad reality" and had virtually destroyed one of the city's most important basilicas. The American and British representatives at the Vatican were bothered by the publication of the letter and expressed their regret that the pope "had failed to raise his voice in some such manner as this" when British civilians, churches, and cultural treasures were being bombed relentlessly by the Germans a few years before.[71]

For his part, the pope let it be known through Montini that he had expected that his British and American friends might have sent a "personal word of sympathy" directly to the pope. As it happened, Pius XII was reputed to be "bitterly disappointed" by their "silence."[72] The pope played the personal angle, too, in a letter he sent to Roosevelt. Although it was intended as a private exchange of views on the Allied bombing campaign, it was hard to escape the conclusion that the pope meant to lodge a kind of informal complaint with the Allied governments. At every chance, Pius XII underscored the unique nature and history of Rome as a "parent of western civilization" and still the center of the Catholic world, a city of "irreplaceable monuments of faith or art and Christian culture."

Since late 1942, Pius XII had been working with American and British officials to have Rome declared an "open city," thereby removing it as a military target and preserving the city's unique cultural and religious heritage. The pope had been pleading his case with Italian officials too, extracting verbal assurances from the Mussolini government that obvious strategic targets would be removed from the city's historic core. Not for the first time, Mussolini's promises proved hollow, a fact the Allies knew well. In practice, then, there was little chance that Pius XII could persuade either Allied authorities or the Italian and later German officials to consider declaring Rome an open city. Near the end of the war, months after Rome had been liberated by the Allies, D'Arcy Osborne quipped that the pope's "consuming desire" to save Rome from the ravages of war ultimately arose because of the rapid Allied military advance, not because of the pontiff's many "exertions."[73]

By mid-September 1943, Rome was firmly under the control of German forces at Marshal von Kesselring's command. Ever since the fall of Mussolini in July and the continued advances on the city by the German army, Vatican officials had been preparing themselves to confront German invasion and occupation of the Eternal City. The fate of the Vatican was uncertain. Rumors from intelligence officers in contact with Cardinal Maglione suggested that the Nazis had drawn up plans for a possible occupation of Vatican City that would involve the forcible confinement of the pope and his removal from Rome, possibly to Munich.[74] Contemporary sources suggest that there even was some vague talk by Hitler about the desirability of removing the pope from Rome. But the evidence is fragmentary, unsubstantiated, and often contradictory. In one account, Nazi Propaganda Minister Josef Goebbels was said to have favored the idea of kidnapping the pope. Yet Goebbels's diaries suggest that it was he who convinced the führer to desist for fear of inflaming public opinion.[75]

The most systematic and deceptively plausible account of a Nazi plot to kidnap the pope came from General Karl Wolff, the S.S. commander in Italy during the war. In sworn testimony given as part of the investigation for the cause to beatify Pius XII, Wolff told of a number of conversations he had had with Hitler at the Wolf's Lair between September and December 1943, in which the führer provided clear instructions that German forces were to occupy Vatican City and effectively kidnap the pope. When asked what he intended to do with the Vatican now that Mussolini had been removed from power, Hitler reportedly said that the Germans would invade the Vatican at once. "Do you think the Vatican will subjugate me?" Hitler reportedly said. "I don't care. . . . Let's drive out that pack of pigs . . . and then we'll apologize . . . for us it's all the same."[76] Hitler's plan, as Wolff recalled it, was to transport the pope to some locale in northern Europe, possibly in Germany, where he would be safe from Allied influence. Hitler and Himmler both were reputed to be keenly interested in securing the Vatican's vast, priceless art collection.

In Wolff's fantastical and self-flattering account, the führer's resolve to put the Vatican under heel and deport Pius XII was tempered only by Wolff's calm exposition of the negative consequences such an action would bring: it would irritate German Catholics, above all, including German Catholic troops, as well as Catholics worldwide.[77] It is unlikely that anything approaching a serious, detailed plan to occupy the Vatican and effectively kidnap the pope ever existed. To be sure, there are a few scattered pieces of evidence from the time—the Goebbels diary, for instance—which suggest that in one of his characteristic flashes of anger, Hitler intimated that he ought to invade the Vatican and clear the place out. But there was never anything like a concerted, coordinated plan, let alone a clear order from the top for German forces to move against the Vatican and the pope with Rome under their command. If anything, Hitler and his advisors resolved that the Vatican and the pope were off-limits, for the time being at least. The Germans seem to have appreciated that any action against the Vatican or the pope had the potential to backfire and arouse Catholic resistance throughout Hitler's Europe.[78]

Whatever Hitler's true intentions, the pope and his advisors, including Cardinal Maglione, believed the story about a possible Nazi occupation of the Vatican and removal of the pope to be credible.[79] Pius XII had resolved to stay put at any rate. Rather than worry about contingency plans in the event of a Nazi invasion of the Vatican, he instructed his diplomatic advisors to consider whether they ought to approach the German ambassador to the Vatican—now Ernst von Weizsäcker—with "an appeal in general terms . . . on behalf of the civilian population of every race, and especially for the weakest (women, elderly, children, the lower classes . . .)." Although it was implicit, the pope must have been referring to Jews, with a view to anticipating how the Nazis intended to deal with Rome's ancient Jewish community.[80] Pius XII was under no illusions about what Nazi occupation meant potentially for the Jews of Rome, and throughout Italy. Even before the full brunt of Nazi occupation bore down on Italy, there were ominous warnings that the thousands of Jewish refugees who had found safe haven in Fascist Italy to that point in the war were threatened with deportation. In early July 1943, in fact, Isaac Herzog wrote to the Irish premier, Eamon de Valera, asking him to "petition" Pius XII on behalf of these Jewish refugees in Italy now facing "certain death."[81]

There were early gestures of papal resolve to spare Roman Jews the fate that had befallen much larger Jewish communities elsewhere in Hitler's Europe. These included the offer of financial assistance when the Nazis demanded that Jewish leaders come up with approximately fifty kilograms of gold or face immediate deportation in late September 1943. In the end, Jewish community leaders graciously declined the pope's offer to lend them the outstanding amount, since other organizations, including Catholic institutions, had helped to make up the difference. The papal offer of assistance was a tangible gesture of aid, however modest.[82]

More consequential was the assistance offered by Catholic religious communities and lay people throughout the city as perhaps as many as 10,000 Jews, including many foreign Jews who were in Rome by this time, sought refuge in monasteries, convents, and private homes. It is estimated that around 100 Jewish refugees were hiding in the Vatican itself, with dozens more in church-related properties in or near some of Rome's major basilicas.[83] Although to date no written evidence of a direct order from the pope to religious communities in the city to shelter Jews has been found, various credible sources confirm that Pius XII did get the word out informally that he approved of and even encouraged this form of shelter and rescue. In October 1943, on the eve of the infamous Nazi roundup of Rome's historic Jewish quarter, Pius XII approved the instruction to lift the so-called barriers of canonical cloister, so as to allow both men and women to be sheltered in female and male religious houses alike.[84] A former Jewish chaplain with the American army in Italy, Captain Harold Saperstein, recalled "from personal experience" his meeting with several Jewish survivors in Rome after the city's liberation in June 1944 and hearing firsthand accounts of papal intervention on their behalf. Saperstein's repeated question to survivors—"How did you survive?"—was met frequently with stories of shelter and aid in convents and monasteries. The chief rabbi of Rome, Israel Zolli, an eventual convert to Catholicism who took the name Eugenio after the pope, told Saperstein that he managed to survive Nazi occupation by finding shelter within the walls of the Vatican itself. Writing in June 1944, Saperstein noted, "It is an interesting fact that the clergy was very sympathetic with the Jews. They took them in and gave them sanctuary and refuge in the churches. Some were given refuge in the Vatican city." Months later, after the war in Europe was over, Saperstein traveled to Belgium, where he learned of the quiet but heroic efforts of Vicar Andre, a parish priest who gave shelter to some 200 Jews during the period of Nazi occupation. Saperstein asked the humble Andre, "Why did you do this . . . placing your life in danger?" The priest responded plainly, "because we have one God and we are all brothers, and the Holy Father instructed that we should do all possible to aid our Jewish brethren." Saperstein noted a similar pattern in France, where Jews found shelter and rescue in churches, convents, monasteries, and seminaries. Writing in September 1944, Saperstein was struck by the parallels with what he had seen in Italy a few months before. It led the Jewish army chaplain to one conclusion: "I have no doubt that in the back of it is the Pope himself, although no definite political statement has been made in this regard."[85]

The valiant efforts of individuals and organizations connected in one way or another to the church to help save Jews demonstrated both the potential and the limitations of Pius XII's policy of diplomatic engagement with authoritarian dictators in predominantly Catholic countries like Italy or Spain. Besides the generic appeals to Christian charity in the face of Nazi terror and his obvious willingness to offer concrete assistance to relief and rescue activities, Pius XII conformed to a predictable pattern of self-imposed restraint and caution consistent with a policy of impartiality rather than rescue. Courageous Catholic rescuers might be able to count on some measure of papal support, but when their efforts became too risky, papal support was attenuated if not withdrawn altogether. The work of the French Capuchin priest Father Marie-Benoît to save thousands of Jews in southern France and then in Rome at the height of Nazi occupation of the city demonstrated how far Pius XII was prepared to go to offer a measure of support for valiant rescue efforts on behalf of the ever-more vulnerable Jews. But it also revealed the effective limits of his resolve on that front.

Starting in 1940 Father Marie Benoît, whose given name was Pierre Petuel, spearheaded rescue efforts on behalf of Jews in southern France, in and around Marseilles, Cannes, and Nice.[86] For his efforts, in fact, the Capuchin priest came to be known during the war as "le Père des Juifs," "father of the Jews." After the war, one journalist dubbed Father Benoît "ambassador of the Jews."[87] With the help of Jewish relief organizations in France and Italy, as well as the Sisters of Sion, a Catholic religious order in Marseilles, Father

Benoît successfully procured food, shelter, and money, as well as identity papers and travel visas, to permit Jews to find safe passage to Spain, Switzerland, or Italy. He worked on his own initiative but was able to count on the support of his superiors in Rome, who knew and approved of Benoît's work. He also could count on the assistance of Italian occupation authorities in southern France, who offered a measure of cover for Benoît's relief and rescue activities. Father Benoît told Pius XII as much when the two met in July 1943 to discuss an ambitious scheme that the Capuchin was trying to organize, to transport upward of 50,000 Jews from France to North Africa via Italy. Benoît's work may have been clandestine, but it was no secret in high-ranking clerical circles in Rome and indeed at the Vatican itself.[88]

Father Benoît's activities in southern France brought constant surveillance and harassment by Gestapo agents; his residence as well as monasteries suspected of harboring Jews were searched periodically, exposing Benoît and Jewish refugees to danger. Concerns for his safety and perhaps too for the viability of his rescue efforts apparently motivated his superiors to summon Benoît back to the Capuchin college in Rome in June 1943, ostensibly to teach theology and offer spiritual direction to seminarians and priests. Benoît was undeterred, continuing from Rome his resistance work and especially his relief and rescue efforts on behalf of Jews, whether in France or in Rome. It is estimated that Father Benoît helped to rescue upward of 4,000 Jews in Rome alone.[89]

So central was Father Benoît to rescue efforts in France and Italy that by September 1943, on the eve of the Nazi occupation of Rome, he had become one of the leaders of the preeminent Italian relief committee for Jewish refugees, the DELASEM (Delegazione per l'Assistenza degli Emigranti Ebrei), an organization that collected sizable funds, in addition to providing false identity papers and finding shelter in homes and religious houses.[90] According to Fernande Leboucher, who worked closely with Benoît, the Vatican offered unconditional and unlimited financial support for Benoît's work. The Holy See pledged to provide "whatever funds would be needed" for the Capuchin's relief efforts, Leboucher maintained, to the tune of several million dollars.[91] Much of the money came from American Catholic sources, in fact, as well as from British sources, and was channeled to Jewish relief work through American and British delegations at the Vatican. This was not the Vatican's money, in other words; but various individuals and agencies associated with the Holy

See, including its own war relief offices and the Secretariat of State, were vital conduits that enabled DELASEM to work on behalf of Jews in Rome and beyond.[92]

That Pius XII was willing to offer assistance to Father Benoît in his relief work was evident when the two men met privately in July 1943. Benoît had not been in Rome for more than a month or so, but already he was devising an ambitious scheme to ferry some Jews out of France via the small zone in the southern part of the country that was occupied by the Italian army. The scheme actually was the brainchild of a group of French and Italian Jewish leaders, including the Italian Jewish banker Angelo Donati, who seized on the strategic potential of Father Benoît's transfer to Rome; in their eyes, Benoît represented a direct channel to the papal court. As Benoît was preparing to leave for Rome in the early summer of 1943, Jewish leaders asked the trusted Capuchin priest to serve as their "intermediary" with Pius XII. They wanted him to meet with the Holy Father, to thank him for his charitable work on behalf of persecuted Jews, but also to implore him to do even more to help Jews suffering growing persecution in Vichy France.

The key to the scheme was to capitalize on the unique set of circumstances posed by the nature of Italian occupation policies toward foreign Jews on the one hand, and the pope's presumed influence over the Mussolini government on the other. Jewish leaders in France and Italy knew that, despite their formal alliance with the Hitler regime, and despite Fascist Italy's own official record of anti-Semitism, the authorities in Italian-occupied France were actively working to protect Jews from German and Vichy French authorities. Father Benoît told Pius XII as much when they met in July 1943, referring to the truly "humane" behavior of Italian officials toward Jews, treatment that was to the great "honor" of the Italian people, Benoît said. He singled out in particular Guido Lo Spinoso, inspector general of public security and Mussolini's representative on Jewish affairs in Nice. Donati and other Jewish relief workers wanted Father Benoît to ask Pius XII to persuade Mussolini's regime to transfer close to 50,000 Jews in France to Italy under the cover of Italian military and civilian operations.[93]

Father Benoît secured a rare private meeting with Pius XII on July 16, 1943. The pope greeted Benoît with his usual warmth and politeness and listened "with great interest" as Benoît told of his rescue work in and around Marseilles. Pius XII reacted strongly to reports of Vichy police persecution of

Jews. "One would not have expected this from France," the pope responded, while pledging to give his full personal attention to Benoît's questions and suggestions.[94]

Father Benoît had much to ask of Pius XII.[95] In a lengthy memorandum replete with detailed appendixes, Benoît chronicled the situation of Jews in France and of his own role in the relief and rescue activities in southern France. But the real purpose of Father Benoît's visit was to ask the pope and the papal diplomatic office for concrete assistance in four specific areas. First, Benoît wondered whether the Vatican could obtain more precise information on the status of Jews deported from France; this amounted to an estimated 50,000 French and foreign Jews, who had been sent to Germany or elsewhere in Hitler's Europe. Benoît provided the pope with secret information about concentration camps in Upper Silesia, and further details on the harsh manner in which deportations from France had been conducted. While distressed by the news, the pope and his advisors insisted there was not much they could do to help in gathering information, since German authorities were refusing to share with the Vatican any information pertaining to the Jews. Second, Benoît requested that the Holy See intervene with German and French authorities to improve the conditions and treatment of Jews currently being held in French camps, asking the pope bluntly, "What might the Holy See be able to do in this regard?" The answer from Pius XII was a disappointing but resounding "probably nothing."

There was an unmistakable air of resignation in Pius XII's response. The pope seemed to think it was futile to press the case with German or French authorities who long had been impervious to criticism of their anti-Jewish policies. But where the pope and his advisors thought they could make a difference, they were willing at least to try, albeit in rather attenuated ways. Pius XII and his diplomatic staff responded favorably to Father Benoît's third request, which was for the pope to help facilitate the repatriation of Spanish Jews currently in France, many of whom were Republicans with Socialist and Communist backgrounds. They had fled to France in the aftermath of Franco's victory in the Spanish Civil War. Not surprisingly, earlier attempts to repatriate Spanish Jews had met with foot-dragging and obstructionism by the Franco regime. Father Benoît pointed out to Pius XII that delay and obstructionism by the Spanish government meant the arrest and deportation of many Spanish Jews in France; any further delay no doubt would put the remaining Spanish Jews in France at risk, hence the urgency of a direct papal appeal to the Franco regime. On this front, the Vatican acted quickly and resolutely. Working through the papal nuncio in Spain, the Holy See pressed the Spanish government to encourage its offices in France to issue entrance visas to all Jews of Spanish nationality, irrespective of their "political tendencies," as Cardinal Maglione put it. It was a thinly veiled critique of the stalling techniques the Franco government had employed to date. The one caveat was that anyone seeking entry into Spain would have to prove their Spanish nationality. The Holy See hoped for, and received, a generous interpretation of the rule; it might have been enough for a would-be Spanish national to have attended some consular event in France, on the occasion of a Spanish national holiday, for instance, to be considered entitled to entrance papers. Franco's regime expected to score some points with the Holy See, explaining to Vatican officials that its authorities in France were being ordered to apply the entrance visa directives with great "generosity." This notwithstanding the fact that many of the Spanish Jews facing persecution in France were Republicans hostile to the Franco regime, for whom France once represented a political safe haven. Still, as the papal nuncio in Madrid, Cicognani, wrote to his superiors at the Vatican, the Franco regime was willing to take these Spanish Jews back as a "policy of generosity."[96] For the Holy See, it was a modest measure of success and a vindication of its policy of diplomatic engagement and behind-the-scenes maneuvering to offer assistance to persecuted Jews.

Father Benoît's fourth request was the most ambitious and would require the greatest commitment of will and effort on the pope's behalf. It was a modified version of the earlier scheme to transfer tens of thousands of Jews from France to Italy under the cover of Italian occupation authorities. By the time Pius XII and Father Benoît met in mid-July 1943, political and military conditions associated with the impending collapse of the Mussolini regime meant that the plan to have these Jews relocated to Italy was no longer feasible. Rescuers like Donati and Benoît persisted, knowing too well that the stakes were high and the situation for Jews was desperate. Benoît assured the pope that the plan still could work, provided that Jews in southern France were relocated to Allied-controlled North Africa instead of Italy, together with any Jews in concentration camps in Italy. The point was to get surviving Jews in France and Italy out of the way of rapidly advancing German forces as Fascist Italy was collapsing. For tens of thousands of Jews, the Italian safe haven was gone, to be replaced by the brutal reality of imminent Nazi occu-pation.[97]

By all accounts, Pius XII listened intently and sympathetically to Father Benoît's impassioned but reasoned and calculated strategies to capitalize on Vatican influence with governments in Italy, Spain, and elsewhere to help as many Jews as possible. It is clear enough that the pope and his diplomatic staff were willing and able to serve as a channel of information and even as a conduit for material aid, when and where they thought it would make a dif-ference. In the case of the scheme to relocate some 50,000 Jews to North Af-rica, for instance, all that Father Benoît and his collaborators could hope for was that the Holy See would continue to press the Italian government to agree to the use of Italian cruise ships to ferry refugees across the Mediterra-nean to North Africa or to encourage American and British officials to finally do something concrete to "save the life of the poor persecuted Jews," as Benoît put it in a report to the Vatican. Thus far, he contended, they had lim-ited themselves "to making speeches and threats."[98] At the very least, it helped Benoît's cause to be able to invoke the pope's personal assurances of support for such relief and rescue initiatives as the tireless "father of the Jews" made the rounds of diplomatic circles in Rome, pressing his case with British, American, and Italian officials.[99]

The logic of Pius XII's preference for dealing with the Nazis by diplo-matic negotiation instead of public protest was tested again by the Nazi roundup of Rome's historic Jewish quarter, which began in the early morn-ing hours of October 16, 1943. In the sweep of the former Jewish ghetto and in targeted raids elsewhere in the city, the SS arrested more than 1,200 Jews, including women and children, and transported them to the drab Military College just across the river from St. Peter's. Within days, the vast majority of those arrested during the roundup were crowded onto trains headed for Auschwitz. Very few—some 17—survived to return to Rome after the war. Most of them were gassed within days of arriving at the notorious death camp.[100]

The Vatican knew firsthand of the brutal conditions the arrested Jews faced during their temporary stay at the Military College from the report of a member of the pope's diplomatic staff, Father Igino Quadraroli, who visited the college the morning of October 17—the day before the mass deportation to Auschwitz. He told a sad tale of "poor Jews" in pitiable conditions, including a woman suffering through premature labor.[101] Some of the arrested or their family members managed to write directly to the Vatican after the roundup, pleading directly with Pius XII to intercede with the Germans on behalf of innocent civilians facing imminent deportation. One woman identified only as "Mme. X" wrote to Maglione to ask whether the pope might secure her release, given that she was older and in poor health, and had been arrested summarily during the roundup simply for being Jewish. It is not clear whether the pope was able to secure her release, or whether he even knew of her anguished plea, along with those of dozens of others who appealed directly to the pope for protection.[102]

The official response from the Vatican was the same as always: the pope was doing everything in his power to help. These efforts, such as they were, remained hidden from public view. In fact, the pope himself remained largely secluded in the chaotic days of the roundup, although he was not altogether inactive. Pius XII first heard of the roundup from a personal friend, the Italian countess Enza Pignatelli Aragona Cortes, who reportedly met with the pope hours after the roundup began with details of the German operation.[103] Pius XII was shocked by the news, so sincerely had he taken the German promise not to move against Jews in Rome after having extorted from them a sizable amount of gold.

The pope's reaction was swift and decisive—Pius XII placed a telephone call that set in motion an immediate if private papal protest against what the Germans were doing to Jews within walking distance of the Vatican. It fell to Maglione to summon Weizsäcker on the very day the roundup took place.[104] Maglione dispensed with the usual diplomatic niceties and directly asked the ambassador to do something immediately on behalf of "those poor people." Maglione noted in particular that it was "painful" for Pius XII, "painful beyond words that here in Rome, under the eyes of the Common Father so many people are made to suffer simply because of their particular background [stirpe]."[105] The allusion to Jews was obvious, if unstated. Weizsäcker understood immediately the implications of Maglione's criticism. He was eager to know how the Vatican intended to proceed should the German operation continue. Maglione held out one of the last instruments of papal influence, which had been withheld for years in favor of diplomatic negotiation. "The Holy See," Maglione said, "would not want to be obliged to express its disapproval." Put simply, if the Nazis did not desist in their operation against

Jews in Rome, the pope would play his trump card, as it were, and issue an explicit public condemnation of Nazi actions. It was a tacit admission that, for all their assurances to the contrary, the pope and his advisors realized that Pius XII still held certain weapons in reserve. For his part, Weizsäcker warned Maglione about the potential consequences of such a public statement, especially since the directives for the roundup had come from the highest offices of the Reich. Maglione was insistent, though, taking Weizsäcker at his word that he was working "to do something for the unfortunate Jews." It might even be best if Weizsäcker saw fit not to mention their conversation. What mattered from the pope's perspective was that something concrete and immediate be done to stop the operation against the Jews in Rome.

Some of Pius XII's critics see this response to the Rome roundup as emblematic of papal silence and the Vatican's diplomatic failure to make a formal and forceful official protest of Nazi actions. They characterize this reaction as evidence that Pius XII was cowed by German threats of unpredictable consequences should the pope go public with a formal protest.[106] An alternative reading sees in this approach the quintessential features of Pacellian diplomacy at work: acting pragmatically and concretely, seeking tangible assistance for those facing imminent deportation. That Maglione, with Pius XII's blessing, should leave it to Weizsäcker's discretion to decide how best to relay the Vatican's objections to the Hitler government was not a sign of weakness. What mattered, after all, was that the Nazis end their operation against Jews in Rome. Saving lives was of paramount importance, and if the indirect, private means of doing so worked best, then a formal public papal condemnation might yet again be held at bay.

Years after the war, the pope's closest confidants—Father Robert Leiber and Mother Pascalina—claimed that Pius XII actually had begun to draft a written protest to denounce Nazi treatment of Roman Jews. They offered differing explanations of why the protest was never issued. Father Leiber reasoned that Pius XII was dissuaded from going public with his protest by both leaders of the Jewish community in Rome and the German bishops. Jewish leaders were said to be worried that it would only make matters worse for the thousands of Jews hiding in church properties across Rome. The German bishops, for their part, were concerned that such a protest would create a "serious crisis of conscience" among German Catholics. Mother Pascalina claimed that Pius XII decided at the last minute to burn the draft statement for fear that, should the Nazis occupy Vatican City, it would give them justification to exact a brutal reprisal against Jews and Catholics everywhere. The pope is purported to have said that if the protest of the Dutch bishops had led to the extermination of 40,000 Jews, "I fear that my own statement . . . would result in the death of 200,000 Jews. I cannot, I should not accept such a responsibility." The pope reportedly stood and watched as the two sheets containing his handwritten draft protest were burned completely in the kitchen of the papal apartment. Mother Pascalina also testified that around this time Pius XII personally authorized her to use his private funds to help facilitate the migration of Jews from Italy to places like Canada and Brazil.[107]

Pius XII's response to the Rome roundup of October 1943 did not end with a meeting of Vatican and German diplomats. The pope is reported to have instructed his trusted nephew Carlo Pacelli to meet with Monsignor Alois Hudal the very day of the roundup. Hudal was rector of the German ecclesiastical college in Rome, and he was known to have a measure of sympathy for the Third Reich. The point of the meeting ostensibly was to pressure the Germans to suspend operations targeting Jews in Rome. In his testimony in support of his uncle's beatification, Carlo Pacelli makes no mention of this meeting with Hudal. Nor did the pope's nephew suggest that Pius XII instructed him to meet with Hudal to help stop the arrest and deportation of Jews. Robert Leiber insisted that Hudal had "no instructions" whatsoever from Pius XII to convey to German authorities the pope's presumed threat of public protest if the action against Roman Jews was not stopped. It is a curious discrepancy that casts doubt on at least a part if not all of Hudal's account.[108] According to Hudal's version of events, after meeting with the pope's nephew, Hudal wrote a letter to General Stahel, the military governor in charge of Rome, to pass along the papal demand to stop the roundup and suspend any planned deportations.[109] If true, Hudal's version of events substantiates the claim that Pius XII intervened directly and efficaciously to prevent the further arrest and deportation of thousands of Jews in Rome.

There is good reason to doubt that Hudal authored such a letter, or even that Pius XII himself or Cardinal Maglione prompted it.[110] The letter was sent to the German Foreign Ministry by Gerhard Gumpert, who worked in Weizsäcker's office and was an aide to Stahel. The letter explained that the "arrest of Jews of Italian nationality," which had begun the morning of October 16, met with severe papal disapproval and might even lead the pope to make the feared "public stand" against the arrests. The advice to Berlin from German officials in Rome was to order "the immediate cessation of these arrests" for the good of Vatican-German relations, and to avoid letting any papal protest turn into an occasion for anti-German propaganda against occupying forces in Italy and beyond.[111]

Stahel sent the letter directly to SS leader Heinrich Himmler, while Ambassador Weizsäcker sent along a letter of his own to the German Foreign Ministry confirming Hudal's account of papal disapproval and the threat of a public condemnation. Weizsäcker acknowledged that the Curia was "dumbfounded" by the roundup, "as the action took place under the very windows of the Pope, as it were." Consequently, anti-German circles close to the Vatican were pressuring Pius XII to dispense with his noted "reserve" in public pronouncements. Given that Catholic bishops in France had spoken out publicly and clearly to condemn operations against Jews in their cities, the reasoning went, Pius XII might now feel compelled to do the same. "The Pope, as supreme head of the Church and bishop of Rome, could not lag behind them," Weizsäcker stated. He even harked back to Pius XI, the combative and "impulsive" pontiff who was much more inclined than Pius XII to issue the kind of forceful public condemnation German officials feared. This was a thinly veiled warning that Pius XII was on the verge of abandoning the path of discreet diplomatic negotiation for the more openly confrontational and public style of his predecessor.[112]

Did this amount to decisive, albeit discreet, action by Pius XII to stay the hand of the SS in defense of Jews in Rome? Some close observers, including British representative Osborne, thought that Maglione's meeting with Weizsäcker in the early hours of the roundup did indeed amount to a private papal protest, which, in turn, worked to convince the Germans to suspend operations against Jews in Rome. Bishop Hudal maintained that when Heinrich Himmler was told of a possible papal protest, the SS leader ordered an immediate stop to the roundup, ostensibly "out of consideration for the special character" of the Eternal City.[113] If this was the case, then a direct line can be drawn between Pius XII's directive to Maglione to approach Weizsäcker the morning the roundup began, and the decision to suspend the operation. Of course, it was the possible threat of a papal condemnation, not any actual statement from the pope, that worried German authorities in Rome; they feared that further arrests and deportations would break the pope's demonstrable resolve to avoid going public with his criticism of Nazi actions. Weiz-säcker assured his superiors in Berlin that the pope was resisting mounting pressure to make a "demonstrative pronouncement against the removal of the Jews from Rome." Such was the measure of Pius XII's commitment to avoid further harm to the Vatican's working relationship with the Hitler government and with occupation authorities in Rome.[114]

In one sense, then, it could be said that Weizsäcker deliberately skewed his reports to Berlin so as to minimize the full extent of papal anger at the roundup of October 16. So much so that, according to the Jesuit historian Robert Graham, Weizsäcker's selective reports contributed in substantive and lasting ways to the "legend" of Pius XII's "silence" during the Holocaust.[115] Weizsäcker came away from his October 16 meeting with Maglione with a clear understanding that the Vatican was threatening a public condemnation if the arrest and deportation of Jews from Rome were to proceed. With Maglione's tacit approval, Weizsäcker chose to relay this message in carefully worded terms designed presumably to avoid angering Hitler's government. In the end, what mattered was that Berlin was made to understand that the threat of a public papal condemnation was real and imminent—this much the Nazi leadership knew, no matter how the ambassador chose to put it.[116]

The extent to which Pius XII's threatened public condemnation of Nazi actions worked to save the Jews of Rome remains an open question. For some historians Maglione's rather tepid intercession at the pope's behest the morning of October 16 could not have been decisive, any more than the warnings coming from Hudal or Weizsäcker. The reasoning goes that the roundup stopped when it did because that was what the SS had planned all along; they simply had never intended a wholesale roundup of Jews in Rome, opting instead for selective screening and deportation.[117] So it was that a few months after the notorious roundup of October 1943, German officials ordered the arrest and deportation of close to 700 Roman Jews; many were sent to the Fossoli concentration camp in Italy, and many of those eventually were deported to Auschwitz. All this happened, as one historian puts it, "without a flicker of a papal protest."[118] And when in March 1944 Hitler ordered the Wehrmacht in Rome to exact swift and unsparing reprisal for partisan killings of German troops, which resulted in the summary execution of more than

300 Italian civilians, including many Jews, Pius XII maintained his stance of public silence.[119]

During the war and for decades after, Pius XII and his men doggedly justified their approach. An influential member of that inner circle, Monsignor Montini (the future Pope Paul VI), recalled in June 1963 that to have protested publicly against Nazi practices, especially against Jews, "would have been not only futile but harmful . . . that is the long and the short of the matter." Robert Leiber echoed those sentiments when he said in 1966, "I simply cannot understand why it is not better understood today why the Pope had to express himself so carefully at the time. . . . If the Pope had protested publicly, what then? What would have happened? We don't know. Hitler did as he liked." And so, Leiber concluded, Pius XII clung to this "firm conviction: that it was better to keep silent."[120]

Limits of Papal Influence:
Pius XII and the Jews of Central and Eastern Europe

If events in Nazi-occupied Rome revealed Pius XII's capacity for direct intervention on behalf of persecuted Jews, and even validated his rationale for using private rather than public means to do so, the practical limitations of his influence were demonstrated starkly by the condition of Jews in Central and Eastern Europe. Even in largely Catholic states, papal influence was curtailed both by the intransigence of openly anti-Semitic puppet governments and by the Vatican's self-imposed policy of avoiding public protest. This was glaringly evident in Slovakia, a fervently Catholic republic established after the Nazi annexation of Czechoslovakia, which was governed as of 1939 by a Roman Catholic priest, Father Joseph Tiso. Although nominally independent, Tiso's Slovakia was closely aligned to the Third Reich, as was seen in its racial laws of September 1941, which mimicked Germany's Nuremberg decrees of 1935. The pope's representative in Bratislava reported that in some respects, the Slovakian anti-Semitic laws were even more severe than their German counterparts.[121]

The contradiction of a traditional Catholic state, headed by a priest, no less, enacting legislation that was at odds with Catholic doctrine was not lost on Pius XII and his advisors. Speaking on the pope's behalf, Maglione wrote

to the Slovakian minister at the Holy See, Karol Sidor, to tell him of the Holy
See's "intense pain" at hearing that profoundly Catholic Slovakia should en-
act laws that openly violated basic Catholic principles. In another one of
the now familiar implicit allusions to Jews, Maglione spoke of the universal
church, which, he said, carried in its womb "people of all background [*stirpe*]"
and therefore looked with "maternal care on all humanity."[122]

Slovakian authorities were unmoved by the Vatican's complaint. After
months of delay in responding, word reached the Holy See that the Slovakian
government intended to resolve its Jewish problem by means of "mass deportation of all Slovakian Jews." They likely would be sent to Galicia or Lublin, "with no regard to age, sex, religion," as the nuncio Giuseppe Burzio reported. One of the more disturbing aspects of the planned deportation was
that it was entirely a Slovakian initiative; there was no pressure coming from
the Germans, who, if anything, demanded that the Slovaks defray the costs
to maintain deportees for up to two weeks. The self-professed Catholic prime
minister Vojtech Tuka told the pope's representative in Bratislava that he saw
nothing "inhumane" or "un-Christian" about the deportation. The nuncio
was incredulous. As he wrote to the Vatican in May 1942, the deportation to
German-occupied Poland meant "certain death" for the vast majority of
some 80,000 Slovakian Jews.[123]

Other sources informed the Vatican in March 1942 that the number of
Slovakian Jews facing imminent deportation to Poland was much closer to
135,000, according to an estimate from Robert Guggenheim, president of
Agudas Jisrael, an international organization of Orthodox Jews. With British
and American officials claiming they could offer nothing in the way of concrete assistance to these threatened Jews, Guggenheim appealed in desperation to the pope to intercede with the Slovakian government to see if innocent civilians might be spared from "atrocious sufferings." Similar pleas came
from other quarters as well, including in an open letter from the Jews of Bratislava to Pius XII.[124] The pope and his diplomatic staff swiftly asked the Slovakian authorities to address the claim of a pending mass deportation of
Jews. The Vatican appealed directly to the Slovakian sense of national identity, which was inextricably bound to Catholicism. It was to be hoped, the
Vatican said, that a country which claimed to adhere to "Catholic principles"
would not adopt such destructive measures.[125]

A telling sign of the practical limits of papal wartime diplomacy came with the start of the mass deportation of Slovakian Jews in late March 1942. From his representative on the ground, Pius XII heard of the brutality of the operation. Chilling accounts crossed the pope's desk of young Jewish girls being accosted by members of the Hlinka Guard, a Fascist-style militia of the Slovak People's Party. The girls were robbed, beaten, stripped, and humiliated, forcibly taken from their families and sent, as Maglione put it in one report, to "perdition," which was a thinly veiled allusion to reports that Jewish girls were being forced into prostitution. Such behavior, Maglione told Slovakian authorities, was a "disgrace, especially for a Catholic country."[126]

Months of direct appeals to Slovakian authorities went nowhere. Despite the strenuous objections coming from the Vatican and from the Slovakian churches, just under 60,000 Jews were deported by the government in the first half of 1942.[127] The plain-speaking Domenico Tardini did not hide the sense of futility that pervaded Pius XII's inner circle. Speaking of the Vatican's dealings with Slovakian officials, Tardini observed, "I don't know whether these steps will be able to stop . . . the lunatics. There are two lunatics: Tuka [the prime minister] who does these things, and Tiso—a priest [the president]—who allows these things to happen." It fell to Tardini to deliver what may very well have been the most succinct expression of Vatican resignation when confronted with the abject failure of its approach to Slovakia. "The sad thing," Tardini noted in July 1942, "is that the president of Slovakia is a priest. Everyone understands that the Holy See can't do anything to stop Hitler. But that it can't stop a priest, who could understand that?"[128]

The question Tardini failed to ask was what effect a public campaign by the pope against the Slovakian government's anti-Jewish measures might have had on public opinion in a fervently Catholic country. With tens of thousands of Slovakian Jews being deported by the fall of 1942, it appears that neither the pope nor his advisors openly questioned the wisdom of continuing with private diplomatic channels, which obviously did not have the desired effect. Instead, the papal court clung stubbornly to its standard line, assuring anyone who asked that the Vatican was doing what it could behind the scenes on behalf of Jews who everywhere were facing what the Vatican acknowledged were "odious" measures. The Secretariat of State insisted that much in particular was being done on behalf of Slovakian Jews.[129]

There was some evidence that Vatican pressure, together with pressure from the Slovakian churches, was having a moderating influence on the government, even though Slovak officials continued to frustrate papal diplomats with their evasive answers to direct questions about the fate of Jews. When in early March 1943 the Holy See received reliable firsthand reports about the imminent deportation of 20,000 Jews from Slovakia, Cardinal Maglione wrote to Monsignor Giuseppe Burzio, the chargé d'affaires at Pressbourg, imploring him to confirm the news and, if accurate, to see what could be done to get the Slovaks to desist. Burzio was able to report that while the deportation was "very likely," it did not seem imminent. Burzio complained that it was hard to get exact information since Slovak authorities were very "reserved" and responded "evasively" to demands for information.[130] The Vatican could take some solace in knowing that even in the face of Hitler's personal intervention in the spring of 1943 to bully Father Tiso into pursuing a more active "solution" to the Jewish question, the president, with the help of Slovakia's bishops, seemed to understand that the planned deportation of Jews was an affront to Catholic doctrine and to divine law. In a pastoral letter from the bishops that was read in all the Catholic churches of Slovakia, President Tiso and the bishops made it clear to German authorities and their collaborators in the Hlinka Guard that the mass deportation of innocent civilians contravened the "natural and revealed laws of God." As much as it may have pleased the Holy See to hear such words from the mouth of Tiso himself, reality intruded to temper any hopes for a reversal in policy. As Burzio put it to Cardinal Maglione, the question was not really whether Jews would be deported from Slovakia, but when and how.[131]

Vatican pressure seemed only to stiffen the resolve of the Tuka faction to follow through with its pledge to solve Slovakia's Jewish problem once and for all. Tuka defiantly told Vatican officials that they had no business meddling in Slovakian affairs, especially on behalf of Slovakian Jews. In a diatribe, Tuka decried the fact that the Vatican and the Slovakian bishops themselves had fallen victim to Jewish influence. All the more reason, he said, to be rid of "these pests." This from a man who considered himself a good Catholic and attended Mass daily.[132] For its part, the Vatican remained undeterred; if anything, it grew more specific in its denunciation of the threatened deportation of Jews. When word reached the Vatican in early May 1943 that the deportations were under way, it renewed its long-standing hope that the Slovak government, in keeping with the country's Catholic tradition and spirit, "would never proceed with the forced removal of persons belonging to the so-called

Jewish race." All the greater was the Holy See's "hurt" and anxiety over news that the deportations were to include the "complete removal" of all Jews in Slovakia; no one was to be spared—not women and children and not even converts to Catholicism. In what was arguably the clearest, most explicit use of its moral authority on behalf of persecuted Jews anywhere, the Vatican said that it was reminding Slovakian officials that the Catholic Church extended its charity to people of "every race." To that end, the Holy See would fall short of its "divine mandate" if it failed to denounce measures that violated the "natural rights" of a group of individuals "for the simple reason that they belong to a certain race."[133]

It was a measure not only of the Vatican's resolve to invoke its moral authority on behalf of persecuted Jews, but also of the practical effects that direct pressure from on high could have on Slovakian authorities, at least for a time. The rumored deportations of the spring and summer of 1943 were suspended indefinitely. Of course, with the coming of direct German military control of Slovakia after August 1944, the deportation of Jews from Slovakia resumed with a vengeance despite continued Vatican protests.[134] In the end, as Burzio reported in late October 1944, papal intervention on behalf of the persecuted Jews came to naught as the Germans energetically seized and deported Jews remaining in Slovakia. Despite the seeming futility of further papal interventions, at least by diplomatic means, the Vatican did make one last attempt to appeal to President Tiso's sense of Christian charity and compassion. This time it was from the highest possible level—a direct message from Pius XII to Father Tiso urging the priest-president to think and act in ways that were in keeping with Tiso's own "dignity" and with his "sacerdotal conscience." The news of the deportations was said to have caused Pius XII "deep pain." Such violence inflicted against so many people simply for reasons of their nationality or ethnicity not only violated basic principles of humanity and justice, the pope said; it was also a black mark on the Slovak people and was being exploited by so-called opponents to discredit the clergy and the church all over the world.[135]

The Slovakia case reveals the paradox inherent in papal intervention on behalf of persecuted Jews. On the one hand, there is a clear record of Pius XII directing his diplomatic representatives to intervene strenuously and repeatedly to stop the planned deportation of Jews from Slovakia, invoking the full moral authority of the Holy See but also appealing to the Catholic conscience of the nation and its priest-president. There is evidence, too, that such direct papal intervention, albeit by private, diplomatic means, worked, at least temporarily or in some limited capacity. According to some estimates, the Vatican's interventions, together with those of the Slovakian churches, Catholic and Protestant, managed to save 25 percent of Slovakia's Jews—about 20,000 people—from the Nazis' Final Solution.[136] On the other hand, it was abundantly clear to Pius XII and his advisors that their influence over Catholic Slovakia, and even over Tiso, only went so far.[137]

To a large extent papal limitations were undoubtedly self-imposed. This was evident in Pius XII's response to events in Hungary following Nazi occupation in March 1944, when the Nazis and a pro-German Hungarian government prepared to deport close to 800,000 Jews from the country.[138] The pope was well represented in Hungary by the widely respected and energetic nuncio Angelo Rotta, one of the few papal diplomats with a truly distinguished record of mustering the full weight of the Vatican's authority to offer assistance to persecuted Jews. The pope and his staff knew of Rotta's consistent efforts on behalf of the Jews and approved of his work wholeheartedly; this surely is some measure of papal resolve to mitigate the worst of Nazi anti-Jewish excesses. Rotta was decisive as the point man in a flurry of diplomatic activity in Vatican circles in 1944 on behalf of Jews threatened with deportation from Hungary and facing certain death in one of the Nazi killing centers. With direct German occupation of the country in the spring of 1944, desperate pleas on behalf of the threatened Hungarian Jews reached the Vatican from the world over, from Jerusalem to London to Washington, all imploring the pope to intercede with the Hungarian regent, Miklos Horthy, to suspend the deportation plans.[139] Jewish authorities in the United States turned to Catholic friends and allies in the hopes of exerting pressure on the pope from within to do or say something on behalf of the threatened Jews in Hungary. Leon Kubowitzki of the World Jewish Congress (WJC) met with French philosopher Jacques Maritain in June 1944 to ask whether some prominent Catholic lay men might be willing to petition Pius XII for a public appeal on behalf of Hungarian Jews. Maritain was not sure whether such a petition would have any effect on the pope. In fact, the French philosopher assumed that any decision about a papal broadcast of some sort rested not with Pius XII but with his "cabinet council of prelates." Kubowitzki had the distinct impression that Maritain, a devout Catholic, was deeply disappointed with the Vatican's policy vis-à-vis Jews. He thought the threat of excommunication might have had some effect earlier, but that it was futile at this late stage to roll out such heavy artillery. After all, what sense would it make to threaten the Hungarians with excommunication when, as Kubowitzki reported in his diary, the Vatican had not "even lifted a finger against the Germans"? Other influential American Catholics doubted whether approaching Pius XII with a petition of some kind would have much of an effect, if any at all. The day after meeting with Maritain, Kubowitzki went to see Father Felix Morlion, a Domincian priest working with the Catholic information bureau Pro Deo. The Belgian prelate told Kubowitzki that, knowing the pope as well as he did, it was unlikely any such petition, even one signed by prominent American Catholics, would have the desired effect. As Morlion described him, Pius XII was a "kind-hearted man, deeply affected and disturbed by the slaughter let loose in Europe." The problem was that the pope was "intimidated by his entourage and by the rules of protocol." Any diplomatic initiative of the kind being proposed on behalf of Hungarian Jews would be left to the pope's "inner circle" of advisors to decide. Only the authoritative intervention of high-ranking American clergymen might succeed at circumventing the pope's entourage; Morlion suggested that someone from the World Jewish Congress contact Edward Mooney, the archbishop of Detroit, who was at the time president of the Board of the National Catholic Relief Committee.[140]

It was all eerily familiar. Nazi invasion and occupation heightened anxieties everywhere about the fate of Jews and inspired pleas for papal intervention from civilians and diplomats alike. In response, the papal representative on the ground sent out diplomatic feelers and then followed a wait-and-see policy. The result was almost always the same: frustration and failure as thousands of Jews, including Jewish converts, faced deportation and death, though the pope's intervention may have saved lives.

One of the remarkable aspects of Rotta's activity in Hungary, at the pope's behest, it must be remembered, is how insistent and explicit Rotta was when protesting with government officials about their treatment of Jews in particular. As Rotta reported to the Vatican in late April 1944, in a meeting with the general secretary of the Hungarian Foreign Ministry, the nuncio, in the name of the pope, complained "seriously" about the government's policies, stressing again the extent to which by virtue of its manner and its reach, the persecution of Jews was "inhumane and anti-Christian." Rotta expressed to Hungarian officials Pius XII's deep personal disapproval and sadness, "to see that Hungary too, which until now boasted that it was a Christian nation, has chosen a path that leads to conflict with the doctrine of the Gospel."[141]

Rotta's clarity and forcefulness were meaningful, to be sure, but they were largely ineffective. Not for the first time, Vatican intervention on behalf of threatened Jews went unheeded, and the deportation of Hungarian Jews to Auschwitz began in the middle of May 1944. Rotta wasted no time in lodging an official complaint—in word but also in writing—with the Hungarian government, this time invoking directly Pius XII's personal interest in the fate of Hungarian Jews. Rotta acknowledged that his note was destined to have little practical effect, but he wanted it on record nonetheless, as testimony to the position his office, and indirectly the Holy See, had assumed when confronted with what Rotta called a "true anti-Jewish obsession" on the part of senior Hungarian officials. Writing to the Hungarian prime minister, Döme Sztójay, and to the Foreign Ministry on May 15, 1944, Rotta was characteristically blunt. In his letter to the Foreign Ministry, he lamented the ongoing persecution of Jews, especially the expected deportation of hundreds of thousands of people. Rotta added, "Everyone knows what deportation means in practice." And in his letter to the prime minister, Rotta invoked Pius XII's fond recollections of his 1938 visit to Budapest, while adding that the Holy Father was profoundly aggrieved by the deportations. Rotta indicated that Pius XII sincerely hoped that he would not be "obliged to raise his voice in protest" against Hungarian policies in his capacity as the universal shepherd of the church and thus the "defender of the rights of all his children."[142] Here, again, was a thinly veiled threat that the pope was prepared to denounce publicly the deportation of Hungarian Jews. Evidently, Pius XII and his men knew that there was still one weapon at their disposal, a trump card that they had been threatening to play, with only modest effect, for years.

In this approach, Pius XII and his diplomatic staff essentially were reactive to news that the Nazi war against the Jews was spreading everywhere, but they did occasionally show signs of taking the initiative. In June 1944, the War Refugee Board (WRB) asked the American delegation at the Vatican to pass along information from a reliable source that the Hungarians were preparing a systematic mass persecution of some 800,000 Hungarian Jews. Most were to be exterminated in Hungary itself, with the survivors to be deported to Poland. The WRB wanted Pius XII to issue a direct personal appeal to the

Hungarian government, using the radio if need be, or via diplomatic channels. In fact, by the time this request reached the Vatican, Pius XII already had
prepared a personal letter addressed to the regent Horthy. In it the pope made
the predictably veiled reference to Jews, whom he referred to simply as "a
large number of unfortunate people" who were suffering tremendously "due
to their nationality or race." Pius XII explained that appeals were reaching
him from various quarters, and he could not ignore them. So Pius XII personally implored Horthy "to do everything within your power so that so many
unfortunate people would be spared further grief and pain."[143]

Initially, the pope's intervention on behalf of Hungarian Jews would appear to have worked, at least to some degree, as the deportations begun in
the summer of 1944 were suspended. For the Vatican, Horthy's affirmative
response to Pius XII in July 1944 could be taken as proof that the pope's long-
standing policy of pursuing diplomatic channels rather than a strong public
declaration was working. Even representatives of Jewish communities and
diplomats alike acknowledged and appreciated the pope's efforts.[144] Not all
Jewish officials agreed, however. After the war, some Jewish authorities who
had been deeply involved in lobbying efforts to get the pope to speak out on
behalf of the threatened Jews of Hungary voiced skepticism about Pius XII's
practical influence over Horthy. Leon Kubowitzki observed in later years that
Horthy's decision to suspend deportations in the summer of 1944 owed more
to pressure and threats from the American government, prompted by the
WJC itself, rather than to Pius XII's rather muted appeal. Kubowitzki was
convinced that the pope had little "effective influence" over "the forces locked
in this tremendous struggle" during the war. Whatever good the church was
able to do at the time, he concluded, was owing to the initiative and goodwill
of individual Catholics and of Catholic institutions at the local level. As for
the pope and the Vatican, Kubowitzki said, they had "no real influence on a
higher international level."[145]

Tragically for hundreds of thousands of Hungarian Jews, Pius XII's successful intervention on their behalf was short-lived. By late summer 1944, after Horthy was toppled by the Nazis and replaced with a puppet regime, mass
deportations resumed. Calls were renewed, mainly in American circles, for
Pius XII to act immediately and decisively, this time taking his message on
behalf of Hungarian Jews directly to the people of Hungary, ideally through
Vatican Radio. Myron Taylor passed along to Pius XII messages from the

World Jewish Congress and the War Refugee Board asking that the pope speak by radio directly to Hungarians and use this forum to call on the Hungarian people, including the clergy, "to temporarily conceal Jews and oppose the deportation and extermination of these people to the full extent of their powers." It was felt that as courageous and as bold as nuncio Rotta had been in working on behalf of Jews, the diplomatic avenue clearly was exhausted. Only a direct public appeal to Catholics to offer help to their persecuted Jewish neighbors could help Hungarian Jews escape an increasingly hopeless situation.[146]

This Pius XII would not do. He felt that a public radio appeal condemning Nazi actions would necessitate a papal criticism of Soviet behavior as well. Ironically, Pius XII had used a similar if inverted rationale in the early part of 1943 when rejecting direct appeals from Hungarian authorities asking the pope to publicly condemn Bolshevism. Pius XII had made it clear to the Hungarians then that the logic of papal neutrality meant that any public denunciation of Bolshevism would necessitate a public condemnation of Nazi persecutions as well.[147] Although the timing and circumstances were dramatically different in the face of the pending deportation of Hungarian Jews in late 1944, Pius XII clung obstinately to the logic of papal neutrality. It may be that said logic actually served as a convenient pretext for papal reluctance to bow to outside pressure calling for decisive public action. In fact, warnings from the World Jewish Congress about a coming wave of persecution against the remaining Jews in Hungary were met with a measure of skepticism in the Vatican. In response to Leon Kubowitzki's plea in late September 1944 for swift preemptive papal intervention on behalf of Jews in Hungary, the papal representative in Washington, Cicognani, maintained that word from the Holy See was that "the situation in Hungary is much less acute, since the persons responsible for the previous persecution have been removed from power." In what was becoming a signature style of papal diplomatic engagement with Jewish authorities, Cicognani asked for hard evidence to back up Kubowitzki's claims, saying it was necessary in order to clarify the "apparently contradictory information" about the Hungarian situation. Cicognani was careful to assure Jewish authorities of the Holy See's continued "vigilance and concern," adding that the church would "leave nothing undone to ameliorate the plight of the unfortunate people of Hungary."[148]

With or without clarification, various factors were conspiring to keep

Pius XII from issuing a forceful public appeal on behalf of the threatened Jews in Hungary. Chief among these was the Allied strategic interest of muting any criticism of Soviet conduct as the Red Army fought its way across Eastern Europe. The prospect of a papal condemnation of both Nazi and Soviet behavior worried British and American officials, mindful of the obvious embarrassment and potential strategic implications of hearing their Soviet allies tarred with the same brush as the Nazis. Sir D'Arcy Osborne telephoned his American colleagues at the Taylor mission to say that he "feared" the pope would speak on radio to address the plight of Hungarian Jews but would also use the occasion to criticize Soviet occupation practices. Osborne said that the pope should be prevailed upon not to say anything about the Soviets, since this could bring "very serious political repercussions." Osborne need not have been concerned. American officials at the Vatican had it from a most reliable source, Domenico Tardini, that the pope had no intention of saying anything at all—not even about the status of Hungarian Jews—precisely because he then would feel compelled to condemn Soviet behavior.[149]

Not for the first time, papal prudence and the pretense of neutrality trumped other considerations of a more strictly humanitarian nature. It helped to reinforce the pope's rationale to know that the Allies themselves preferred public silence over a stinging rebuke of Soviet excesses. Papal silence on the fate of Hungarian Jews in Nazi hands was the price to be paid for the overriding political and military implications of criticizing the Soviet Red Army, which remained the bulwark against Hitler's ambitions in the East. No doubt Pius XII worried about other repercussions as well. As American intelligence data suggested, Hitler's government reacted angrily to persistent signs of papal intervention, even if by private means. According to one intelligence report, the Hitler government was especially bothered by the Vatican's "objection to the violently anti-Semitic policy."[150] This response was further evidence that Hitler and the Nazis were paying close attention to everything the pope said and did, and evidently were more aware of the potential power of a papal condemnation than even the pope himself.

Called upon to condemn publicly Nazi policies against Jews, Pius XII chose to exercise prudence and restraint, all in the name of avoiding a greater evil. It is clear now that this approach preserved the institutional integrity of the church throughout Nazi-occupied Europe. This, in turn, furnished papal representatives with the concrete means with which to assist persecuted

Jews and other victims of Nazi brutality. But questions lingered. Were such prudence and caution appropriate for the Vicar of Christ? Was it the behavior of a prophet, a martyr, or a saint? With millions of innocent civilians already dead, and thousands more facing a similar fate, what greater evil could there be?

6

A New World Order

As had been his tradition since becoming pope in 1939, Pius XII used the feast of his namesake, Saint Eugene, to address the Sacred College of Cardinals on June 2, 1945. It had been less than a month since the unconditional surrender of the German army and the fall of the Third Reich. Hitler and most of the Nazi leadership were either dead or in custody, while many others were in hiding and on the run. The defeat of Nazi Germany freed Pius XII from the self-imposed constraints that had tempered his public responses to Nazi policies. Allied victory in Europe ought to have freed him to address squarely the Nazi racial war.

The pope's address did contain a few rehearsed allusions to "the many crimes committed against mankind," and to the use of "exquisite scientific methods to torture or eliminate people who were often innocent." Pius XII made special mention of the persecuted church of Germany, and of the systematic campaign against the Polish clergy. He even spoke explicitly about Nazi crimes committed against "the unfortunate youth of Germany," presumably for having bequeathed to them a country in ruins, materially and spiritually.[1] But he offered no special word of acknowledgment or comfort to the Jews. This omission was further evidence of his unwillingness or inability to grasp the true nature and scale of the Nazi war against the Jews and its consequences. Although no one yet had a precise sense of the numbers to quantify the catastrophe, Pius XII knew from his own sources that entire Jewish communities in parts of Europe had been destroyed. Even when more precise information reached the pope and his staff just after the war, telling of the scale of the Final Solution, they reacted with surprise and incredulity, even skepticism. But any frank talk about the thorny problem of lingering anti-Semitism throughout Europe, let alone the historical legacy of anti-Judaism, was out of the question. As we have seen, Pius XII was not indifferent to the fate of millions of Jews; nor was he oblivious to the enormous challenges facing Jewish organizations struggling to salvage what they could of Jewish life in Europe. He simply refused to accept the premise of Christian responsibility for Hitler's crimes. Moreover, he had other priorities.

The main thrust of the pope's speech to the cardinals in June 1945 was to articulate those priorities, chief of which were the moral and material reconstruction of Europe and the coming of a new world order. His speech echoed his 1939 Christmas Eve sermon on the five points of a "just and honorable peace," a statement of principle that echoed the Atlantic Charter of 1941, the Anglo-American plan for the postwar era.[2] Pius XII continued to defend the principle of national self-determination and security, invoking too the rights of ethnic minorities, as he had in 1939. He envisioned a genuine program of disarmament by all the major powers. And he hoped for the establishment of new international organizations to regulate the affairs of states and correct the mistakes and oversights of preceding organizations.

The pope's vision for the postwar era rested above all on the principles that had guided his political philosophy from his earliest days as a papal diplomat: a stable and unified Germany, fully integrated into the family of European states and acting as a spiritual, cultural, and political bulwark against Communism. This vision of a new European order made Pius XII one of the earliest advocates of a geopolitical arrangement premised on integration and cooperation among former enemy powers. It was a model for Europe's future that sought to move beyond the era of competitive nationalism that had caused two great wars. For some commentators, the pope's blueprint for Europe made him something of a political prophet—a kind of founding father of European unification who looked to the Continent's future by urging a rediscovery of its Christian past. When he died in October 1958, the French newspaper *Le Monde* argued that Pius XII's commitment to the idea of a "united Europe" was one of the great projects of his political life.[3]

It would be an exaggeration to consider Pius XII one of the fathers of the European Union, but he was one of the earliest advocates of European integration, which he hoped would be achieved in conjunction with a rediscovery of the Continent's Christian heritage. The call for Europe's spiritual reawakening had a pragmatic goal: to contain and ultimately defeat the Communist scourge. No matter what the Soviets had done to help defeat the Third Reich, Pius XII never wavered in the conviction that, together with the pagan nationalism and racialism of the Nazis, the atheistic materialism of Soviet Communism constituted one of the great heresies of the modern age. Worse still, Communism's growing appeal in places like Italy and France constituted an immediate strategic threat in the very heart of Christian Europe. With the memory of 1919 always fresh in his mind, Pius XII warned ominously in June 1945 of the "mobs of dispossessed, disillusioned, disappointed and hopeless men" in every corner of the Continent, potential recruits to join what he called "the ranks of revolution and disorder," thus paving the way for "a tyranny no less despotic than those for whose overthrow men planned."

In his speech to the cardinals in June 1945, Pius XII offered a carefully crafted justification of his wartime policies, which turned on a selective reading of the events of the preceding decade. He sought to absolve the church, the papacy, and even the mass of ordinary Germans of responsibility for the crimes of Nazism. He spoke fondly of his time living and working among the German people he loved and admired so much; he described that period as "twelve of the best years of our mature age." His first explicit moral condemnation of Nazism as a "satanic specter" came as part of his attempt to absolve the German people of the sins of the Third Reich. As he had on other occasions during the war, within weeks of the German surrender Pius XII took up the argument against the notion of collective guilt. Choosing his words carefully, he said that he hoped Germany could be reborn after "the guilty have expiated the crimes they have committed." The pope also sought to redeem in the court of public opinion his own policy and that of his predecessor in pursuing formal diplomatic relations with Hitler's Germany in 1933, and preserving formal ties right to the end, despite years of constant tension and repeated violations of the terms of the 1933 agreement. With a certain measure

of defensiveness, Pius XII insisted that the Vatican had long denounced Nazism as incompatible with Christian doctrine, pointing to a stream of "protests" to the German authorities, culminating in the searing papal condemnation of 1937, which, the pope recalled, only made matters worse for the
persecuted German church.

The centerpiece of Pius XII's postwar apologia was that Catholics in Germany and in all of Nazi-occupied Europe—and clergy in particular—had "en-
dured indescribable sufferings for their faith and for their vocation." It was as
if Nazism's greatest crime was that it had declared an unholy war against
Christianity. In a report from August 1945, Pius XII's staff offered a detailed
assessment of the Nazi persecution of Catholics in Germany and in parts of
German-occupied Europe. It served to buttress the evolving narrative of a
Nazi crusade to destroy the Catholic Church. The report reiterated long-
standing complaints dating back to the 1930s about repeated Nazi violations
of the 1933 concordat, the closure of Catholic parochial schools, and the attempt to teach the Nazi *Weltanschauung* in place of the Catholic catechism, as
well as the arrest, confinement, and execution of thousands of priests and
religious. The pattern of persecution carried over into Nazi-occupied Europe, in places like France, Belgium, and Holland. Among the clergy, Pius XII
reasoned, no group had suffered more than Polish clerics—close to 3,000 of
them had been imprisoned in concentration camps, beaten, and tortured,
leaving few survivors by war's end.[4] Indeed, it was thought that people of
faith would find some solace in hoping that the ultimate sacrifice paid by so
many clerics might be taken by God as reparation for Nazi crimes.[5]

In the Shadow of Auschwitz: Pius XII and the Jews after the Shoah

If Pius XII could afford a few words to acknowledge the "unfortunate youth
of Germany" or the valiant martyrdom of Polish priests, then surely the spiritual leader of the Christian world could acknowledge the fate of European
Jews. So reasoned several leading Jewish and Catholic figures in the months
and years after the war. For Jewish authorities, papal support entailed more
than a public statement condemning all forms of anti-Semitism. There were
practical ways in which spirited papal intervention could help the decimated
Jewish communities to recover what they could, physically, culturally, and
spiritually. For Jewish organizations mounting a massive relief effort on be-

half of survivors, the identification and return of Jewish children who had survived the Holocaust by finding shelter in Catholic convents and monasteries or in Catholic families was a top priority.[6] It was impossible to know just how many Jewish children had survived the Holocaust.[7] It was also impossible to know how many of these child survivors were still in Catholic convents or households.[8] The first challenge was to find these children. The survivors, even those who had been baptized as Catholics, had to be returned to their parents, relatives, or appropriate Jewish organizations. For Jewish authorities, raising child survivors as Jews was essential to the survival of the Jewish people.[9]

For the Vatican the matter was not so straightforward. In the first place, neither Jewish organizations nor church officials in Rome or elsewhere in Europe had specific details about how many child survivors were in Catholic hands at the end of the war or even where they were. More challenging, though, was the doctrinal and pastoral dilemma posed by Jewish children who had been baptized as Catholics during the war, some reportedly of their own volition. What was to be done about a Jewish child who had been baptized during the war and whose parents had returned at war's end and were now asking for their child to be returned? What was to be done about Jewish children, baptized or not, who were orphaned?

For Jewish authorities, the answer was obvious, and they resolved to let Pius XII hear it. In September 1945, Leon Kubowitzki, secretary of the World Jewish Congress, went to Rome with the encouragement of the Italian Jewish leader Raffaele Cantoni. Contacts in the American delegation to the Vatican helped Cantoni secure for Kubowitzki a private audience with the pope. Kubowitzki intended to ask Pius XII to issue an authoritative encyclical condemning anti-Semitism, but he also hoped to enlist the pope's help in finding Jewish child survivors in Catholic institutions and directing that they be returned to their families or to Jewish organizations. Representatives of the Italian Jewish community implored Kubowitzki to express their gratitude for papal efforts on their behalf during the war. A hesitant Kubowitzki agreed, realizing that Italian Jews were "truly grateful" to the pope and to Catholics for helping them survive the Nazi occupation.[10]

Far from the cold and aloof caricature of Pacelli that already was taking hold in the popular imagination, Kubowitzki found the pope to be warm and hospitable. "His eyes were shining," Kubowitzki recalled, "and a smile full of kindness weaved round his lips."[11] The two men settled into a cordial but frank conversation with Franklin C. Gowen of Myron Taylor's office listening quietly. To Kubowitzki's expression of gratitude, Pius XII replied simply, "We have done it with all our affection." When Kubowitzki spoke of some six million Jewish victims of the Holocaust, the pope readily acknowledged the nature and extent of the tragedy, saying simply, "It is terrible. And in what cruel way they died." "But now everything is over," Pius XII added; "the persecutions have come to an end." Kubowitzki agreed that the priority now had to be reconstruction, and he made two specific requests of the pope. The first was for a papal statement that addressed some of the theological and biblical roots that undergirded centuries of Christian anti-Jewish sentiment. Pius XII reflected for a moment and said he would consider the matter "with good will." The second request was that any surviving Jewish children in Catholic hands be returned to the Jewish community. According to Kubowitzki's account, the pope was "obviously astonished" to hear of such cases and asked, "But are there many?" Kubowitzki explained that while most child survivors had been returned, Jewish organizations were meeting with "difficulties in certain cases," citing in particular instances in France, Belgium, and Holland. In keeping with his cautious nature, or maybe simply stalling for time, Pius XII asked Kubowitzki to produce a memorandum on the subject and to provide him with statistics. "We should like to study the problem," the pope said. "We shall devote our full attention to it." Kubowitzki promised to deliver just such a report, and the meeting ended on a personal note, with Pius XII asking about the fate of Kubowitzki's own family. Upon hearing that they were well and in America and Belgium, the pope ended the audience, saying, "I was glad to see you. May God Bless you."[12] Kubowitzki thought he detected a "note of triumph or irony" in the pope's smile as the two parted company, but he could not be sure.[13]

The promised memorandum never materialized because quantifiable data proved hard to find.[14] Kubowitzki claimed in later years that after his meeting with the pope, he had attempted to follow up on the various complaints he had heard about Jewish children in the custody of Catholic religious houses. But his investigations came to naught. For the most part, he found, Jewish children had been "recovered by other means," though he did not say what those means were. His account makes it clear that not long after meeting with Pius XII, Kubowitzki concluded that there was nothing substantive to report to the pope; nor was there anything further that the pope could be asked to do to facilitate the return of the child survivors.[15]

That Pius XII and his advisors were at a loss as to how to respond to Jewish concerns over the custody of child survivors was made clear when Gerhart Riegner of the Geneva office of the World Jewish Congress met with Monsignor Montini in November 1945. Evidently Kubowitzki's visit had not done much to sensitize the papal entourage to the issue of child survivors in Catholic institutions. Riegner was in Rome as the WJC representative at a meeting of 25,000 Jewish survivors who had found refuge in Italy. The delegation had come to Rome to meet with Pius XII and to thank him for his efforts on their behalf. Raffaele Cantoni accompanied Riegner to the Vatican to meet with Montini.

The meeting did not go well. Riegner asked for intervention at the highest levels to locate child survivors and return them to their families. The discussion that followed was, in Riegner's words, "extremely painful for me." He said later that it was "one of the most dramatic and unhappy undertakings in my life."[16] Most disconcerting of all was that Montini openly "contested" Riegner's claim that close to a million and a half Jewish children had perished in the Holocaust. Montini thought the figure "inflated." Riegner cited as an example the case of Hungary, where, on the basis of prewar data, one would expect to find 100,000 Jewish children. Instead, Jewish organizations to date had managed to find only 8. Montini scoffed at the claim that hundreds of thousands of children in Hungary and elsewhere in Europe had been killed, saying, "That is not possible. They probably emigrated." Riegner pointed out that tens of thousands of Jewish children in Hungary would have had neither the means nor the freedom to travel very far in Nazi-occupied Central Europe. Montini's stance seemed to soften as the conversation wore on. Riegner had the sense that perhaps only then did Montini begin to comprehend the full scale of the tragedy. Even so, the caution that had long characterized papal diplomacy was evident. As Pius XII had done with Kubowitzki, Montini asked Riegner for specifics. "Point out to me where these children are," Montini reportedly said, "and I will assist you in recovering them." Riegner replied curtly, "If I knew that, I wouldn't need you."[17]

The Jewish leaders who met with the pope did not impute the Vatican's careful response to sinister motives. How, then, to explain the Vatican's hesitant, noncommittal reaction? Surely part of the answer lies in the absence of

solid evidence to document the nature and scale of the issue. Riegner identified the problem as one of perception, a lack of understanding. During
the war and in its immediate aftermath, Riegner reasoned, neither the pope
nor his senior advisors realized just what had happened to the Jews. As
Riegner put it, "Ignorance of the scope of the tragedy persisted. That is a
simple fact."[18]

When he met with Pius XII in March 1946, Isaac Herzog, the chief rabbi
of Palestine, similarly came away with the impression that Pius XII was surprised to hear of the full extent of what Herzog called "the Jewish people's
disaster." The pope also seemed surprised to hear that anti-Semitism was still
widespread in Poland. Like Kubowitzki, Rabbi Herzog had gone to the Vatican not only to ask Pius XII to make a statement condemning anti-Jewish
sentiment, but also to enlist the pope's help in finding child survivors in Catholic care. As before, Pius XII asked first for a memorandum. Herzog detected
something of a diplomatic ploy in this request. In his report of the meeting
Herzog noted, "I asked him to issue a decree [on anti-Semitism] but he hesi-
tated to give this to me. They say he is a diplomat. In this regard, it was once
said of a certain rabbi that he was clever and I said: 'a rabbi should not be
clever, he should be wise.' The Pope is clever . . . he promised to help me if I
ran into difficulties."[19] This time around, though, the requested memorandum was prepared, and Herzog delivered it to the pope a couple of days after
their first meeting. Even with a written report in hand, the pope and his staff
asked for more precise information. Vatican officials told Herzog that the
pope would consider issuing wider directives to church institutions only on
the condition that Herzog himself "investigate the incidents" as he made his
way through Europe.[20]

Herzog set out across war-torn Europe to seek out information on the
fate of Jewish communities everywhere, including child survivors in Catholic
care. He went first to Paris, where he met with papal nuncio Angelo Roncalli,
the future Pope John XXIII. The two men knew each other well from Roncalli's days as nuncio in Istanbul, where he had worked to rescue Jews from
Europe. Although the details of the meeting remain obscure, it seems clear
that after his conversation with Herzog, Roncalli sought the Vatican's guidance on how he and the French bishops should respond to Herzog's request
for assistance. The matter was submitted to the Holy Office, which issued
five directives to guide the local churches.[21] It is telling that in the covering

remarks transmitting the instructions to Roncalli, the Pope's under-secretary of state, Domenico Tardini, began by saying that in the opinion of the "Eminent Fathers" of the Holy Office, "if possible, there should be no response to the Grand Rabbi of Palestine." The Vatican directed church officials not to communicate in writing with Jewish authorities, presumably to avoid committing anything definitive to paper.

When a response was deemed necessary, the first step was for church officials to conduct their own investigations and handle each case separately. Jewish children who had been baptized validly, even if under the auspices of a rescue and shelter effort, were not to be "entrusted to institutions that would not be in a position to guarantee their Christian upbringing." If the children had been given to Catholic institutions or to Catholic families by their parents, and if the parents returned to reclaim them, then those children ought to be returned to their families, but only if the children had not yet been baptized. In the case of orphans who had not been baptized, the church claimed to be responsible for them and so could not abandon them to "any persons who have no rights over them, at least until they are in a position to choose for themselves."[22] The note transmitting the instructions ends with the solemn statement that "this decision of the Holy Congregation of the Holy Office has been approved by the Holy Father."

Jewish leaders were not the only ones dissatisfied with the pope's response, which had the feel of deferral and avoidance rather than spirited moral leadership. The most notable Catholic voice in favor of a papal statement that would come to terms with what had transpired during the Holocaust was that of the renowned French philosopher Jacques Maritain, arguably the most influential Catholic thinker of the twentieth century. His was a prophetic voice in the interwar era urging Catholic thinkers to speak and write about Jews and Judaism in respectful terms and to guard against "all hatred and contempt against the Jewish race and the religion of Israel."[23] Having spent most of the war in exile in the United States, where he had helped to animate the intellectual spirit of the French Resistance, Maritain was tapped by General Charles de Gaulle to serve as French ambassador to the Holy See, a position Maritain occupied between 1945 and 1948.[24]

Given his evolving concern with Catholic responses to the Jewish question, Maritain turned to the Vatican after the war for spiritual leadership in coming to terms with the painful legacy of Christian anti-Semitism, which, he believed, was all too evident in the Holocaust. Writing to Montini in July 1946—in friendship, Maritain said, not as an ambassador, though he must have presumed that his letter would reach the pope—he asked Pius XII to say something about the almost "supernatural" hatred of Nazi anti-Semitism, which had claimed the lives of millions of European Jews in the most "savage" way imaginable. He reminded the Vatican that the Nazis had "liquidated" six million Jews during the war, had "massacred" thousands of Jewish children, and that thousands more had been "torn from their families and stripped of their identity." He asserted, "Nazism proclaimed the necessity of removing Jews from the face of the earth (the only people that it wanted to exterminate *as a people*)," thereby underscoring the unique nature of the Nazi war against the Jews.[25] Maritain acknowledged that the pope had done much during the war to "save and protect the persecuted," and he recognized Pius XII's "condemnations of racism that have won for him the gratitude of Jews and all those who care for the human race." Maritain even claimed that he accepted the "wisdom" of the pope's rationale for not referring specifically to Jews in his wartime pronouncements, lest he make matters worse for the persecuted. But now that Nazism had been defeated, Maritain asked, had not the time come for Pius XII to say something specifically about the enormous tragedy that had befallen European Jews? What Jews and Christians needed above all, he said, was "a voice—the paternal voice, the voice par excellence, that of the Vicar of Jesus Christ—to tell the truth to the world and shed light on this tragedy." In other words, even if others were not willing to speak the truth, the pope should do so.

Maritain was asking Pius XII to lead rather than to follow, to demonstrate moral clarity and spiritual leadership. He left no doubt that in asking this of the pope, he was not only pleading on behalf of the Jews but also defending the integrity and authority of the church's teaching and of its claims to be a witness to truth in the world. He wanted the pope to show courage in acknowledging "the part that many Catholics had in the development of anti-Semitism," and to express "la vraie pensée de l'Église," that is, "the true thought of the Church . . . striking at a cruel and evil error, as well as being a work of justice and reparation."

Evidently Pius XII did not see the logic of, or need for, a papal statement to serve as a work of reparation. That would mean accepting some measure of Catholic responsibility for what had transpired. Pius XII saw no such responsibility, or at least refused to acknowledge it publicly. When the pope and Maritain met just a few days after Maritain sent his letter to Montini, Pius XII assured the French philosopher that the matter had been addressed more than adequately in a meeting with Jewish groups several months earlier.[26] It was settled. Pius XII had said all he was going to say on the matter; a painful chapter of recent history was closed.

Maritain knew otherwise. Just a few weeks earlier, the Polish town of Kielce had witnessed what the *New York Times* called the "worst anti-Semitic outbreak" since the end of the war. In scenes that were eerily similar to episodes from the past, fictitious tales of Jewish ritual murder of gentile children sparked mob violence against local Jews; some forty Jews were killed in the violence.[27] Word of a renewal of anti-Semitic violence, in Europe and beyond, is what had prompted Maritain to approach the Vatican in the first place. A flabbergasted Maritain noted in his diary that the Vatican newspaper was dismissing the Kielce violence as "non racial." It was clear, he wrote, that "Catholic conscience is poisoned" by anti-Semitism and that "something has to be done."[28] In his letter to Montini, Maritain had singled out as especially disconcerting the role that Catholics continued to play in the "development" of anti-Semitism in Europe and also in South America.

Later that summer Maritain met with Leon Kubowitzki in Paris, where the two men exchanged stories of their respective papal encounters. Maritain said that he had found both the pope and Montini "friendly" to the idea of an encyclical on anti-Semitism but added that he suspected the pope and his advisors were "afraid" to take such a decisive step. Maritain purportedly admitted to Kubowitzki that he was profoundly saddened by the pope's "silence" during the war in light of what had happened to the Jews; there was no escaping the fact that Pius XII had made every attempt to avoid speaking directly about the persecution of the Jews, confining himself to statements of a general nature. A confounded Kubowitzki asked Maritain why the pope would not want to have his name associated with such an encyclical. A path-breaking statement on the legacy of Christian anti-Semitism "would have a deep and lasting influence and would be of considerable historic significance." To this Maritain replied, "I would not hesitate to answer in the affirmative, if we were speaking about his predecessor."[29]

There is no mistaking the fact that Pius XII and his advisors were crafting a narrative of heroic papal intervention on behalf of persecuted Jews during the war, which conveyed a clear Catholic conscience in the aftermath of the Holocaust. Even before the war ended, for instance, Monsignor Tardini told officials in Myron Taylor's office that approximately 6,000 Jews in Rome had been given "refuge and succour" by the Vatican during the Nazi occupation of the city. Tardini estimated that between the time the Germans arrived in Rome in early September 1943 and the Allied liberation of the city in early June 1944, some 180 Catholic institutions and religious houses, including pontifical universities, had provided "asylum" to Jews, as well as to several prominent Italian anti-Fascists, some of whom were Communists and Socialists. Tardini told Taylor that the Vatican preferred not to have this information made public for fear of Nazi and Fascist reprisals in occupied territories while the war was still being fought.

The pope and his senior advisors were framing the narrative of papal action on behalf of persecuted Jews lest the story be skewed by elements with a political agenda hostile to the church.[30] In a meeting at the Vatican with the Supreme Arab Council of Palestine in early August 1946, Pius XII ventured further than ever before in speaking of the persecution of European Jews, referring to his many "condemnations" of the "persecutions" that "fanatical anti-Semitism" had unleashed against the Jewish people. Called yet again to take sides in a thorny geopolitical matter, this time over the state of Palestine and the growing impetus for the creation of a Jewish state in the Holy Land, Pius XII made it clear to the Arab leaders, as he had to the Jewish leaders in the preceding months, that he intended to continue his policy of "complete impartiality." He was careful to add, perhaps mindful of the emerging tendency to question his behavior during the war, that the impartiality demanded of the Vicar of Christ did not mean "indifference" to the plight of all peoples, regardless of their ethnic, cultural, or religious background. All peoples could count on Pius XII to help achieve a just and peaceful coexistence.[31]

Part of constructing a narrative of papal action on behalf of Jews entailed widely publicizing praise for Pius XII that came from grateful Jewish communities during and after the war. In February 1944, Rabbi Isaac Herzog wrote to Pius XII saying that the "people of Israel will never forget what His Holiness and his illustrious delegates, inspired by the eternal principles of religion . . . are doing for our unfortunate brothers and sisters in the most tragic hour of our history." Chaim Weizmann, future president of Israel, said during the war that "the Holy See is lending its powerful help whenever it can, to mitigate the fate of my persecuted co-religionists."[32] One of the most evocative expressions of gratitude came from Israel Zolli, the chief rabbi of Rome during the Second World War. Near the end of the war, Zolli claimed to have a mystical experience that led him to convert to Catholicism. By his own admission, he took on Pius XII's Christian name—Eugenio—as a sign of gratitude for the pope's efforts to save thousands of Roman Jews.[33]

Publicly expressed Jewish gratitude carried considerable currency in Vatican circles, which were highly sensitive to the charge of papal inaction. Vatican sources triumphantly reported that expressions of gratitude from Jews everywhere were crossing the pope's desk. At the height of the war, the pope had referred to such appreciation from Jewish organizations as proof that his policies, although unpopular among certain groups, were working in concrete ways to help the persecuted Jews. Writing in April 1943 to Bishop von Preysing of Berlin, who, we know, continued to implore Pius XII to do more on behalf of the remaining German Jews, the pope pointed out how authoritative statements, whether from the bishop of Rome or from the German bishops themselves, could go only so far in influencing the Hitler government. This was another way of saying that private diplomatic channels had been tried, but to no avail. At the same time, Pius XII spoke confidently of the Holy See's charitable work on behalf of "non-Aryan Catholics," as well as those of the Jewish faith. The pope said,

> This action has necessitated a great deal of patience and disinterestedness on the part of the executive arms of Our relief organizations in meeting the expectations—one might even say demands—of those asking for help, and also in overcoming the diplomatic difficulties that have arisen. Let us not speak of the very large sums in American money which We have had to disburse on shipping for emigrants. We gave those sums willingly because the people were in distress. The money was given for love of God, and We were right not to expect gratitude on earth. Nevertheless, Jewish organizations have warmly thanked the Holy See for these rescue operations.[34]

After the war, Pius XII could count on similar expressions of Jewish gratitude to bolster his defense of papal wartime action, and to respond to claims of papal inaction. In late November 1945, *L'Osservatore Romano* reported on a meeting between Pius XII and a delegation from the Congress of Jewish Refugees in Italy, a group composed mainly of Polish Jews recently freed from Nazi concentration camps. The delegation had asked to meet with Pius XII to thank him personally for his "generosity" in offering assistance to Jews during the "terrible period of Nazi-Fascist persecution." In his address to the group, Pius XII studiously avoided any talk of Catholic responsibility for the tragedy that had befallen European Jews, saying only that the "abyss of discord, hatred and persecution" that had opened between "peoples and races" was caused by "doctrines of error and intolerance, which are contrary to the true spirit of human and Christian kindness." He interpreted this visit by a group of Jewish survivors as "an intimate testimonial of the gratitude" to the church and to Catholics who proved themselves able to "rise above narrow and arbitrary limits fixed by selfishness and racial hatreds." Mindful that thorny political questions were already being raised about the future of Europe's diminished Jewish communities, with renewed talk of a Jewish state in the Holy Land, Pius XII insisted that the church could not speak to "questions of a political and territorial character." Instead, it would confine itself to its "religious mission" and to helping furnish "the basis for the solution of those questions with justice and equity." This was a diplomatic way of conveying Pius XII's long-standing reservations about the prospect of a Jewish state in Palestine, which would find more explicit and authoritative expression in the coming years.[35]

The pope's oratory was true to form. His measured statement was pastoral and political, sensitive in its acknowledgment of Jewish suffering yet shrewd in assigning blame for the catastrophe to errors of doctrine that sprang not from the heart of the church but from a fundamental violation of divine law. Yet despite the public projection of confidence and self-assuredness in his response to the Nazi persecution of Jews, in private Pius XII seems to have had some moments of doubt over his decision to restrain his public statements about the Hitler regime, whether about the fate of Jews or about Nazi behavior in general. Writing in his diary in October 1941, Angelo Roncalli recorded that in a meeting with Pius XII, Pacelli had asked him whether the pope's "silence" vis-à-vis Nazism was being misunderstood and judged unfavorably. Writing to the German archbishop Josef Frings in March 1944, Pius XII acknowledged that it was "painfully difficult to decide whether reserve and prudent silence or frank speaking and forceful action are called for."[36] Pius XII obviously wrestled with the nagging doubt that history would judge him harshly for his failure to condemn more directly Nazi atrocities.[37]

Pius XII and the Remaking of Europe

Many critics emerged at war's end to cast stones at Pius XII's wartime leadership, especially at his reluctance to confront the Fascist dictators forcefully in public. The British diplomat Sir Oliver Harvey wrote to D'Arcy Osborne referring to Pius XII as "Mr. Facing-both-Ways, being all things to all men who are not Communists." Harvey's reasoning echoed criticism first seen in Catholic circles in the early weeks of Pacelli's pontificate, namely, that Pius XII "failed to pronounce clearly against German atrocities, or against the fire bombings of civilian populations." For this reason, the British diplomat concluded, the pope's many "fine speeches and exhortations inevitably fall flat." The spiritual father of Catholicism was thus doomed to play a marginal role in postwar world affairs.[38]

In his reply to Harvey, D'Arcy Osborne, who was not above criticizing the pope, said that he found it "difficult" to answer the charges being leveled against him. Osborne knew well that many "good" British Catholics, as he called them, agreed that Pius XII had played an "ignoble role" during the war in his failure to speak out publicly and directly against Nazi atrocities. Yet Osborne admitted a certain measure of understanding of the pope's approach, saying that it arose fundamentally from Pius XII's "attitude of meticulous and seemingly pusillanimous neutrality."

Ironically, perhaps, Osborne had not always been so empathetic in his assessment of the policy of papal neutrality. In a secret report to Prime Minister Winston Churchill in July 1945, Osborne described Pius XII as "timorous, irresolute and averse to irrevocable action." Having observed the pope and his *modus operandi* from a unique and intimate perspective for the duration of the war years, Osborne was conflicted in his assessment of Pius XII. "It is impossible not to admire the saint or to like and respect the man," Osborne wrote. But he admitted that "it is less easy to esteem the diplomat, the politician, the Pontiff."[39]

In his correspondence with Harvey, though, Osborne seems to have returned to his more empathetic perspective on the ever-contested Pius XII, perhaps if only to counter what he saw as excessive, unbalanced, or uninformed criticism. He explained to Harvey that, whatever the impression may be to the outside world, Pius XII "is genuinely convinced . . . that he specifically condemned all Nazi war crimes in his public speeches during the war." Nothing could shake the pope from this opinion, Osborne added. For his own part, Osborne could not agree with Harvey's indictment not simply of Pius XII's silence in the face of Nazi war crimes but also of the pope's seemingly "tender" way of dealing with clerical collaborators—mentioning by name Cardinal Suhard of Paris, Cardinal Innitzer of Vienna, and Archbishop Stepinac of Zagreb. On the matter of the clergy in particular, Osborne saw no point in Harvey's suggestion that the pope ought to have removed Stepinac after his trial and conviction in 1946, as an institutional censure for collaboration with Ante Pavelić's Ustaša regime. As for the charge that Pius XII was "tender" with collaborators such as Marshal Petain of Vichy France, Osborne observed that the Vatican's dealings with the Petain government did not mean that it approved of Petain's policies.

Osborne reasoned that it was difficult for anyone to understand papal policy, let alone lay persons and non-Catholics. There were so many "imponderables" that conditioned papal responses to events well beyond a pope's control. So Pius XII's apparent silence might be the result of his genuine hope that by remaining neutral and above all being seen to remain neutral, the papal office could work constructively to bring about a quick and workable peace settlement. And while certain papal decisions might appear "inscrutable, confusing and, on occasion, reprehensible" to practical minds, Osborne admitted, it should be borne in mind that the Vatican is not only supranational and universal, but also "fourth-dimensional." In other words, when the pope and his advisors assess contemporary events and chart a course for papal policy, they "reckon in centuries and plan for eternity."

Long after he left his post at the Vatican, in fact, amid the gathering controversy over Pius XII's wartime role occasioned by Hochhuth's play *The Deputy,* Osborne offered an exceedingly flattering portrait of the embattled pontiff. "So far from being a cool (which, I suppose implies cold-blooded and inhumane) diplomatist," Osborne wrote in a 1963 letter to *The Times* of London, "Pius XII was the most warmly humane, kind, generous, sympathetic (and, incidentally, saintly) character that it has been my privilege to meet in the course of a long life." Osborne acknowledged, as he had back in 1947, that

Pius XII was concerned with maintaining "meticulous neutrality between the warring countries." He acknowledged too that the pope was pro-German; more precisely, he was "pro-German Catholic." But Osborne had no doubt of Pacelli's sensitivity to the "human suffering" caused by the war, or of the pope's universal compassion and charity for all peoples, "quite irrespective of nationality or faith." He concluded that the enormous challenges facing the wartime pope were exacerbated by the effective limits of his power. After all, Osborne asked, "what could he effectively do?"[40]

General Charles de Gaulle, who met with Pius XII in late June 1944, was impressed by Pacelli's "sensible and powerful" thinking. De Gaulle remarked that Pius XII "judges everything from a perspective that surpasses human beings, their undertakings and their quarrels. . . . One feels that the supernatural burden that he alone carries in the world weighs down on his soul, but he bears it willingly, certain to the end, sure of the way." De Gaulle appreciated Pius XII's "lucid thought," which was focused on "consequences" and on the policy of the church, "on what it does, on its language, on the way it is conducted." For de Gaulle, Pius XII's lucidity in thought and resolute action explained why, as supreme pontiff, "he displays the gifts of authority, of influence, of the eloquence given him by God." De Gaulle concluded effusively, "Pious, compassionate, political—in the highest meaning these can assume— such does this pontiff and sovereign appear to me because of the respect that he inspires in me."[41] No doubt it helped the pope's image that the two men shared a broadly similar vision of a new Europe grounded on cooperative political and economic relations among Germany, France, and Italy.[42]

Still, questions lingered in Allied circles about the wisdom of Pius XII's wartime policies and about his capacity for decisive leadership. Pacelli continued to confound diplomats and intelligence officers who struggled to offer a definitive reading of how he worked. One line of reasoning in intelligence circles had it that Pius XII's "temperament" made him vulnerable to pressure from his small but tightly knit entourage. When Luigi Maglione died in late summer 1944, the pope decided not to appoint a successor, relying instead on the under-secretaries Tardini and Montini. For a time it was rumored that Archbishop Spellman, whom Pius XII named a cardinal in early 1946, was a leading candidate for the position. Everyone knew that Spellman was close to the pope, and, with the growing prestige and influence of American Catholicism, it made sense that an American prelate should be considered for one of the most powerful positions in papal government. Some journalists even mused aloud that there might soon be "an American Pope."[43]

Pius XII never chose a replacement for Maglione, serving out the remainder of his pontificate—some thirteen years—without a secretary of state.[44] This created considerable frustration among the Vatican's diplomatic corps; it also exacerbated the pope's isolation from the other organs of church governance. Whereas Maglione had met with diplomats at least once a week, foreign diplomats could now meet with the pope directly only every few months. Access to the pope became even more difficult as Pius XII faced recurring bouts of serious illness. Writing to the French Foreign Office in early 1954, French Ambassador Wladimir d'Ormesson reported that a kind of "absolute dictatorship" had come to characterize Pius XII's pontificate, though he admitted readily that it was a rather benign and mild form of rule. This was to be expected, given the pope's "sensitive and hesitant" temperament and his reputation for deliberating carefully, to the point of procrastinating, but it was a form of dictatorship all the same, which saw Pius XII growing ever more detached from the day-to-day life of the church.[45]

Even some high-ranking cardinals, including the prefects who ran the curial offices in Rome that administered church affairs around the world, could not conceal their frustration with the management of the papal schedule and the increased difficulty in gaining direct access to the pope. The powerful French cardinal Eugène Tisserant complained to the French ambassador that the pope was too involved and yet simultaneously too detached from the administration of church affairs. On the one hand, Pius XII seemed almost obsessed by the diplomatic files, scrupulously reviewing even minor dispatches; on the other hand, the prefects of the various Congregations met with the pope only every two weeks or so. Even then, the meetings were said to be rather perfunctory, with the pope seeming to pass over important substantive discussions.[46]

Others who worked closely with Pius XII on a daily basis complained that while the pope was a careful and deliberative leader, he at times exhibited prudence and caution that could translate into inaction or procrastination. Father Leiber, the Jesuit priest who enjoyed privileged access to Pius XII, admired Pacelli deeply but felt the pope was overly sensitive and a perfectionist, all of which detracted from his capacity to be a truly great leader.[47]

It was no secret that Pius XII was a solitary figure, maintaining great reserve even among his closest associates. Father Leiber once said the pope rarely ever spoke to his advisors in a "leisurely, relaxed manner." As closely as he worked with Tardini and Montini, it is said that Pius XII probably dined with them only once in ten years.[48] Pius XII certainly guarded his thoughts jealously, especially those pertaining to individuals who worked in church administration. As Leiber put it, Pius XII "was most careful not to give a judgment about these personalities, especially if it could be interpreted less favorably."[49] Despite his preference for solitude, Pius XII surrounded himself with an inner circle of close advisors, official and unofficial, who made up the rather confined and rarified world Pius XII occupied in the last decade of his life. The pope's most intimate circle was dominated not by staff members of the Secretariat like Tardini or Montini but by the German Jesuits Robert Leiber, Wilhelm Hentrich, and Ivo Zeiger. Even Pius XII's personal confessor, Augustin Bea, was a German Jesuit. Originally from Baden, Bea taught Scripture studies at the prestigious Pontifical Gregorian University in Rome and the Pontifical Biblical Institute. It was to Bea that Pius XII turned for assistance in compiling the 1943 encyclical, *Divino Afflante Spiritu*, which *Time* magazine once described as akin to a "declaration of independence" for Catholic biblical scholars."[50] Bea, who was named a cardinal in 1959, was one of the leading figures of the Second Vatican Council and a pioneer in Catholic-Jewish relations.

Mother Pascalina Lehnert and the other German-speaking sisters of the papal household rounded out the German contingent that dominated Pius XII's inner circle.[51] The pope also relied on the counsel of clerical confidants such as Cardinal Franceso Marchetti Selvaggiani and Monsignor Ludwig Kaas, who had been in Rome by Pacelli's side since 1933. The American prelate Monsignor Francis Spellman, then archbishop of New York and, like Kaas, a friend and confidant to Pacelli since the 1920s, was said by American intelligence officials to be "the only friend of the Pope who can dine with him." This was no small feat given Pacelli's obsessive preference for dining alone.[52] Among lay persons, the pope's nephew Carlo Pacelli and Vatican City director Enrico Galeazzi enjoyed privileged access to Pius XII, meeting with him frequently, almost every evening at the height of the war. That Pius XII relied on his nephew to handle high-level matters was made clear when he sent

Carlo to North America after the war to secure material aid for Italian reconstruction—part of the pope's efforts to procure resources from abroad in order to stem rising Communist fortunes in Europe.

On the eve of the 1952 local elections in Rome, in which the Communist and Socialist parties threatened to win power, Pius XII relied on his informal network of trusted confidants to convey his policies. Having resolved to encourage Italy's Christian Democrats to countenance an electoral alliance with the parties of the Right as part of a great Center-Right, anti-Communist coalition in the elections, Pius XII asked the Jesuit priest Father Riccardo Lombardi to speak directly with Alcide De Gasperi to urge the Christian Democratic leader to consider an electoral alliance with the Right.[53] De Gasperi dismissed the idea as politically dangerous to the long-term viability of a centrist Catholic party in postwar Italian politics.

Apparently disappointed with the premier's response, Pius XII ordered Lombardi to pay De Gasperi's wife a visit, or so the Jesuit recorded in his diary. If direct pressure from the Vatican on the leader of the Christian Democrats would not work, surely his wife, Francesca, herself a devout Catholic, would be easier to persuade. Lombardi traveled to the De Gasperi country home outside Rome, not far from the papal summer residence at Castel Gandolfo. It was a decidedly unpleasant encounter. Lombardi, who was renowned for his thundering public exhortations, recorded in his diary that he found himself literally "screaming" at De Gasperi's wife, who responded in kind; it was enough to attract the concern of puzzled police officers standing nearby. Like her husband, Francesca De Gasperi saw in Lombardi's machinations the ugly side of ecclesiastical interference in political affairs.[54]

Through this tightly controlled but unofficial network the pope's postwar policies were communicated to other Vatican offices. The role of the German Jesuit Ivo Zeiger in helping to apply papal policy after the war offers another example of decision-making in Pius XII's inner circle. Zeiger was a former rector of the German College in Rome and a widely respected expert in church law. Pius XII appointed him to the Vatican Mission in Kronberg in 1945, working alongside American bishop Aloisius Muench to organize the massive papal relief effort in Germany and address the tricky question of church-state relations in a country occupied by foreign powers. Papal relief work entailed an unprecedented mobilization of material resources, money above all. The campaign was a tremendous success. Muench helped to procure close to five million dollars, much of it from the charitable donations of American Catholics.[55]

Father Zeiger was something of an *éminence grise* in Pacelli's inner circle. By virtue of his training and extensive network of contacts, he exercised significant if underestimated influence over papal policy. It helped that Zeiger was well known in church circles in Rome and above all that he enjoyed Pius XII's personal trust. As Father Leiber noted, "Zeiger knew Rome." He was fluent in Italian, having lived and worked in the city for years. He had an intimate knowledge of the inner workings of church governance, and he had contacts in clerical circles in and around the Vatican. Of course, Zeiger knew his own country just as well if not better and appreciated the challenges a defeated Germany now faced.[56]

Zeiger's personal relationship with Pius XII dated back to the 1930s, when he worked closely with the future pope and Monsignor Kaas to finalize the details of the 1933 *Reichskonkordat*. The pope's personal trust went a long way after 1945 to magnifying Zeiger's importance. Although other people assigned to the Vatican Mission in Kronberg were nominally more powerful, it was Zeiger who had direct access to Pius XII and also to the German bishops. This made him an indispensable conduit between the Vatican and the bishops on the ground, and Pius XII had long placed enormous stock in preserving the relationship between the German bishops and the bishop of Rome. In the words of Monsignor Alberto Giovanetti of the Vatican's Secretariat of State, who worked on papal relief in Germany, Zeiger may have had no formal title in the papal relief commission's work, but he was for all intents and purposes "the real man of the Mission" because of the practical authority invested in him by Pius XII. Even Bishop Muench, who carried the formal title as the pope's representative to Germany, relied on Zeiger to deliver reports on the situation of the German church directly to Pius XII.

Muench learned quickly that this was just as Pius XII wanted it, that the pope preferred to work directly through Leiber, Zeiger, and Pascalina Lehnert. The fact that Mother Pascalina was in charge of the vast Vatican warehouse filled with material supplies—food, clothing, printing paper, Bibles, and catechism books—coupled with her unfettered access to the pope, gave the indomitable Pascalina Lehnert far greater influence than her position as papal housekeeper would suggest. Of all the people surrounding Pius XII, Bishop Muench discovered, it was Mother Pascalina who was to be "informed of all developments" and kept abreast of conditions in Germany.[57] Even into the 1950s, after Muench had been appointed officially as papal nuncio in West Germany, Mother Pascalina remained an important Vatican conduit on matters related to postwar Germany's social and economic recovery.[58] As Muench came to appreciate, Pius XII's housekeeper seemed to have a hand in virtually everything that transpired in and around the pope.

This included his concern for the situation in Germany, which the pope had declared to be his top priority at the end of the war. Meeting in July 1946 to discuss the future of papal relief efforts in Germany, Muench remarked on Pius XII's "great love" for the German people, who faced enormous challenges. Although he rejected outright the notion of a collective German guilt for the crimes of Nazism, Pius XII was not oblivious to the destructive legacy of Hitler's regime; nor was he insensitive to the logic of holding Germany accountable in some way for its actions. In an address to the cardinals in early June 1947, the pope put it plainly: "We well know indeed the extent and the gravity of the unspeakable horrors with which a defeated system covered the face of Europe; nor do We wish to lessen the enormity of its guilt." But it was dangerous for the victors to think they could or should act with impunity in dealing with the vanquished. To ensure a lasting peace, Pius XII insisted, the victors should take care to avoid employing the very tactics for which the vanquished were being punished.[59]

It did not take long for Muench to realize that the pope's heart and mind were still very much in Germany. He recorded in his diary in November 1948 that Pius XII was "more interested in affairs of [the] Church in Germany than in any other part of the Church." Another Vatican insider told Muench that Pius XII had no faults other than "that he loves Germans too much."[60] It was about more than loving the Germans too much—Pius XII made a speedy resolution of the postwar German crisis a top priority. The problems facing a defeated, demoralized, and occupied Germany were enormous: an acute refugee crisis that exacerbated conditions of poverty, hunger, and disease; thorny questions about the fate of prisoners-of-war and accused war criminals; the severe "disruptions" to the internal organization and communal life of German Catholicism; and Germany's politically uncertain future, which also meant uncertainty for the future of church-state relations, an issue especially close to Pius XII's heart.[61]

The pope obviously clung to the memory of his experiences as a nuncio in Germany, so much so that his policy toward that country after 1945 was driven by assumptions and expectations that had been formed decades earlier under different circumstances. One veteran Vatican watcher quipped to Muench that the pope evidently "thinks that he is still nuncio in Germany."[62] Nowhere was this more problematic than in the pope's attitude on the status of the 1933 concordat. Pius XII reasoned that the agreement he had negotiated in good faith with the legitimate German government of the day remained valid even after the fall of Hitler's Germany, and so should be incorporated into any future constitutional arrangement to emerge for a new German state. It remained one of the core principles of Pacelli's political philosophy: the first and essential condition for the freedom and vitality of German Catholicism rested on a legal formula to regulate church-state relations. Pius XII urged his representatives to hold firm in defending against any serious or unilateral revision to the substance of the 1933 agreement. He warned Muench not to allow himself to be intimidated by his German counterparts.

Pius XII knew from his own experience as nuncio that one should "talk up to Germans, stand firm."[63] There was no disputing Pacelli's success as nuncio in the 1920s in formalizing historic agreements with governments in Bavaria and Prussia. But the situation had changed by the late 1940s. Even some of his advisors complained that Pius XII failed to appreciate fully the sea change in German politics wrought by Nazism, its defeat in war, and the foreign occupation that followed. As Muench confided to his diary, the German federal republic that was taking shape in the years after 1945 did not have the same power or freedom of action as previous German states. However, Pius XII refused to recognize just how unprecedented the situation was after 1945.[64] Just as when he was nuncio, and then through his years as Vatican secretary of state, Pacelli trusted himself more than anyone to understand German affairs and to defend the interests of German Catholicism.

The Cold Warrior

Pius XII proved himself similarly capable of combative leadership in the great confrontation with Communism after 1945. It was not opposition at any cost. He continued to hold fast to one of the fundamental principles of his political philosophy: to work with any form of government, irrespective of ideology, toward workable, mutually beneficial accommodations between church and state. The result was something of a hybrid papal response to the Communist threat in Europe and elsewhere in the world, one that was bound to alienate supporters and critics alike.

Pius XII was unmistakably alarmed about the potential spread of Communism in Western Europe and the Americas. In the words of the French ambassador Wladimir d'Ormesson, Pius XII was "obsessed" with the Communist threat.[65] Luigi Gedda, one of the leading lay persons in Italy's Catholic Action movement, recalled being summoned to the Vatican by a worried Pius XII in late January 1948. It was at the start of an intense campaign to elect the first parliament of Italy's post-Fascist republic, and the Italian Communist and Socialist parties seemed to be headed for certain victory at the polls. Pius XII was visibly agitated at the prospect of a Communist electoral victory, and frustrated by the seeming inability of the Christian Democrats, the Catholic party, to stem the rising Communist fortunes. In desperation, he turned to the ostensibly apolitical Catholic Action, an organization of Catholic laity, to help get out the Catholic vote against the Leftist parties. For Pius XII, the prospect of a Communist victory in Italy was unthinkable. The pope made it clear to Gedda that there was too much at stake in these elections to leave Catholic interests in the hands of the fractious and seemingly inept Christian Democrats. Worried that it was too late to stem the Communist tide, Pius XII readily deferred to Gedda's superior organizing skills. The pope appreciated in particular Gedda's original ideas for using mass media and the existing capillary networks of Catholic Action to get out the Catholic vote, especially in the south.[66] In fact, to do what he could to thwart a Communist victory at the polls, Pius XII instructed one of his nephews to visit the United States and Canada on the eve of the vote, hoping to procure grain to alleviate the food shortage, which Pius XII believed was one of the material causes of rising Communist popularity.[67]

Pius XII's anxiety over the Communist threat was predictable enough, given his memory of the toxic dynamic created by revolutionary ferment in Germany and the reaction to it when Hitler's political career began in the early 1920s. Before the war's end, Pius XII and his staff already were hearing that in areas under Soviet control Polish Catholics were facing persecution and harassment from a different but equally implacable enemy. Reports told eerily familiar accounts of Catholic priests being arrested and held incommunicado, and of "subtle efforts" by Polish authorities to "undermine" the church's position in Polish society. Poland was only the beginning. Pius XII and his advisors watched anxiously as Communist parties, backed by Moscow, came to influence and eventually control Hungary and other heavily Catholic countries in Eastern and Central Europe. There were also growing fears for the religious freedoms of Catholic minorities in Yugoslavia, Albania, and elsewhere.[68]

Faced with obvious Soviet transgressions of religious freedoms and the norms of civility and decency, Pius XII displayed a remarkable capacity for forceful public opposition, as well as energy and imagination in rallying an array of instruments—spiritual and political—to arm a new generation of Christ's soldiers. In his annual Christmas address of 1946, for instance, he was clearly attacking the increasingly popular Italian Communist and Socialist parties—both of which had close ties to Moscow—when he told Italians that the choice they faced as voters was "to be either with Christ, or against Christ."[69] It was a stark admonition to voters in an overwhelming Catholic country to reflect well on the spiritual consequences of an ostensibly political choice.

The soldiers of Christ had been summoned to battle again. When in December 1948 Communist officials in Hungary tried Cardinal Jozsef Mindszenty for treason and sentenced him to life imprisonment, Pius XII showed no hesitation. In mid-February 1949, the pope convened a special meeting of the College of Cardinals to address the Mindszenty case. The solemn venue was meant to underscore the gravity of the situation and the depths of the pope's alarm and anger. Later that month, he addressed the people of Rome, telling them of the "cry of indignation" that the arrest had elicited from the bishop of Rome. "Can the Pope be silent," Pius XII asked, "when a State, exceeding the limits of its competence, arrogates to itself the power to suppress dioceses, to depose Bishops, to upset the organization of the Church, and to reduce it below the minimum requirements for the effective cure of souls?" Gone was any trace of that circumspection that the world had come to expect of Pius XII's speeches during the war. Here, finally, was the kind of address so many people had been hoping for when the full brunt of Nazi occupation was bearing down on helpless civilian populations, especially the Jews.

American diplomats familiar with papal circles believed that the pope had deliberately adopted an unambiguously combative approach. Those at the

Vatican reported that he was gratified by the enthusiastic public response to his address, seeing it as confirmation of his decision to speak publicly in such unequivocal ways. The time for accommodation and engagement, it seemed, was over. As one diplomat put it, Pius XII's "tone and bearing was that of a militant leader who was prepared to engage the enemy at whatever cost."[70] Not content simply to cast off the mask of public neutrality or maintain oratorical restraint, the pope approved in July 1949 a controversial move by the Holy Office to threaten with excommunication anyone with known Communist affiliations.[71] This was as clear an indication as any of Pius XII's determination to combat Communism with every means at his disposal, in this case using a rare and powerful form of internal punishment reserved for the gravest of ecclesiastical crimes. It was expected to have the greatest force in France and Italy, where, the pope knew, a growing number of Catholics, clerics even, were flirting openly with movements and ideas that espoused radical social change. With France and Italy boasting the largest Communist parties in the Western world, talk of a Communist victory at the ballot box was no mere fantasy.

Exacerbating the pope's anxiety was the widespread assumption in certain Vatican circles—namely, among a group of Jesuits associated with the influential journal *La Civiltà Cattolica*—that "fifth columns" of Soviet Communism were active in Western Europe, poised to exploit widespread popular discontent and social crisis to serve the cause of Soviet expansion. Often referred to as the *partito romano,* the Roman faction, this group of Vatican insiders, whose leading exponent was Cardinal Alfredo Ottaviani of the Holy Office, urged Pius XII to forge an even closer alliance with Western governments, especially the Truman administration, as part of a multifront crusade to defend Western civilization.[72] By virtue of its clerical training and cultural outlook, the Roman faction saw the pope—a Roman born and bred—as its ideal leader.[73]

As we have seen from his responses to the 1948 Italian election, it was no secret to anyone that Pius XII shared the Roman faction's mistrust of Italy's Christian Democrats. This, despite the party's growing electoral fortunes during Italy's democratic transition. Although it was the dominant party of politically active Catholics, it contained internal currents on both the Left and the Right of the political spectrum. Because of what he perceived to be its fractious and at times indecisive nature, Pius XII had serious doubts about the party's capacity to confront the domestic Communist menace. He was concerned, too, that its leader, the devoutly Catholic Alcide De Gasperi, was prone to consider hazardous political coalitions with Italy's growing Communist and Socialist parties. One of Italy's most dominant postwar politicians, the enigmatic Giulio Andreotti, recalled that Pius XII thought of Christian Democracy as a political means to achieve religious ends. Apparently, American observers who first became acquainted with Italy's nascent Christian Democracy in the last year of the Second World War similarly assumed that political Catholicism in Italy was a branch of the Vatican, with De Gasperi as a kind of "Vatican spokesperson." It would take time and considerable effort by De Gasperi and his allies to convince the Americans otherwise.[74]

Pius XII knew well that De Gasperi was too independent to take orders from the Vatican, let alone to act as its spokesperson. He did not much trust De Gasperi or the entire enterprise of creating a vibrant, autonomous political party to act as a Catholic voice in the public realm. The pope had what Giulio Andreotti described as an unyielding philosophy about Catholics in politics, which made him deeply suspicious of a Catholic political party that was open to working with its political opponents.[75] Pius XII was also wary of certain reformist currents within Christian Democracy, which tended to the moderate Left of the political spectrum and had included vocal critics of the Vatican's approach to Mussolini's Italy in the interwar era. Notable among them was the Sicilian priest Luigi Sturzo, a politician who was forced into exile in the early 1920s for his criticism of Fascism and the church's policy of accommodation with the Mussolini regime. When in 1945 Sturzo, who was living in the United States, expressed the hope of returning to Italy, Pius XII balked at the idea. It was not just that Sturzo had long refused to accept on principle the terms of the Vatican's 1929 treaty with Italy. Pius XII also worried that if Sturzo trumpeted a pro-republican line at a time when Italians were deciding the fate of their monarchy, Pius XII would be in the uncomfortable position of having to defend the monarchy. The pope apparently feared that this would split Catholic loyalties and lead to the creation of a Catholic monarchist party, an eventuality that neither the pope nor De Gasperi welcomed. Nor did it help Sturzo that Pius XII felt him to be too lax about the dangers of Communism and too friendly with the Left.[76] Sturzo did return to Italy in 1946 and eventually was named senator for life in the Italian parliament, where he continued to defend the ideal of an autonomous

Catholic political movement working to preserve and promote parliamentary democracy and freedom.[77]

De Gasperi, like Sturzo before him, felt the personal sting of papal disapproval. As we have seen, on the eve of critical local elections in Rome scheduled for 1952, Pius XII and exponents of the Roman faction urged the Christian Democrats to consider forming a broad electoral alliance with parties of the Right, including those with monarchist and even neo-Fascist sympathies. A victory for the Communist and Socialist parties in the capital of the Catholic world in the midst of the heightening tensions of the Cold War would have represented a stinging defeat and embarrassment for the Vatican.[78]

Pius XII made no secret of his anxiety over the outcome of these local elections and the serious repercussions for Italy and the world should the Communist and Socialist parties score a symbolic victory at the polls. He told one Christian Democratic parliamentarian in the fall of 1951 that "things are going badly." The pope was especially worried about news reaching him from across Italy of "Communist activity which grows ever more audacious," spurred on, he said, by the movement's "growing numbers." Pius XII wanted the Catholic politicians to be "stronger" in facing down the Communist threat; what was needed especially, the pope said, was for decisive action on the part of Italy's Christian Democratic rulers to address the underlying issues that were fueling the rising Communist prospects.[79] In a conversation with Father Riccardo Lombardi—often referred to as "God's microphone" for his oratorical flair and evangelical fervor—Pius XII acknowledged that the Jesuit was right in saying that the church in Italy was in need of reform and renewal, but the most pressing challenges were political. Talk of reform, renewal, and revival were all well and good, the pope acknowledged, but the immediate problem was the pending elections in Rome. "If the Communists win in Rome, in Italy," Pius XII warned, "it will cast a shadow on the entire world: France would become Communist, and then Spain and then all of Europe."[80]

De Gasperi held his ground in the face of considerable political and personal pressure from the Roman faction. One source of pressure was the bombastic Father Lombardi, whose confrontation with Francesca De Gasperi, while typical of his style, was viewed with disfavor in Vatican circles. In fact, a few months after the meeting with De Gasperi's wife, Lombardi met with the pope and spoke in such an intemperate manner that Pius XII decided that it was best never again to meet with Lombardi one-on-one.[81] More serious and direct pressure on De Gasperi came from Monsignor Pietro Pavan, a professor at the Lateran pontifical university and an expert on Catholic social thought. Pavan's work was well known to Montini and others at the Secretariat of State.[82]

In late 1951 Pavan was tapped by Monsignor Tardini to approach De Gasperi to discuss the state of Italian political affairs. The first meeting took place at De Gasperi's apartment in central Rome in early December 1951.[83] It was, as Pavan recorded, a cordial and respectful meeting. Pavan explained that he had come at the pope's behest to convey to the Italian leader Pius XII's "great concern" about the pending local elections in Rome and the consequences for the papacy and the church if the parties of the "extreme Left" won power.

De Gasperi responded that while he could appreciate the pope's anxiety, he felt Pius XII was not being fully informed of all the good work the government was doing to promote Italian reconstruction and, by extension, alleviate the conditions that were fueling rising Communist popularity. He politely rejected the pope's suggestion of a rapprochement with the parties of the Right, especially the neo-Fascist Italian Social Movement. De Gasperi said he was convinced that the "healthy forces" eventually would win. He also pointed out that since the Communist and Socialist parties could claim upward of 40 percent of the popular vote, removing them from the political scene could provoke a "civil war," which in turn could spread beyond Italy's borders.[84]

Pavan reminded De Gasperi that on these last points, the pope was clear: Communism was "enemy number 1." Without saying so directly, the Vatican was telling De Gasperi to worry less about the threat of neo-Fascism and more about the clear and present danger posed by Italy's Left parties. In a tone that was half-joking, half-serious, De Gasperi pointed out to Monsignor Pavan that if the Communists were to come to power, even if briefly, De Gasperi would be the first to be hanged.[85]

Eventually the pope relented, and the vague plans for some kind of anti-Communist electoral front for the Rome elections never materialized.[86] The entire episode provides important insights into Pius XII's mind-set and *modus operandi*. Clearly, he feared a Communist victory in Rome or Italy, and he doubted whether the Christian Democrats could defend church interests adequately in the public realm. So great was his anxiety about the Communist threat, and so deep was his suspicion about the Christian Democrats, that he was persuaded to consider a politically volatile electoral alliance that could have compromised the integrity of Italian political Catholicism at a delicate moment in Italy's postwar history. Yet when he came up against De Gasperi's principled opposition and realized that dissension in the Catholic ranks would only hasten a Communist victory, his habitual pragmatism won out, and he quietly dropped the matter. For all of his misgivings about De Gasperi and the Christian Democrats, the pope realized that they remained the strongest, surest voice for the church in Italian politics. He concluded that there was little to be gained, and much to be lost, by dissension in the Catholic ranks. And Pacelli had never been one to insist on getting his way when he saw that it was futile or counterproductive.

Even still, Pius XII did not easily forgive De Gasperi's intransigence. In June 1952, after the much-anticipated Rome elections saw De Gasperi's centrist line affirmed, the Italian leader asked for an audience with Pius XII, hoping for papal blessings on the occasion of his thirtieth wedding anniversary. It was a deeply personal request from a devout Catholic, not a political request from the leader of the Italian government. The pope refused. It fell to Montini, who shared De Gasperi's centrist orientation, to explain that Pius XII thought it inopportune so soon after the Rome elections to meet with the leader of the Christian Democrats. Such a meeting, he said, would give the impression of papal support for the victors, while reinforcing the mistaken impression of collusion between the Vatican and the Christian Democrats. In reality, it was nothing more than a deliberate snub, and De Gasperi knew it. He made it clear through Italian officials at the Holy See that whatever his personal feeling, the Vatican had to answer to the Italian people for the snub. "As a Christian I accept the humiliation," De Gasperi wrote, but as head of the Italian government and as Italy's foreign minister, "the dignity and authority that I represent and which I cannot shed even in private matters, demands that I express my astonishment at such a remarkable refusal, and . . . reserve the right to ask the Secretariat of State for clarification."[87]

Pius XII may have come to regret the way he had treated De Gasperi in the wake of the Rome elections. Toward the middle of August 1952, he sent Monsignor Pavan to meet with De Gasperi a second time, ostensibly to discuss a possible electoral alliance between the Christian Democrats and monarchist elements in future elections. Again, De Gasperi held his ground. His party was oriented along Center-Left lines, he said, but open to the Right. Since it did not have the numbers to govern alone, it depended on the political support of a number of diverse political factions. If the party were to affiliate exclusively with parties of either Right or Left, De Gasperi reasoned, it would be torn by internal divisions and bereft of key electoral support from its broad base of solidly centrist voters. Any move to either extreme of the political spectrum would be the death knell of the Christian Democratic experiment.

Monsignor Pavan thought it best for De Gasperi to meet directly with Pius XII to explain this philosophy. It may be that the pope was reaching out to De Gasperi, through an intermediary, to make up for his slight to the Italian leader back in June. With the unpleasant memory of that episode still fresh in his mind, De Gasperi was cautious but tactful. He said that he more than welcomed a meeting with the pope, but he underscored that as leader of his party and as head of the government, he would not take the risk of asking for a meeting unless he was assured that it would be granted. An emotional De Gasperi added that if Pius XII judged his political approach to be mistaken, then the veteran Catholic politician would retire from public life. "I am a Christian," De Gasperi said, "and I am nearing the end of my days and never will I act against the expressed will of the Holy Father." While no doubt sincere, De Gasperi may have been posturing, sending the pope a subtle reminder of his unquestionable success in laying the foundations for the Christian Democrats' dominance of Italian political life.[88]

Some Vatican insiders, including Montini, cautioned against aligning the papacy too closely with any one party, government, or bloc of states. Not that anyone at the Vatican had any serious doubts that mutual interest dictated a close working relationship between the Holy See and the Western powers, especially the United States. It was clear enough in the aftermath of the war that defending Christian civilization in a renewed Europe would depend on the military and financial might of the emerging superpower of the Western world. So enthusiastic was the pope about the prospect of American financial backing for European reconstruction in the form of the Marshall Plan that Monsignor Montini described Pius XII as "almost American."[89] Pius knew how much European recovery depended on the generosity of the American government and people.[90]

For all its pretense at neutrality, the Vatican realized that its interests coincided more generally with those of the Truman administration and the Western capitalist democracies. This did not mean, though, that the pope was prepared to sacrifice the papal neutrality he had defended so assiduously. Pius XII was obsessed about the red menace, but he was too temperate to allow it to cloud his judgment to the point of abandoning what had long been a signature of his diplomatic style and political philosophy: engagement and conciliation with secular governments, irrespective of their ideological or political nature.[91] He was too much the pragmatist, too much of a realist, to believe that a bona fide crusade against Soviet Communism, waged on various fronts and through various means, was either desirable or feasible. So while Pius XII would play the part of anti-Communist crusader, he also kept open the lines of communication with the Communist world—and more specifically with the ordinary people in Communist countries—hoping to avoid irrevocable ruptures that would serve no one's interest.[92] He declared in his Christmas address of 1951 that those who demanded of the church a "renunciation of her neutrality and a definite election in favor of one or the other side" failed to understand that the church was a mystical entity, not an "earthly power" or "world empire." Consequently, Pius XII said, "there can be no question of the Church renouncing her political neutrality for the simple reason she cannot serve purely political interests."[93]

As he had during World War Two, then, Pius XII would attempt to steer papal diplomacy deftly down a path of political neutrality between the two emerging power blocs. Once again, however, pretensions to papal neutrality would prove both elusive and illusory.[94] For one, Pius XII was shrewd enough to realize that, in the initial postwar period at least, Vatican and Catholic interests throughout Europe coincided most closely with those of the Western powers, especially the United States. It was more than a matter of a shared aversion to Communism. As we saw above, Pius XII and his men knew that Europe's material reconstruction—which they considered the most obvious way to stem the rise of Communism—depended ultimately on growing U.S. economic clout and the willingness of the United States to expend its wealth strategically. At the same time, there were limits to Vatican–U.S. cooperation in the crusade against Communism in Central and Eastern Europe. The Americans might be content with a would-be policy of containment, but the Holy See could not afford such limitations, ever-more mindful of the vulnerable condition of Catholic interests in Communist regimes everywhere. In fact, some historians argue that by 1948 the Catholic Church was effectively on its own when it came to dealing with Communism behind the Iron Curtain.[95]

Further eroding papal claims to neutrality between the two blocs was the mutually reinforcing dynamic of increasing Communist control and outright persecution of the Catholic Church in Eastern Europe, and Pius XII's hardline response, which was to reject the possibility of Catholic collaboration of any kind with Communist parties and regimes.[96] In practice, taking a hardline stance against Communist regimes in places like Poland and Hungary put Catholic leaders and institutions in those countries in difficult, perhaps even untenable positions. After all, what was true of the Catholic Church in Nazi Germany was true of the church in many Communist-bloc countries where cooperation with Communist officials was the best way to avoid increased repression.[97] Many Catholics in the Communist bloc—from bishops to the laity—did appreciate the pope's resolute spiritual leadership and discerned in his private dealings with them the same measure of trust and discretion he had shown the German bishops who had written to Rome during World War Two seeking guidance on how best to respond to German occupation.[98]

Even still, the 1950 decision of the Polish hierarchy, led by the new primate Archbishop Stefan Wyszynski, to conclude a formal agreement with the Polish government met with Pius XII's sharp disapproval. The Polish bishops had not sought let alone received the Vatican's approval to conclude such an agreement, and now, the Holy See feared, Catholic leaders elsewhere would see fit to follow suit. Domenico Tardini expressed the sentiment of the papal court when he remarked to the British representative at the Vatican that the decision by the Polish hierarchy was "simply disastrous." Faced with the stark and unenviable choice of publicly denouncing the agreement or saying nothing, Pius XII and his diplomats said nothing.[99]

The fact that Poland's most powerful Catholic prelate was arrested in 1953 and imprisoned for several years would seem to vindicate Pius XII's reasoning that hopes for a *modus vivendi* between the church and Communist regimes were illusory. The story goes that when Wyszynski, whom Pius XII had named a cardinal in 1953, went to Rome in 1957, after having been released from prison the previous year, he was snubbed by Pius XII. Some reports suggested that Wyszynski had to wait almost a full week before the pope would agree to see him. The Communist press seized on the story and distorted the facts so that what was an entirely expected delay was inflated into a story of papal disapproval for Wyszynski's policy of engagement with the Polish state.

In later years, when asked about the incident, Cardinal Wyszynski scoffed at talk of a papal snub, insisting that, far from being given the cold shoulder by Pius XII, he had found a warm and emotional welcome at the papal court. Pius XII, he said, had wept openly for the fate of the Polish church. During Wyszynski's installation as cardinal, a visibly shaken pope had told him that for someone who had known three years in prison, there was added significance to the tradition which says that the deep red of the cardinal's cap symbolized a readiness to shed blood for the faith.[100]

If there was any lingering animosity between Pius XII and Cardinal Wyszynski stemming from their disagreement about how best to deal with Communist regimes, it was not apparent when Pius XII was being considered for sainthood after his death. Wyszynski described Pius XII as "an exceptional man" with "eminent Christian virtue," and he defended the pope's approach during the heady early years of the Cold War, especially in the 1950s, when Pius XII avoided making speeches that dealt too explicitly with the delicate political situation in Poland, focusing instead on matters of a religious or pastoral nature.[101]

Pius XII's response to Wyszynski when he became a cardinal suggests that there may be something to the claim that in the last years of his life, the combative cold warrior of the immediate postwar era gradually adopted a more conciliatory approach in dealing with the Communist world. Some historians argue that after the excommunication order issued by the Holy Office in 1949, Pius XII began sending signals to Communist leaders in the Soviet Union and throughout Eastern and Central Europe of the Vatican's willingness to work toward an accommodation between church and state behind the Iron Curtain. A telling gesture of the pope's opening to the East came in July 1952, when Pius XII issued an open letter to the people of Russia. It followed his letter earlier that year to the Catholic Church in China. In tone and style, these papal messages to peoples living under Communist regimes bore obvious similarities to earlier addresses directed to those living under Nazism. While he intended to signal the Vatican's willingness to deal with the legitimate political authority of the day, the pope also made it clear that any accommodation between church and state presupposed certain fundamental principles. These included, above all, rights and freedoms for individuals, especially religious freedom. In the letter to Catholics in China, Pius XII used language that was strikingly similar to any number of his utterances, public or private, regarding the church's relationship with the Fascist dictatorships of the interwar era. The Catholic Church, he wrote, expressed no preference for any one form of government over another. It respected the natural desire of a people to adopt the form of government consistent with its traditions and values. Hence the pope's consternation to hear of the persecuted Catholics of China, of the repression of the charitable works of so many Catholic religious working in schools and hospitals, and of priests and bishops forcibly removed from their posts or prevented from practicing freely and openly the sacramental life of the church.[102]

Whatever their intended impact, such papal statements were carefully crafted forms of public diplomacy that allowed the pope to appear as a willing participant in dialogue with civil authorities while also registering a thinly veiled protest against the state's treatment of its Catholic minorities. And as he had done in his dealings with Hitler's Germany and Mussolini's Italy, Pius XII complemented his rather restrained public statements with diplomatic maneuvers, sending signals behind the scenes that the Vatican was serious about its desire to reach a workable accommodation with Communist states, especially with the Soviet bloc. Until Stalin's death in 1953, the few tentative contacts between the Vatican and the Soviets came at the pope's initiative. Stalin did not take these initiatives seriously, nor did he care to see the papacy's international prestige and influence enhanced in postwar Europe. The story has been told repeatedly of Stalin's alleged quip to Roosevelt at Yalta, questioning the logic of involving the pope in discussions about Europe's future: "The Pope? Who is he? How many divisions does he have?" Pius XII apparently caught wind of the story and was offended by it. According to his personal physician, Riccardo Galeazzi-Lisi, when the pope read the news of Stalin's death in 1953 he grinned and said: "Joseph Stalin is dead. Now he will see how many divisions We have up there!"[103]

Vatican Ratlines

As we have seen, in the years after the war, Pius XII had directed Vatican resources toward a massive and multifront relief effort.[104] Among the earliest and most successful initiatives was one that worked with governments in South America to encourage the migration of thousands of refugees displaced by war. By professing a particular concern with the plight of Catholic refugees, and appealing to the self-interest of pro-Catholic governments in such places as Argentina, which might be eager to see European Catholic migrants settle in their country, the Vatican hoped to do something concrete on behalf of the nominally baptized Jews, who, like all of European Jewry, were desperate to find a safe haven.

In the confusion and chaos of the refugee crisis, these Vatican-backed emigration schemes were easily manipulated by a small handful of nefarious characters, including some well-placed Roman Catholic clerics, to help secure the escape of known or suspected war criminals.[105] In a top-secret report prepared for the State Department in May 1947, Vincent La Vista reported on the details of a well-defined "German organization . . . for the illegal emigration of Germans to South America." There were similar organizations for other nationalities and groups, including Jewish refugees, all with offices in Rome headed almost entirely by Roman Catholic prelates. Several such networks ran from parts of Germany and Central Europe through to Spain or Portugal and then on to South America. The Italian ratline, though, arguably was the most important and certainly one of the busiest of the smuggling networks, with Vatican-related organizations and properties playing an operative role.[106] According to La Vista's report, by 1947 the Vatican had become "the largest single organization involved in the illegal movement of emigrants."[107]

So it was that among the thousands of displaced persons who were passing through Rome after the war, there were dozens if not hundreds of known or suspected war criminals and escaped POWs. They could count on Vatican-affiliated relief organizations to help them obtain passports for foreign travel from the International Red Cross under false pretenses. On the basis of information culled from someone identified only as "the notorious Dr. Willy Nix"—whom La Vista identified as the head of the Free German Committee in Italy and under investigation by Italian authorities yet enjoying the "benevolent protection of the Vatican"—intelligence agents dissected the process by which legitimate relief operations were being manipulated, with the Vatican's tacit approval, it seemed. Individuals whom Nix knew or suspected of being wanted by Allied authorities for involvement in war crimes or as escaped POWs were issued false identification papers and travel documents. The would-be refugees were then put in touch with a Father Bayer, whom La Vista identified as the "Vatican representative" dealing with the German line of the emigration scheme, or with one Father Carlos, also identified as affiliated with the Vatican. With the help of some well-connected lay persons who were said to be close to the Vatican, the fugitives could secure food and other material necessities, including reference letters and perhaps even the promise of paid employment once they arrived in South America.

This "chain of refugees," as La Vista called it, worked seamlessly and efficiently because of individuals like Willy Nix and Father Bayer, who enjoyed "Vatican connections." Vatican connections, it was believed, begat connections with government and businesses in Argentina and other receiving countries. Official travel papers issued by the International Red Cross, unwittingly in most cases, gave these fugitives the cover of legality. So did Vatican relief efforts. Seen from the perspective of suspicious intelligence officers, the emigration schemes had all the appearances of a bona fide Vatican-backed ratline to clandestinely ferry to safety hundreds if not thousands of Nazis and Nazi collaborators, all under the cover of an otherwise legitimate objective. "The justification of the Vatican for its participation in this illegal traffic is simply the propagation of the Faith," La Vista reported. It was the familiar refrain of Vatican neutrality, this time applied to relief efforts aimed at helping refugees, regardless of their nationality or political affiliations.

According to La Vista's report, the Vatican made no secret of its eagerness to help such people regardless of their political feelings, "as long as they are anti-Communist and pro-Catholic." As a result, large numbers of former Nazis were going to Italy with the express purpose of obtaining false travel papers, and then leaving promptly via Italian or Spanish ports for Latin America, mainly for Argentina. The popularity of Latin American destinations prompted further investigation by field agents and revealed the Vatican's operative role. La Vista explained that "in those Latin American countries where the Church is a controlling or dominating factor, the Vatican has brought pressure to bear which has resulted in the foreign missions of those countries taking an attitude almost favoring the entry into their country of former Nazi and former Fascists or other political groups, so long as they are anti-Communist." Legwork by members of Myron Taylor's staff confirmed that there was some substance to this claim. Taylor's assistant J. Graham Parsons reported in August 1947 that his contacts at the Panama delegation in Italy confirmed that Panama was eager to admit emigrants who clearly had no Communist affiliation or leanings. The net effect of this unwritten rule, Parsons concluded, was that "persons possessing a fascist background are favorably considered" to settle in the country. And so it was, it seemed, with other Latin American states.[108]

The State Department took La Vista's report seriously and acted quickly to take up the matter with Vatican officials and with representatives of the International Red Cross in Geneva. It would seem that no one in the Taylor mission suspected that the pope himself or any of his close advisors knew of the scheme, let alone authorized it. Consequently, the officials couched their concern in terms of a friendly warning that the legitimate cause of aiding refugees was being exploited by a small but active group eager to capitalize financially and politically on the trafficking of wanted war criminals. As Parsons put it to Vatican officials, the U.S. government was concerned that "unscrupulous persons, often engaged in illicit and clandestine activities, had been able increasingly to secure documentation for travel through the unwitting assistance of charitable organizations and governments and institutions cooperating therewith." Sir D'Arcy Osborne of the British Legation to the Holy See dismissed as "completely untrue" allegations that Vatican relief schemes, and in particular the Pontifical Aid Commission (Pontificia Commissione di Assistenza, or PCA), would "knowingly promote or abet the emigration and resettlement in South America of war criminals."[109]

What troubled certain American officials the most, though, was the likelihood that among those securing travel documentation through bogus means were large numbers of Soviet agents: Communist operatives who were exploiting the messy nature of refugee relief work in Rome to reach the United States. The notorious Willy Nix was said to be a double agent. Decrying what it called the "wholesale victimization of agencies engaged in humanitarian work," the State Department asked the Vatican to join it in pursuing "further precautions against illicit travel" of this kind, lest "unfriendly agents" be allowed to undermine the "integrity of nations" and besmirch the reputation of genuine humanitarian work on behalf of refugees. It was a telling sign of the fast-approaching Cold War that American officials were more concerned that Soviet agents might be infiltrating U.S. territory than that suspected war criminals might be evading justice with the help of charitable organizations funded generously with donations from the American public. La Vista estimated that upward of 100,000 Russian agents were flowing illegally in and out of Italy through Vatican-related channels. This is an implausibly high number and casts a shadow of doubt on the reliability of the information La Vista was drawing upon to reach such alarming conclusions. In the tense and uncertain atmosphere of the nascent Cold War, the frightening prospect of thousands of Communist agents entering the United States by means of a messy illegal emigration network operating apparently with the Vatican's tacit approval sounded alarm bells in American diplomatic and intelligence circles; the ethical concerns raised by the prospect of war criminals' fleeing from justice was of secondary concern.[110]

Could the pope's fear of Communism, bordering on paranoia, according to some observers, have led the supremely cautious Pius XII to accept some degree of association with the postwar ratlines? It will not do to speak simply of Vatican ratlines, as if Pius XII had declared it the official policy of the Holy See to sponsor the clandestine escape of war criminals. Nor is it fair to take the nefarious actions of some working for Vatican relief organizations as proof of the pope's direct knowledge and involvement. When Parsons spoke to Monsignor Walter Carroll in August 1947 to report on La Vista's findings, Carroll responded with assurances that he would bring the matter to the attention of the highest Vatican authorities. But, he added, the agencies listed in La Vista's report, like the ones headed by Bishop Hudal, were "not connected with the Vatican."[111] What was true of Hudal was true also of men such as Father Bayer or the Croatian priest Krunoslav Draganović, who was helping a sizable number of Croatian Fascists escape through Rome under the auspices of the PCA, which enjoyed financial support from American Catholics.[112] As the Jesuit historian Father Robert Graham said when acknowledging Draganović's schemes, "Just because he's a priest doesn't mean he represents the Vatican. It was his *own* operation. He's not the Vatican."[113]

There is some evidence to show that, at the very least, Pius XII knew that small paramilitary groups of former generals and soldiers, whose wartime records were murky at best, were forming "under-cover resistance groups" to engage in "guerrilla warfare against Russians." This is what the pope told Aloisius Muench when they met in September 1947. Although Muench's record of their meeting is sketchy, it confirms that Pius XII was told that Muench's name had been mentioned in an American military intelligence report on these purported resistance groups. Muench hastened to assure the pope that he had "never discussed political matters" with foreign nationals said to be part of a gathering counter-revolutionary resistance movement to fight Soviet Communism.[114] It remains unclear what Pius XII thought of such initiatives one way or another.

A few American intelligence reports from the last year of the war suggested that Pius XII was serious about the idea of creating a kind of Catholic super-state in the heart of Europe, something akin to the old Austro-Hungarian Empire, to act as a bulwark against the Soviet menace.[115] The Italian priest Luigi Sturzo dismissed as "absurd" the tales of an actual "Vatican plan" to restore monarchies in parts of Europe as a way of thwarting Communism. No doubt some in the church might prefer a hereditary monarch to an elected leader, Sturzo conceded, but the pope and his advisors were not among them. Sturzo reasoned that "those responsible for Vatican policies are too wide-awake not to perceive the poverty and danger of any such maneuver. . . . It is, in short, a scheme for a different century."[116]

The more pertinent question is whether Pius XII was so blinded by his fear of Communism that he was led into abandoning his well-known prudence to embrace such immoral and illegal schemes. According to historian Michael Phayer, Pius XII led the Western world "in an unethical fight against communism." Phayer insists that the pope "did not hesitate to flout principles of justice in pursuit of a pragmatic goal that was necessary to protect the Catholic Church, or so the pontiff thought." In this version, the normally circumspect Pius XII allowed the Vatican's legitimate refugee relief initiatives to be manipulated for the illicit purpose of shepherding such mass murderers as Adolf Eichmann to safety.[117] Or Pius XII became the powerful protector of murderous men like Ante Pavelić, the Croatian Ustaša leader who reportedly found temporary shelter in Vatican properties on his way to Argentina. In a similar vein, there is some evidence to suggest that Pius XII gave tacit approval to the clandestine work of Father Draganović and afforded the Croatian priest—who was described even by American intelligence operatives as a "war criminal" and a "fascist"—shelter and protection in Vatican properties. It is telling, perhaps, that according to one CIA report, within days of Pius XII's death in October 1958, Vatican officials asked Draganović to leave the College of St. Jerome, where he had been living and working with impunity since the latter part of the war.[118]

It makes for a good story, but is it true? It is conceivable, of course, that Pius XII at least knew of the ratline operations. It is possible, too, that the pope authorized such operations and instructed his staff to provide the necessary financial and material resources needed to pull off the great escape of notorious war criminals. Michael Phayer is convinced that Father Draganović's role directly implicates Pius XII. The fact that someone working for a Vatican organization could be so deeply enmeshed in the ratlines scheme, Phayer concludes, is proof positive of "the direct involvement of Pius XII himself."[119] Drawing on evidence from the diplomatic and intelligence reports of the time, the Argentine journalist Uki Goñi has written that the documentation proves "not only how Pius XII was fully aware of the sanctuary provided to war criminals at Roman ecclesiastical institutions, but also how he personally liaised with the Nazi-smuggling operation at the Croatian Confraternity of San Girolamo [Saint Jerome]." This, Goñi says, despite the Vatican's repeated denial that the pope had any knowledge of, let alone direct dealings with, the work of men like Draganović.[120]

According to reports from the Counter Intelligence Corps (CIC) agent Robert C. Mudd, some 100 Ustaša were in hiding at the Saint Jerome seminary, hoping to escape to Argentina through Vatican channels, and with the full knowledge of the Vatican and Argentine government.[121] Mudd described how Draganović and others working with the Vatican's relief efforts were able to move in and out of Vatican City effortlessly, shielded by the diplomatic immunity afforded official Vatican vehicles. Draganović's work with Ustaša trying to flee to South America, Mudd reasoned, "definitely links him up with the plan of the Vatican to shield these ex-Ustashi nationalists" and help them reach South America. Mudd was convinced that the Vatican was counting on the "strong anti-communist feelings of these men," and thus wanted to help facilitate their migration to South America "in any way possible to counteract the spread of Red doctrine."

That the Vatican and associated organizations had become the epicenter of illegal emigration movements just after the war is clear enough. Writing to the Supreme Allied Commander in November 1946 on the search for Pavelić, a political advisor in the Foreign Office stated bluntly that it was "increasingly clear that many of the more important quislings [that is, traitors] are taking refuge under the wing of the Church" in Italy. Confounding the situation was the unlikelihood that Italian police could be persuaded to search for men like

Pavelić if it meant entering church property, unless, of course, the Vatican it-self could be "persuaded into active cooperation."[122] Adding to this certainty was the fact that Allied officials believed the Vatican was dragging its feet on expelling from the Vatican proper such men as former Nazi diplomat Baron von Weizsäcker. American Secretary of State James Byrnes wrote with con-cern at the start of 1946 to Robert Murphy, Truman's advisor on Germany, complaining of the Vatican's "negligible" assistance in turning over former "enemy aliens" to Allied officials.[123] American representatives at the Vatican tried to reassure Washington that the Vatican wanted to be rid of former Ger-man diplomats as soon as possible, but the pope wanted certain assurances that men like Weizsäcker and their families would be treated fairly and hu-manely when they left the confines of Vatican City.[124] Harold Tittmann wrote that the Vatican was "most anxious" to see former German diplomats leave, but was concerned "only with the appearances and with its own prestige as charitable and impartial institution." The pope and his staff were especially sensitive to how German Catholics might perceive their collaboration with the powers that now occupied their country. As Harold Tittmann explained, the Vatican fully expected German Catholics to play a central role in the "fu-ture rehabilitation" of Germany.[125] It was out of a similar concern for the ef-fect on public opinion of so many death sentences being meted out to former German and Italian generals, along with the logic of Christian compassion and forgiveness, that Pius XII could appeal to Allied authorities all the way to Truman to commute the death sentences of convicted war criminals.[126] Among those for whom the pope sought clemency was General Anton Dos-tler, the commander of the 75th German Army Corps, condemned to death by a U.S. military tribunal in Rome in October 1945 for having ordered the execution of unarmed American POWs. The Vatican wanted Dostler's life spared solely on compassionate grounds. The American member of the Vati-can diplomatic office, Monsignor Carroll, assured U.S. officials that Dostler was a devout Roman Catholic and a "deeply religious man." The pope's ap-peal in this instance, as in most cases, was politely acknowledged by the rele-vant Allied authorities, then promptly ignored.[127]

The diplomatic and military officials who fielded the many papal requests for clemency could accept the pope's interventions as emanating from hu-manitarian impulses, even when appeals were made on behalf of accused mass murderers.[128] By the second half of 1947, though, American and British officials were finding it harder to hide their frustration with the Vatican's failure to acknowledge that religious institutions in Rome, affiliated in one way or another with the Vatican, likely were harboring known or suspected war criminals. Nowhere was this more obvious than in the case of a group of Croatian Ustaša generals and POWs whom the Yugoslavs wanted extradited to face trial as war criminals. Some Allied officials believed that Pius XII was actively pleading the case of these Croatian nationals in order to keep them from the hands of the Yugoslavian Communist leader Tito. Pius XII's distrust of the Yugoslav Communists was no secret to the Allied representatives who worked closely with the pope. According to Myron Taylor, the pope saw Tito as a "cruel, ambitious dictator of the worst type . . . utterly unreliable and dangerous."[129]

This did not alleviate the frustration of the American and British officials who wanted the pope to understand the enormous damage the matter was doing to the Holy See's moral credibility. A case in point was the Vatican's slow response to queries about the whereabouts of the Croatian political and military leaders actively being sought as war criminals by the Yugoslavian government. The former Independent State of Croatia, which after 1941 undertook a murderous campaign targeting civilians, mainly Serbs and Jews, had taken hundreds of thousands of lives. Forced conversions of orthodox Serbs to Catholicism, the legal and economic marginalization of Jews, concentration camps and systematic mass murder—such was the nature of Ustaša brutality, which even some German officials believed was excessive.[130] During the war, Pius XII and his staff certainly were well aware of the brutal nature of an ostensibly pro-Catholic regime and of the particularly vulnerable situation of some 40,000 Jews in Croatia. Religious leaders in Croatia, both Jewish and Catholic, together with relief and rescue organizations from Italy, implored the Holy See to see what could be done to get Croatian Jews, including those who had converted to Catholicism, out of harm's way; this might entail allowing them to travel to Italy or to remain in those parts of the former Yugoslavia currently occupied by Italian troops who were expected to be accommodating. Like his counterparts in other parts of occupied Europe, the Vatican's envoy in Zagreb, Giuseppe Marcone—who carried the title of apostolic visitor rather than nuncio since there were no formal diplomatic ties between the Holy See and the Ustaša regime—persistently entreated the Croatian authorities to listen to the dictates of morality and Christian charity. He enjoyed, at best, very modest success.[131]

While it is true that the Holy See refused to recognize formally the Ustaša regime, it is also the case that Pius XII declined to issue anything like a strong public denunciation of murderous behavior being carried out ostensibly in the name of Catholic Croatia. Not surprisingly, then, after the war Yugoslavian authorities were prone to view the Vatican's attitude toward former Ustaša leaders with deep suspicion. The most notorious among the Ustaša who were reportedly being sheltered in Vatican-related property were Ante Pavelić, the Ustaša leader himself, who had met with Pius XII at the Vatican in 1941. Reports had it that even Hitler's Serbian wartime collaborator, General Milan Nedic, found shelter in Vatican property, though such claims were contradicted by word reaching Allied authorities that Nedic had committed suicide while in custody in early February 1946.[132]

Allied authorities had known for some time that the Vatican took issue with Yugoslavia's widespread demands for handing over war criminals and so-called quislings, reasoning that some individuals were being unjustly accused presumably because of their opposition to the Yugoslav Communists. Such was the case with Monsignor Gregory Rozman, the bishop of Ljubljana, who was characterized as a suspected quisling and interned at the Klagenfurt camp in Austria. In late January 1946, American and British officials learned that the pope himself wanted the Allies to allow Bishop Rozman to flee to northern Italy, to find refuge in a Benedictine abbey at Praglia, near Padua.[133] As Allied officials had it from the Vatican, the abbey was a "centre of refuge" for Yugoslav priests and seminarians, and thus would be eminently "suitable" for Rozman. Osborne relayed the pope's request to the Foreign Office, saying that he hoped the Allies would be amenable. They were not, at least not while investigations were still ongoing to determine whether there was evidence to warrant handing Rozman over to Yugoslavia to be tried. Allied officials, the Americans in particular, had doubts about the Yugoslav charges against Bishop Rozman. There was, in the words of one British official in Belgrade, "nothing that can be called concrete evidence against Rozman." American officials at Belgrade went even further and questioned Yugoslav motivations, to the point of suggesting that the charges against Rozman were "propagandistic" and were part of the Tito government's "campaign against the Church in Yugoslavia."[134] Even still, so long as doubts about Rozman's wartime activities remained, and there was little question that he had expressed anti-Allied views during the war, Allied authorities did not want him leaving the Klagenfurt area, let alone traveling into northern Italy to find church-backed refuge. In fact, the Foreign Office and the British representative at Belgrade wanted Osborne to let the pope know that the existence of a small "community" of Yugoslav priests near Padua, even if they were bona fide refugees in need of the church's humanitarian assistance, nevertheless could fuel the Yugoslavian government's suspicions to the detriment of Catholic interests in the country.[135]

There were no such doubts about men like Nedic or Pavelić. The thought that they might be finding shelter in Rome from people associated even loosely with the Vatican caused predictable consternation among American and British officials. And although there remained serious doubts about whether such a high-profile figure as Pavelić was given sanctuary in Vatican properties in Rome, Allied authorities had it from the Yugoslavs that at least five men who were being sought by the Yugoslavian government were indeed in Rome, living in Vatican properties, apparently at the Oriental Institute in Rome.[136] The Yugoslav government claimed to have learned that a "large number" of wanted war criminals were managing to escape Italy and make their way to South America, with the active assistance of the Vatican's Pontifical Aid Commission in the form of visas and financial assistance procured under false pretenses.[137]

Having agreed to work with the Yugoslavian government on helping to bring suspected war criminals and quislings to trial, the Foreign Office counseled a direct approach to the Vatican to see whether they might respond proactively. In fact, by the start of 1947, the Foreign Office was eager to wash its hands of the affair, asking that Yugoslavia deal directly with the Vatican about inquiries related to the five former Ustaša presumed to be enjoying Vatican cover.[138] This the Yugoslav government did in early February 1947.

Osborne, who knew the court of Pius XII better than any other foreign diplomat, had his doubts about Vatican cooperation. He warned that there should be no talk whatsoever of anything like a "forced search" of Vatican territories by the authorities in search of suspected war criminals.[139] The Vatican's resentment, not to mention Catholic opinion in England, would be all the greater, Osborne reasoned, in light of the fresh wounds lingering from the arrest, trial, and eventual conviction in October 1946 of Archbishop Aloysius Stepinac, the most powerful prelate in Croatia. For Marshal Tito's regime, by virtue of his dealings with the Ustaša, Archbishop Stepinac clearly was guilty of collaboration. It mattered little to Yugoslavian officials that Stepinac had denounced Ustaša excesses during the war; Allied officials themselves were inclined to regard Stepinac's wartime record as questionable. The Vatican, for its part, had no doubt about true Yugoslavian intentions. It considered the Stepinac trial a farce; the archbishop was an innocent pawn in a dangerous game of early Cold War politics whose unfair arrest and sham trial were but the opening salvo in a war against Catholicism in the new Yugoslavia.[140]

Even still, the Foreign Office wanted Osborne to send a clear signal to the Vatican that the alleged harboring of known or suspected war criminals was a dangerous game that could only hurt church interests in the long run. As a Foreign Office dispatch from M. S. Williams put it to D'Arcy Osborne at the start of January 1947, the likes of Nedic and Pavelić were "not Thomas à Beckets"—a stark warning to the Vatican to avoid making martyrs out of brutal war criminals.[141] Osborne delivered this message to the Vatican, speaking with Tardini, who was able to confirm that the pope had instructed church-related institutions to exercise greater vigilance when being asked to "entertain guests," which was to say, harbor refugees. Pius XII ordered that such shelter was to be given only with the approval of a "higher authority." This could be taken as one way of saying diplomatically that anyone being housed in church property was going to be allowed to stay there at the pope's discretion, albeit with due consideration for the concerns of friends and allies in postwar reconstruction. Osborne had his doubts about papal cooperation. He wrote to a colleague in the Foreign Office to say that "if they [Ustaša refugees] were in Vatican territory I do not believe for a moment that the Pope would give the order for their surrender." But Osborne was speaking here about a hypothetical. Given what Tardini had said about the pope's recent instructions against harboring refugees, Osborne himself was inclined to believe that the five suspected quislings had already left their Roman refuge.[142]

Osborne's reports suggested that the Vatican was not willing to accept responsibility openly for what certain organizations attached to its massive postwar relief efforts might be doing to harbor suspected war criminals and to help them evade justice by escaping to the Americas. When they met in early February 1947, Osborne and Tardini discussed charges from the Yugoslavs that a number of wanted Ustaša were being helped to escape from Europe to South America under the guise of the charitable work of the PCA, a clear allusion to Father Draganović's work based out of Saint Jerome College.[143] In fact, by late 1946 some British diplomatic officials had been convinced that Pavelić was in Italy and that his precise whereabouts were known to Draganović alone.[144] When Tardini tried to disassociate the Vatican's Secretariat of State from Draganović and the day-to-day functioning of the Pontifical Aid Commission, Osborne retorted sharply that whatever its precise connection to the Vatican, the aid commission "was a Vatican organization and the instrument of papal charity, and that consequently responsibility for it could not be disavowed."[145] Tardini's attempt to disassociate his office from the pontifical relief commission strained the limits of credulity, and so Osborne called him to account. Clearly, British officials were not impressed with this apparent attempt to absolve the pope of any responsibility for activities taking place under the guise of organizations that Pius XII himself had established. Nor were they pleased with the Vatican's apparent unwillingness to cooperate with Allied authorities, and with the Tito regime, in handing suspected war criminals over to the Yugoslavs. As J. R. Colville of the Foreign Office's Southern Department observed, "I am afraid the Vatican have not been helpful. . . . The plain fact is that the [Roman Catholic] Church apparently has no wish to come to terms with Tito and is willing to support his enemies." Colville went on to say, "But if Pope Pius XII wishes to assume the mantle of Gregory VII . . . he can do it better than by harboring Ustashi."[146] When the Vatican intervened with Allied authorities on behalf of Miroslav Spalaicovich, former Yugoslavian representative to Paris who took refuge in Italy after the war, pleading that the aged and ailing man was in no condition to be extradited to Yugoslavia to face trial, the Southern Department of the Foreign Office wrote to the Political Advisor's Office at Caserta to suggest that the Vatican be made aware that there was compelling evidence to substantiate Spalaicovich's guilt. It was a diplomatic way of saying for the record what officials were saying privately—that on the matter of former Ustaša and other wartime collaborators, the Vatican risked being on the wrong side in the judgment of history.[147]

Indeed, there was a growing conviction that the pope approved of the scheme to shelter a certain number of Croatian Fascists from Yugoslavian justice. One British official wrote in late 1947 that

> there has been much evidence to show that the Vatican has permitted the encouragement both covert, and overt, of the Ustashi. . . . This wholly undesirable organization has not only been collectively responsible for vile atrocities on an immense scale during the war but has ever since its inception made use of murder as a normal political weapon. There is surely all the difference between giving shelter to, let us say, dissident Slovene priests, and giving positive aid to a creature like Pavelić?

From Walter "Red" Dowling at the U.S. State Department came understanding and even appreciation for the Vatican's "humanitarian attitude towards criminals who may have shown any indication of repentance." But the Pavelić case was different. "It seems to me," Dowling told J. Graham Parsons at the Taylor mission, "that Pavelić's peculiarly unsavory record would make it difficult for the Church to afford him protection."[148]

It is assumed that Pavelić had found his way to Rome by the spring of 1946, and remained there until the end of 1948, when he was able to escape to Argentina, presumably via a Vatican ratline. By 1947, American and British authorities had grown more earnest in their search for Pavelić. The Yugoslav case found a receptive audience with the American diplomat John Moors Cabot, who was uniquely placed to evaluate the likelihood of a Vatican-Argentine connection. He was stationed in Argentina until 1947, when he was moved to the American Embassy in Belgrade, Yugoslavia. Moors Cabot heard directly from Tito about the Ustaša who were said to be hiding in Italy and Austria. In a letter to the U.S. State Department in June 1947, he wrote, "Some arrangement has been worked out with the Vatican and Argentina by which collaborationist Yugoslavs will be helped to emigrate [*sic*] to Argentina." He seems to have realized that the "arrangement" had the blessing of his own government. Indignantly, he questioned the practical as well as ethical consequence of such an arrangement not only for the Vatican but also for the United States, which risked compromising its "moral obligations" if it allowed such a scheme to continue. "How we can defend this record before the

UN if the Yugoslavs take it there I do not know, and there are increasing evidences they will. As I see it we may then be forced either to accept a humiliating decision against us or so manipulate things as to show that we also consider [the] UN a mere instrument of power politics."[149]

For some time, all manner of rumor surrounding Pavelić's whereabouts had been swirling in diplomatic and intelligence circles. The most conclusive evidence pointed to Pavelić being sheltered in Rome, where, it was said, he enjoyed some very powerful backing at the Vatican. If Pavelić were in Rome, American intelligence reports concluded, he was most likely being sheltered at the College of St. Jerome, a property that enjoyed the extraterritorial sovereignty afforded to Vatican properties by virtue of the church-state accords. So if American and British officials wanted him arrested and extradited to Yugoslavia, there was no other means than to implore the Vatican and Pius XII directly to help facilitate Pavelić's apprehension. The few intelligence reports produced at the time suggested that the Vatican resisted this pressure, and instead urged the British and Americans to think of Pavelić as a potential strategic ally to help remove the Communist Tito. As CIC agent William Gowen wrote, the Ustaša leader's "contacts are so high and his present position is so compromising to the Vatican, that any extradition of subject would be a staggering blow to the Roman Catholic Church."[150] But intelligence reports of this kind were notoriously unreliable, based as they were on scarce and often inaccurate information about the world of the Vatican—a world to which intelligence operators and even diplomats had very limited access, if any at all. Getting accurate information about the Vatican entailed piercing a veil of secrecy; it meant breaching what David Alvarez aptly describes as "a wall of silence and discretion" put up by the small handful of senior individuals who guided papal diplomacy and guarded zealously—under oath, in fact—the Vatican's secrets.[151]

It is not surprising, then, that the reports of Pavelić's whereabouts were wildly inconsistent, so much so that no one in diplomatic or intelligence circles could verify for certain where the Croatian Ustaša leader was, or where he was likely to go. Some reports placed him in British or American custody; others had him living in hiding in Switzerland. One story located Pavelić in Argentina by May 1947, fresh off a passenger ship from Genoa, bedecked in clerical clothing and surrounded by a veritable "retinue" of Catholic clerics. As Parsons noted when reporting all this to Dowling at the State Department, it was difficult to take any of these stories seriously since Pavelić, "like Kilroy, seems to be everywhere."[152]

After a brief but intense search to pinpoint Pavelić's whereabouts, the hunt for the Nazi collaborator was stopped abruptly in the late summer of 1947. The message that reached CIC Rome was "HANDS OFF."[153] In a curious reversal, CIC agent William Gowen, whose father worked with the Taylor mission at the Vatican, abandoned his earlier insistence that Pavelić be surrendered immediately and recommended that the hunt be called off. How to explain Gowen's change of heart? Some have speculated that the younger Gowen was feeling the influence of a powerful coterie of well-placed officials close to the pope, including Montini, the British representative Osborne, and also members of Taylor's staff, including Harold Tittmann and Gowen's father.[154] Perhaps he was, but it seems more likely that word was out that the complex world of underground escape routes was operating under the unofficial patronage of the Allied powers. The search for Pavelić in Vatican environs went cold.

Despite the seductive allure of its sensationalistic elements, the damning indictment of Pius XII's purported involvement in the so-called Vatican ratlines rests on shaky foundations. In fact, there really were no Vatican ratlines as such. Claims to that effect have long been based on highly selective reading of partial and sometimes dubious intelligence reporting of the immediate postwar era. There simply is no direct, credible evidence to prove that Pius XII knew of such schemes or that he personally approved and helped to finance them using funds from, among others, charitable donations intended for postwar relief efforts. Given his propensity for caution and probity, it seems unlikely that he would have dared to authorize such questionable operations, fraught not only with ethical but also with strategic and symbolic dangers for the Holy See and for all of Catholicism. Was his mistake to have trusted too much the discretion of his advisors or other cardinals in the Curia, or Allied authorities, for that matter, who saw some strategic opportunities in the ratline operations? After all, the operation of the notorious ratlines depended more on the strategic interests of the Western powers on the eve of the Cold War than on papal patronage.[155]

While Pius XII cannot be directly implicated in the ratlines operations, he cannot be absolved of complete responsibility for the use, or rather misuse, of Vatican-related institutions and relief structures. Pleas of innocence based on ignorance of the dubious dealings of prelates like Father Draganović or Bishop Hudal, whom the Vatican entrusted with delicate aspects of postwar papal aid, were bound to be met at the time—and ever since—with a measure of incredulity if not derision. True, it was possible for the pope or the Secretariat of State to claim, as each did, a plausible deniability about such activities, especially if, as seems likely, the schemes were known to only a few officials. What is more, when he was informed that religious institutions like Saint Jerome College purportedly were being used to shelter wanted war criminals, Pius XII ordered heightened surveillance, presumably to keep such things from happening again. Even still, if not Pius XII himself then someone or some persons with influence in the Vatican provided a measure of legitimacy and protection to Draganović and Hudal, who, in turn, twisted papal relief into a tool for escape.

This speaks to a paradoxical quality of Pius XII's administration of Vatican affairs. On the one hand, the pope governed with singular authority over certain areas, namely, the political and diplomatic offices of the Holy See. Indeed, foreign diplomats marveled at the discipline shown by Vatican officials, confounded and frustrated though they were by their secrecy. Not even American or British clerics who were working for the Holy See could be cajoled by their fellow nationals into breaking the code of silence.[156] On the other hand, the internal discipline exhibited in the political and diplomatic offices of the Vatican was not always replicated in other branches of papal administration. Pius XII's administration was not immune to tensions, conflicts, and internal competition. Indeed, the fault lines arguably were deepened by the pope's renowned capacity to procrastinate and to deliberate so carefully as to delay decisive action. Making matters worse was an increasing tendency for Pius XII to rely on an informal, unofficial network of trusted advisors to handle practical matters like the organization and distribution of papal relief. In the absence of the formal structures of discipline and control employed in the diplomatic offices, and given the enormity and the urgency of the postwar refugee crisis, it appears that a few people with access to resources, like Draganović and Hudal, also enjoyed considerable latitude to improvise and delegate as they saw fit, at least for a time.

Evocative talk of Vatican ratlines must therefore yield to the more mundane but nonetheless troubling possibility that the postwar escape routes exploited a certain dysfunction and inattention in the administration of Vatican affairs. There was also the lack of political will on the pope's part to see Vatican resources enjoined in a campaign to mete out victor's justice, especially when, as in the case of Yugoslavia, the victors were Communists who seemed determined to persecute the Catholic Church. Either way, the story of the ratlines with its many unanswered questions casts a long shadow on Pius XII's otherwise heroic efforts to help rebuild the Continent after a cataclysmic war. The intersection of papal relief work with the culture and system of postwar escape suggests at the very least a disturbing lack of transparency and accountability in the use of relief resources, if not simple naiveté and poor judgment in the administration of relief.

7

The Universal Pope

In a biting critique of the curial culture of the late 1940s, the outgoing French ambassador to the Holy See and venerable philosopher Jacques Maritain complained to French officials that the so-called Government of the Church actually governed little and administered much. It performed not so much a leadership role in the church as a regulatory function, protecting the store, as it were. Citing Chateaubriand, Maritain referred to the Curia as a "monarchical government ruled by old men." It was futile, then, to look to Rome for new ideas or what Maritain called "evangelical initiatives." Meaningful change, he concluded, would have to emerge "spontaneously" among the wider church community. Papal Rome, Maritain stated, "keeps watch, exercises prudence, directs in order to control, takes its time and takes account of the times."[1]

Though he was sensitive to the conflicting demands made of papal leadership, Maritain attributed to Pius XII's character and style of governance the increasingly stultified intellectual atmosphere in Catholic thought in the years after 1945. He saw Pius XII's approach to leadership as antithetical: on the one hand, the pope encouraged free and open debate on fundamental matters pertaining to doctrine, liturgical practices, or scriptural interpretation; on the other, he acted as a severe doctrinal enforcer, containing or suppressing trends in research that strayed too far from orthodox teachings. The pope who issued pioneering statements to stimulate reform in certain areas of church life at the same time allowed a reactionary and repressive culture to fester, to the point of authorizing formal censures of some prominent Catholic theologians.

Many of Pius XII's advisors and admirers admitted that in the latter part of his pontificate especially the papal court exhibited a tendency toward inertia, stagnation, and reaction. For a faithful critical thinker like Jacques Maritain, it was especially lamentable that Pius XII gave free rein to the "archaic methods" and mentality of the men of the Holy Office. Denouncing the "abuses" flowing from the secretive manner in which the doctrinal watchdog scrutinized the work of Catholic scholars, Maritain singled out the incompetence and "mediocrity" of many of the advisors (consultors) called upon by the Holy Office to lend expert opinion in highly specialized fields of study. Given that there was no centralized, cohesive method to the Holy Office's work of doctrinal surveillance and enforcement, this left far too much latitude to ad hoc denunciations from individual sources to individual cardinals. It was not unusual for vague and unsubstantiated charges, motivated by personal rivalry or politics, to reach the ear of one curial cardinal or another, tripping a censorious alarm among the doctrinal watchdogs of the Holy Office. For all its power, the office was characterized by what Maritain described as a "surprising provincialism."[2]

Tensions within the church of Pius XII over doctrinal matters intensified through the late 1940s and reached a crescendo after the publication of the papal encyclical *Humani Generis* (August 1950). In it, Pius XII condemned what he saw as the "false theories" of modern philosophies that were affecting the work of Catholic thinkers—whose adherents were labeled by critics as exponents of a *nouvelle théologie*, a "new" theology that threatened to undermine the very foundations of the church's teaching.[3] Concerned that the essence of the Christian message gradually was being lost and growing unintelligible and irrelevant in the lives of believers, the exponents of the so-called new theology argued in favor of a return to Scripture and to the writings of the Fathers of the Church. This, they hoped, would pave the way for a rediscovery of the true dynamism of the Christian faith.[4] It would mean peeling back layers of deeply rooted and officially sanctioned explanations of the foundations of the faith.

For Pius XII, this trend in Catholic theology bordered on open contempt of the supreme teaching authority of the church. More than simply a response to the *nouvelle théologie,* then, *Humani Generis* was intended to discourage the movement. "It is true," Pius XII wrote, "that Popes generally leave theologians free in those matters which are disputed in various ways by men of very high authority in this field; but history teaches that many matters that formerly were open to discussion, no longer now admit of discussion." Pius XII acknowledged that the encyclical did not in itself "demand consent" of the theologians, since such papal letters did not carry the full weight of the "supreme power" of the pope's teaching authority. But he made it clear that some things were no longer open for debate.[5]

The will of Pius XII was clear enough: there was room in the church for research and debate on a host of issues, including, for instance, the doctrine of evolution, but within well-defined limits. One could talk about evolution from a Catholic perspective so long as one accepted the precept that the human body comes from both "pre-existent and living matter," in other words, that humans have a soul that is created "immediately" by God. At the same time, Pius XII refused to tolerate any serious Catholic engagement with the idea of "polygenism," an argument against the idea that Adam was the "first parent of all," created by the one, true God. Pius XII dismissed such talk as "conjectural opinion" and said definitively that "the children of the Church by no means enjoy such liberty" to research and discuss the theory.

There were limits to what Catholic scholars could research, write, and teach about interpreting Scripture. As the author of the encyclical that freed Catholic exegetes from a literal interpretation of the Bible, Pius XII was eager to encourage continued critical-scientific study of the sacred texts of the Hebrew Bible and the Gospels. One had to be vigilant lest the Catholic scholar fall prey to an excessive historicism, to the point of emptying the texts of their divine inspiration and message. Pius XII conceded that the Sacred Books contained passages that drew upon the metaphors, symbols, and traditions of the ancient communities in which the texts were formed. Yet he insisted that whatever the sacred writers took from the culture of their day, they did so "with the help of divine inspiration." This rendered "immune from any error" the fundamental spiritual truth of the Sacred Books.[6]

In his crusade to preserve Catholic doctrine, the critics say, Pius XII and the conservative prelates who had come to dominate his circle in the last years of his pontificate effectively slowed the push for much-needed reform to church structure and teachings. The practical effects of this authoritative papal intervention were felt by the French and German theologians who were considered the leading lights of the *nouvelle théologie*. It was not so much what the pope himself had said in the encyclical as how a small group of prelates close to the pope and at the Holy Office—Fathers Leiber and Hentrich, Monsignor Ottaviani, Father Garrigou-Lagrange—exploited their influence with the pope and in the Roman Curia to deal forcefully with what they saw as excessively "progressive" trends emanating from French Jesuit circles.[7]

The French Dominican theologian Yves Congar recalled that from 1947 until 1956, he faced "an uninterrupted series of denunciations, warnings, restrictive or discriminatory measures and mistrustful interventions" from official circles in Rome.[8] Even Maritain and others, like the American Jesuit theologian John Courtney Murray, found themselves in the crosshairs of at least some of the doctrinal watchdogs in the Curia; they were spared an official censure only by the death of Pius XII.[9] In an atmosphere that recalled the antimodernist crusade of the early twentieth century, the French Jesuit theologian Henri de Lubac was to be kept away from seminary teaching and his books removed from library bookshelves and Catholic bookstores.[10] It is said that soon after succeeding Pius XII as Pope John XXIII, Angelo Roncalli made it known that he was pained by the atmosphere created by *Humani Generis*, complaining that he had learned of the papal document only through the newspapers.

Despite all this, Pius XII cannot be caricatured so easily as the architect of an archconservative, reactionary, and monolithic church culture. Pius XII could be temperate, judicious, and forgiving when he saw fit. Henri de Lubac, for instance, would make peace with the Curia and even win the praise and confidence of Pius XII. Writing through Augustin Bea in March 1958, the pope wanted to assure de Lubac that he had a "lively interest" in the French Jesuit's books, especially in the controversial *Méditations sur l'Eglise,* and, moreover, that he was impressed by the "scientific soundness" of de Lubac's work. Bea noted that Pius XII expected great things from such a great mind working for the "good of the Church"; the pope was encouraging him "to continue with much confidence your scientific activity from which much fruit is promised for the Church."[11]

It is of no small significance that Roncalli, the pope who would convene the Second Vatican Council and thereby spark enormous transformations in

Catholic life, lauded Pius XII as a "great teacher of the Faith," together with the illustrious church fathers. Roncalli saw in Pius XII's work a winning formula for grappling with modernity that allowed the church to profess its unchanging faith in an ever-changing world, for the good of all peoples.[12] Indeed, for Pacelli's two immediate successors, Roncalli and Montini, it was Pius XII himself who was the real spiritual father of the council. Montini reasoned that the corpus of Pius XII's teachings was a "vast and fruitful preparation for the doctrinal and pastoral words" of the council.[13] Whereas critics saw in Pius XII a pope out of touch with reality and out of step with the age, Montini saw "a friend of our times," someone open to "dialogue" with the many expressions of modernity, albeit informed by an unyielding commitment to the universal and absolute truths of the Gospel. It was good and just to remember him, Montini concluded, and above all to follow his lead.[14]

Over the course of his difficult pontificate, Pius XII issued a steady stream of authoritative teachings and decisions—more than forty encyclicals in all, to say nothing of the hundreds of letters and speeches. His teachings can be grouped into three distinct but related categories: theological-ecclesiological, social-political, and moral-ethical. The broad range of his teaching was marked by a complex mixture of continuity and change. The result was, and continues to be, a contradictory and at times ambiguous legacy for the doctrinal and organizational life of the church. In some ways, Pius XII was a pioneering pope who broke the mold of papal leadership and cast a new one, by insisting that the pope speak frequently to the church and to the world on a host of issues and to the widest possible range of social categories.

The German Jesuit Augustin Bea, one of the most influential voices at the Second Vatican Council calling for change in Catholic attitudes toward Jews and Judaism, predicted that history would rank Pius XII as one of the truly great popes of all time. As a renowned expert in biblical studies and Pacelli's personal confessor after 1945, Bea brought a unique perspective, insisting that it would take decades if not centuries for Pius XII's "gigantic work" on behalf of the church and humanity to be fully understood and appreciated.[15] "Pius XII remains a doctor of the Church for the future too," Bea wrote in 1959, "even if officially he has not (or not yet) been declared such." A few years later, as he meditated upon Pacelli's influence on the life of the church and especially in the work of the Second Vatican Council, Bea went so far as to say "that the teaching spread by Pius XII has become the spiritual air that we constantly breathe without even being aware of it." Like Roncalli and Montini, Bea saw Pius XII's legacy as "fundamental" for the council, especially because of its comprehensive attempt to reconcile the ancient but unchanging truths of Christian faith to contemporary realities. Pius XII thus had left the church well placed to "re-conquer modern man to faith, to the Church, to Christ and to God."[16]

Pius XII's capacity to be progressive was evident during the Second World War, with the publication in 1943 of two pioneering encyclicals, *Mystici Corporis,* on the church as the mystical Body of Christ, and *Divino Afflante Spiritu,* on promoting biblical studies. These were followed in 1947 by the encyclical *Mediator Dei,* which addressed the subject of the liturgy and encouraged new ways of thinking about Catholic worship. While far from revolutionary, all three encyclicals were to have a profound influence on the reforms instituted in the 1960s by the Second Vatican Council.[17] *Divino Afflante Spiritu* arguably was the most consequential. Its subject matter—how Catholics were to interpret the Bible—was esoteric, even banal when juxtaposed with the barbarous events that enveloped war-torn Europe. Nevertheless, it was a momentous publication that was bound to have a profound, lasting effect on the way Catholics related to the sacred texts of their faith. Timed to coincide with the fiftieth anniversary of Leo XIII's encyclical *Providetissimus Deus* (November 1893), which offered papal counsel on the proper way for Catholic scholars to engage in "the study of Biblical science," *Divino Afflante Spiritu* served to offer clarity and a new sense of purpose and direction to Catholic biblical scholarship even at such a turbulent moment in global affairs. The practical effect of Leo XIII's encyclical had been to hamper and suppress the work of a school of biblical scholars who wanted to understand sacred Scripture through the lens of the critical-historical method. Their purpose was not to challenge the divine nature or inspiration of the holy books but simply to submit the books to critical study that drew upon emerging methods and sources of the historical sciences and to situate the sacred texts in their proper historical and cultural context.

With one authoritative statement, Pius XII changed the way the church related to its sacred texts.[18] Far from working under the constant threat of suspicion if not censorship, Catholic biblical scholars effectively were being directed by the pope to employ what Pius XII described as the "art of textual criticism." Catholic Bible studies were freed from the shackles of a literalist approach to scriptural interpretation. The point was not to undermine or question the divine nature of the sacred texts or to empty the Bible of its divine message. To the contrary, Pius XII called for a critical method of studying the Bible precisely so as to cut through the layers of translations and transcriptions to get to the heart of the original source. "Let the Catholic exegete undertake the task," Pius XII declared, "of all those imposed on him the greatest, that namely of discovering and expounding the genuine meaning of the Sacred Books." In exercising their work, he added, Catholic biblical scholars ought to remember that their "foremost and greatest endeavor should be to discern and define clearly the sense of the biblical words . . . so that the mind of the author may be made abundantly clear."

To make the mind of the author abundantly clear was to render more plainly and directly the scriptural basis for the Catholic faith and its practices. It also meant acknowledging how discoveries in such fields as archaeology had deepened understanding of the social and cultural world of biblical Israel, including ancient language and symbols.[19] With an eye to the Catholic encounter with modernity, Pius XII invited biblical scholars to find ways of making their work accessible not only to other scholars but also to priests, to the men charged with teaching Christian doctrine to the people. The esoteric work of critical scholars was, to the pope's mind, a way of helping "all the faithful to lead a life that is holy and worthy of a Christian."

Commentators refer to the "prompt and dramatic" influence on Catholic biblical studies of Pius XII's teaching on biblical interpretation. No doubt the development toward this more liberal approach had been a long time coming, the logical outcome of decades of internal debate and discussion among Catholic scholars over how best to reconcile critical biblical scholarship with the fundamental articles of the Catholic faith. Still, it took the decisive intervention of Pius XII, and in particular his own comfort in the capacity to reconcile textual criticism with the articles of faith, to translate decades of internal wrangling into official Catholic teaching.[20]

In March 1964, a few months after being elected Pope Paul VI, Giovanni Battista Montini, one of Pius XII's closest advisors over the years, paid homage to his predecessor as he unveiled the imposing bronze monument to Pius XII in St. Peter's Basilica. It was an effusive testament to a long, virtuous life of Christian service. Montini spoke admiringly of Pius XII's "complete devotion" to the papal office and his capacity to reflect deeply on the nature of that office. Montini admired Pacelli's understated but profound spirituality and religious piety, to say nothing of his asceticism and work ethic despite chronically fragile health. What to others appeared to be a pedantic attention to minor details was, to Montini's mind, a "rare ability" to understand how the proper ordering of so many "small things" mattered to getting the "big things" right. Other observers recalled how studiously and diligently the pope worked to prepare his statements, paying close attention to every detail, from background research to the meticulous reading and revision of every last sentence, every last word. Those who worked with the pope understood that Pius XII did all this out of a genuine sense of duty, with an elevated sense of the papal office. Domenico Tardini recalled that Pius XII liked to say that the pope "must speak as pope." This meant preparing carefully, methodically, for every public address, to the point of delving into highly specialized studies in such areas as science and medicine.

Especially noteworthy was his interest in atomic physics and medical ethics, two expansive and rapidly developing fields that Pius XII had the foresight to see were going to challenge traditional Christian faith and practice in unprecedented ways. Far from shirking away from advances in scientific and medical research or retreating behind the illusory protection afforded by a reactionary orthodoxy, Pius XII boldly entered the fray of scientific and medical research. He grappled openly and in sophisticated ways with cutting-edge research, mindful of the need to make new discoveries and advances fit with the essence of the Christian claim. In his presentations to the Pontifical Academy of Sciences, which counted among its members some of the most illustrious scientists of the day, Pius XII could dazzle with his mastery of complex questions of quantum mechanics, all the while relating findings in scientific research back to the age-old moral and philosophical questions of life.[21]

Pius XII's many addresses in the areas of science, medicine, and bioethics—which numbered in the hundreds—reveal a very different Pius XII from the diplomat-pope of the war years. There is scarcely a trace of the cautious restraint of the pope's wartime oratory, little evidence of the tendency toward circumlocution that characterized his speeches at the height of World War Two. In these speeches, Pius XII seemed fully alive to the prophetic and the evangelical dimension of papal leadership. At the opening of the seventh annual meeting of the Pontifical Academy of the Sciences in February 1943, the pope acknowledged the "capital importance" of certain discoveries and inventions stemming from what he called "artificial transformations" in the nucleus of the atom. Such pioneering scientific discoveries, he said, raised fundamental questions about the very nature of the universe and of "existence" itself. Therein lay the importance of acknowledging the path-breaking work of scientists while insisting that this work play itself out against the backdrop of ultimate questions about the natural order, its origins and destiny.

In this respect, Pius XII hoped to serve as a bridge between two worlds—faith and reason, the supernatural and the natural. There was no question in his mind which of them reigned supreme. Still, it was significant that the spiritual head of the world's largest religious denomination was prepared to engage in dialogue with the world of science in the middle of the twentieth century. Pius XII thus signaled that he was open to finding ways of reconciling faith and reason, religion and science. Rather than retreating into a reactionary obscurantism, Pius XII insisted that faith could not escape from certain dictates of reason and its method. But he insisted equally that science could not escape the dictates of natural law and the moral universe. His exposition was technical, pastoral, and poetic all at once—a veritable *tour de force* of oratory. He called on scientists to admire the great "theater" of human life with all its wonders, the epic drama that featured the "grandeur of man" at center stage. All the human sciences, Pius XII concluded, from anatomy to physics to psychology, medicine, and even politics—all of them, he said, together constituted a great "hymn to God," and all human endeavors were governed by the moral dictates of conscience. A decade later he would have occasion to revisit the subject of nuclear technologies, praising the many potential benefits of nuclear advancements while warning ominously of what he called the "homicidal and suicidal madness" evident in the arms race. The former were testimony to the grandeur of man, the latter to the consequences of a science unmoored from morality and ethics.[22]

This was Pius XII speaking as he thought a pope should speak. His task and tone were educative and pastoral. He stood before the professionals not as one of them but as the Vicar of Christ and the bishop of Rome—a pastor to the whole human family. It was true that he wanted to speak competently to the specialists in the technical language of their field. But he knew his own limits.[23]

His authority was evident whenever Pius XII sought to remind his audiences both of the limits and of the ultimate purpose of any form of scientific inquiry. Speaking to a group of astronomers in May 1957, Pius XII demonstrated an appreciation for the critical methods by which scientific knowledge was advanced. At the same time, he used the opportunity to caution the modern scientist not to be seduced by the excitement of discovery into thinking himself "lord of the cosmos." He wanted scientists to remember that the "truth" which every researcher seeks exists ultimately "on a higher plane than that of scientific research." The "moral universe," the pope continued, "transcends the physical world"; consequently, he reasoned, "every gain made by science is on a lower plane than that of man's personal destiny—the ultimate aim and purpose of his existence—and of the relations which unite him to God." Speaking to a group of geophysicists in 1954, Pius XII intoned that the human mind "remains subject in its essence and in its activity to the supreme command of a Divine Creator." And he warned about the perils to society of a life of the mind detached from a proper, holistic, integrated sense of the nature and purpose of human life. More than just a warning, though, it was a call for scientists to exercise moral and civil responsibilities. "Knowledge divorced from the rest of life," Pius XII warned, "becomes sterile, nay dangerous. The scientist is above all a man face to face with his destiny, and from him, more than from others, will be required an accounting for the good and the evil that he has done."[24]

In asserting the primacy of morality and ethics in the face of would-be advances in scientific research, Pius XII restated in contemporary terms fundamental Catholic teachings about the nature of human life and the dignity of the person. In these ethical admonitions, the pope spoke plainly about the lessons of the recent past, evoking the lingering specter of Nazism and the great human tragedies wrought by science and medicine unmoored from morality. In a wide-ranging address to an association of Italian Catholic midwives in October 1951, Pius XII reiterated in unequivocal terms Catholic doctrine forbidding artificial means of contraception or insemination. The speech captured the pope's skill at blending a defense of orthodoxy with recognition that Catholics had to adapt, or rather respond effectively, to the spread of knowledge and new technologies, together with rapidly changing social mores. In speaking to this group of women on intimate matters related to marriage, sexuality, and contraception, Pius XII proved that he could be orthodox and modern—albeit within definite limits—at the same time. He reiterated orthodox Catholic teaching, which held that contraceptive practices, in particular sterilization, constituted "a grave violation of the moral law." The same applied to abortion, even in cases when the health or life of the mother was endangered.[25] No one, not even the so-called public authority—that is, the state—had any right to permit such a practice, even less to authorize its use against "innocents." The matter had been settled definitely by his predecessor's encyclical on marriage (*Casti connubbi*, December 1930) and reinforced at Pacelli's instruction by the Holy Office in early 1940, in response to the widespread use of sterilization in Nazi Germany.[26]

Alongside this resolute defense of orthodoxy, though, the pope took the first tentative steps toward official acceptance of the methods of natural family planning. In a gesture that anticipated by over a decade the Second Vatican Council's call on the laity to assume a more active role in the life of the church, Pius XII called on Catholic midwives to exercise their "professional apostolate" in defense of the church's conception of the meaning and dignity of human life. In leaving the door open to ongoing debate and research on methods of natural family planning, Pius XII told the women that it was their responsibility—not the priest's—to instruct and counsel married couples about moral and ethical methods of family planning, in keeping with church teaching.[27]

Ironically, the pope pilloried for his seeming "silence" during the Holocaust was concerned near the end of his life that he had written and said too much during his pontificate. Speaking in May 1957 to Father Antoine Wenger, then editor of the French Catholic newspaper *Le Croix*, Pius XII admitted to worrying that perhaps by issuing so many letters and speeches over the course of a long pontificate he had contributed to an "inflation of the papal word."[28] Some critics at the time agreed that Pius XII perhaps was speaking too frequently and too expansively on matters far beyond his competency. The result was not so much the inflation of papal words as their trivialization.[29] Such criticism reflected a dramatic reversal of expectations from those placed on Pacelli at the height of World War Two, when it was his persistent silence that reputedly was damaging the moral prestige of the papacy.

The Coming of Global Catholicism

In the area of social and political commentary, Pius XII spoke out in general terms about the threat to religious freedom posed by the spread of atheism, but also more specifically about the campaigns of repression and persecution inflicted on Catholics in Eastern Europe and China.[30] There were signs, too, of an evolving doctrine of religious freedom that could articulate basic precepts of human dignity beyond the traditional concern for the rights and privileges of Catholics, be they in a majority or a minority. Despite having felt the chilled censorious atmosphere of the last years of Pacelli's pontificate, John Courtney Murray a few years later lauded Pius XII's political teachings for having furnished a "badly need aggiornamento," or updating, of the church's doctrine on religious freedom. What Pius XII did was to encourage a "change in the state of the . . . question" on religious freedom. While his was not yet a fully articulated doctrine of religious freedom per se, Courtney Murray reasoned that Pius XII had carefully discerned the "signs of the times" in realizing that the growth of personal freedoms demanded the application of state power in a manner consistent with what the pope called the "dignity and freedom of the citizenry." For Courtney Murray, it was especially important that during the Second World War, Pius XII had warned consistently against an excessive and inappropriate use of state power in ways that conflicted with the "personal rights and duties of man." In this respect at least, Pius XII could be seen as both a transitional and a transformational figure. At the very least, Pacelli had come some way from the near-exclusive concern for the religious rights of Catholics exhibited during his tenure as papal nuncio in Germany and then as secretary of state.[31]

After the war, Pius XII prayed for peace in Palestine in the face of the political, military, and social crises that resulted from the establishment of the state of Israel, reserving special mention for the "thousands of refugees" who were driven to "wander from their fatherland in search of shelter and food." Then there was the "grievous" news of damage and outright destruction to the sacred sites of Christianity, especially within the "Holy City" of Jerusalem. News of damage to the holy places affirmed Pius XII in repeating his call for Jerusalem and other religious sites to be under the patronage and protection of the international community.[32] In the encyclical letter *Fidei Donum* (April 1957), Pius XII addressed the state of Catholic missions around the world. Africa merited special attention, the pope said, since the church there continued to strive "to forward her work among the heathen multitudes." Although "healthy progress" had been made in bringing the Gospel to that diverse continent, there were signs that "seeds of trouble are being sown . . . by the proponents of atheistic materialism." The letter was intended as an appeal to Catholics around the world to lend material and moral assistance to the vital work of the missionaries—who were far too few in number—so that "the message of saving truth may be brought to what is called 'darkest' Africa, where some 85,000,000 people still sit in the darkness of idolatry." At the time of his death in late 1958, there was clear evidence that Pius XII's attention to Africa as fertile grounds for evangelization was paying dividends. Under Pacelli's pontificate, the number of Catholics in Africa rose from 5 million to well over 20 million.[33]

Although his language harked back to outmoded conceptions of Europe's civilizing mission, there were unmistakable signs that Pius XII appreciated the need to move beyond the colonial mentality of previous eras, with its accompanying political and economic systems of servitude. In an implicit but clear-minded critique of old-world colonialism and of the ongoing tensions in Africa and Asia between indigenous populations and their erstwhile European colonizers, Pius XII in 1956 expressed solidarity with the "non-Europeans who aspire to full political independence." The lingering practices and mentality of old-world colonialism, the pope warned, were bound to fuel antagonism among indigenous populations which, in turn, would leave them vulnerable to the deceptive allure of Communist ideology. In his Christmas address of 1955, Pius XII declared, "Let not those peoples be denied a fair and progressive political freedom and [let them not be] hindered in its pursuit." In his last encyclical from June 1958, *Ad Apostolorum Principis,* which dealt with Communism and the church in China, Pius XII reiterated his teaching from earlier in the decade declaring "that the Catholic Church is a stranger to no people on earth, much less hostile to any. With a mother's anxiety, she embraces all peoples in impartial charity."[34]

Closer to home, the aging Pius XII showed a remarkable awareness of the social, economic, and cultural transformations that were challenging the Catholic laity in the West to question the relevance of church doctrine in their daily lives. Mindful of the growing appeal of domestic Communist and Socialist parties in Western Europe, Pius XII spoke frequently to workers and students, assuring them of the church's awareness of social questions and issues of economic fairness. Pius XII forcefully and persistently reiterated Catholic rejection of the Marxist class warfare thesis and defended private property rights; he also restated the church's commitment to such principles of social justice as the "just wage" for workers. In various venues and through diverse media, Pius XII urged Catholics to reject the extremes of Communist and capitalist economic systems, and work instead for a system ordered by a proper Christian sense of the dignity of the human person.[35]

In the area of church governance, one of the most consequential responsibilities of a pope is to appoint bishops and name cardinals, from whose ranks are drawn electors and future popes, as well as the heads of the influential offices of the Roman Curia. In this area of church life, Pius XII also broke new ground and helped lay the foundations for a truly global Catholic community. Evidence of his commitment to the internationalization of church governance was evident in the early months of his pontificate, when he appointed twelve indigenous bishops from Asia and Africa. The importance of the moment was not lost on Catholics in the old world. One French parish magazine, for instance, praised the new pope's appointments as "both an affirmation of the University of the Church and a condemnation of all racism." Pius XII's bold move was praised in 1939 as "a continuation of his predecessor's work" but also as "a fine response to the errors of Germanic racism."[36] Could it be that ordinary Catholics saw something in the new pope, something of his true intentions toward Nazism, that eluded the diplomats and heads of state?

Pius XII made history again after the war when in 1946 and 1953, respectively, he named as cardinals Thomas Tien of China and Valerian Gracias of India. They were the first indigenous Catholics of their respective nations to sit in the College of Cardinals.[37] The 1946 Consistory—the first of only two times in his long pontificate that Pius XII appointed new cardinals—was a historic step toward the internationalization of the central government of the church. It was also an opportunity for Pius XII to reward American Catholics for their stalwart moral and material support of Vatican policies through the war years with the appointment of leading American prelates as cardinals: Francis Spellman of New York, Edward Mooney of Detroit, Samuel Stritch of Chicago, and John Glennon of St. Louis. News coverage seized on the novelty of the occasion. For the first time in history, a contingent of cardinal designates, including Bishop Tien of China, traveled by air to receive the customary red hat. In a telling sign of the state of affairs in Italy at war's end, Vatican tailors did not have enough material to outfit all of the new cardinals with the robes proper to their new offices, leaving the American designates and Bishop Tien to borrow from the wardrobes of several deceased American cardinals.[38]

Speaking to the new cardinals in February 1946, Pius XII acknowledged publicly that his decision to appoint so many new cardinals from outside the traditional Catholic bastions of Europe reflected a deliberate strategy to underscore at the highest levels of church governance the "supranational character" and "universal unity" of the church. The pope took care to distinguish the church's sense of its global nature and mission from what he called "modern imperialism." The church, Pius XII declared, "is not an Empire," at least not in the way the modern world and modern states conceived of the term. In fact, he said, the two were diametrically opposed to each other at a fundamental level. For Pius XII, the universalism of the church sought first and foremost to preserve and promote individual identity and the dignity of the human person. The church worked to "model and perfect" the image of the divine in each individual as the proper foundation for a fair, just, and secure human society. The imperialism of the modern nation-state worked in the opposite sense, seeking expansion for its own sake and exploiting people to serve that end. For Pius XII, the selfish, self-serving territorial ambition that underlay modern imperialism had been and continued to be the cause of discord, insecurity, and instability in global affairs. It was the universalism of the church, Pius XII insisted, that offered the surest guarantee of meaningful, durable peace among nation-states and within societies.[39]

It could be said that no pope to that point had done more than Pius XII to foster a truly global Catholicism, giving spiritual inspiration and concrete material assistance to Catholic missionaries and local ecclesiastical authorities in Africa and Asia. Pius XII realized too that old-world assumptions about spreading the church's message would have to change to adapt to newfound realities. Speaking in 1955, he acknowledged explicitly the need to start thinking differently about the nature of the church's history and its mission. While recognizing that for many people Christianity's history was tied intimately to the West, the pope said that it was important to remember that the church "is conscious of having received her mission and task for all time to come and for all men, and consequently of being tied to no determined culture. . . . She is . . . ready to maintain contact with all cultures." This echoed a message Pius XII had sent to the Christians of India a few years before, when he insisted that the church respected indigenous cultures and customs and would compel "no one to adopt foreign ways of living." After all, he said, the church "belongs to the East as well as the West."[40]

In this sense, then, the church alone constituted what Pius XII described as the "perfect society"—a truly universal community that "embraces and unites all men in the unity of the mystical body of Christ." Each individual and all peoples, he said, therefore are called to come to the church, to the house of the Father, as he saw it. This call was a far cry from the "imperialistic tendencies of the day," Pius XII insisted. Deprived of a moral foundation and freed from all ethical restraints, the modern state, in its domestic affairs and in its international relations, pursued its naked material self-interest even after the war with a ruthless disregard for human life and for the integrity of entire communities. The results were everywhere to see in postwar Europe: the mass movements of people, the expulsions and the deportations ordered by governments to displace groups from their lands and their roots, and in the "violent separation" of countless families. Invoking the 1931 encyclical *Quadragesimo anno,* Pius XII proposed a Catholic alternative: an order within and among states that placed the whole human person, attendant with his full dignity and freedom as a child of God, at the very heart of the social order. Far from expressing vague and abstract philosophical principles, Pius XII insisted that there were practical matters at stake: basic questions about freedom, justice, equality, and authority in the communal life of society; about how to balance personal dignity and freedom with the common good; about how to organize the communal life of the "social body," as he put it, so that government and authority are exercised in ways that serve the individual and the common good, and not the other way around. A truly Christian social order, Pius XII believed sincerely, was the only concrete antidote to what he decried as the "degradation of man" and the "humiliating condition" wrought by mass society in modern times.[41] This was no call for retreating into some medieval Christian utopia, but rather a challenge to modernity to find its way back to the true source and purpose of human dignity and the common good.

Death of a Pope

At the end of October 1950, after returning from his usual solitary walk through the Vatican gardens, Pius XII told Mother Pascalina and the sisters of the household that he had just witnessed a "strange spectacle." Against an otherwise clear sky, the sun had suddenly darkened and then was encircled by a blazing ring of light, as if on fire. The pope watched transfixed without any harm to his eyes as the sun then moved gently from side to side. The next day he asked the sisters to accompany him on his walk, hoping they, too, would behold the wondrous sight. "Did you see?" Pius XII asked them as he watched in awe. "It was the same as yesterday." The sisters saw nothing. For Pius XII, though, there was no doubt that what he had seen was real. He could even interpret it as perhaps a celestial sign of favor on a momentous declaration he was set to issue that very day: the Dogma of the Assumption, the controversial move to enshrine in official church teaching an ancient but contentious belief in Christian tradition that upon her death the mother of Jesus was taken body and soul into heaven. The pope claimed to witness the spectacle of the sun a week later, and then again a year later while he was at the papal vacation residence at Castel Gandolfo. He even asked the Vatican Observatory whether its sophisticated instruments had detected anything unusual on those days. The records showed nothing out of the ordinary.[42]

These visions came to Pius XII amid a transitional phase in his pontificate and in global affairs. The year 1950 had been especially busy on various fronts, marked by numerous public functions to commemorate the Holy Year and by the release of a spate of encyclicals and speeches. Pius XII simultaneously steered a course for the church in changing international affairs while fulfilling what might be considered the most vital function of the papal office: to preserve and promote the coherence and consistency of Catholic doctrine while maintaining the unity of an increasingly diversified global Catholic community. It was estimated that at the time Pius XII died in 1958, the global Catholic population was just fewer than five hundred million—the single largest religious denomination. About half of all Catholics lived in Europe, and Catholics constituted the overwhelming majority in Central and South America. But sizable Catholic minorities were growing in North America, in the United States in particular, and in Asia and Africa. The economic influence of American Catholicism far surpassed the demographic presence of U.S. Catholics. Estimates had it that donations coming from American Catholics—who numbered around thirty-six million—translated into more than half of all Vatican revenues. Without the concrete material support of the American church, the Vatican's massive relief efforts, and its missionary work in Africa and Asia, would have been inconceivable. The fact was not lost on Pius XII, who did more than any pontiff in history to promote American prelates to positions of influence at the highest levels of church governance.[43]

In the early 1950s, papal concerns about postwar European reconstruction evolved into more generalized Cold War anxiety about the spread of Communism across the globe. There was a growing sense in the Vatican's diplomatic offices that crises in other parts of the world ought now to come to the fore of the Vatican's attention. Writing in 1953 to Bishop Aloisius Muench, Monsignor Montini complained about the many ordinary Germans who continued to write to the Holy See, and usually to the pope directly, asking for material assistance—for clothing, food, employment—or sometimes beseeching the Vatican to help in the sale of valuable artwork to aid German families in their economic recovery. Montini told Muench that with Germany's economic recovery well under way, it was time for Germans to "help each other" rather than continue begging the pope for aid. The Vatican now had to attend to more pressing concerns in other parts of the world, from the Middle East to Asia, and other areas of Europe.[44]

The globalization of the church made for a fuller papal agenda than ever, even as the aging Pius XII struggled through bouts of life-threatening illnesses. Those who had occasion to meet with Pius XII in those years marveled at the pontiff's sustained capacity for long days of work filled with meetings, study, and prayer. In private correspondence, the pope's personal confessor, Augustin Bea, documented the genuine concern among his advisors that Pius XII was pushing himself too hard, still keeping long hours, meeting with groups of pilgrims and dignitaries, and continuing to write and deliver speeches on a wide array of topics. Bea felt compelled to tell the pope of his concern. "The Pope refuses to discuss the subject," Bea wrote in 1956. On another occasion Bea observed in his personal papers that Pius XII "does not spare himself because his sense of duty is too strong to allow this."[45]

In fact, Pius XII's personal habits changed hardly at all as the pope grew older. Aloisius Muench recorded in his diary in October 1953 that the pope "has grown old since I saw him two years ago—illness of last winter took much of him." The meeting ended with a warm embrace between the two men, with Pius XII thanking a deeply moved Muench for his work on behalf of the church in Germany.[46] Within a few months of that meeting, in February 1954, the pope fell gravely ill. Muench recorded in his diary that reports about Pius XII's health were "not good." The Vatican was not saying much about the pope's condition, and what it was saying was, to Muench's mind, "unsatisfactory." This only served to fuel rampant speculation in the media, with some reports claiming that Pius XII was suffering from a form of severe depression, while others concluded that the pope was suffering from gastritis, ulcers, or possibly even stomach cancer. Reliable information from the pope's inner circle confirmed that Pacelli indeed was suffering from some kind of digestive ailment, a problem that had plagued him since childhood. Muench recorded in his diary that those with access to the papal court were preparing for Pacelli's imminent death. The pope was said to be in a fragile state. Weeks without solid food had left the gaunt Pacelli emaciated. Discreetly, Muench prepared the draft of an obituary for the news agencies.[47]

By early April 1954, Pius XII was on his way to recovery, though concerns about his delicate health persisted. In December rumors began to swirl of yet another medical crisis. Some reports said that the pope had suffered a heart attack, while others suggested that the stomach ailments of earlier in the year had returned with a vengeance. This was more than speculation. Pius XII was on the precipice, again, of a life-threatening illness whose precise nature or origins were never made quite clear. The pope's health deteriorated to the point where he was administered his last rites. A team of physicians kept constant watch while his circle of advisors prepared for the inevitable. Father Robert Leiber reportedly said of the pope, "If he lives until Christmas, we can thank God."[48] Those closest to Pius XII took some comfort in knowing that well before falling ill, the pope had spoken openly of his mortal end. He even claimed to have had a kind of revelation about his own passing, telling his inner circle, "I will die suddenly, but I have asked for one day to prepare myself."[49]

As he straddled the line between life and death near the end of 1954, Pius XII experienced another one of his visions. The pope confided the episode to a number of close friends, including his private secretary, Father Hentrich, who recorded Pacelli's version of events in his diary.[50] Pius XII also shared the story with Father Virginio Rotondi, an Italian Jesuit who went to visit the ailing Pacelli on the morning of December 2. Pius XII told Rotondi flatly, "This morning I saw the Lord." The pope proceeded to explain how the day before he had heard a voice alerting him to expect a vision. The next day, having received Holy Communion, Pius XII prayed the traditional *Anima Christi* prayer. As he uttered the words, "In the hour of my death call me," Pius XII says that

Jesus appeared and stood next to him. Convinced that his earthly pilgrimage was ending, Pius XII continued with the prayer, proclaiming, *"Et iube me venire ad te*—And bid me come unto Thee."

The apparition ended, and Pius XII recovered. His time was still a few years off. As he lay convalescing in the days after the vision, he confided to Cardinals Eugène Tisserant and Nicola Canali that he was "disappointed" to have survived.[51] Each successive health scare left the aging pontiff weaker and dependent, physically and emotionally, on a small and increasingly restricted circle of attendants and confidants. The narrow and rarefied world of the papal court grew more insular, with competing agendas and petty jealousies combining to accentuate the dawning awareness of a pending transition in power. Mother Pascalina was the reputed cause of persistent discontent among Vatican insiders who resented her overbearing manner and excessive influence over the pope. Cardinal Mario Nasalli Rocca di Corneliano, a longtime Vatican insider who had known Pacelli since the early 1930s, concluded that Mother Pascalina's influence over Pius XII was "significant," especially in matters concerning internal Vatican affairs and the Holy See's dealings with Germany, Bavaria, and Switzerland. Nasalli Rocca recalled hearing Domenico Tardini complain bitterly about this situation in colorful language. It was said that Mother Pascalina was aware of her power and influence, and that she was not above exercising her privileged access to Pius XII to settle personal scores. She reportedly was overheard boasting once about having convinced the pope in 1946 to delay naming Monsignor Borgoncini-Duca a cardinal. Presumably this was in retribution for certain suspicions Borgoncini-Duca— a long-serving member of the Congregation for Extraordinary Ecclesiastical Affairs—had raised while Pacelli was nuncio in Berlin about Lehnert's relationship with the future Pius XII and about the propriety of her role in the nuncio's office.

Given his rectitude and sense of responsibility to the papal office, it is difficult to imagine that Pius XII would allow himself to be influenced by anyone, let alone the head of his household, in something as important as the appointment of a cardinal. This is not to say that Mother Pascalina played a trivial role in papal circles. The former deputy-editor of *L'Osservatore Romano*, Cesidio Lolli, agreed that Mother Pascalina exercised considerable influence in and around the papal court, and not only over household matters. She could be overly zealous at times in controlling access to the pope, to the point of trying to limit the frequency and duration of Lolli's important meetings with Pius XII to discuss revisions of papal statements set to be published in the Vatican's official mouthpiece. Lolli recalled an incident in which Lehnert interrupted one of his meetings with Pius XII to remind the pope that it was time for dinner. The pope gave Mother Pascalina a stern look and kindly asked her to leave.

In later years, Mother Pascalina dismissed such claims, saying that in all her time working for the pope, she had never once interrupted an important meeting.[52] To Lolli, Pius XII undoubtedly had enormous respect and even abiding affection for Mother Pascalina, especially for her superior organizational skills. The pope made no secret of his admiration for Mother Pascalina's administration of the Vatican warehouse, which she ran with exacting precision in wartime and during postwar reconstruction to help coordinate the massive papal relief effort. Pius XII was convinced that her skills in this regard were second to none. As he put it to Lolli, "She is good at what she does." Father Wilhelm Hentrich, for sixteen years Pius XII's private secretary, recalled the pope's reaction when Mother Pascalina broke her foot and was hospitalized: a distraught Pius XII heaped praise on the Bavarian nun, saying that without Mother Pascalina, he would have died a long time ago. Beyond appreciating her indispensable role in the running of the papal household, Pius XII knew that he could trust Mother Pascalina to follow his orders in the handling of the papal relief efforts, no small thing for a pope who ruled in a highly personalized manner and counted on the informal network of his inner circle to execute some of the more important pieces of papal policy. Often when Pius XII met privately in the evenings with his nephew Carlo and Enrico Galeazzi, ostensibly to discuss matters related to the administration of Vatican City, it was not uncommon for the pope to invite Mother Pascalina to be present.[53]

Clearly, then, Lehnert was something more than the pope's housekeeper, even though she held no formal position in the Vatican's power structure. Cardinal Mario Nasalli Rocca di Corneliano acknowledged in later years that, from what he saw of how the papal court worked, Mother Pascalina was indeed an influential figure.[54] To be sure, she enjoyed the trust and respect of influential prelates who were especially close to Pius XII, including Cardinal Faulhaber of Munich and Cardinal Spellman of New York. There was no question that Mother Pascalina oversaw the papal relief effort with an iron fist, and that she sometimes lacked tact when dealing with high-ranking clerics. Invariably, this ruffled a few feathers, especially among certain influential members of the Roman Curia. After Pius XII's death, Mother Pascalina would pay the price for her authoritarian and domineering manner, as was evident in the rumors that circulated in Roman circles and in the press alleging among other things that she and the sisters may have profited materially from their privileged access to the pope and to the papal relief warehouse. To a person, the other members of Pius XII's inner circle of aides and confidants, while acknowledging Mother Pascalina's at times overbearing manner, dismissed such allegations as unfounded and grossly unfair.

There could be no doubt as to Mother Pascalina's sincere devotion to the pope, and to the simple, self-effacing manner in which she and the other sisters went about serving the Holy Father.[55] What mattered above all to the formidable Bavarian sister was the pope's confidence in her honest and capable work, and this Mother Pascalina enjoyed in spades. Still, it is difficult to imagine that Pius XII would allow Mother Pascalina to interfere in sensitive church affairs. It was one thing to involve her in decisions pertaining to the distribution of papal relief. It was something else altogether to envision Pius XII turning to Mother Pascalina for advice on matters relating to church governance like the naming of bishops.[56]

There were signs that an ailing Pius XII was losing his renowned control over his own entourage, evidence that age and illness were taking their toll on his capacity for lucid judgment and effective governance. A telling indication of waning papal control, at least over some members of the pope's inner circle, came when news broke in the Italian media late in 1955 of Pius XII's purported visions of Christ a year before. Father Rotondi told the story of the pope's vision to a popular Italian magazine, even though Pius XII had sworn him to secrecy. News spread quickly to media around the world, prompting the Vatican's newspaper to issue a statement saying that the pope "certainly neither desired nor approved" of the so-called indiscretion that led to the reporting of his vision.[57] But the Vatican did not deny the actual claim of a purported vision, which many took to be confirmation that the pope really did profess to have seen visions. The remarkable nature of the claim was not lost on commentators in either the secular or the Catholic media. As reported in the British Catholic weekly The Tablet, "There is, we believe, no authenticated record of a vision of Christ being experienced by any earlier Pope other than St. Peter himself." Of course, other popes in history had claimed to see visions of one kind or another, but, as *The Tablet* concluded, Pius XII's claim "is the only example we can find of a vision of any kind being attributed to a Pope for more than a thousand years."[58]

The publicity surrounding the pope's fantastical claims embarrassed some Catholics. After all, it was one thing to hear that Pius XII was seeing things, but another thing entirely to think that the stories of visions were being publicized deliberately by the Holy See, as if to lend to Pius XII an aura of sanctity. The pope's advisors found themselves in a delicate situation. They could hardly deny outright any talk of visions and apparitions, especially with Pius XII insisting that what he had experienced was real. "I can tell you," the pope said to Domenico Tardini, "the others might think it was a sick man's hallucination." Pius XII insisted, "This morning, while I was assisting at Holy Mass, for an instant I saw Our Lord. It was only an instant, but I saw Him clearly."[59] As the pope's personal confessor, Augustin Bea was uniquely positioned to offer insights into the matter. Writing to one skeptical critic, Bea insisted that it was "certain" that Pius XII had experienced the vision described in news reports, saying specifically that Pius XII "is convinced that it was *not* an illusion."[60] Whatever they may have thought of the pope's purported visions, members of his inner circle could not ignore that Pius's claims to have seen Christ coincided with a remarkable recovery from a dreadfully serious illness, one that had seen the long-serving pope at death's door near the end of 1954. Bea unhesitatingly described the pope's recovery after December 1954 as nothing short of a "miracle."[61]

Although Pius XII maintained a full and active schedule, with no signs of altering his routine of constant work until the early-morning hours, the effects of age and declining health were readily evident. Meeting with Aloisius Muench in May 1957, Robert Leiber assured the American prelate that Pius XII continued to follow German affairs more closely than any others, and still read attentively all of Muench's reports. The pope was in relatively good health, but he tired more easily and his face showed obvious signs of fatigue. Leiber was convinced that should Pius XII suffer another bout of pneumonia, he likely would not recover.[62] When Muench met with the pope a week later, he found Pius XII in a sprightly mood. In the course of a forty-five-minute discussion that was dominated, as always, by talk of German affairs, the pope managed to get in a highly offensive joke, knowing presumably that Muench would not object: Hitler and Moses meet in heaven. Hitler apologizes for his treatment of the Jews and then asks Moses whether he started the fire of the burning bush. This was an apparent allusion to presumed Nazi responsibility for the Reichstag fire of 1933, although Muench's mention of the episode in his diary does not elaborate on what Pius XII was trying to say. It may have been merely an ill-conceived and flippant remark, or perhaps it betrayed anti-Jewish prejudice carefully hidden from public view. Either way, the insensitive remark showed little of the refined probity for which Pacelli was renowned.

When Muench saw Pius XII again in June 1958, he was surprised to find the pope in remarkably good health. As had been the case for several years, though, Pius XII seemed fixated on the afterlife. He told Muench that, having reached the ripe old age of eighty-two, he was eager to "go to heaven." In late September 1958, Pius XII began exhibiting symptoms of the digestive problems that had afflicted him in the previous bouts of illness.[63] The return of persistent hiccups was especially alarming. The pope admitted that he was feeling ill, so much so that he cancelled his weekly public audience. Vatican Radio announced simply that the pope was not able to speak publicly because of a "slight indisposition."

In fact, Pius XII was dying. For a few days he managed to continue working, meeting with individuals and groups, including some seven hundred American pilgrims who were introduced to the pope by his old friend and confidant Cardinal Spellman. The persistent hiccupping was impossible to miss. He took a decisive turn for the worse on Saturday, October 4, when he was forced to cut short his address to a group of Italian plastic surgeons, but not before he decried the immorality of surgery performed "only to satisfy vanity or the caprice of fashion" while acknowledging instances when plastic surgery may be legitimate, even necessary.[64] Later that evening, while trying to work at his desk, Pius XII said he felt ill and fainted.

Undeterred by the illness that slowly was consuming his already frail body, Pius XII insisted on making a public appearance on the balcony of the papal residence at Castel Gandolfo. This would be his last public appearance, to members of the International Congress of Public Notaries. It was clear to everyone who saw him that day that the situation was critical. One of the pope's physicians, stomach specialist Antonio Gasbarrini, was immediately summoned from Venice to Rome. In the early-morning hours of Monday, October 6, Pius XII suffered what Vatican officials were describing as "cerebral circulatory disturbances." It was a stroke. The pope was paralyzed and falling in and out of consciousness. His personal secretary, Father Wilhelm Hentrich, administered the last rites. Other physicians were called to the pope's bedside, including the discredited Riccardo Galeazzi-Lisi, the half-brother of the powerful Vatican City official and papal confidant Enrico Galeazzi. Galeazzi-Lisi, who was an ophthalmologist, began caring for Pius XII when Pacelli was secretary of state and is said to have earned Pacelli's eternal gratitude for helping to relieve chronic headaches attributed to eye strain. This, together with the noteworthy family connection, doubtless explains why Pacelli appointed Galeazzi-Lisi his personal physician upon becoming pope in 1939. The physician fell out of favor with the pope, however, after attempting to sell to the press his personal diaries—reportedly to the tune of $12,000 U.S.—detailing Pius XII's health crisis of 1954.[65]

How, or why, Galeazzi-Lisi had been readmitted into Pius XII's good graces and allowed to be part of a reserved team of specialists to treat the dying pontiff was a question very much on the minds of Vatican observers in the weeks and months following Pacelli's death. That such a dubious figure should have been invited to join a team of noteworthy specialists to treat the pope in his final days may be owing to the decisive influence of Mother Pascalina. One account suggests that when Pius XII fell gravely ill in early October, the sisters of his household, unable to locate Gasbarrini, turned to the disgraced Galeazzi-Lisi. An unapologetic and emboldened Galeazzi-Lisi took to giving press conferences in the days after Pius XII died, to the Vatican's great embarrassment. He told the press, among other things, that it was the pope himself who had called the discredited physician to Castel Gandolfo the weekend Pacelli fell ill, asking for a "complete check."[66] As it happened, the man who a few years earlier had fallen out of favor with Pius XII found himself a protagonist in the dramatic final moments of Pacelli's life, and he would earn a measure of infamy for his bizarre behavior in the days following the pope's death.

The gravity of the pope's condition was made evident on October 6, when Vatican officials asked the clergy and the faithful of Rome to pray for their bishop. Churches across the city filled spontaneously as ordinary Romans gathered to offer prayers. The Vatican switchboard was inundated with calls from around the world, including from Italian President Giovanni Gronchi, asking for more information about the pope's condition and extending prayers and good wishes for his recovery. Aside from the obvious human dimension to news of a dying man, there were affairs of state at play. After all, Pacelli had been a deeply influential figure in the church and in global affairs for decades and had governed as pope in a highly personalized and centralized manner. It was not lost on outside observers that for most of his pontificate Pius XII had ruled without a secretary of state. Nor had he bothered to name a cardinal *camerlengo* (chamberlain) whose task it would be to manage church affairs in the interim between the pope's death and the election of a successor, the very role Pacelli had assumed so resolutely when Pius XI died in 1939. The absence of a formal chamberlain would leave the immediate transition in the hands of the French cardinal Tisserant, then dean of the Sacred College. The urgency of filling the vacancy was evident in the haste with which the cardinals chose one of their Italian counterparts, the accomplished papal diplomat Benedetto Aloisi Masella, to serve as interim camerlengo until after the election of the new pope.[67]

In the tense hours that followed, there were occasional hopeful signs of a recovery. A medical bulletin issued on Tuesday, October 7, said that Pius XII was "completely conscious." According to Cesidio Lolli, the pope was "perfectly lucid" throughout the day; he even asked to listen to a part of Beethoven's first symphony. The pope was well enough, in fact, to receive visitors, including his younger sister Elisabetta, and Monsignor Angelo dell'Acqua, then head of the general affairs section of the Secretariat. Days away from death, Pacelli was still conferring with his staff about church affairs.[68]

All hope of recovery was dashed the following morning when Pius XII suffered another stroke and fell into a coma. Official bulletins later that day said explicitly that the pope's condition offered "little hope" and had "progressively become more serious" despite vigorous treatment. Pius XII's nephews were summoned from Rome to Castel Gandolfo, where they found their uncle drifting in and out of consciousness. In a last, fleeting moment of lucidity, when he awoke to see Carlo Pacelli standing at his bedside, Pius XII asked, "What are you doing here? Get to work!" A few hours later, Pius XII lost all consciousness and, as his nephew put it, entered into his "agony."[69]

As Pacelli lay dying in a nondescript room on the second floor of the papal summer residence, away from the noise emanating from the crowd gathered below in the square in front of Castel Gandolfo, thousands of people, from the faithful to curious onlookers, descended on St. Peter's Square in Rome to keep vigil. Among them was a group of German pilgrims who had filled twelve buses for the long drive to Rome. Vatican Radio broadcast the Mass that was being celebrated just beyond the pope's bedroom by his long-time aide Domenico Tardini, and invited listeners to continue praying for the pope so that "God's will be done."[70]

On Thursday, October 9, Eugenio Pacelli breathed his last. The time was 3:52 A.M. The official cause of death was heart failure. Pacelli was surrounded by his nephews, by Mother Pascalina and the other sisters of the household, and by members of the papal staff, including the German Jesuits Hentrich and Leiber, and by Monsignor Tardini. It was Tardini, in fact, who intoned the *Magnificat,* popularly known as the Canticle of Mary, the great exhortation of Mary's assent to God's plan for salvation. Tardini was overheard saying that a saint was about to enter the gates of heaven.[71] Vatican Radio made the announcement of the pope's death a few minutes later. Church bells across the Eternal City tolled as a group of the faithful lingered before dawn in St. Peter's Square; some wept openly, while others fell to their knees to pray for the repose of Pacelli's soul. One woman expressed the sentiment of many mourners around the world when she said simply, "A saint has left us."[72]

The pope's last words reportedly were, "Pray, pray, pray that this unhappy situation for the Church may end."[73] A sick and infirm pope, one who was incapacitated physically or mentally, truly could not function for very long in an institution where he alone has the authority to make the most consequential decisions in spiritual or administrative affairs. Complicating matters was the absence of clear provisions, either in church law or by tradition, for how church affairs were to be administered when the pope was incapacitated. The absence of a powerful, resolute secretary of state—such as Pacelli had been in the last months and weeks of Ratti's pontificate—further fueled anxiety and uncertainty in curial circles and beyond about who was in charge as Pius XII lay dying. It fell to Cardinal Tisserant and a handful of cardinals of the Curia to form what reports described as an "informal directorate of cardinals" to attend to certain administrative matters during the pending papal transition.[74]

Signs that the Pacelli era was over were readily apparent within hours, even minutes, of Pius XII's death. Wilhelm Hentrich, the pope's personal secretary, left the papal palace immediately after hearing physicians confirm that the pope was dead.[75] His work was complete. News agencies reported seeing Mother Pascalina leaving Castel Gandolfo with two suitcases and a bird cage that held Pius XII's pet birds, including his favorite, a goldfinch named Gretel.[76] When she arrived at the Vatican in the hours after the pope died to assist Cardinal Tisserant in ordering Pius XII's personal effects before sealing the papal apartment, part of the ritual of the transition of papal power, Mother Pascalina found an official of the papal Noble Guard at the gates to block her entry. She was told brusquely never again to set foot on Vatican soil, although it is not clear whether any such formal orders were ever given, and, if so, by whom. As she recalled in later years, only the direct intervention of Cardinal Tisserant allowed her to gain entry into the Vatican palaces.[77]

At Castel Gandolfo, it fell to the sisters from Menzingen to help with the preparations for Pacelli's funeral. With the same reverence and devotion that had won them Pacelli's undying gratitude and loyalty in life, Mother Pascalina and the sisters served him in death, carefully dressing his body in preparation for the exposition of the corpse. It was to Mother Pascalina that Cardinal Tisserant turned to ask whether Pius XII had left anything in the way of a last will and testament. Tisserant understood that Mother Pascalina's privileged relationship with Pius XII made her indispensable to a smooth and orderly transition of power. Other Vatican insiders wondered about personal papers that the pope may have kept in his private study at Castel Gandolfo or in the Vatican, documentation that might be relevant to Vatican affairs, especially to the political and diplomatic business of the Secretariat of State. Mother Pascalina knew that in 1956 the pope had hastily composed a kind of spiritual testament, after having a premonition that he would die suddenly. It was written on the back of a scrap of paper, which he kept under lock and key in his desk in the papal apartment at the Vatican. With Mother Pascalina and Carlo Pacelli present, Tisserant was able to secure the pope's testament, which would be read to the entire Sacred College of Cardinals. With this vital step in the transition ensured, Cardinal Tisserant ordered the papal apartment to be closed and sealed off until the election of a new pope. As for Pius XII's personal papers, Mother Pascalina told the interested Vatican officials —in particular Monsignor dell'Aqua of the Secretariat of State—that he had left the members of his staff explicit orders to burn everything upon his death. This Mother Pascalina did, with the help of Sister Maria Corrada, the pope's cook.[78]

Tales of personal papers and even of a secret reform proposal left behind by the deceased pope persisted as the solemn rites of the papal funeral began. In the weeks after Pius XII died, rumors swirled about "diaries" that the pope reportedly had left but that had since disappeared. Some Vatican insiders apparently believed there might be some truth to the claim, hence the inquiries made of Mother Pascalina. In the hands of long-standing Vatican critics, like the Italian Communist newspaper *L'Unità*, the story evolved into a typical tale of Vatican intrigue, with Mother Pascalina and the pope's nephews at the center. Even the *New York Times* reported on the claim that after Pius XII's death, Vatican authorities saw Mother Pascalina carrying a "bulging briefcase" out of the papal residence and handing it over to an unidentified character waiting at the walls of Vatican City. The Communist daily opined that the man in question may have been one of the pope's nephews, or perhaps an "agent" working for the West German government. The pope's nephews denied the claim, while German and Italian authorities dismissed the entire report as "absurd."[79]

By late morning on October 9, Pius XII was lying in state at Castel Gandolfo. He was clothed in a plain white silk cassock adorned with embroidered vestments and a red velvet cape with an ermine trim, his head crowned with a stunning gold miter. On his feet were soft velvet shoes with embroidered gold crosses.[80] Thousands of mourners, from leading Italian statesmen and high-ranking Catholic prelates to ordinary citizens filed past the bier to pay their final respects. It was reported that some local Communists were in attendance to pay homage to the pope who had opened the doors of the papal palace to hundreds of refugees during the war, including partisans and Jews. Cardinal Spellman went to extraordinary lengths to be present at the papal palace. The New York–bound ship on which he was traveling at the time of the pope's death made an emergency stop in Portugal, and from there he was flown to Rome.[81]

In the late afternoon, the motorcade left Castel Gandolfo to escort the body of Pius XII to St. Peter's. Tens of thousands of mourners and onlookers lined the highway to Rome, with crowds sometimes spilling onto the streets to get a closer look or even quickly touch the hearse carrying the body of the pope whom many Romans credited with helping to deliver the city from the worst excesses of war. Angelo Roncalli, the cardinal archbishop of Venice, who in a matter of weeks would be chosen to succeed Pacelli, marveled at the historic turnout of ordinary Romans to pay homage to their bishop. He confided to his diary that it was unlikely any Roman emperor had ever received such popular acclamation.[82]

The funeral cortege was late in arriving at the Church of Saint John Lateran, the Cathedral of the Diocese of Rome, where funeral rites were celebrated. Finally, the remains were carried to the Vatican. Throngs of mourners and onlookers continued to line the route that led from Saint John Lateran to St. Peter's, passing through the heart of the ancient city, and along the modern Corso Vittorio Emanuele, which crossed in front of the storied streets and neighborhoods of Pacelli's youth. The pope's nephews, Francesco's sons Carlo, Marcantonio, and Giulio Pacelli, walked behind the hearse.

The bells of St. Peter's tolled as the procession wound its way through the heart of the ancient city, beckoning Pius XII to his final resting place. The crowds that lined the route to the Vatican flowed into St. Peter's Square, which was filled to capacity. Pius XII lay in state in St. Peter's, in the apse just beyond Bernini's monumental canopy, which towers over the main altar. He was to be interred in the crypt beneath the majestic basilica, just steps from Peter's tomb. For admirers, it was only fitting that Pacelli should be laid to rest near the tomb of the first pope; after all, it was he who had ordered the definitive investigation of the crypt beneath the basilica, where researchers found compelling evidence to confirm what tradition had long held was the burial site of Saint Peter, the first pope.[83]

The bier was flanked by members of the Noble Guard, a colorful, symbolic remnant of the papal military forces of a bygone era. From dawn to dusk for three consecutive days, tens of thousands of people filed past the bier as the guards kept constant vigil. Detracting from the majestic solemnity of the moment were signs that the pope's body was decomposing rapidly. Observers noted that the eyes of the guards and others keeping vigil at the bier of Pius XII "smarted and watered." Evidence of rapid decomposition was impossible to ignore as thousands of mourners continued to file past the body. It was the first of a series of undignified episodes connected to the pope's former personal physician, Riccardo Galeazzi-Lisi. Inexplicably, the disgraced doctor was charged with the task of embalming the pope's body, even though he had no expertise in that area. Galeazzi-Lisi told the press that, together with the plastic surgeon Oreste Nuzzi, he had embalmed the pope's body using a method called "aromatic osmosis," which consisted of transmitting resins and oils into a corpse by means of a semi-permeable membrane—in effect a cellophane sheet that was placed over the body for twenty hours. The sheet was removed when Pius XII's body was prepared for return to Rome. Even as word of the botched embalmment emerged, Galeazzi-Lisi boasted grandiosely to the press that the method used was similar to the way that Christ's body would have been prepared after his crucifixion. It had the advantage of avoiding any injections or evisceration of the corpse, Galeazzi-Lisi said, and would preserve Pius XII's corpse indefinitely.[84]

For Galeazzi-Lisi, it was the beginning of the end of a bizarre association with the papal court that befuddled Vatican insiders, the Italian medical profession, and Vatican watchers everywhere. His rift with the pope over his attempt to sell details of Pius XII's earlier health crisis was no secret. That the discredited doctor was allowed back into the pope's inner circle even after this episode was taken by many in the pope's entourage as a sign of Pius XII's charity and compassion. It seems likely, too, that the pope was inclined to at least tolerate Galeazzi-Lisi's presence in papal circles as a sign of respect to the doctor's eminently more serious and infinitely more influential half-brother Enrico Galeazzi. It is impossible to rule out the possibility that Pius XII himself wanted Galeazzi-Lisi nearby as he struggled with declining health.

Galeazzi-Lisi's continued presence in the papal entourage even after the controversy of the mid-1950s could be taken as a sign of the pope's munificence, but it also raises questions about Pius XII's judgment. One Milan newspaper put it bluntly: "How could Pius XII entrust his health for so many years to a quack?"[85] The dubious qualifications and character of the chief papal physician were painfully obvious when Galeazzi-Lisi created something of a media sideshow as Pius XII lay dying, and in the days and weeks after Pacelli's death. The first sign of trouble came when media outlets in Rome printed news of the pope's death at Castel Gandolfo almost a day before it actually happened. A pool of reporters had arranged to pay Galeazzi-Lisi, who was at the dying pope's bedside, to give them some signal from a window of Castel Gandolfo—the waving of a handkerchief—to alert them when the pope had expired. Evidently some Italian reporters camped outside the papal palace mistook a fluttering curtain as the decisive signal and passed on the erroneous word of the pope's death. Monsignor Angelo dell'Aqua rushed from Castel Gandolfo back to the Vatican to deny the rumor. By order of the local police, the news reports were retracted.[86]

There was worse to come. In the days and weeks after Pius XII died, news stories from Italy recounted in vivid detail Pacelli's death agony. Even more shocking was the publication in newspapers around the world of Pius XII on his death bed, his face and body physically marked by the predictable signs of suffering. In time it became clear that the source of information about the pope's final hours and of the distasteful photographs was none other than Galeazzi-Lisi.[87] The doctor's attempts to profit from his personal care of the pope, which had been thwarted a few years earlier, finally succeeded. In addition to his own detailed clinical notes of Pacelli's final hours, which recorded even the minutest detail of the patient's vital signs, Galeazzi-Lisi managed to sneak in a camera to photograph the dying pontiff. His personal diary and the photos were to be sold to the highest bidder; one report suggested that Galeazzi-Lisi wanted just over $3,000 U.S. for pictures of the pope's death throes, and about the same for a detailed account of the pope's final hours. Pacelli's former personal physician even charged money to tell his story of the dubious embalming method. Various Italian dailies published the details of Pius XII's final agony, and the story was reprinted in newspapers around the world, albeit with certain "crude" details excised.[88]

The Vatican was indignant. The whole sordid episode was an affront not only to the memory of a great pope but also to the personal dignity of the deceased man. Vatican officials denounced the publication of such distasteful reports without naming Galeazzi-Lisi directly. His days as a Vatican insider were over. The only official sign of displeasure with Galeazzi-Lisi came with the publication in *L'Osservatore Romano* of the doctor's letter to Cardinal Tisserant tendering his resignation. The Vatican organ reported tersely, "The resignation has been accepted," adding that Galeazzi-Lisi's position as papal physician had ended formally with Pius XII's death. News reports also confirmed that the College of Cardinals had ordered Vatican City police to bar the doctor from Vatican territory. More serious trouble awaited the unscrupulous physician. In December 1958, Rome's Medical Association barred him from practicing in Italy. At the same time, Galeazzi-Lisi faced the prospect of a criminal investigation. The Italian prime minister, Amintore Fanfani, launched an inquiry to determine whether Galeazzi-Lisi should be punished under Italian law, by virtue of the 1929 Lateran treaty, which made public insults against the person of the pope a punishable offense akin to insults against the president of the Italian Republic.[89]

Pius XII was laid to rest in the crypt beneath St. Peter's on October 13, 1958. It was the anniversary of the Miracle of the Sun, the purported celestial sign promised in an apparition of the Virgin Mary to three peasant children at Fatima, Portugal, in 1917, and akin to the spectacle Pius XII claimed to have seen in 1950, a fitting bookend for a life punctuated by an intense devotion to the cult of the Madonna. The funeral was a historic event: the first papal funeral to be televised to a potential audience of some twenty million people, with millions more around the world following the rites broadcast in various languages from Vatican Radio. Evidence that this was the dawn of the television age was obvious from the "candid shots" broadcast in the two-hour ceremony. The Prefect of Pontifical Ceremonies was shown muttering directions under his breath, while a lay dignitary wearing the colorful garb of a Spanish aristocrat played with his sword. These quizzical moments could not detract from the solemnity and the simple majesty of the event: the catafalque bearing the body of Pius XII stood at the heart of the basilica, circled by a contingent of Swiss Guards and by the officiating prelates, the cardinals of the Sacred College first among them.

It was early evening when the coffin of Pius XII was lowered into the crypt of St. Peter's by pulleys erected next to the central altar of the basilica, to the sounds of the ancient *Benedictus* hymn. In his last will and testament, Pius XII had pleaded with those charged with caring for his mortal remains not to erect grand monuments to his memory. "It would be good enough if my poor mortal remains," he wrote, "are placed simply in a holy place, the more obscure the better." The niche in the papal crypt beneath St. Peter's, a spot Pius XII himself reportedly chose, truly was a holy place for Christians. But lying as it was across from the tomb of Saint Peter—the "rock" on whom the Church of Christ was to be built—Pacelli's tomb could hardly be considered obscure; this place was the very seat of the papal office and the heart of Roman Catholic Christianity. Was there a more fitting burial place for the man who, at his ordination more than a half-century earlier, had described himself simply as *Eugenio Pacelli, Roman,* and had lived all of his adult life as a dutiful prelate working in Saint Peter's shadow?

Epilogue

A Virtuous Life?

"The world pauses on the death of a Pope." So began an editorial in *Life* magazine in October 1958 that eulogized Eugenio Pacelli as "the most impressive living symbol of the spiritual which the world knew." Here was a man of his times, and yet a man for all times, someone at ease with the trappings of modernity but with the prophetic foresight to adapt an ancient and unchanging faith to a changing global reality. From the mundane features of his daily routine—his use of an electric razor, say, or a typewriter and dictaphone—to the more consequential and "far harder work" of applying Catholic teaching to "a bewildering variety of grimly concrete situations," in everything he said and did, Pius XII truly was a "modern Pope." Not since the time of Saint Thomas Aquinas had the church seen one of its own so willing and able to offer what *Life*'s editorial called "a comprehensive spiritual comment on the temporality around him," sharing original and authoritative insights on a diverse and "inexhaustible" range of topics—from women's fashions, to the effects of television on family life, to the virtues of space exploration, to the dangers of irresponsible use of pharmaceutical drugs or the ethical use of painkillers for terminally ill patients. Pius XII wanted not so much to come to terms with the modern world as to transform it, to sanctify and ready it for its redemption.[1]

This and other early assessments of Pius XII's life and work suggested that he had been a good pope, perhaps even great. It was said that he transformed the papacy into an actor in global affairs, increasing its prestige and its influence by advocating for humanity in a time of crisis and uncertainty. An editorial in the *Wall Street Journal* concluded that Pius XII "made a distinguished mark on Western institutions," above all by showing "that the real basis of those institutions is moral force." Commentators observed that although some would have liked the pope to have spoken out more forcefully against Nazism during the war, there was no doubt that he was anti-Nazi and anti-Fascist. He was also prescient in his fight against Communism. Pius XII was, in the words of one commentary, "strongly anti-Communist when many Western leaders were not." It was a quality of Pacelli's leadership that resonated with Polish Cardinal Stefan Wyszynski, who knew firsthand the true nature of the Nazi and Soviet systems. Speaking to thousands of mourners in Warsaw on the eve of Pacelli's funeral, Wyszynski praised Pius XII for his uncompromising, consistent opposition to "the abominable totalitarian systems" and for his defense of "universal human rights."[2]

Church leaders everywhere were unanimous in their praise for the deceased pontiff. Admittedly, it would have been difficult for churchmen in positions of power to say otherwise. Still, even erstwhile critics were effusive in their admiration. Archbishop Joseph P. Hurley, who had worked with some measure of disagreement under the pope during and after the war, said from St. Augustine, Florida, that he was "inexpressibly grieved at the death of his Holiness Pope Pius XII." One of the sharper critics of Pius XII's wartime role, Hurley nevertheless managed to muster a positive assessment of the deceased pontiff. Pius XII was a "man of peace," Hurley conceded, who "taught us to fight our way with Christian fortitude up through materialistic darkness to the light of grace." The primate of Canada, Archbishop Maurice Roy of Quebec, said, "A great Pope has just died," while Bishop Fulton J. Sheen of New York remarked, "We have lost a father on earth, but have gained an ambassador of the peace to plead in heaven for our wounded world." Pacelli's old friend Cardinal Spellman remarked on a personal note that "[t]hose who have been privileged with the intimacy of a deeper friendship have ever come from his presence stimulated with the realization that they have been in the presence of the Vicar of Christ." From Hong Kong, Bishop Lawrence Bianchi declared, "The Catholics of Hong Kong have special reason to lament the death of Pope Pius XII. Time after time he showed special favor to us."[3]

There was no shortage of voices from the Jewish world praising the late pontiff for his work on behalf of the persecuted Jews. This may come as a surprise, given the firestorm of controversy that has followed Pius XII since the 1960s. Whether it was because a full understanding of the Holocaust had yet to mature or because sensibilities about the role of powerful institutions like the papacy had yet to change, as they would during the cultural revolution of the 1960s, up to the time he died, Pius XII generally was admired by Jewish communities everywhere. Israeli President Itzhak Ben-Zvi asked the country's ambassador in Rome to pass along his condolences to the Vatican, referring to himself as "spokesperson" for the numerous Jewish refugees saved "from death and torture" by Pius XII's interventions during the war.[4] Golda Meir, Israeli foreign minister at the time, sent a telegram to the Vatican, mourning the pontiff's death and praising his work on behalf of the Jewish people during the years of "Nazi terror." The chief rabbi of Jerusalem, Isaac Herzog, wrote to the Vatican to say that the death of Pius XII was a loss for all the "free world," and that Catholics were not alone in mourning his loss. Before the start of a concert on the day the pope died, Leonard Bernstein led the New York Philharmonic Orchestra in a moment of silence to acknowledge the passing of a "great man," Pope Pius XII. In the words of Pinchas Lapide, a former Israeli diplomat in Italy, never before had a pope been thanked with such warm praise by the Jewish communities of the world for the work he had done on behalf of the persecuted Jews of Europe. Rome's chief rabbi, Elia Toaff, said something similar in the days after Pius XII died. "More than any other people," he remarked, "the Italian Jews had experienced the great pity and supreme generosity of the pontiff during the unfortunate years of persecution and terror, when it seemed to them they had no open way of escape." Toaff went on to provide tangible evidence of the pope's work on behalf of Italian Jews, referring to "the papal ruling to open the doors of convents and parish houses" to the persecuted Jews.[5]

Although the cause to have Pius XII declared a saint does not rest on his purported rescue and relief work on behalf of Jews, and others, during World War Two, his promoters point to the testimony of witnesses like Toaff to demonstrate that through an extraordinary exercise of *prudence,* Pius XII saved many, many lives. This is what matters, they say, not what the pope said or did not say either during or after the war. For some people, the word *prudence* suggests a certain measure of cowardice and selfishness; the prudent person is someone who avoids making the difficult and even risky decisions for the sake of self-preservation.[6] But for the spiritual and intellectual tradition in which Pius XII was steeped, prudence is considered to be the "mother" of all virtues—that practical wisdom that determines moral and ethical action, in keeping with God's laws. Following Aristotle, Thomas Aquinas defined prudence as "right reason in action." *Omnis virtus moralis debet essens prudens,* Aquinas held: "All virtue is necessarily prudent." All of the ethical virtues—justice, fortitude, and temperance—are grounded in and molded by the virtue of prudence. Put in lay man's terms, only the prudent person can be good, fair, and temperate.[7] To act prudently is not to act perfectly, without fault or misjudgment. The prudent person, called to act in practical ways in the world, meditates and deliberates. He seeks counsel from history and from the learned, and tries to discern the will of God while weighing the risks and benefits as well as the potential consequences of a given course of action. The Book of Proverbs (14:15) has it that the prudent man "looks where he is going." Another version puts it this way: the "clever consider their steps."

Whatever we might say about him or however we might judge his actions, there can be no doubt that Pius XII always looked where he was going, always considered his steps. For his many critics, this suggests that Pius XII was more clever than prudent. Others, by contrast, reason that by carefully considering his steps, by refusing to speak out explicitly against the systematic persecution of Jews in particular, Pius XII wisely preserved the church's capacity for concrete action, however limited or inadequate. Indeed, as we have seen, the Vatican's Secretariat of State itself boasted to Allied officials near war's end that the Holy See could be credited with making it possible for Rome's many religious institutions and residences to offer shelter and assistance to some 6,000 Jews in Rome during the Nazi occupation of the city.[8] Other estimates cited by established historians such as Renzo De Felice and Meir Michaelis—and accepted by such eminent scholars as Sir Martin Gilbert—put that number at around 4,000 Jews who found shelter and survival in dozens of Rome's religious institutions, not to mention the thousands of others who found refuge in private homes.[9] For the advocates of Pius XII, the salient point is this—without the pope's approval, albeit indirect and private, such systematic and effective succor would not have been feasible.

The absence of substantive documentation to trace the courageous rescue efforts of religious orders and ordinary citizens directly back to the pope and the Holy See has not discouraged promoters from building what they say is a solid argument grounded on an eminently logical inference. Indeed, to the criticism that Pius XII failed to protest forcefully in public when the Nazis began the roundup of Rome's Jews, his promoters argue that by virtue of his prudent, pragmatic approach, he helped save the lives of the vast majority of Rome's Jewish community. From the historical records currently available, we know that in places like Budapest many thousands of Jews found shelter and ultimately survival thanks to the efforts of papal representatives acting apparently with Pius XII's blessing and material assistance. Other evidence shows that through his representatives, Pius XII protested forcefully when the Slovak government began to deport approximately 80,000 Jews to Auschwitz. There are many more such wartime records that document Pius XII's knowledge of and support for various initiatives by papal representatives and church institutions to protect tens of thousands of European Jews. Mostly, it did not help but sometimes it did. And lives were saved.

Yet the cause to have Pius XII made a saint will always be dogged by a great imponderable that lingers over Pius XII's policy of avoiding public confrontation with the Hitler regime. It is the standard by which his pontificate has been judged wanting by so many critics, no matter what might be said about rescue and relief efforts. *What if* Pius XII had issued a forceful, unequivocal condemnation of Nazism and especially its persecution of Jews? *What if* the pope had directed his representatives and all European Catholics to resist Nazi policies actively? How many more Jews, and others, might have been saved?

It is impossible to provide properly historical answers to such imponderables. It might be a useful analytical tool to speculate on possible outcomes of a different approach from the pope during the Holocaust. It is clear enough that Pius XII *could* have spoken out more clearly, more explicitly, to denounce the Nazi persecution of Jews and others, including Catholics. He could have directed Catholic agencies and the Catholic faithful to make anti-Nazi resistance a religious crusade or the rescue of Jews and other victims a religious duty. So, yes, Pius XII could have done things differently. But we can never say with certainty that a different approach would have produced a different outcome. The approach he chose—to avoid public confrontation and thus avoid a greater evil, as he put it—is all we have to go by. How do we assess this approach? That is the question.

Or it is one question. If we widen our lens and view the whole of Pius XII's life and pontificate, the question emerges: where in the long, travailed history of the papacy, an institution with ancient roots that has seen its share of sinners and saints, does Pope Pius XII sit?[10] While the study of Pius XII's full legacy awaits its historian, there is a strong argument to be made that taken as a whole his reign over the church was consistent with the moral, pastoral, and political leadership expected of the Vicar of Christ. Pius XII fulfilled the complex papal role as well as anyone of his generation, or any generation, could. He maintained decent working relationships with all the major constituencies of the Catholic community. While resolutely defending the claims of papal supremacy, Pius XII generally was respectful of the authority of local bishops. He sought their counsel and showed himself willing and able to defer to their discretion, especially in instances where the application of a universal standard risked having untold adverse effects according to local, regional, or national circumstances. He preached but also practiced the noblest sense of the religious calling, marrying asceticism and self-denial with an elevated sense of the priest's vocation, all the while taking decisive first steps toward a greater opening to the laity. In many respects, he governed the internal affairs of the church with a firm but flexible, pragmatic sensibility. He left the Vatican's finances arguably in better shape than ever in modern times and helped to bolster the material position of the Holy See through a deft reliance on the growing financial power of American Catholics in particular.[11] At the time of his death, there were more Catholics in the world than ever before, and they were spread out across the globe further than ever before. There were more non-Italians in the governing offices of the church, too, including the College of Cardinals. It is little wonder that just twenty years after Pius XII died, the world would see the election of the first non-Italian pope in well over 400 years.

We return to where we started and remember that, despite the caricatures and mythic versions, Pius XII was a person, not an institution. As he readily acknowledged in his last will and testament, Eugenio Pacelli, like anyone, had many deficiencies and shortcomings. He hurt, offended, and scandalized a good many people, Catholics and non-Catholics—sins of commission and of omission for which this pious and God-fearing man sincerely asked forgiveness in his last testament. In death, as in life, Pius XII remained polarizing, enigmatic, and elusive, even to those who knew him.[12] Temperate and cautious by nature and training, Pius XII could also be severe and unyielding. Reflective and self-critical to the point of self-doubting at times, he could also be stubbornly self-assured and self-righteous. While ruling with a strong, resolute hand in some areas of church life, he sometimes seemed to govern little and thus delegated to a narrow clique of informal confidants responsibility for delicate papal affairs. Broad-minded, intellectually curious, and prescient, he allowed a reactionary, inquisitorial culture to fester—to the personal and professional detriment of some of the church's most intelligent, creative, and faithful servants.

In the parable of the good shepherd from John's Gospel, the sheep hear the shepherd's voice and follow him because, Jesus says, they recognize his voice. Can we say that Pius XII called his own sheep; that he let his voice be heard for them to follow? And not just his followers but others who, to borrow again from Scripture, did not belong to his fold? For, as Jesus admonishes in the same parable, "these also I must lead, and they will hear my voice, and there will be one flock, one shepherd."[13] Perhaps no failure—personal or pastoral—was greater than Pius XII's inability or unwillingness to lend his singularly authoritative voice to arouse the individual and collective conscience in a humanitarian defense of European Jews before and during the war. After the war, when the self-imposed restraints of neutrality had been removed, Pius XII either failed to perceive or refused to accept the obvious spiritual need for a public accounting of what had transpired in the heart of Christian Europe. This is not to say that he was anti-Semitic or hard-hearted in the face of the catastrophe that befell Jews and others during World War Two. We know that he was neither of these things. It was simply that he failed to appreciate how a word from the foremost spiritual leader of the Christian world could serve as a powerful symbol and practical impetus for action during the war, and for atonement and reconciliation after.

To accept the need for atonement entailed accepting a degree of Catholic-Christian responsibility for the theological and cultural antecedents of the Holocaust. Pius XII simply did not see the logic of that premise, and so he refused to accept it. It was for this reason that a respectful but disappointed Jacques Maritain wrote in 1948, after having failed to extract from Pius XII a strong public statement acknowledging the painful legacy of Christian anti-Semitism, to express his doubts about the pope's political and diplomatic choices. He wondered whether Pius XII's diplomacy conformed to the evangelical function of the papal office. Maritain realized, of course, that the papal office made conflicting, often incompatible demands of the men who occupied the Chair of Saint Peter. There were times when papal leadership was more juridical and political than pastoral and evangelical, what Maritain ascribed to the "realism" of Saint Peter, as opposed to the profound, brilliant insights of a Saint Paul or the "evangelical love" of a Saint John. For observers like Maritain, it was hard to deny that, at least in the first part of his pontificate, Pius XII was more the diplomat than the evangelist. Maritain concluded wistfully that, judging from the first part of the pontificate through the war years and just beyond, Pius XII always appeared "more worried about achieving practical results by means of political and diplomatic prudence and by acts of charity" than by offering clear, resolute "witness" to the Christian claim through the proclamation of "words that could shake the conscience of all peoples."[14]

One could argue, as we saw above, that Maritain failed to appreciate how Pius XII's concern with achieving "practical results" by means of "political and diplomatic prudence" actually may have saved lives. But his salient point was another—once the war was over and circumstances had changed, prudence demanded that the pope play the part of the evangelist rather than the diplomat. To do nothing, to say nothing, was not the kind of leadership one expected from the Vicar of Christ. Maritain suspected that Pius XII himself realized as much, and anguished over it.

So it is understandable that even among those who loved and admired Pius XII, there was—and is—some ambivalence about the cause to have Pius XII declared a saint. Indeed, even those who knew Pacelli the best seem to have been divided over whether he merited the honor of sainthood. Domenic Tardini and Augustin Bea, both of whom worked side-by-side with Pacelli for years, were convinced of the merits of the cause. Bea was an early albeit informal proponent of the cause to have Eugenio Pacelli declared a saint. The year after the pope died, Bea wrote, "Pius XII was not a martyr in the usual sense of the term. Even so, he was a martyr: a martyr to his duty, to his love for the church, to his love for souls."[15] Bea concluded that there was ample proof that Pius XII "died in the odor of sanctity." Apparently even Pope John XXIII was on record as saying that he thought Pius XII would be canonized someday.[16] Father Robert Leiber, by contrast, who worked as closely with Pius XII as anyone else, was not so sure. When asked about the merits of Pius XII's cause for sainthood, Leiber is reported to have remarked, *"Grande si, santo no"*—great, yes, but not a saint.[17]

On December 19, 2009, Pope Benedict XVI approved the decree that acknowledges simply "the heroic virtues of the Servant of God Pius XII (Eugenio Pacelli), Pope, born in Rome 2 March 1876, died at Castelgandolfo 9 October 1958." With this simple decree, Pius XII moved one step closer to sainthood, even if serious benchmarks have yet to be reached before the controversial wartime pope can be declared a saint. The Catholic Church teaches that the purpose of the virtuous life is "to become like God." To have exhibited "heroic virtues" in his lifetime is to say that Pius XII gave extraordinary witness in word and deed to the Christian virtues, among them prudence, fortitude, and temperance. Above all, it is to underscore that he made the three theological virtues—faith, hope, and charity—the cornerstone of his conscience and actions. This was manifest in his renowned asceticism and spirituality, his Marian devotion, his work as a diplomat during the First World War and later as pope on behalf of prisoners-of-war and refugees, his prophetic warnings about the evils of nationalism and atheistic materialism, and even in his cautious response to the many demonstrable crimes of Nazism. In all this, his promoters say, Pius XII practiced the Christian virtues in an extraordinary way.

It is entirely understandable that for many people, especially for Jewish communities around the world, such a conclusion simply does not square with the facts. To many people, Benedict XVI's decision appears premature and insensitive, given the many wounds in Jewish-Catholic relations. However, to say, as Benedict has done, that Pius XII exhibited "heroic virtues" is not to render a final verdict on the questions about his wartime activities. Nor is it to suggest that Pacelli was a perfect man, or that his life's work before and after becoming pope was without its ambiguities and shortcomings. Benedict's point, simply, is to say that Eugenio Pacelli lived as a virtuous man striving in extraordinary ways to be like God.

The extent to which he succeeded awaits final judgment.

ABBREVIATIONS

NOTES

ACKNOWLEDGMENTS

INDEX

Abbreviations

AAS   *Acta Apostolicae Sedes.* Vatican City: Typis Polyglottis Vaticanis

ACS   Archivio Centrale dello Stato, Rome

       Fondo Segreteria Particolare del Duce (Carteggio Riservato)

       Fondo Segreteria Particolare del Presidente del Consiglio
       Alcide De Gasperi

       Fondo Ministero della Cultura Popolare

ACUA American Catholic History Research Center and University
      Archives, Catholic University of America, Washington, D.C.

ADSS *Actes et documents du Saint-Siège relatifs à la seconde guerre
      mondiale,* ed. Pierre Blet, Robert A. Graham, Angelo Martini,
      Burkhart Schneider. Vatican City: Libreria Vaticana, 1965–1981,
      12 vols.

       vol. 1: Le Saint-Siège et la guerre en Europe, 1939–1940

       vol. 2: Lettres de Pie XII aux évêques allemands, 1939–1944

       vol. 3: Le Saint-Siège et la situation religieuse en Pologne et
          dans les Pays baltes, 1939–1945, 2 vols.

       vol. 4: Le Saint-Siège et la guerre en Europe, juin 1940–juin
          1941

       vol. 5: Le Saint-Siège et la guerre mondiale, juillet
          1941–octobre 1942

       vol. 6: Le Saint-Siège et les victimes de la guerre, mars
          1939–décembre 1940

       vol. 7: Le Saint-Siège et la guerre mondiale, novembre
          1942–décembre 1943

       vol. 8: Le Saint-Siège et les victimes de la guerre, janvier
          1941–décembre 1942

       vol. 9: Le Saint-Siège et les victimes de la guerre, janvier–
          décembre 1943

       vol. 10: Le Saint-Siège et les victimes de la guerre, janvier
          1944–juillet 1945

vol. II: Le Saint-Siège et la guerre mondiale, janvier 1944–mai
1945

ARSI — Archivium Romanum Societatis Iesu, Rome

ASMAE — Archivio Storico Diplomatico del Ministero degli Affari Esteri
Italian, Rome

> Fondo Ambasciata d'Italia presso la Santa Sede
> Fondo Ministero dell'Africa Italiana

ASV — Archivio Segreto Vaticano, Vatican City

CDJC — Centre de documentation juive contemporaine, Paris

CZA — Central Zionist Archives, Jerusalem

DBFP — E. L. Woodward and Rohan Butler, eds., *Documents on British
Foreign Policy: 1919–1939*. London: H.M. Stationery Office, 1956

DDI — Documenti Diplomatici Italiani

DGFP — Documents on German Foreign Policy, 1918–1945

FO — Foreign Office

FRUS — Papers relating to the Foreign Relations of the United States,
Department of State, Washington, D.C.

ISA — The Israel State Archives, Jerusalem

Kennedy Papers — Joseph P. Kennedy Personal Papers, John F. Kennedy
Presidential Library and Museum, Boston

Muench Diaries/ — The Cardinal Aloisius Muench Papers, ACUA
Muench Papers

NA — The National Archives, Kew, Richmond, Surrey, United
Kingdom

NARA — National Archives and Records Administration, College Park,
Maryland

NCWC — National Catholic Welfare Conference/United States
Conference of Catholic Bishops, ACUA

Positio Summ. — Congregatio De Causis Sanctorum, P.N. 1088, ROMANA,
Beatificationis et Canonizationis Servi Dei PII XII (Eugeni
Pacelli), Summi Pontificis (1876–1958), *Summarium: Depositiones
Testium* (Rome, 1999)

RG: Record Group — RG 59: General Records of the Department of State Records of
the Personal Representative of the President to Pope Pius XII
(Myron C. Taylor Mission)

> RG 226: Records of the Office of Strategic Services
> RG 319: Records of the Army Staff

Von Hügel — Manuscript papers of Baron Friedrich von Hügel, University of
Collection — St. Andrews, University Library Special Collections, Scotland

Yad Vashem — International Institute for Holocaust Research, Jerusalem

Vita Documentata — Congregatio De Causis Sanctorum, P.N. 1088, Romana,
Beatificationis et Canonizationis Servi Dei PII XII (Eugeni
Pacelli), Summi Pontificis (1876–1958), *Positio Super Vita,
Virtutibus et Fama Sanctitatis* (Rome, 2004)

Notes

Prologue

1. The translation is from the Jewish Publication Society, Tanakh, translation 1985.
2. This was written in May 1956, two years before he died. Pius XII's last will and testament was published in the Vatican newspaper *L'Osservatore Romano* on October 9/10, 1958. It is reproduced in part in Andrea Tornielli, *Pio XII: Il Papa degli Ebrei* (Casale Monferrato: Edizioni Piemme, 2001), 34–35.
3. Many thanks to Rev. Murray Watson, biblical scholar at St. Peter's Seminary in London, Ontario, for helping me with the proper translation from the Latin and with the scriptural reference of the Miserere psalm.
4. For further description of the Pius XII monument in St. Peter's, see Father Giovanni Giuliani, OFM Conv., *Guide to St. Peter's Basilica* (Rome: A.T.S., 1995), available at http://saintpetersbasilica.org/Docs/GuideSPB1.htm; Niccolo Suffi and Kate Marcelin-Rice, *St. Peter's—Guide to the Square and the Basilica* (Vatican City: Libreria Editrice Vaticana, 1998). The work of Francesco Messina, including the Pius XII monument, is the subject of Mario Pancera, "La poesia di Messina è nascosta nel bronzo," *Arte* 277 (September 1996): 94–99.
5. Pius XII used the phrase "Soldiers of Christ" in his first encyclical, *Summi Pontificatus*, "On the Unity of Human Society," October 20, 1939.
6. Rolf Hochhuth, *The Deputy,* trans. Richard and Clara Winston, preface by Dr. Albert Schweitzer (Baltimore: Johns Hopkins University Press, 1997); originally published and staged in Germany as *Der Stellvertreter* in 1963.
7. Hochhuth, *The Deputy,* Act Two, 101. The story about Pius XII's staff taking his calls on their knees, which is without foundation, was asserted in recent years by Gary Wills, "The Vatican Monarchy," *New York Review of Books,* February 19, 1998. For further descriptions of Pacelli's daily routine and temperament, see Douglas

Woodruff, "Quest of Perfection: Some Personal Impressions of Pius XII," *The Tablet,* October 18, 1958, 330–331.

8. Hochhuth, *The Deputy,* Act Two, 101–102.

9. Ronald J. Rychlak, *Righteous Gentiles: How Pius XII and the Catholic Church Saved Half a Million Jews from the Nazis* (Dallas: Spence, 2005).

10. The useful phrase is by Joseph Bottum, "The End of the Pius Wars," *First Things* 142 (April 2004): 18–24.

11. *The Tablet,* June 29, 1963, 714.

12. Robert C. Doty, "Pope Paul Opens Way to Sainthood for John and Pius," *New York Times,* November 19, 1965, 1. For more on the "politics" of canonizing Pius XII, see Kenneth L. Woodward, *Making Saints: How the Catholic Church Determines Who Becomes a Saint, Who Doesn't and Why* (New York: Simon and Schuster, 1990); and Michael W. Higgins, *Stalking the Holy: The Pursuit of Saint-Making* (Toronto: House of Anansi Press, 2006).

1. The Black Nobility and Papal Rome

1. This story is recounted in numerous sources, including Marvin R. O'Connell, *Critics on Trial: An Introduction to the Catholic Modernist Crisis* (Washington, DC: Catholic University of America Press, 1994), 23; and Owen Chadwick, *A History of the Popes, 1830–1914* (New York: Oxford University Press, 1998), 305.

2. Quoted in Robert Graham, *Vatican Diplomacy: A Study of Church and State on the International Plane* (Princeton, NJ: Princeton University Press, 1959), 182. In fact, well before the capture of Rome, Pius IX had made defense of papal temporal power a leitmotif of his papacy. See his address *Maxima Quidem,* June 9, 1862, and the encyclical Pius IX, *Quanta Cura,* "Condemning Current Errors," December 8, 1864, which contains the infamous condemnation of liberalism in the Syllabus of Errors.

3. Ludovico Pratesi, *Il rione Ponte* (Rome: Newton Compton, 1994).

4. Marcantonio Pacelli, "Questi pseudo storici," *Strenna dei Romanisti* 55 (1994): 389–393; Andrea Tornielli, *Pio XII: Eugenio Pacelli; Un uomo sul trono di Pietro* (Milan: Mondadori, 2007), 8.

5. According to Father Edoardo Cerrato, procurator general of the Congregation of the Oratory of Saint Philip Neri, traditionally the first floor of the palazzi in the neighborhood in which Pacelli was raised was called the "piano nobile," or the "noble floor," reserved for the aristocracy, usually the actual owners of the large building. In conversation with the author, Chiesa Nuova, Rome, December 16, 2010.

6. The story reportedly was told to Ilse-Lore Konopatzki by Pacelli's sister Giusep-

pina. Ilse-Lore Konopatzki, *Eugenio Pacelli: Pius XII; Kindheit und Jugend in Doku-menten* (Salzburg: Pustet, 1974), 13.

7. *Vita Documentata,* 2–3.

8. On Ernesto Pacelli, see Benny Lai, *Finanze e finanzieri vaticani tra l'Ottocento e il Novecento: Da Pio IX a Benedetto XV* (Milan: Mondadori, 1979), 132–196. See also John F. Pollard, *Money and the Rise of the Modern Papacy: Financing the Vatican, 1850–1950* (Cambridge: Cambridge University Press, 2005), 69–72.

9. Tornielli, *Pio XII: Eugenio Pacelli,* 8; Rafaelle De Cesare, *The Last Days of Papal Rome, 1850–1870,* trans. Helen Zimmern (London: Constable, 1909), 13; Pacelli, "Questi pseudo storici," 390. To date, the authoritative biography of Pius IX remains Frank Coppa, *Pope Pius IX: Crusader in a Secular Age* (Boston: Twayne, 1979). For a discussion of the administrative reforms after 1850, see page 113.

10. De Cesare, *Last Days of Papal Rome,* 80–81.

11. Ibid., 88.

12. Coppa, *Pope Pius IX,* 101–102, 105–106, 113.

13. Ibid., 105–106.

14. An excellent, concise summary of these measures can be found in Arturo Jemolo, *Chiesa e Stato in Italia dalla unificazione agli anni settanta* (Turin: Einaudi, 1977), ch. 2, Il Risorgimento (dalla proclamazione del Regno d'Italia alla morte di Pio XII e di Vittorio Emanuele II), 20–46; and Denis Mack Smith, *Italy: A Modern History* (Ann Arbor: University of Michigan Press, 1959), 89.

15. "European Mail News," *New York Times,* October 10, 1879.

16. An informative and highly readable survey of papal history is Eamon Duffy, *Saints and Sinners: A History of the Popes,* 3rd ed. (New Haven: Yale University Press, 2006).

17. It may be useful to note that the 1917 Code of Canon Law provided the philo-sophical rationale to consider the Catholic Church and the Apostolic See as having legal personality in Italian and international law, with the recognized legal capacity to enter into agreements with other nations or political entities. For general commentary on the Code of Canon Law, including discussion of the 1917 Code, which Pacelli helped to prepare, see John P. Beal, James A. Coriden, and Thomas J. Green, eds., *New Commentary on the Code of Canon Law* (New York: Paulist Press, 2000). See especially the commentary on Canon 3 of Book I, and also a useful commentary by Robert T. Kennedy, ch. 2, "Juridic Persons," 154–176.

18. For fascinating insights into background preparation for the 1929 agreements see the notes of Francesco Pacelli, brother to the future Pius XII, who, of course, helped to steer negotiations on behalf of the Holy See to a successful conclusion. See Re: Convenzioni Laternanensi—Trattative, 1926–1927, ASV, AES, Italia, peri-

odo IV, pos. 702, fasc. I–VI. See especially fasc. II for a detailed but incisive analysis by Francesco on the legal-juridical status of the Holy See. The text of the pacts can be found as an appendix to John Pollard, *The Vatican and Italian Fascism, 1929–32: A Study in Conflict* (Cambridge University Press, 1985), 197–215.

19. Graham, *Vatican Diplomacy,* 25.

20. Chadwick, *History of the Popes,* 271.

21. Graham, *Vatican Diplomacy,* 25.

22. Ibid., 191–192.

23. Mack Smith, *Italy,* 97.

24. Ibid. Some historians even speak of a "catholicization" of Italian life, and a "flowering of religion" despite the progressive secularization after Unification. See Victoria De Grazia, *How Fascism Ruled Women: Italy, 1922–1945* (Berkeley: University of California Press, 1992), 243–244.

25. De Cesare, *Last Days of Papal Rome,* vi.

26. Ibid., vi–vii.

27. So argues John Cornwell, *Hitler's Pope: The Secret History of Pius XII* (New York: Viking, 1999), 13–14.

28. Recollections of Giuseppina Pacelli in Konopatzki, *Eugenio Pacelli,* 11–18.

29. Giuseppina was born in 1872, followed by Francesco in 1874, Eugenio in 1876, and Elisabetta in 1880.

30. *Positio Summ.,* 213.

31. *Positio Summ.,* 407–420.

32. The depositions of Pius XII's nephews can be found in *Positio Summ.,* 212–233 (Carlo Pacelli), 384–392 (Marcantonio Pacelli), 407–420 (Giulio Pacelli).

33. The essay is taken from one of the few surviving notebooks from Pacelli's childhood. The essay was written sometime in 1889, and is reproduced in Igino Giordani, *Pio XII: Un grande papa* (Turin: Società Editoriale Internazionale, 1961), 14–15; and in Konopatzki, *Eugenio Pacelli,* ch. 2, Selbstdarstellung des dreizehnjährigen Schülers, 19–28, see 23 for a copy of one page of Pacelli's original journal.

34. *Vita Documentata,* 3–4, 6–7; *Positio Summ.,* 2, 78, 213. On the purported visions connected to the Marian cult, see Andrea Tornielli, "Pio XII e Fatima 'Ho rivisto il miracolo,'" *Il Giornale,* February 28, 2008, 21.

35. *Positio Summ.,* 11. See Domenico Tardini's recollections in *Pio XII* (Vatican City: Libreria Editrice Vaticana, 1960), published in English as *Memories of Pius XII* (Westminster, MD: Newman Press, 1961), especially at pages 35–36, 73–74, for commentary to this effect.

36. See Nazareno Padellaro, *Portrait of Pius XII* (London: J. M. Dent, 1956), 10–11.

37. Cornwell, *Hitler's Pope,* 17.

38. My thanks to Father Edoardo Cerrato, procurator general of the Congregation of the Oratory of Saint Philip Neri in Rome, for sharing with me his insightful

research on the life and work of Father Lais, in records preserved at the Archives of the Congregation at the Chiesa Nuova in Rome; personal correspondence, December 2010.

39. For more insight into these grassroots initiatives of the time, see also Salvatore De Angelis, *I veri amici del popolo: Biografie di pii sacerdoti del clero romano* (Rome: Leonina, 1927).

40. *Positio Summ.*, 213.

41. Edoardo A. Cerrato, "Ricordo di tre Pontefici," *Annales Oratorii, Annuum Commentarium De Rebus Oratorianis A Procura Generali Confoederationis Oratorii S. Philippi Nerii Editum* 7 (2008): 121–123. Again, my thanks go to Father Edoardo Cerrato for pointing me to this source.

42. *Positio Summ.*, 97.

43. The story is recounted in the *Vita Documentata*, 4.

44. So recalled Giacomo Martegani, the Jesuit editor of *La Civiltà Cattolica*, in *Positio Summ.*, 205.

45. *Vita Documentata*, 4–5. See also Kees Van Hoek, "Love for Nature, and People, Born in Studious Boyhood," an excerpt of Van Hoek's pietistic biography of Pius XII, published in parts in the *Washington Post*, March 20, 1950, 9B.

46. Van Hoek, "Love for Nature."

47. Carlo Piersanti, *Origini, vicende e glorie, del "Collegio romano" e del Liceo gimnasio "E.Q. Visconti"* (Rome: A. Signorelli, 1958), 128–129. See also Piersanti's deposition in *Positio Summ.*, 195–197.

48. Essay is in Konopatzki, *Eugenio Pacelli*, 194.

49. Spellman is quoted by Pascalina Lehnert in her memoir, *Pio XII: Il privilegio di servirlo*, trans. M. Guardacci (Milan: Rusconi, 1984), 50.

50. The story of Guido Mendes was reported by Mark Segal, "Ramat Gan Physician Recalls Schooldays with Pius XII," *Jerusalem Post*, October 10, 1958. It has been re-told repeatedly in some of the more apologetic literature. See Rabbi David G. Dalin, *The Myth of Hitler's Pope: How Pope Pius XII Rescued Jews from the Nazis* (Washington, DC: Regnery, 2005), 54, 73; Tornielli, *Pio XII: Eugenio Pacelli*, 23–24; and Sergio Pagano, "Eugenio Pacelli e l'amico ebreo," *L'Osservatore Romano*, October 9, 2011. See also *Vita Documentata*, 25.

51. Thomas à Kempis, *The Imitation of Christ*, trans. Leo Sherley-Price (London: Penguin Books, 1952); Anne O'Hare McCormick, "New Pope Praised Fight on Heresies," *New York Times*, March 3, 1939, 1.

52. McCormick, "New Pope Praised Fight on Heresies"; and "Habemus Papam," *Time*, March 13, 1939, 38. Kennedy's recollections are recorded in an entry dated March 15, 1939, Kennedy Papers, Papers 8.2.2, Ambassador Correspondence, Subject File: Pope Pius XII—Coronation, Box 130.

53. Lehnert, *Pio XII*, 14–15.

54. *Positio Summ.*, 3–4.

55. *Positio Super Vita et Virtutibus*, Vol. IV, *Documenta et Bibliographia Selecta* (Rome, 2004), 85–86.

56. *Positio Summ.*, 3.

57. *Positio Documenta*, Vol. IV, Document 20, "Dichiarazione del Segretario Generale della Università Gregoriana all'Archivista della medesima a proposito della immatricolazione di Eugenio Pacelli alla Facoltà di Filosofia (1895) e dei premi ottenuti e della iscrizione alla Facoltà di Diritto Canonico (1899)," at 95.

58. Tornielli, *Pio XII: Eugenio Pacelli*, 29; Philippe Chenaux, *Pio XII: Diplomatico e pastore* (Milan: San Paolo, 2004), 26. In his notes, Tornielli points to some useful primary sources, namely, the original manuals with rules for the Colleges, "Regole da osservare dagli alunni e convittori dimoranti nell'Almo Collegio Capranica" (Rome, 1867); and "Manuale di pietà per uso degli alunni dell'Almo Romano Collegio" (Rome, 1902).

59. H. Richard Niebuhr described Leo XIII's era as an "epoch-making pontificate." See his *Christ and Culture* (New York: Harper and Row, 1951), 138.

60. Pius XII, *Summi Pontificatus*, "On the Unity of Human Society," October 20, 1939, no. 2.

61. Vincenzo Paglia, "Note sulla formazione culturale del clero romano tra Otto e Novecento," *Ricerche per la storia religiosa di Roma* 4 (1980): 175–211. For further information on the modernist influence at the Apollinare, see Lorenzo Bedeschi, "Circoli modernizzanti a Roma a cavallo del secolo (con documenti inediti)," *Studi Romani* 18, no. 2 (1970): 189–215; and "Il gruppo radicale romano," *Fonti e documenti* 1 (1972): 9–344.

62. John McGreevy, *Catholicism and American Freedom: A History* (New York: Norton, 2004).

63. Chadwick, *History of the Popes*, 278–279.

64. Ibid., 330. In his desire to propose a model of the church as a creative element in the modern era, Leo XIII issued important and consequential encyclicals; these were authoritative documents that outlined orthodox Catholic teaching on a host of issues. Arguably the two most important encyclicals were Leo XIII, *Aeterni Patris*, "On the Restoration of Christian Philosophy," August 4, 1879, on the revival of the philosophy of Saint Thomas Aquinas, and Leo XIII, *Rerum Novarum*, "On Capital and Labor," May 15, 1891, which addressed the condition of the working class and offered the classic formulation of what today is generically described as Catholic social teaching.

65. James Collins, "Leo XIII and the Philosophical Approach to Modernity," in *Leo XIII and the Modern World*, ed. Edward T. Gargan, 179–209 (New York: Sheed and Ward, 1961); Raymond H. Schmandt, "Life and Work of Leo XIII," in *Leo XIII and the Modern World*, 38.

66. Bernard Lonergan, "Aquinas Today: Tradition and Innovation," *Journal of Religion* 55, no. 2 (April 1975): 165–180.

67. See Robert A. Ventresca, "'A Plague of Perverse Opinions': Leo XIII's *Aeterni Patris* and the Catholic Encounter with Modernity," *Logos: A Journal of Catholic Thought and Culture* 12, no. 1 (Winter 2009): 143–168; and Thomas J. A. Hartley, *Thomistic Revival and the Modernist Era* (Toronto: Institute of Christian Thought, University of St. Michael's College, 1971), 8, 22–29. Hartley's useful study relies heavily upon the earlier research of Roger Aubert and Francesco Duranti. See Aubert, "Aspects divers du néo-thomisme sous le pontificat de Leon XIII," in *Aspetti della Cultura Cattolica nell età di Leone XIII,* ed. Giuseppe Rossini (Rome: Cinque Lune, 1961), 133–227, 246–248, 410–414; and Duranti, "La rinascita del tomismo a Perugia. Appunti per una storia del neotomismo," *Aquinas* (1962): 249–294. Consider also a study by Mons. Antonio Piolanti, at the time vice-president of the Pontifical Academy of Saint Thomas Aquinas, on Pius IX's interest in Thomism and his patronage of the work of Thomists like Sanseverino, Taparelli, Zigliara, and others in the decades before *Aeterni Patris.* Piolanti's basic point is to argue that *Aeterni Patris* was the culmination of a broader "cultural movement" to revive Thomism which matured, he says, during Pius IX's long and eventful pontificate. See Antonio Piolanti, *Pio IX e la Rinascita del Tomismo* (Vatican City: Libreria Editrice Vaticana, 1974).

68. This according to one Lanzoni, quoted by Paglia, "Note sulla formazione culturale del clero romano," 204.

69. Paglia, "Note sulla formazione culturale del clero romano," 204.

70. Eugen Weber, *Action Française: Royalism and Reaction in Twentieth Century France* (Stanford: Stanford University Press, 1962), 220.

71. Tornielli, *Pio XII: Eugenio Pacelli,* 32–33.

72. Ibid., 33.

73. Lawrence F. Barmann, *Baron Friedrich von Hügel and the Modernist Crisis in England* (Cambridge: Cambridge University Press, 1972), 62–63. See von Hügel, *Diaries,* January 26, 28, and 31; February 2, 6, 16, and 23; March 15 and 28, 1896, all in Von Hügel Collection. My thanks to Ashleigh Ross for her research assistance at St. Andrews University Library.

74. On Duchesne, see the excellent, brief survey by O'Connell, *Critics on Trial,* 55–57.

75. See Alfred Loisy, *Mémoires pour servir à l'histoire religieuse de notre temps* (Paris: Émile Nourry, 1930), 1:421.

76. Quoted by Michael De La Bédoyère, *The Life of Baron Von Hügel* (London: J. M. Dent, 1951), 95.

77. Loisy, *Mémoires,* 1:422.

78. Lawrence Barmann reasons that von Hügel and Pacelli lost touch after 1897. See Barmann, *Baron Friedrich von Hügel,* 64. By contrast, Michael De La Bédoyère sug-

gests that von Hügel stayed in touch with Pacelli for several years after the apparent change in Pacelli's attitude toward modernist ideas. See De La Bédoyère, *The Life of Baron von Hügel,* 125, 250. There is even some suggestion that von Hügel solicited Pacelli's assistance sometime around 1910 to clarify the status of his son-in-law, who was suspended from the Pontifical Noble Guard, ostensibly for technical reasons, but perhaps for the baron's unpopular association with the now-discredited and disgraced modernists. Von Hügel may have hoped that the Pacelli family's connections to the Noble Guard could help his son-in-law's cause, although there is no evidence that it did.

79. Paglia, "Note sulla formazione culturale del clero romano," 184–185. Paglia draws from the guidelines for the Seminario Romano in the Archives of the *Seminario Romano Maggiore* (ASRM), DO 21, Regola, part. I, cap. 8.

80. For a vivid description of the Roman "effect" on young seminarians, see Giuseppe De Luca, *Il cardinale Bonaventura Cerretti* (Rome: Edizioni di storia e letteratura, 1971), 89; Salvatore Minocchi, *Memorie di un modernista* (Florence: Vallecchi, 1974), 228.

81. Paglia, "Note sulla formazione culturale del clero romano," 181.

82. Eugenio Pacelli, "Amore orante e obbediente al Papa," *Sursum Corda* 21 (1938): 1–5; also in Paglia, "Note sulla formazione culturale del clero romano," 189.

2. The Diplomat's Vocation

1. See Robert A. Ventresca, *From Fascism to Democracy: Culture and Politics in the Italian Election of 1948* (Toronto: University of Toronto Press, 2004), 107. The historian David Blackbourn speaks of Pacelli's Marian devotion and anti-Communism often being "fused." See Blackbourn, *Marpingen: Apparitions of the Virgin Mary in Nineteenth-Century Germany* (New York: Knopf, 1994), 351. See also William Christian, "Religious Apparitions and the Cold War in Southern Europe," in *Religion, Power and Protest in Local Communities: The Northern Shore of the Mediterranean,* ed. Eric R. Wolf, 239–266 (Berlin: Mouton, 1984).

2. *L'Osservatore Romano,* April 4, 1899, 3; see also Tornielli, *Pio XII: Eugenio Pacelli; un uomo sul trono di Pietro* (Milan: Mondadori, 2007), 35–36.

3. See the deposition of Elisabetta Pacelli, *Positio Summ.,* 4.

4. From the deposition of Isidoro Marco Emanuel, former bishop of Speyer, Germany, *Positio Summ.,* 814.

5. For this description of the Secretariat of State's organizational structure at the start of the twentieth century, I have relied on David Alvarez's excellent article, "The Professionalization of the Papal Diplomatic Service, 1909–1967," *Catholic Historical Review* 75, no. 2 (April 1989): 233–248.

6. See my entry on Gasparri in the *Encyclopedia of Modern Christian Politics,* vol. 1,

ed. Roy P. Domenico and Mark Y. Hanley (Westport, CT: Greenwood Press, 2006), 229–230.

7. This account, perhaps apocryphal, is in Margherita Marchione, *Shepherd of Souls: A Pictorial Life of Pope Pius XII* (New York: Paulist Press, 2004), 20.

8. *Vita Documentata,* 40.

9. See Alvarez, "Professionalization," 233–248. See also R. A. Ventresca, "'A Plague of Perverse Opinions': Leo XIII's *Aeterni Patris* and the Catholic Encounter with Modernity," *Logos: A Journal of Catholic Thought and Culture* 12, 1 (Winter 2009): 143–168. For a general survey of the situation of the papacy after Italian Unification and the loss of the papal states, see Owen Chadwick, *History of the Popes, 1830–1914* (Oxford: Oxford University Press, 1998), especially 330.

10. David Alvarez, *Spies in the Vatican: Espionage and Intrigue from Napoleon to the Holocaust* (Lawrence: University Press of Kansas, 2002), 126–127.

11. An excellent explanation of the organizational structure of the papal diplomatic service can be found in Alvarez, "Professionalization," 236–238.

12. Alvarez, "Professionalization," 234.

13. Alvarez's "Professionalization" contains some fascinating insights into the composition of the papal diplomatic service in the period from just before the First World War to around Vatican II. Most of his data are drawn from the *Annuario Pontificio,* published at the Vatican, for the periods 1909 to 1968.

14. Alvarez, "Professionalization," 238–239.

15. Along with Pacelli's work on the codification of canon law, Gasparri relied on him to help compile the so-called White Book, or *Libro bianco,* which was the Holy See's official response to the 1905 rupture in formal diplomatic relations between France and the Holy See. It was titled *La separazione dello Stato della Chiesa in Francia. Esposizione documentata* (Rome: Tipografia Vaticana, 1905). An official, concise summary of *Libro bianco* was published in the Jesuit journal *La Civiltà Cattolica,* "Il 'Libro Bianco' e L'apostasia officiale della Terza Repubblica Francese," vol. 1 (Anno 57—1906): 129–149.

16. Gasparri is quoted in Giordani, *Pio XII: un grande papa* (Turin: SET, 1961), 36.

17. Ibid., 36.

18. The original documents for the codification papers are housed at the Vatican Secret Archives, Commissione (Pontificia) per la codificazione del Diritto Canonico, or simply *Commissione Codice Diritto Canonico;* Indice 1164. A review of several of the boxes of this voluminous file confirms that Pacelli's contributions to the project were essentially administrative and clerical, rather than substantive.

19. In fact, the 1917 Code of Canon Law that Eugenio Pacelli helped to compile governed the Roman Catholic Church for sixty-six years until it was revised and replaced by the 1983 Code authorized by Pope John Paul II. For further information on the Code of Canon Law, see, among others, Constant van de Wiel, *History of*

Canon Law (Louvain: Peeters, 1991); James A. Coriden, *An Introduction to Canon Law* (New York: Paulist Press, 1991).

20. In 1912, Pacelli published a short but highly technical, dense treatise on the so-called personality and territoriality of laws, especially in canon law. It was an erudite attempt to advance a cutting-edge interpretation of an ancient question then under review by the Vatican's foremost experts in church law. See Eugenio Pacelli, *La personalità e la territorialità delle leggi specialmente nel diritto canonico: Studio storico-giuridico* (Rome: Tipografia Poliglotta Vaticana, 1912). See the useful commentary by Dino Staffa that serves as an Introduction to the French translation of Pacelli's study, *La personnalité et la territorialité des lois: Particulièrement dans le droit canon; Étude historique-juridique* (Rome: Scientia Catholica, 1945). At the time, Staffa was professor at the Pontificium Institutum Utriusque Iuris.

21. Eugenio Pacelli, *La personalità e la territorialità delle leggi.* My analysis is based on a reading of the French translation, *La personnalité et la territorialité des lois,* 11.

22. Pacelli, *La personnalité et la territorialité des lois,* 16–17.

23. For the long history of the pontifical diplomatic academy, whose faculty counted prominent church men of the nineteenth and twentieth centuries, including future popes Gioacchino Pecci (Leo XIII) and Giacomo Della Chiesa (Benedict XV), as well as influential Vatican secretaries of state Rampolla and Merry del Val, see *La Pontificia Accademia ecclesiastica, 1701–1951* (Vatican City: Tipografia della Poliglotta Vaticana, 1951). See in particular A. M. Bettanini's essay in this collection, which offers unique insights into Pacelli's teaching style with glimpses into his thinking: A. M. Bettanini, "Pio XII insegnante di diplomazia nella Pontificia Accademia ecclesiastica: Riccordi di un accademico," 71–74.

24. *Positio Summ.,* 815.

25. Bettanini, "Pio XII insegnante di diplomazia," 74. Pacelli had been named a monsignor by Pope Pius X in 1905.

26. Cornwell, for instance, speaks of signs of "special favor" bestowed upon Pacelli. See John Cornwell, *Hitler's Pope: The Secret History of Pius XII* (New York: Viking, 1999), 47–48.

27. ASV, AES contains the original documentation pertaining to the negotiations. For further detail see Philippe Chenaux, *Pie XII: diplomate e pasteur* (Paris: Cerf, 2003), 421.

28. Chenaux, *Pie XII,* 93. The best English-language biography of Benedict XV is John F. Pollard, *Benedict XV: The Unknown Pope and the Pursuit of Peace* (London: Continuum, 1999).

29. See Italo Garzia, *La questione romana durante la prima guerra mondiale* (Naples: Edizioni Scientifiche Italiane, 1981); see also ASV, Segr. Stato, Guerra (1914–1918), for original documentation pertaining to, among other things, Pacelli's visit with Emperor Franz Josef. For a useful overview in English of Pacelli's 1917 mission, see Charles J. Herber, "Eugenio Pacelli's Mission to Germany and the Papal Peace

Proposals of 1917," *Catholic Historical Review* 65, no. 1 (January 1979): 20–48. For further context about papal representation in Germany, see Michael F. Feldkamp, *La Diplomazia Pontificia* (Milan: Jaca Book, 1995); and Alvarez, *Spies in the Vatican,* 58, 70.

30. On Aversa's passing, see AAS, 9 (1917), 256.

31. *Positio Summ.*, vol. 1, pars I, 69. See also Robert A. Ventresca, "The Virgin and the Bear: Religion, Society and the Cold War in Italy," *Journal of Social History,* vol. 37, no. 2 (Winter 2003), 439–456.

32. *Vita Documentata,* 50.

33. See *Positio Summ.*, 79; *Vita Documentata,* 21; Giordani, *Pio XII,* 47.

34. *Positio Summ.*, 5, 49, and 408.

35. Antonio Scottà, *La conciliazione ufficiosa: Diario del barone Carlo Monti 'incaricato d'affari' del governo italiano presso la Santa Sede (1914–1922),* 2 vols. (Vatican City: Libreria Editrice Vaticana, 1997); Giorgio Rumi, preface to Scottà, *La conciliazione ufficiosa,* 1:49–50.

36. Quoted by Giordani, *Pio XII,* 47. The original citation, in German, can be found in Ludwig Kaas, *Eugenio Pacelli: Erster Apostolischer Nuntius beim Deutschen Reich; Gesammelte Reden* (Berlin: Germania, 1930), 26.

37. Emma Fattorini, *Germania e Santa Sede: le nunziature di Pacelli fra la Grande guerra e la Repubblica di Weimar* (Bologna: Società editrice il Mulino, 1992), 46.

38. An excellent summary of the 1917 papal peace initiative that is drawn largely from the diplomatic correspondence between Gasparri and Pacelli can be found in Angelo Martini, "La Nota di Benedetto XV ai capi delle nazioni belligeranti (1 agosto 1917)," *La Civiltà Cattolica* 4 (1962): 417–429; and Martini, "La Preparazione dell'Appello di Benedetto XV ai governi belligeranti," also in *La Civiltà Cattolica,* 4 (1962): 119–132. For further reading see also Giorgio Rumi, ed., *Benedetto XV e la pace, 1914–1918* (Brescia: Morcelliana, 1990).

39. These included such guarantees as freedom of the seas; simultaneous disarmament of the belligerent powers with international sanctions for noncompliance; the appointment of an arbitrator or some such body to monitor and enforce disarmament; the surrender of any seized colonial territories; and commitments to convene a peace conference to resolve outstanding territorial matters, including redrawing the map of central Europe and the Balkans. See *Vita Documentata,* 85–86; see also Fattorini, *Germania e Santa Sede,* 21.

40. *Vita Documentata,* 86; quoted in Michael F. Feldkamp, *Pius XII und Deutschland* (Göttingen: Vandenhoeck und Ruprecht, 2000), 26. See also Ernesto Vercesi, *Il Vaticano, l'Italia e la guerra* (Milan: Mondadori, 1928), 166.

41. Correspondence between Gasparri and Pacelli, which includes Pacelli's reports back to the Holy See of his meetings with the kaiser, are in ASV, AES, Germania P.O. 415, and discussed in detail in Martini, "La Nota di Benedetto XV."

42. Kaiser Wilhelm recounts this meeting with Pacelli in his somewhat dubious

memoirs, written while in exile at Doorn, Holland. Published originally in German as *Ereignisse und Gestalten aus den Jahren, 1878–1918* (Leipzig: Koehler, 1922); English translation *My Memoirs: 1878–1918* (London: Cassell, 1922). See especially ch. 11, "The Pope and Peace," 258–265, where the former kaiser writes of his 1917 meeting with Pacelli.

43. See Pacelli to Gasparri, June 30, 1917, and November 15, 1917, ASV, AES, Germania P.O. 415.

44. Pacelli's reports to Gasparri of his meeting with the kaiser and other German leaders were being intercepted and studied by Italian intelligence, as is evident in the Sonnino paper intercepts. See Pacelli to Gasparri, June 1917, Papers of Baron Sidney Sonnino (1847–1922) (University Microfilms, 1968), N. 16–30, no. 1464, par. 117. Sonnino was the Italian foreign minister from November 1914 to June 1919.

45. Fattorini, *Germania e Santa Sede*, 51.

46. Rapporto del nunzio apostolico Eugenio Pacelli al cardinal Pietro Gasparri, "Risposta del Governo Imperiale alla Lettera Pontificia sulla pace," September 14, 1917, in ASV, AES, SE 216/IV, N. 1046, reproduced in the Appendix to Fattorini, *Germania e Santa Sede*, 289–290.

47. Quoted by Martini, "La Nota di Benedetto XV," 428n29, reproduced in *Vita Documentata*, 101.

48. Pascalina Lehnert, *Pio XII: il privilegio di servirlo* (Milan: Rusconi, 1984), 36–39.

49. Ibid., 13–15.

50. Ibid.

51. See the deposition of Cardinal Nasalli Rocca di Corneliano, *Positio Summ.*, 473.

52. Lehnert, *Pio XII*, 35–36.

53. For an excellent summary of the nature of Munich Catholicism and its political implications in the years after 1918, see Derek Hastings, "How 'Catholic' Was the Early Nazi Movement? Religion, Race, and Culture in Munich, 1919–1924," *Central European History* 36, no. 3 (2003): 383–433, especially 385–386.

54. Funk's 1922 essay is quoted and discussed at length in Hastings, "How 'Catholic' Was the Early Nazi Movement?" 388–390.

55. The other "best friend" was American prelate Aloisius Muench, future cardinal and Pius XII's point man in the papal relief efforts for postwar Germany after 1945; Pacelli appointed Muench as nuncio to Germany in 1950. Faulhaber left Muench his "favorite ring" and a gold-plated statue of St. Michael that had adorned Faulhaber's desk in Munich for years. See Muench's diary entry for July 16, 1952, in Diaries, Reminiscences, and Notebooks, Vol. 15, May 1, 1952, to August 16, 1952, Aloisius Muench Papers, ACUA.

56. On the establishment of the Berlin nunciature and the appointment of Diego von Bergen as German representative to the Holy See, see ASV, AES, Germania

(1917–1922), pos. 1716–1718, fasc. 897, n. 1716, Berlino, 1917–1921., RE: Nunzio Apostolico accreditato a Berlino e Ambasciata presso la Santa Sede.

57. Pacelli to Gasparri, June 3, 1920, ASV, AES, Germania (1917–1922), pos. 1716–1718, fasc. 897, n. 1716. Berlino, 1917–1921, Re: Nunzio Apostolico accreditato a Berlino e Ambasciata presso la Santa Sede.

58. Among Pacelli's many reports from this time, see Pacelli to Gasparri, "Sulla rivoluzione in Baviera," November 15, 1918, ASV, AES, Baviera 129, no. 10856.

59. Robert Paxton, *Europe in the Twentieth Century*, 4th ed. (Belmont, CA: Wadsworth, 2005), 137. An excellent survey of the revolutionary climate in postwar Bavaria is Alan Mitchell, *Revolution in Bavaria 1918–1919: The Eisner Regime and the Soviet Republic* (Princeton, NJ: Princeton University Press, 1965).

60. David Clay Large, *Where Ghosts Walked: Munich's Road to the Third Reich* (New York: Norton, 1997), 77.

61. See Pacelli to Gasparri, "Sulla rivoluzione in Baviera," November 15, 1918, ASV, AES, Baviera 129, no. 10856.

62. According to a dispatch intercepted by the Italian authorities, Pacelli wrote to Gasparri advising of his trip to Rorschach, which began around November 21, 1918. See Pacelli to Gasparri, November 21, 1918, Sonnino Papers, dispatch N. 21072, n. 7505, par. 66.

63. Parts of Eugenio's letter to Francesco, which is held in the Pacelli family's private archives, are reproduced in Tornielli, *Pio XII: Eugenio Pacelli*, 111–112.

64. Pacelli to Gasparri, "Sulla seconda rivoluzione in Baviera," February 23, 1919, ASV, AES, Baviera 129, no. 12163.

65. When he was pope, Pacelli even alluded to the incident during a tense meeting with the Italian ambassador (Alfieri) in 1940. This account of Pius XII's meeting with Alfieri is provided in various sources, including in the deposition of J. Neuhausler, *Positio Summ.*, 704.

66. Large, *Where Ghosts Walked*, 88; Hastings, "How 'Catholic' Was the Early Nazi Movement?" 393.

67. Pacelli to Gasparri, "Sulla Nunziatura e la Repubblica dei Consigli," April 18, 1919, ASV, AES, Germania P.O. 442, no. 12572.

68. Pacelli to Gasparri, "Sulla seconda rivoluzione in Baviera," February 23, 1919, ASV, AES, Baviera 129, no. 12163.

69. Ibid.

70. Large, *Where Ghosts Walked*, 120.

71. Emma Fattorini suggests that the Holy See in general saw Germany as a cultural bulwark against the spread not only of Bolshevism but also of Slavic Orthodoxy and "masonic laicism" from Western Europe. See Fattorini, *Germania e Santa Sede*, 165.

72. Pacelli to Gasparri, Re: Rapporti della Nunziatura Apostolica di argomento po-

litico e vario, April 12, 1919, ASV, AES, Baviera (1918–1921), no. 89308, pos. 67, fasc. 43, N. 67 (Continuazione); and Pacelli to Gasparri, "Sulla Situazione politica," March 28, 1919, ASV, AES, Germania 442, no. 12429.

73. Pacelli to Gasparri, "Situazione politica in Germania. Questione bolscevica," August 18, 1920, ASV, AES, Germania 442, no. 17673. Pacelli was reporting his conversation with the Bavarian minister von Kahr.

74. Pacelli expressed his concerns in a letter to his brother Francesco in December 1919, in which Eugenio writes of his support for the *Einwohnerwehr*, the counterrevolutionary civil guards that were eventually suppressed by the German government. See Eugenio Pacelli to Francesco Pacelli, December 6, 1919, Pacelli family archives, quoted by Tornielli, *Pio XII: Eugenio Pacelli*, 111–112. Pacelli's letters to his brother are contained in the Pacelli family archives, which are privately held by the Pacelli family in Rome.

75. Pacelli to Gasparri, "Situazione politica in Germania. Questione bolscevica," August 18, 1920, ASV, AES, Germania 442, no. 17673.

76. See Klaus Epstein, *Matthias Erzberger and the Dilemma of German Democracy* (Princeton, NJ: Princeton University Press, 1959), vii.

77. See his report "Contro l'Istruzione religiosa nelle scuole di Baviera," January 28, 1919, ASV, AES, Baviera 229.

78. For a comprehensive history of the Civil Guards, see David Clay Large, *The Politics of Law and Order: A History of the Bavarian Einwohnerwehr, 1918–1921* (Philadelphia: American Philosophical Society, 1980).

79. Large, *Where Ghosts Walked*, 126, 134.

80. Ibid., 140–141.

81. See, for instance, Pacelli to Gasparri, Re: Rapporti della Nunziatura Apostolica di argomento politico e vario, April 14, 1920, ASV, AES, Baviera (1918–1921), pos. 67, fasc. 44, n. 67 (Continuazione).

82. The letter from Eugenio to Francesco from Munich, dated December 6, 1919, is quoted in Tornielli, *Pio XII: Eugenio Pacelli*, 111–112.

83. David Clay Large argues that the suppression of the Civil Guards constituted a "windfall" for Hitler and the fledgling Nazi movement because many members of the Guards flowed directly to the NSDAP and its paramilitary force, the SA. See Large, *Where Ghosts Walked*, 143.

84. Consider the report from Lorenzo Schioppa (Uditore of the nunciature) to Gasparri, "I precedenti della controrivoluzione in Germania e le sue conseguenze," March 25, 1920, ASV, AES, Germania 438, no. 16180, reproduced in Fattorini, *Germania e Santa Sede*, 344–348.

85. Pacelli to Gasparri, "Le elezioni politiche del Reich germanico," June 10, 1920, ASV, AES, Germania 442, no. 16998, also reproduced in the Appendix to Fattorini, *Germania e Santa Sede*, 349–351.

86. Ibid.

87. See Pacelli's reports to Gasparri of his meetings with Gustav von Kahr, then head of the Bavarian government, which took place in September 1923, ASV, AES, Baviera 2. See also Pacelli's reports of Hitler's failed Beer Hall Putsch from November 1923, in Baviera 3; ASV, Arch. Nunz. Monaco 396/7; see also Chenaux, *Pie XII,* 139–141.

88. See Pacelli to Gasparri, November 9, 1923, ASV, AES, Baviera 3; ASV, Arch. Nunz. Monaco 396/7; see also Chenaux, *Pie XII,* 140.

89. Pacelli to Gasparri, November 12, 1923, ASV, AES, Baviera 3; ASV, Arch. Nunz. Monaco 396/7.

90. Chenaux, *Pie XII,* 140–141; see Pacelli to Gasparri, November 14, 1923, ASV, AES, Baviera 3; ASV, Arch. Nunz. Monaco 396/7.

91. Quoted by Chenaux, *Pie XII,* 141; original is in Pacelli to Gasparri, May 1, 1924, ASV, AES, Baviera 3; ASV, Arch. Nunz. Monaco 396/7.

92. Franz von Papen, *Memoirs,* trans. Brian Connell (London: Deutsch, 1952), 126. For further details of Pacelli's time in Berlin, see the deposition of Isidor Markus Emanuel, the future bishop of Speyer, in *Positio Summ.,* 816; see also *Positio Summ.,* 97.

93. Pacelli to Gasparri, December 7, 1923, Re: Sul nuovo Cancelliere del Reich, Sig. Marx in ASV, AES, Germania 1922–1930. Re: Rapporti delal Nunziatura Apostolica su argomenti politici e vari, ASV, AES, pos. 511, fasc. 21, no. 29126.

94. See *Vita Documentata;* cf. AAS, 21 (1929): 521–535, for copy of the agreement; Pacelli's letter to Braun is also in AAS, 21 (1929): 536–539.

95. Quoted in the deposition of Hans Struth, *Positio Summ.,* 54.

96. Eugenio Pacelli to Francesco Pacelli, November 23, 1929, Pacelli family archives, quoted in Tornielli, *Pio XII: Eugenio Pacelli,* 158.

97. See the recollections of Friedrich Muckermann in his memoirs, *Im Kampf zwischen zwei Epochen: Lebenserinnerungen* (Mainz: Matthias-Grünewald, 1973), cited by Michel Deneken, "Le cardinal Faulhaber à archives ouvertes," *Revue d'Allemagne* 36, no. 2 (2004): 178, n13.

98. Pacelli's speech is here quoted in a deposition by Hans Struth, editor of the Catholic periodical *Feuerreiter,* who followed closely Pacelli's work as nuncio in Berlin. See *Positio Summ.,* 53.

99. See the deposition of Mons. Dott. Isidor Markus Emanuel, in *Positio Summ.,* 819. Emanuel wrote about Pacelli in *Sieben Jahre in roten Talar* (Speyer: Pilger, 1970), 153–155.

100. Full text of the Lateran Pacts of 1929 and related documents can be found in John F. Pollard, *The Vatican and Italian Fascism, 1929–1932* (Cambridge: Cambridge University Press, 2005), app. I, II, and III, 195–216.

101. Pollard makes the convincing argument that, despite widespread expectations,

the period that followed the signing of the 1929 pacts actually witnessed "more conflict between the Vatican and the Fascists than in the preceding seven-year period that had begun with the March on Rome." See Pollard, *The Vatican and Italian Fascism*, 2–3.

102. Pollard, *The Vatican and Italian Fascism*, especially ch. 6, for the best concise summary of the so-called crisis of 1931.

103. Pius XI, *Non Abbiamo Bisogno*, "On Catholic Action in Italy," June 29, 1931, no. 44.

104. Notable among them were Giuseppe Pizzardo, Ottaviani, and Borgoncini-Duca. See Chenaux, *Pie XII*, 168–170.

105. Italian Ambassador to Berlin, Aldrovandi, to Minister of Foreign Affairs Grandi, Berlin, December 10, 1929, in DDI, ser. 7, vol. 8, 245–246.

106. Clerical and lay informants working for the Italian political police depicted Pacelli as a very capable diplomat but perhaps not quite fit for the job of Vatican secretary of state. For valuable insights into the way Italian officials were reading the Vatican through the lens of informants, see Carlo M. Fiorentino, *All'ombra di Pietro: La Chiesa Cattolica e lo spionaggio fascista in Vaticano, 1929–1939* (Florence: Le lettere, 1999).

107. Pollard, *The Vatican and Italian Fascism*, 156; see De Vecchi interview with Pacelli, DDI, ser, 7, vol. 10. For G. Ogilvie Forbes's report, see Thomas E. Hachey, ed., *Anglo-Vatican Relations, 1914–1939: Confidential Annual Reports of the British Ministers to the Holy See* (Boston: G. K. Hall, 1972), 196.

108. Informants at the Vatican working for Mussolini's political police similarly singled out Pizzardo and Ottaviani for their influence within papal diplomatic circles. For a full discussion of Pizzardo in particular as a kind of *éminence grise* of papal diplomacy, see Fioriento, *All'ombra di Pietro*, 85–129.

109. Alfred Baudrillart, *Carnets du Alfred Baudrillart*, ed. Paul Christophe (Paris: Editions du Cerf, 1994–2003), 714, 818–819.

110. It is difficult to say whether there was any substance to the rumor, which was passed along to the Mussolini government from its paid informants at the Vatican in the first half of 1934. See Fioriento, *All'ombra di Pietro*, 98.

111. So argues John Pollard, *The Vatican and Italian Fascism*, 177.

112. Ottaviani, "Pio XI e I suoi Segretari di Stato," in *Pio XI nel trentesimo della morte (1939–1969). Racconti di studi e di memorie*, ed. Carlo Colombo (Milan: Opera Diocesana per la preservazione e diffiusione della fede, 1969), 499.

113. *Carnets du Cardinal Baudrillart*, December 26, 1928–February 12, 1933, 676.

114. D. O. Osborne, "Leading personalities at the Holy See," June 24, 1938, FO 371/22441.

115. For a fascinating discussion of the administrative developments in church governance in the 1920s and 1930s, drawn mainly from the recently released archives for the pontificate of Pius XI, see Roberto Regoli, "Il Ruolo della Sacra Congregazione degli Affari Ecclesiastici Staordinari durante il Pontificato di Pio XI," in *Con-*

vegno internazionale: la sollecitudine ecclesiale di Pio XI alla luce delle nuove fonti archivistiche, Vatican City, February 27, 2009. On the growth of the Congregation's staff, see 193–194.

116. There are several instructive book-length studies that look at the internal discussions in papal circles in the 1930s about how to respond publicly to the doctrinal challenges posed by excessive nationalism, racism, Communism, and the "totalitarian" ambition of Fascist and Communist regimes. See Hubert Wolf, *Pope and Devil: The Vatican's Archives and the Third Reich,* trans. Kenneth Kronenberg (Cambridge, MA: Belknap Press of Harvard University Press, 2010); and Danilo Menozzi and Renato Moro, eds., *Cattolicesimo e totalitarismo: chiese e culture religiose tra le due guerre mondiali* (Brescia: Morcelliana, 2004).

117. See Roberto Regoli, "Il ruolo della Sacra Congregazione degli Affari Ecclesiastici Staordinari," 206–216, 227–228. The records of the joint sessions from 1937, one to deal with Ethiopia, the other with the Vatican's relations with Germany, are in the ASV, AES, Rapporti delle Sessioni, anno 1937, Session 1374, stampa 1269, Ordinamento ecclesiastico dell'Etiopia, 11 March 1937, and AES Rapporti delle Sessioni, anno 1937, Session 1376, stampa 1271, Germana. Situazione religiosa e politica—Discorso dell'E.mo Cardinale Mundelein, Castelgandolfo, June 20, 1937.

118. See Cardinal Siri's recollection in *Positio Summ., Pars II,* 597.

119. From the so-called Pacelli notebooks, Fogli di udienza del Cardinale Eugenio Pacelli, Segretario di Stato di Pio XI (1930–1939), ASV, AES, Stati Ecclesiastici, IV Periodo, P.O. 430b, fasc. 360, audience of February 19, 1934; and P.O. 430a, fasc. 349 (1933–1934), audience of March 2, 1934.

120. Neuhausler, *Positio Summ.,* 704.

121. For general information on Cramer-Klett, see the obituary "Baron Von Cramer-Klett," *New York Times,* June 1, 1938, 23. A more detailed portrait of the baron can be found in Ludwig Benedikt von Cramer-Klett, *Theodor Freiherr von Cramer Klett: Weg und Wirken eines christlichen Mannes* (Aschau: Chiemgau, 1966).

122. For various letters and newspaper clippings sent to the Vatican's secretary of state about possible Catholic collaboration with National Socialism, see Situazioni Politica—Rapporti intorno alla relazione tra I cattolici e il nazionalsocialismo, ASV, AES, 1930–1932, pos. 606, fasc. 117 and 118. For a sample of conservative disdain or distrust of the parties of the extreme Right, see Cramer-Klett to Pacelli, August 1, 1931, n. 2123/31. On Cramer-Klett's arrest, see ASV, AES, Germania, Periodo IV, pos. 666, fasc. 223, no. 3288/35.

123. A secret U.S. State Department report from 1943 that surveyed the political role of German Catholic bishops since World War One identified Faulhaber as the backbone of Bavarian Catholic hostility toward the Weimar Republic. See U.S. Department of State, Washington DC, Reference Division, September 6, 1943, tracking no. 097.3 Z 092 #1212.

124. Although he makes no explicit mention of Pacelli or the Vatican, and only pass-

ing reference to German Catholicism, for an excellent explanation of the relationship between German conservatives and Nazism, see Jeremy Noakes, "German Conservatives and the Third Reich: An Ambiguous Relationship," in *Fascists and Conservatives: The Radical Right and the Establishment in 20th Century Europe*, ed. Martin Blinkhorn (London: Unwin Hyman, 1990), 71–97.

125. John Zeender, "Germany: The Catholic Church and the Nazi Regime, 1933–1945," in *Catholics, the State and the European Radical Right, 1919–1945*, ed. Richard J. Wolff and Jorg K. Hoensch (Highland Lakes, NJ: Social Science Monographs, 1987; distributed by Columbia University Press), 92–118.

126. For further reading on these influential German prelates, see Richard Rolf, "The Role of Adolf Cardinal Bertram in the Church-State Struggle in Nazi Germany" (Ph.D. diss., University of California at Santa Barbara, 1975); Ulrich von Hehl, *Katholische Kirche und National Sozialismus im Erzbistum Koln 1935–1945* (Mainz: Matthias-Grünewald-Verlag, 1977); Ludwig Volk, S.J., "Lebensbild," in *Akten Kardinal Michael von Faulhaber 1917–1945*, ed. Andreas Kraus (Mainz: Matthias-Grünewald-Verlag, 1978).

127. The many reports from Orsenigo and Torregrossa can be found, for instance, in ASV, AES Germania, 1932–1934, pos. 627, fasc. 144: Elezioni Presidenziali e Politiche.

128. Michel Deneken, "Le cardinal Faulhaber à archives ouvertes," *Revue d'Allemagne* 36, no. 2 (2004): 175–193, here at 178.

129. Robert A. Krieg, "The Vatican Concordat with Hitler's Reich," in *America*, September 1, 2003.

130. As John Zeender observes, in the two years or so before Hitler became chancellor, the German bishops "chose first to march on Nazism in different formations, its members initially separated into several regional conferences; all condemned certain basic Nazi doctrines like race superiority; some did so publicly, others restricted condemnation to a general directive to pastors in their provinces. Some conferences explicitly prohibited Catholics from entering the party; others did not." See Zeender, "Germany: The Catholic Church and the Nazi Regime," 96.

131. For a general history of the German Center Party, see Ellen Lovell Evans, *The German Center Party, 1870–1933: A Study in Political Catholicism* (Carbondale: Southern Illinois University Press, 1981). For a more recent analysis, one that focuses in particular on the decisive role of Franz von Papen, see Larry Eugene Jones, "Franz von Papen, the German Center Party, and the Failure of Catholic Conservativism in the Weimar Republic," *Central European History* 38 (2005): 191–217.

132. See Gordon A. Craig, *Germany, 1866–1945* (Oxford: Oxford University Press, 1981), ch. 15, for an ever-instructive summary of the Brüning government and the eventual collapse of Weimar.

133. Craig, *Germany*, 541–542.

134. The many reports from Orsenigo and Torregrossa can be found, for instance, in ASV, AES, Germania, 1932–1934, pos. 627, fasc. 144: Elezioni Presidenziali e Politiche. On the fact that the Catholic vote was holding steady, see, for instance, Torregrossa to Pacelli, Munich, April 26, 1932, n. 3821; and Orsenigo to Pacelli, Berlin, August 2, 1932, "Le elezioni politiche," n. 4959.

135. See, for instance, Orsenigo to Pacelli, Berlin, August 2, 1932, "Le elezioni politiche," ASV, AES Germania, 1932–1934, pos. 627, fasc. 144: Elezioni Presidenziali e Politiche, n. 4959.

136. Torregrossa to Pacelli, Munich, April 26, 1932, n. 3821; Orsenigo to Pacelli, Berlin, April 12, 1932, n. 4183, both in ASV, AES, Germania, 1932–1934, pos. 627, fasc. 144: Elezioni Presidenziali e Politiche.

137. Torregrossa to Pacelli, Munich, April 30, 1932, ASV, AES Germania, 1932–1934, pos. 627, fasc. 144: Elezioni Presidenziali e Politiche, n. 3828.

138. This was in response to a suggestion made by Heinrich Köhler, as recalled in his *Lebenserinnerungen*, 300–301, quoted by William L. Patch, Jr., *Heinrich Brüning and the Dissolution of the Weimar Republic* (Cambridge: Cambridge University Press, 1998), 132.

139. Quoted in Patch, *Heinrich Brüning*, 147.

140. See Stewart A. Stehlin, *Weimar and the Vatican, 1919–1933: German-Vatican Diplomatic Relations in the Interwar Years* (Princeton, NJ: Princeton University Press, 1983), 358–360.

141. The Pacelli diaries contain only passing reference to this meeting between the cardinal secretary of state and Brüning; see Pacelli's meeting with German chargé d'affaires, July 17 and August 14, 1931, in ASV, AES, P.O. 430b, fasc. 357 (1931).

142. See Brüning's controversial and sometimes suspect memoirs. In German as *Memoiren, 1918–1934* (Stuttgart: Deutsche Verlags-Anstalt, 1970), 135–136. See also the French translation, Brüning, *Memoirs 1918–1934* (Paris: Editions Gallimard, 1974), 98–99.

143. See, for instance, the 1931 annual report from the British chargé d'affaires, G. Ogilvie Forbes, to the British Foreign Office, in Thomas E. Hachey, ed., *Anglo-Vatican Relations, 1914–1939: Confidential Annual Reports of the British Ministers to the Holy See* (Boston: G. K. Hall, 1972), 210.

144. Audience of March 4, 1933, ASV, AES, Stati Ecclesiastici, P.O. 430a, fasc. 348 (1933). For a recent and very insightful review of Pius XI's responses to Hitler (and to Mussolini), see Emma Fattorini, *Hitler, Mussolini and the Vatican: Pope Pius XI and the Speech That Was Never Made* (Cambridge: Polity Press, 2011).

145. Brüning, *Memoirs*, 260; in German original at 359.

146. Ibid., 261; in German original at 360.

147. See the transcripts of an interview Father Colman conducted with Bishop Josef

Frings in November 1963, as part of Colman's research for the Muench biography, in ACUA, Muench Papers, Series 13: Biography, box 60, folder 3, 11–12; John Tracy Ellis, "Fragments from My Autobiography, 1905–1942," *Review of Politics 36*, no. 4 (October 1974): 565–591, especially at 584–586, where Ellis tells of his encounters at Harvard with an embittered Brüning.

148. Brüning's version of events can easily be misconstrued to depict Pacelli as more comfortable dealing with the Nazis than the future Pius XII was at the time. William Patch agrees with this assessment, citing a number of sources. See Patch, *Heinrich Brüning*, 189, including note 64. For some detailed critiques of Brüning's recollections of his meeting with Pacelli, see "Brüning contra Pacelli," in *Katholische Kirche und Nationalsozialismus. Ausgewählte Aufsätze*, ed. Ludwig Volk (Mainz: Matthias-Grünewald, 1987), 315–320.

149. See, for instance, several reports to this effect from Orsenigo to Pacelli, including May 29, 1932, n. 4501; June 11, 1932, n. 4584; August 1, 1932, telegram no. 55; August 2, 1932, "Le elezioni politiche," n. 4959, all in ASV, AES, Germania, 1932–1934, pos. 627, fasc. 144: Elezioni Presidenziali e Politiche.

150. Patch, *Heinrich Brüning*, 291.

151. From the notes of Pacelli's meeting with French ambassador, in ASV, AES, Stati Ecclesiastici, P.O. 430b, fasc. 359 (1932–1933), audience of February 1, 1933.

152. Notes from Pacelli's meeting with German ambassador, February 24, 1933; meeting with Italian ambassador, February 24 and March 3, 1933, in ASV, AES, Stati Ecclesiastici, P.O. 430b, fasc. 359 (1932–1933).

153. Notes from Pacelli's meeting with the Italian ambassador, March 14, 1933, and March 17, 1933, ASV, AES, Stati Ecclesiastici, P.O. 430b, fasc. 359 (1932–1933).

154. See Georg May, *Ludwig Kaas, Der Priester, der Politiker und der Gelehrte aus der Schule von Ulrich Stutz* (Amsterdam: B. R. Grüner, 1982), 3:325–327; see also Brüning's *Memoiren*, 663–664.

155. See John Zeender, "Germany: The Catholic Church and the Nazi Regime," 97–98; see also Zeender, "The Genesis of the Concordat of 1933," in *Studies in Catholic History in Honor of John Tracy Ellis*, ed. Nelson H. Minnich, Robert B. Eno, and Robert Trisco (Wilmington, DE: M. Glazier, 1985), 617–644. Zeender agrees with the view of Klaus Scholder, who sees a connection between the Center Party's eventual parliamentary support for the Enabling Act, and the Hitler regime's start of concordat negotiations. See Klaus Scholder, *Die Kirchen und das dritte Reich*, vol. 1: *Vorgeschichte und Zeit der Illusionen, 1918–1934* (Frankfurt: Ullstein, 1977), 300–322, 482–534.

156. See Franz von Papen's *Memoirs*, 279–280. For an insightful chronology of Kaas's role in the first half of 1933, see Guenter Lewy, *The Catholic Church and Nazi Germany* (London: Weidenfeld and Nicolson, 1964), 64–65.

157. See the Brüning papers at Harvard, Brüning manuscript memoirs, 351–352; and

Memoiren, 630–631, 656–674, quoted by Patch, *Heinrich Brüning,* 295. After the Enabling Act was adopted, the Italian ambassador to the Holy See asked Pacelli whether the Vatican or the German bishops had given instructions to the Center Party to support the Hitler government. As he records in his personal papers, Pacelli said no such instructions had been issued. See audience of March 14, 1933, ASV, AES, P.O. Stati Ecclesiastici, 430b, fasc. 359 (1932–1933).

158. See Patch, *Heinrich Brüning,* 296 n68; for Hitler's comments to his cabinet, see Alphons Kupper, ed., *Staatliche Akten über die Reichskonkordatsverhandlungen 1933* (Mainz: Matthias-Grünewald-Verlag, 1969), 236–237.

159. Patch, *Heinrich Brüning,* 299.

160. So said Zeiger in conversation with the American archbishop Aloisius Muench, during informational conversations in early 1947, as Muench recorded in his diary for January 1, 1947, Muench Papers, Diary, vol. 5, at ACUA.

161. Orsenigo to Pacelli, March 24, 1931, in Volk, *Kirchliche Akten,* 4. Pacelli's response here was recorded after his meeting with Pius XI on March 28, 1933, ASV, AES, Stati Ecclesiastici, P.O. 430a, fasc. 348 (1933).

162. On early papal support for the Hitler government, see Faulhaber's papers on his meeting with Pius XI as reported to Bavarian bishops in Ludwig Volk, ed., *Akten Kardinal Michael von Faulhaber,* vol. 1: *1917–1934* (Mainz: Matthias-Grünewald-Verlag 1975), 660–662.

163. Deneken, "Le cardinal Faulhaber," 179.

164. According to William Patch, Cardinals Bertram and Faulhaber realized already by April 1933 that their statement to take back their previous "bans and warnings" about Nazism actually lowered the episcopates' standing and provoked the disillusionment of Catholics suffering from Nazi persecution. See Patch, *Heinrich Brüning,* 300–301; original statements to this effect from Faulhaber, for instance, can be found in the *Akten Faulhaber,* 714–716. Revealing insights can be gleaned from the correspondence exchanged among Pacelli, Kaas, and various German bishops surrounding the negotiation of the *Reichskonkordat,* as published in Ludwig Volk, *Kirchliche Akten Über Die Reichskonkordatsverhandlungen 1933* (Mainz: Matthias-Grünewald-Verlag, 1969), Reihe A: Quellen—Band 11, for example at 66–80.

165. See Ludwig Kaas, "Der Konkordatstyp des faschistischen Italiens," *Zeitschrift fur auslandisches offentliches Recht und Volkerrecht* 3 (1933): 488–522; Kaas diary, April 7–18, 1933; Kaas to Bergen, November 19, 1935, in Kupper, ed., *Staatliche Akten,* 2–17, 495–496, all cited by Patch, *Heinrich Brüning,* 301 n82.

166. Quoted by Lewy, *The Catholic Church,* 69–70. Original documentation is Clive to Foreign Minister, April 22, 1933, in DBFP, ser. 2, vol. 5, doc. 85, 156.

167. Papen to Bergen, Berlin, May 26, 1933, in DGFP, ser. C, vol. 1, doc. 263, 491–492.

168. Papen to Hitler, July 2, 1933, in DGFP, ser. C, vol. 1, doc. 347, 622–624.

169. Extract from the Minutes of the Conference of Ministers on July 14, 1933, in DGFP, ser. C, vol. 1, doc. 362, 651–653.

170. DBFP, ser. 2, vol. 5, 1933, doc. 227, 383. See also Brüning's *Memoiren*, 670–672.

171. Pacelli to Schioppa, Vatican, July 15, 1933, in Volk, ed., *Kirchliche Akten*, n. 86, 162–163.

172. Ibid.

173. See the memo by Hermann-Josef Schmitt, a Center Party official, on a visit to Pacelli in February 1934, in Volk, ed., *Kirchliche Akten*, 304–305.

174. For further details about the actual dissolution of the Center Party, see Patch, *Heinrich Brüning*, 302–303, nn86,87; for original documentation, see, for instance, memo by Hermann-Josef Schmitt on a visit to Pacelli in February 1934, in Volk, ed., *Kirchliche Akten*, 304–305; on Brüning's recollection of the decision to dissolve the party, see his *Memoiren*, 673.

175. For revealing insights into how the German bishops and the Holy See were thinking about these matters in the spring and summer of 1933, see, for instance, Faulhaber's memo regarding conversation with Papen, June 10, 1933; Betram to Pacelli, June 23, 1933; the memo by Fr. Leiber dated June 29, 1933, all in Volk, ed., *Kirchliche Akten*, 61–63, 76–68, 88–89.

176. See, for instance, Bergen to Foreign Ministry, June 30, 1933, in DGFP, ser. C, vol. 1, doc. 341, 611; and Bergen to Neurath, July 3, 1933, in ibid., doc. 351, 635.

177. See R. H. Clive, Annual Report, 1933, January 1, 1934, in Hachey, *Anglo-Vatican Relations*, 241–261, especially 251–252.

178. Audience of July 29, 1933, ASV, AES, Stati Ecclesiastici, P.O. 430b, fasc. 360 (1933–1940).

179. See Father Robert Leiber's argument that the Vatican attitude to the concordat reflected two previous moves within Germany proper: the first was the Center Party's support of the Enabling Act, and the second the German bishops' statement in late March 1933 withdrawing their erstwhile condemnation of the Nazi movement. Leiber, "Reichskonkordat und Ende der Zentrumspartei," *Stimmen der Zeit* 167 (1960–1961): 213–223, here at 220–221.

180. Audience of November 5 and 10, 1933, ASV, AES, P.O. 430a, fasc. 349 (1933–1934).

3. Conflict and Compromise

1. See the "Short Note on a Discussion on September 5, 1933," which Eugen Klee, the chargé d'affaires of the German Embassy to the Holy See, sent to the Foreign Ministry in Berlin, September 6, 1933, in DGFP, ser. C, vol. 1, doc. 418, 782–785.

2. The "exchange of notes" between the Vatican and the German government, most of which came from Pacelli directly, can be found at ASV, AES; also reproduced in part in Dieter Albrecht, ed., *Der Notenwechsel zwischen dem Heiligen Stuhl*

und der Deutschen Reichsregierung, vol. 1: *Von der Ratifizierung des Reichskonkordat bis zur Enzyklika "Mit Brennender Sorge"* (Mainz: Matthias-Grunewald-Verlag, 1965); volume 2 covers the years 1937–1945 (Mainz: Matthias-Grunewald-Verlag, 1969). See also Michele Maccarrone, *Il nazionalsocialismo e la Santa Sede* (Rome: Editrice Studium, 1947); and the *Vita Documentata* of the *Positio Summ.*, vol. 1, 446–448.

3. See "Short Note on a Discussion on September 5, 1933," DGFP, ser. C, vol. 1, doc. 418, 782–785.

4. Memorandum by the Chargé d'Affaires of the Embassy to the Holy See [Klee], September 7, 1933, DGFP, ser. C, vol. 1, doc. 419, 786, and doc. 422, 789.

5. Memorandum by the Chargé d'Affaires of the Embassy to the Holy See to the Foreign Ministry, September 12, 1933, DGFP, ser. C, vol. 1, doc. 425, 793–794.

6. The Ambassador to the Holy See [Bergen] to the Foreign Ministry, October 14, 1933, DGFP, ser. C, vol. 1, doc. 501, 927–928.

7. Quoted by Guenter Lewy, *The Catholic Church and Nazi Germany* (New York: McGraw-Hill, 1964), 116–117.

8. See, for instance, the Promemoria prepared by Pacelli, dated October 19, 1933, in *Der Notenwechsel*, 1:51–57. See also ASV, AES, Germania, IV, 1934–1936, P.O. 666, fasc. 220: Nuovo Governo Hitler.

9. See *Vita Documentata*, vol. 1, 448, cited in Maccarrone, *Il nazionalsocialismo e la Santa Sede*, 29–32.

10. See the German government's Promemoria dated January 15, 1934, reproduced in *Vita Documentata*, vol. 1, 487; and Maccarrone, *Il nazionalsocialismo e la Santa Sede*, 37–40.

11. Audience of December 18, 1933, ASV, AES, Stati Ecclesiastici, P.O. 430a, fasc. 349 (1933–1934).

12. See Pacelli's Promemoria dated January 31, 1934, reproduced in *Der Notenwechsel*, 1:51–57.

13. Consider, for instance, the long list of complaints the Holy See lodged with the Nazi government in July 1939, a few months into Pacelli's pontificate. These are reproduced in *Der Notenwechsel*, vol. 2, n. 27, 85–94.

14. See, for instance, on Cramer-Klett's arrest, Vasallo to Pacelli, Munich, August 14, 1935, n. 4832: Arresto del Barone Cramer-Klett; Orsenigo to Pacelli, Berlin, November 1, 1935, n. 14971; Pacelli to Orsenigo, November 13, 1935, n. 3826/35; and Orsenigo to Pacelli, Berlin, November 23, 1935, n. 15186, Oggetto: colloquio con Ministro Esteri; all in ASV, AES, Germania, IV Periodo IV, 1934–1936, P.O. 666, fasc. 223, "Nuovo Governo Hitler." Other Vatican archive files pertaining to the Nazi campaign against the Catholic Church are in ASV, AES Germania, Periodo IV, P.O. 645, fasc. 162–171 (1933–36). Re. Concordat with Reich; and P.O. 650, fasc. 194–200 (1933–37). AES Germania, Periodo IV, P.O. 692, fasc. 260–263 (1935–38).

This last file deals with the arrest of priests and persecution of Catholics and includes a letter from Pacelli condemning violations of the concordat.

15. From Pacelli's notes of a meeting with Dr. Buttmann, June 17, 1935, and a meeting with Ambassador Bergen, September 13, 1935, in ASV, AES, Stati Ecclesiastici, P.O. 430b, fasc. 362 (1935).

16. The "nota di protesta," January 29, 1936, ASV, AES, Germania, Periodo IV, P.O. 692, fasc. 260, 261 (N. 312/36).

17. For more on this wave of arrests and subsequent trials, see Maccarrone, *Il Nazionalsocialismo e la Santa Sede*, 90–97; and John S. Conway, *The Nazi Persecution of the Churches, 1933–1945* (New York: Basic Books, 1968).

18. The "nota di protesta," January 29, 1936, ASV, AES, Germania, Periodo IV, P.O. 692, fasc. 260, 261 (N. 312/36).

19. Ibid.

20. Bergen to Neurath, January 4, 1936, DGFP, ser. C, vol. 4, doc. 482, 963–967.

21. March 13, 1936, DDI, ser. 8, vol. 3, doc. 449, 508.

22. According to Philippe Chenaux, it was Hudal more than anyone who pressed the line about finding a *modus vivendi* with the Nazi state, an approach supported by Monsignor Kaas. On Hudal and Pacelli, see Chenaux, "Pacelli, Hudale et la question du nazisme (1933–1938)," *Rivista di storia della Chiesa in Italia* 57 (2003): 133–154, which is drawn in part from the Hudal archives, Archivio Storico di Santa Maria dell'Anima. See also ASV, AES, Germania 4, 336.

23. Faulhaber to Pacelli, Munich, December 27, 1937, in *Akten Faulhabers*, vol. 2, nos. 690, 461.

24. Pacelli to Faulhaber, Vatican, November 16, 1936, in *Akten Faulhabers*, vol. 2, no. 575, 197–198.

25. Michel Deneken, "Le Cardinal Faulhaber à Archives Ouvertes," *Revue d'Allemagne et des Pays de langue allemande* 36, no. 2 (2004): 175–193, here at 181–182.

26. Emma Fattorini, *Pio XI, Hitler e Mussolini: la solitudine di un papa* (Turin: Einaudi, 2007), 54–55; T. V. Lehnert, *Positio Summ.*, 80.

27. Fattorini, *Pio XI, Hitler e Mussolini*, 54–55.

28. See Giovanni Miccoli, *I dilemmi e I silenzi di Pio XII* (Milan: Mondador, 2000), 160. Pacelli's notes on this are in Audience of March 22, 1935, ASV, AES, Stati Ecclesiastici, P.O. 430a, fasc. 351 (1934–1935).

29. Audience of March 20, 1936, ASV, AES, Stati Ecclesiastici, P.O. 430b, fasc. 363, n. 26.

30. See De Vecchi's memorandum to Mussolini dated April 18, 1931, in DDI, ser. 7, vol. 10, doc. 207, 318–319.

31. Audience of April 10, 1931, ASV, AES, Stati Ecclesiastici, P.O. 430b, fasc. 356 (1930–1931).

32. Audience of November 12, 1933, ASV, AES, Stati Ecclesiastici, P.O. 430a, fasc. 347 (1932–1933).

33. Quoted by Carlo Fiorentino, *All'ombra di Pietro: la Chiesa cattolica e lo spionaggio fascista in Vaticano: 1929–1939* (Florence: Casa editrice le lettere, 1999), 37. The original is in ACS, Ministero della Cultura Popolare, Gabinetto, b. 198, fasc. "Zanetti." Anno 1935. Fiorentino notes that in the numerous Fascist espionage papers conserved at the Central State Archives in Rome, there is no specific file reserved for Pacelli, nor for other high-ranking Vatican officials like Montini, Tardini, or Ottaviani.

34. An excellent summary of this radical turn in Fascist policy, both foreign and domestic, is offered by Alexander De Grand, "Mussolini's Follies: Fascism in Its Imperial and Racist Phase, 1935–1940," *Contemporary European History* 13, no. 2 (2004): 127–147.

35. Peter C. Kent, "Between Rome and London: Pius XI, the Catholic Church, and the Abyssinian Crisis of 1935–1936," *International History Review* 11, no. 2 (May 1989), 252–271. See also, among others, Lucia Ceci, *Il papa non deve parlare: Chiesa, fascismo e guerra d'Etiopia* (Rome: Laterza, 2010). On the insights provided by the careers and papers of chief protagonists, see Renzo De Felice, "La Santa Sede e il conflitto italo-etiopiano del diario di Bernardino Nogara," *Storia contemporanea* 8, no. 4 (1977): 823–834; and Carlo Felice Casula, *Domenico Tardini (1888–1961): L'azione della Santa Sede nella crisi fra le due guerre* (Rome: Studium, 1988); Mario Casella, *Gli ambasciatori d'Italia presso la Santa Sede dal 1929 al 1943* (Lecce: Congedo, 2009); Nicolas G. Virtue, "A Way Out of Isolation: Fascist Italy's Relationship with the Vatican during the Ethiopian Crisis," in *Collision of Empires: Italy's Invasion of Ethiopia and Its International Impact,* ed. G. Bruce Strang (Farnham: Ashgate, forthcoming).

36. D. G. Osborne, "Leading Personalities at the Holy See," FO 371/22441, June 24, 1938.

37. Lucia Ceci, "La Mancata Lettera di Pio XI a Mussolini per fermare l'aggressione all'Etiopia," *Studi Storici* 3 (2007): 817–840, here at 820. The official version of the speech was published first in French in *L'Osservatore Romano* on August 29, 1935, followed by an Italian version on September 1, 1935. Indispensable insights into the entire episode can be found in Domenico Tardini's diaries, which have been edited by Carlo Felice Casula, in the biography by Casula, *Domenico Tardini,* 384–386. For a more comprehensive and highly instructive survey of the incident and its significance, see Lucia Ceci, "Santa Sede e guerra in Etiopia: a proposito di un discorso di Pio XI," *Studi Storici* 44, no. 2 (2003): 511–525.

38. See *Discorsi di Pio XI,* ed. Domenico Bertetto (Turin: Società editrice internazionale, 1960), 3:386–390, especially 389.

39. As we will see below, this plea against the war was to be the essence of a private letter the pope intended to send to Mussolini in September 1935. See here audience of September 20, 1935, Pacelli notebooks, ASV, AES, Stati Ecclesiastici, P.O. 430a, fasc. 352.

40. These purported comments were hearsay, and appear to have been passed along from the French delegation at the Holy See to the British. See S. K. B Assante, "The Catholic Mission, British West African Nationalists, and the Italian Invasion of Ethiopia, 1935–1936," *African Affairs* 73, no. 291 (April 1974): 207–208, which draws from documentation in the Foreign Office archives in the UK, FO 371/19135, Hugh Montgomery, British League to the Holy See to Sir Samuel Hoare, Foreign Secretary, September 16, 1935.

41. For the Italian case, see, among other sources, Claudio M. Betti, *Colonialismo e missioni. Autorità coloniali e missionari in Etiopia (1885–1896)* (Rome: Ariani, 1990); and Betti, *Missioni e colonie in Africa Orientale* (Rome: Studium, 1999).

42. See DDI, Pignatti-Mussolini, December 14, 1935 [ser. 8], vol. 2, doc. 854, 836–837.

43. Audience of August 30, 1935, ASV, AES, Stati Ecclesiastici, P.O. 430b, fasc. 362 (1935).

44. Some revealing insights into Tacchi-Venturi's contacts with the Mussolini government emerge from his personal correspondence, which is conserved and accessible to researchers at the Jesuit Archives in Rome, ARSI. See, too, the instructive work of Robert A. Maryks, *Pouring Jewish Water into Fascist Wine: Untold Stories of (Catholic) Jews from the Archive of Mussolini's Jesuit Pietro Tacchi Venturi* (Leiden: Brill, 2011).

45. For Pacelli's account of meetings with Pignatti in December 1935, see the audience of December 6, 1935, Pacelli notebooks, ASV, AES, IV, P.O. 430b, fasc. 362 (1935) [n. 146]. See also Colloquio del P. Tacchi Venturi col Duce, December 14, 1935, ASV, AES, Italia, IV, 967, Conflitto Italo-Etiopico, vol. II, ff. 256–260.

46. See the lengthy notes compiled by Domenico Tardini in the fall-winter of 1935, in ASV, AES, Italia, 967, Conflitto Italo-Etiopico, vol. 1 bis.

47. Letters from Pignatti to Mussolini, October 13, 1935, doc. 335, 310–312; November 15, 1935, doc. 645, 623; November 19, 1935, doc. 664, 639; December 10, 1935, doc. 827, 810–811, all in DDI, ser. 8, vol. 2. For evidence that the British were puzzled by the absence of a public papal condemnation of Italian aggression, see FO 371/19227; FO 371/19135.

48. Quoted by Charles-Roux, *Huit Ans au Vatican, 1932–1940* (Paris: Flammarion, 1947), 143. The letter was dated October 2, 1935.

49. See Charles-Roux, *Huit Ans au Vatican*, 138–143, 156, 229–233. See also Fattorini, *Pio XI, Hitler e Mussolini*, 71.

50. See Pignatti to Mussolini, January 17, 1936, in DDI, ser. 8, vol. 3, doc. 71, 93–95.

51. "Nota del Sig. Bernardino Nogara con una visione pessimistica della situazione italiana," January 8, 1936, ASV, AES, ITALIA, 967, Conflitto Italo-Etiopico, vol. II, ff. 364–367. See also in the same, Audience of January 2, 1936, in which Pacelli recounts meeting with Tacchi-Venturi with instructions to approach Mussolini urging a calm, restrained, and reasonable public and private response to the other powers, especially England.

52. Pignatti to Mussolini, January 17, 1936, DDI, ser. 8, vol. 3, doc. 71, 93–95.

53. See February 1, 1936, doc. 158, 197; April 3, 1936, doc. 570, 631–633; April 24, 1936, doc. 751, 798–799, all in DDI, ser. 8, vol. 3. For the corresponding Vatican files, see Pacelli's notes, Pacelli and Charles-Roux, audiences of April 11 and April 12, 1936, ASV, AES, Stati Ecclesiastici, P.O. 430b, f. 363, n. 32 and n. 33.

54. For a good general survey of the Ethiopian campaign and its consequences, see G. Rochat, *Le guerre italiane 1935–1943. Dall'impero d'Etiopia alla disfatta* (Turin: Einaudi, 2005).

55. Pacelli and Magaz, audience of September 10, 1936, ASV, AES, Stati Ecclesiastici, P.O. 430b, fasc. 364 (1936–1940) [n. 7]. See also Fattorini, *Pio XI, Hitler e Mussolini,* 90–91.

56. Fattorini, *Pio XI, Hitler e Mussolini,* 92–93.

57. *Discorsi di Pio XI,* 3:556. For firsthand documentary accounts of Pacelli's handling of the Spanish Civil War, see the Pacelli notebooks, ASV, AES, Stati Ecclesiastic, P.O. 430a, fasc. 353, and P.O. 430b, fasc. 364.

58. Pacelli and Charles-Roux, audience of August 6, 1936, ASV, AES, Stati Ecclesiastici, P.O. 430b, fasc. 363 (1936); see also from the same file the audience of August 12, 1936, in which Pacelli recounts details of his meeting with the Spanish ambassador to the Holy See.

59. Ibid.

60. Quoted by Fattorini, *Pio XI, Hitler e Mussolini,* 104. Full original text is in AAS, 31 (1939), 151–154.

61. See, for instance, a letter written by Pacelli, August 15, 1937, in ASV, Arch. Nunz. Madrid, b. 968, fasc. 6, Roma Rapporti Politici, which is discussed in Fattorini, *Pio XI, Hitler e Mussolini,* 100–101.

62. Pacelli's various addresses as cardinal secretary of state can be found in Pie XII, *Discours et panegyriques (1931–1938)* (Paris: Maison de la Bonee Presse Cinq, 1939); also in Italian as *Discorsi e panegerici (1931–1938)* (Vatican City: Tipografia Poliglotta Vaticana, 1956). The Lourdes speech is from April 26, 1935, in *Discours et panegyriques,* 205–206.

63. For further details, see Chenaux, "Il cardinale Pacelli e la questione del nazismo dopo la enciclica 'Mit Brennender Sorge,' (1937)," *Annali dell'Istituto storico italo-germanico in Trento* (Bologna, 2006): 265–267. The AES files for France are rich with documentation that confirms the heightening fear in papal circles of grow-

ing Communist influences over French workers and youth, including increasing numbers of Catholics. See, for instance, reports in ASV, AES, IV Periodo, Francia, P.O. 795 and P.O. 796–797.

64. Pio XII, *Discours et panegyriques*, 228–229.

65. So says Charles-Roux in his memoir, *Huit Ans au Vatican*, 232.

66. Pio XII, *Discours et panegyriques*, 381.

67. See John Pollard, "American Catholics and the Financing of the Vatican in the Great Depression: Peter's Pence Payments, 1935–1938," paper presented at the Pius XI and America Conference, Brown University, October 29–30, 2010. My thanks to Professor Pollard for his permission to use and cite his work.

68. Pacelli quoted by Gannon, *The Cardinal Spellman Story* (Garden City, N.Y.: Doubleday, 1962), 107. For semi-official Vatican commentary see "Il Cardinale Pacelli a Nuova York," *L'Osservatore Romano,* October 10, 1936.

69. For a brief summary of the life and times of Nicholas Frederic Brady, who was chairman of New York Edison Co., see *Time,* April 7, 1930.

70. "Pulse Taker," *Time,* October 19, 1936, 37–38; and "Vatican State Secretary Sails for U.S. Today," *Chicago Daily Tribune,* October 1, 1936, 2.

71. The Vatican's files on Pacelli's visit and on the origins of what became the Taylor mission are rather thin and not yet fully accessible, but they allow for some insights nevertheless. See, on the 1936 Pacelli visit, ASV, Delegazione Apostolica Stati Uniti, V, P.O., 194, Visita negli USA del Cardinale Eugenio Pacelli (26–37–39). Further correspondence regarding talks toward some kind of diplomatic rapport between the Holy See and the Roosevelt administration can be found in ASV, AES, America IV, P.O. 237, fasc. 65. For broader commentary on the gradual rapprochement, so to speak, effected largely with the help of Spellman and other members of the American Catholic hierarchy, see Gerald P. Fogarty, *The Vatican and the American Hierarchy from 1870 to 1965* (Stuttgart: Hiersemann, 1982).

72. "Pacelli Urges World Peace, Blesses Many," *Washington Post,* October 23, 1936, X1.

73. "Pacelli Ends a 6,500 Mile Plane Tour over U.S.," *Chicago Daily Tribune,* November 1, 1936, 7; "Cardinal Pacelli Ends Plane Tour," *New York Times,* November 1, 1936, 12.

74. Quoted by Gannon, *The Cardinal Spellman Story,* 114.

75. "Pacelli Lunches with Roosevelt," *New York Times,* November 6, 1936, 1.

76. For an instructive analysis of the impact of Pacelli's 1936 visit and the behind-the-scenes maneuvers that lead eventually to the naming of Myron C. Taylor as FDR's "personal representative" to the Holy See in 1939, see Gerald P. Fogarty, S.J., "Roosevelt and the American Catholic Hierarchy," in *FDR, the Vatican, and the Roman Catholic Church in America, 1933–1945,* ed. David B. Woolner and Richard G. Kurial (New York: Palgrave Macmillan, 2003), 11–43.

77. Gannon writes that after Pacelli's visit to Hyde Park, "things began to happen. Barriers dropped." Gannon, *The Cardinal Spellman Story*, 154.

78. For general surveys of the relationship between American culture and Roman Catholicism and the Vatican, see John McGreevy, *Catholicism and American Freedom* (New York: W. W. Norton, 2003); and Peter R. D'Agostino, *Rome in America: Transnational Catholic Ideology from the Risorgimento to Fascism* (Chapel Hill: University of North Carolina Press, 2004).

79. For excerpts of Faulhaber's notes of the January 1937 meeting and subsequent correspondence with Pacelli, see *Akten Faulhabers*, January 23, 1937, no. 609, vol. 2, 282 onward.

80. Lewy, *The Catholic Church and Nazi Germany*, 156.

81. Pius XI, *Mit Brennender Sorge*, "On the Church and the German Reich," March 14, 1937, para. 11.

82. Ibid., para. 8.

83. This is from Pius XII's famous address to the cardinals, June 2, 1945, here discussed by Martin Rhonheimer, "The Holocaust: What Was Not Said," *First Things* 137 (November 2003): 18–27.

84. See Angelo Martini, S.J., *Positio Summ.*, 512; Pascalina Lehnert, *Positio Summ.*, 103–104. For further discussion of Cardinal Faulhaber's role in drafting the encyclical, see Angelo Martini, S.J., "Il Cardinale Faulhaber e l'enciclica 'Mit Brennender Sorge,'" *Archivium Historiae Pontificiae* 2 (1964): 303–320.

85. See *Vita Documentata*, I, 590, n. 18. See also H. A. Raem, *Pius XI. und der Nazionalsozialismus. Die Enzyklika "Mit Brennender Sorge" vom 14 marz 1937* (Paderborn-Munich-Vienna-Zurich, 1979). To compare Faulhaber's earlier draft and the final version, see *Der Notenwechsel*, vol. 2, 1937–1945, Appendix 7, 404–443.

86. See ADSS, vol. 6, 2:424. See also Miccoli, *I dilemma*, 451 n130.

87. See, for instance, March 13, 1936, DDI, ser. 8, vol. 3, doc. 449, 508; and especially DDI, ser. 8, vol. 3, doc. 752, 799–800.

88. Pignatti to Ciano, June 15, 1936, doc. 275, 326–327; and Pignatti to Ciano, June 19, 1936, doc. 316, 365–366, both in DDI, ser. 8, vol 4.

89. See *Positio Summ.*, Pars I, 512.

90. So argues Giovanni Miccoli in *I Dilemmi*, 159–160. Apparently Pius XI reviewed at least three drafts of the encyclical. See *Der Notenwechsel*, vol. 1, Appendix 7, 402–433.

91. *Mit Brennender Sorge*, para. 22.

92. Ibid., para. 33, 34.

93. Even though papal encyclicals like *Mit Brennender Sorge* were clear in some respects, translating this clarity into practice was not so straightforward, especially when bishops and theologians turned to articulate concrete guidelines and policies to reflect the doctrinal principles contained in papal pronouncements. For a

fascinating insight into this dynamic, see Claudia Koonz, "Ethical Dilemmas and Nazi Eugenics: Single-Issue Dissent in Religious Contexts," in *Resistance against the Third Reich, 1933–1990,* ed. Michael Geyer and John W. Boyer (Chicago: University of Chicago Press, 1994), 15–38. See also Beth Griech-Polelle, "Image of a Churchman-Resister: Bishop von Galen, the Euthanasia Project and the Sermons of Summer 1941," *Journal of Contemporary History* 36, no. 1 (2001): 41–57; and Michael Burleigh, *Death and Deliverance: "Euthanasia" in Germany, c. 1900–1945* (Cambridge: Cambridge University Press, 1994).

94. Faulhaber to Pacelli, January 21, 1937, in *Akten Faulhabers,* vol. 2 (1935–1945), no. 608, 282.

95. See details of Faulhaber's meeting with Pacelli, January 15, 1937, in *Akten Faulhabers,* vol. 2, no. 605, 276, and no. 607, 281.

96. For an excellent summary of Murri's "reconciliation" with the church, see Lorenzo Bedeschi, "La Reconciliazione di Murri con la Chiesa," *Civitas* 28, no. 9 (1977): 3–28.

97. A measure of Nazi anger at the Vatican and an impulse in certain Nazi circles to accelerate attacks against the church can be seen in a Gestapo report from *Der Welt Kampf,* Munich, September 1938, which discusses methods to use in the persecution of the Catholic Church. A copy of this can be found in the Vatican archives, ASV, AES, Germania, IV, no. 738 P.O., 1938–1945, fasc. 354, foll. 54.

98. The lengthy diplomatic complaint was delivered by von Bergen to Pacelli, Berlin, April 15, 1937, and is reproduced, in English translation, in DGFP, doc. 646, 951–954.

99. Pacelli and Charles-Roux, audience of April 23, 1937, ASV, AES, Stati Ecclesiastici, P.O. 430b, fasc. 364 (1936–1940), [n. 68].

100. See the German Foreign Ministry to the German Embassy to the Holy See, Berlin, April 7, 1937, in DGFP, ser. D, vol. 1, doc. 642, 945.

101. See Lewy, *The Catholic Church and Nazi Germany,* 158–159. For a cursory but revealing reading of the German discussion of Hitler's visit to Rome, see DGFP.

102. See Chenaux, "Il cardinale Pacelli e la questione del nazismo," 268; Chenaux draws upon M. Casella, "La crisi del 1938 fra Stato e Chiesa nella documentazione dell'Archivio Storico del Ministero degli Affari Esteri," *Rivista di storia della Chiesa in Italia* 54 (2000), 102.

103. Quoted by Miccoli, *I Dilemmi,* 160. For the relevant Vatican files pertaining to Hitler's visit to Rome and the non-visit with the pope, see ASV, AES Germania, IV, P.O. 724, fasc. 339, 1937–1938; and P.O. 735, fasc. 353, 1938. For German reaction to the pope's statement on May 4, 1938, see DGFP, ser. D, vol. 1, doc. 710, 1038.

104. For the rich documentation chronicling the Holy See's perspective on the German response to *Mit Brennender Sorge,* see ASV, AES, Germania, IV, 1937–1938, P.O. 720, fasc. 323.

105. Pacelli and von Bergen, audience of April 15, 1937, ASV, AES, Stati Ecclesiastici, P.O. 430b, fasc. 364 (1936–1940), [n. 63–65].

106. Pacelli's long note to Bergen, from the Vatican, April 30, 1937, is in DGFP, ser. D, vol. 1, doc. 649, 956–966.

107. See "Dopo il congresso di Norimberga," L'Osservatore Romano, September 15, 1937. The day before the article appeared, Pacelli met with the pope to read aloud his draft of the article and get Pius XI's approval. Pacelli's handwritten notes to the draft indicate that the pope was greatly pleased and jokingly assigned his pupil the highest grade possible. See ASV, AES, IV Germania, P.O. 720, fasc. 323, foll. 14–18.

108. See Cicognani's report to Pacelli, with the accompanying documentation, October 3, 1937, in ASV, AES, Germania, IV, 1937–1938, P.O. 720, fasc. 354, foll. 6–13.

109. See ASV, AES, Germania, IV, P.O. 720, fasc. 324, foll. 35–38.

110. ASV, AES, Germania, IV, P.O. 720, fasc. 323, foll. 20–25.

111. See "Mundelein Scores Nazi Government," New York Times, May 19, 1937, 11.

112. Bergen to Pacelli, May 24, 1937, Rome, in Der Notenwechsel, vol. 2, 20–21.

113. For the diplomatic exchanges between Pacelli and members of the German delegation at the Vatican, see Der Notenwechsel, vol. 2, 20–30, for May to June 1937. See also Angelo Martini, S.J., "Pio XII e Hitler," La Civiltà Cattolica 116, no. 1 (1965): 342–354, especially at 344.

114. The minutes of the joint session can be found in ASV, AES, Congregazioni miste, Rapporti delle Sessioni, "Relazione, Germania: Situazione Religiosa e Politica Discorso dell'E.MO Cardinale Mundelein," anno 1937, Sessione 1376, Stampa 1271.

115. Pacelli and Charles-Roux, audience of January 28, 1937, no. 32, and Pacelli and Pignatti, audience of January 29, 1937, no. 33, both in ASV, AES, P.O. Stati Ecclesiastici, 430b, fasc. 364 (1936–1940).

116. "Spagna, Situazione Religiosa e Politica," June 14, 1937, ASV, AES, Congregazioni miste, Rapporti delle Sessioni, anno 1937, Sessione 1375, Stampa 1270.

117. Audience of February 8, 1938, ASV, AES, Stati Ecclesiastici, P.O. 430b, fasc. 364 (1936-1940), n.133.

118. "Nuove trattative tra la S. Sede ed il Reich," ASV, AES, Germania, IV, P.O. 731–733, 1937–1952, fasc. 346.

119. Audience of October 31, 1938, ASV, AES, Stati Ecclesiastici, P.O. 430b, fasc. 364 (1936–1940), [n. 130].

120. Pacelli's memorandum to Ambassador Kennedy, which has been referred to as "the Pacelli report," was compiled sometime in April 1938, and sent by Kennedy to James Roosevelt at the White House on April 19, 1938. J. P. Kennedy Papers at the John F. Kennedy Presidential Library and Museum. Many thanks to Charles Gallagher, S.J., for bringing this to my attention. Many thanks also to the Joseph

P. Kennedy Papers Donor Committee as well as the archivists at the Kennedy Library in Boston for facilitating my research into the Joseph P. Kennedy collection in August 2009.

121. Robert S. Wistrich, *Hitler and the Holocaust* (New York: Modern Library, 2001), 61–66.

122. Orsenigo to Pacelli, November 15, 1938, in ASV, AES, 1938, P.O. 742, fasc. 356. Copies of the original can be found in RG 76, "Reichskristallnacht," United States Holocaust Memorial Museum. Many thanks to Suzanne Brown-Fleming for sharing with me the results of her research into the copious Vatican archives files now held by the USHMM. See Brown-Fleming, "The Vatican and the Nazi Movement, 1922–1939: New Sources and Unexpected Findings on the Vatican's Response to *Reichskristallnacht*," in *Lessons and Legacies IX: Memory, History and Responsibility: Reassessments of the Holocaust, Implications for the Future,* ed. Jonathan Petropoulos, Lynn Rapaport, and John K. Roth (Chicago: Northwestern University Press, 2010), 203–214. Orsenigo's letter was published many years ago in the ADSS, vol. 6, Appendix 4, 536–537.

123. Orsenigo to Pacelli, November 19, 1938, ASV, AES, Germania, 1938, P.O. 742, fasc. 356; also in ADSS, 6, Appendix 5, 538.

124. See letter sent from Pacelli's office dated January 9, 1939, to bishops in Europe but also Canada, the United States, Latin America, and Australia, on Pius XI's behalf. In ASV, AES, Stati Ecclesiastici, 1938–1939, P.O. 575, fasc. 606 bis.

125. Quoted by Brown-Fleming, "The Vatican and the Nazi Movement." The original can be found in ADSS, 6, 539, no. 1.

126. Pacelli's response, which was dated December 3, 1938, can be found in the ADSS, 6, 539.

127. Pacelli, *Discours et panegyriques,* 506.

4. A Tremendous Responsibility

1. The story is told in Andrea Tornielli, *Pio XII: Eugenio Pacelli. Un uomo sul trono di Pietro* (Milan: Mondadori, 2007), 292.

2. For Pacelli's role as *camerlengo* in certifying the pope's death, see coverage by Camille M. Cianfarra, "Death at 5:31 A.M.," *New York Times,* February 10, 1939, 1–2. Camille Cianfarra, "Vatican Conclave Is Set for March 1," *New York Times,* February 22, 1939, 10.

3. See here the account provided in the *Vita Documentata,* vol. I, Pars II, 699; Emma Fattorini, *Pio XI, Hitler e Mussolini: la solitudine di un papa* (Turin: G. Einaudi, 2007), 213–214.

4. The text is reproduced in Fattorini, *Pio XI, Hitler e Mussolini,* 240–244. Significantly,

the full text of the address was not published until 1956, under John XXIII, who had it published in AAS, 51 (February 1959), 131–139.

5. See Tornielli, *Pio XII: Eugenio Pacelli*, 292–293.

6. Galeazzo Ciano, *The Complete Unabridged Diaries of Count Galeazzo Ciano, Italian Minister for Foreign Affairs, 1939–1943*, ed. Hugh Gibson (Garden City, N.Y.: Doubleday, 1946), 251 (1939).

7. Giuseppe Dalla Torre, *Memorie*, 2nd ed. (Verona: Arnaldo Mondadori Editore, 1967), 139–140. The original in Italian reads that Pacelli was convinced "che una aperta trattativa sarebbe state più efficace, capace anzi di superare le difficoltà attuali fino a condurre a un'intesa continua e completa, a rendere insomma la Conciliazione effettiva a vantaggio della Chiesa e dello Stato."

8. *Ciano Diaries*, 1939, 250.

9. Ibid., 251–252.

10. All of this is recounted in fascinating detail in a memo drafted by Tardini and conserved in the ASV, AES, pos. 576, fasc. 607. For an instructive commentary, see Fattorini, *Pio XI, Hitler e Mussolini*, 214.

11. Hubert Wolf, *Pope and Devil: The Vatican's Archives and the Third Reich* (Cambridge, MA: Belknap Press of Harvard University Press, 2010), 210.

12. Georges Passelecq and Bernard Suchecky, *The Hidden Encyclical of Pius XI* (New York: Harcourt Brace, 1997). For a properly critical assessment of what the encyclical did or did not represent, see Michael Marrus, "The Vatican on Racism and Antisemitism, 1938–39: A New Look at a Might-Have-Been," *Holocaust and Genocide Studies* 2, no. 3 (Winter 1997): 378–395; and Giovanni Miccoli, "L'Enciclica mancata di Pio XI sul razzismo e l'antisemitismo," *Passato e presente* 15, no. 40 (1997): 35–54.

13. The secret dossier is available in the original in ASMAE, Ambasciata d'Italia presso la Santa Sede, busta 143, which is reproduced in Mario Casella, "La crisis del 1938 fra Chiesa e Stato nella documentazione dell'Archivio Storico del Ministero degli Affari Esteri," *Rivista di storia della chiesa in Italia* 54 (2000): 91–186; see the appendix at 140–186. Pucci was a well-connected prelate and thus a highly prized informant for the Italian government. See David Alvarez, *Spies in the Vatican: Espionage and Intrigue from Napoleon to the Holocaust* (Lawrence: University Press of Kansas, 2002), 156–157; and especially Carlo Fiorentino, *All'ombra di Pietro: La Chiesa cattolica e lo spionaggio fascista in Vaticano, 1929–1939* (Florence: Casa editrice le lettere, 1999), 7–40. Fiorentino reasons that Pucci was able to maintain access to the papal court because the Vatican, well aware that he was passing information on to Italian authorities, nevertheless saw him as a useful conduit to the Italian government and thus potentially helpful in promoting a good working relationship with the Mussolini regime.

14. For the British report, which was signed by Charles Wingfield, January 12, 1935, see Thomas E. Hachey, ed., *Anglo-Vatican Relations, 1914–1939: Confidential Annual Reports of the British Ministers to the Holy See* (Boston: G. K. Hall, 1972), 263.

15. Camille Cianfarra, "Hailed by Throngs," *New York Times*, March 3, 1939, 1.

16. Pascalina Lehnert, *Positio Summ.*, 82; Carlo Pacelli, *Positio Summ.*, 215; Giulio Pacelli, *Positio Summ*, 410.

17. "Most Eminent Princes," *Time*, February 27, 1939, 26.

18. Quoted by Camille Cianfarra, "Vatican Conclave Is Set for March 1," *New York Times*, February 22, 1939, 10.

19. So argues Lapide in his *Roma e gli ebrei*, where he reproduces part of the SD report on Pacelli cited by Tornielli, *Pio XII: Eugenio Pacelli*, 308. See also Gilbert report from Berlin to Sec. State in Washington, dated February 18, 1939, in RG 59, 1930–1939: Central Decimal File, 865D.502/8–866A.911, Box No. 6901.

20. For an excellent summary of the intrigue behind the conclave, see David Alvarez and Robert A. Graham, *Nothing Sacred: Nazi Espionage against the Vatican, 1939–1945* (London: Frank Cass, 1997); see especially "The Final Interrogation Report: Albert Hartl." See also Alvarez, *Spies in the Vatican*, ch. 4; and Owen Chadwick, *Britain and the Vatican during the Second World War* (New York: Cambridge University Press, 1986), 20, 33–43.

21. The story is told in compelling detail by Alvarez, *Spies in the Vatican*, 170. See also Alvarez and Graham, *Nothing Sacred*, 65–66.

22. Alvarez, *Spies in the Vatican*, 170–171; Chadwick, *Britain and the Vatican*, 42.

23. Cianfarra, "Vatican Conclave Is Set for March 1," *New York Times*, February 22, 1939, 10.

24. As Enrico Galeazzi, one of Vatican City's top administrators, told U.S. Ambassador Joseph P. Kennedy, a "thorough search" of the Sistine Chapel before the vote did yield one "very small" dictaphone. Only he and Pacelli were aware of the minor security breach as voting began. For the ambassador's impressions of the coronation and private audience with Pius XII, see Kennedy Papers, 8.2.2 Ambassador's Correspondence, Subject File: Pope Pius XII—Coronation, Box 130, March 13, 1939, 2–3. I would like to thank the Donor Committee of the Joseph P. Kennedy Papers for their kind permission both to study this valuable documentary record and to use it here.

25. See the recollections of Cardinal Pellegrinetti, *I Diari del Cardinale Ermenegildo Pellegrinetti, 1916–1922*, ed. Terzo Natalini (Vatican City: Vatican Archives, 1994), v–vi.

26. Cianfarra, "Cardinal Pacelli Is Elected Pope," *New York Times*, March 3, 1939, 1, 3; Tornielli, *Pio XII: Eugenio Pacelli*, 303–305.

27. For various accounts of the balloting, see the following: Cianfarra, "Cardinal Pacelli Is Elected Pope," *New York Times*, March 3, 1939, 1, 3; the recollections of

Isidoro Marco Emanuel, former bishop of Speyer, Germany, in *Positio Summ.*, II, T. XV, 814; Tornielli's account in *Pio XII*, 303–304, which draws from an account of the conclave published in *La Revue Nouvelle*. The diary kept by Cardinal Pellegrinetti during the conclave, if taken as credible—and there is no reason it should not be—suggests that Pacelli crossed the needed threshold by a small margin (he cites the figure of forty-two; the details are somewhat fuzzy, though). See *I Diari del Cardinale Ermenegildo Pellegrinetti*, v–vi.

28. According to Joseph Kennedy, Galeazzi confided in him that all but one of the twenty-six "foreign" cardinals had voted for Pacelli on the first ballot—the lone exception may have been American Cardinal O'Connell. According to Galeazzi, Pacelli did end up with unanimity by the third ballot.

29. For these firsthand recollections, see Pascalina Lehnert, *Positio Summ.*, 82; and *I Diaria del Cardinale Pellegrinetti*, vi.

30. See Cerejeria's testimonial in the *Positio Summ.*, II, 613.

31. This story is told by Camille Cianfarra, "Pius XII Was Calm during the Voting," *New York Times*, March 4, 1939, 3.

32. Cianfarra, "Pius XII Was Calm during the Voting," *New York Times*, March 4, 1939, 3; Tornielli, *Pio XII: Eugenio Pacelli*, 304.

33. Cerejeria, *Positio Summ.*, 613.

34. Galeazzi, *Positio Summ.*, 293.

35. Tornielli, *Pio XII: Eugenio Pacelli*, 305–306; Lehnert, *Positio Summ.*, 117.

36. Cianfarra, "Hailed by Throngs," *New York Times*, March 3, 1939, 1.

37. Anne O'Hare McCormick, "New Pope Praised Fight on 'Heresies,'" *New York Times*, March 3, 1939, 1.

38. ACS, Rome, Ministero della Cultura Popolare, Gabinetto, b. 80, fasc. Città del Vaticano, sf. 3—S.S. Pio XII, Pignatti to Alfieri, March 1939.

39. See Kennedy Papers, 8.2.2. Ambassador Correspondence, Subject File, Pope Pius XII—Coronation, Box 130.

40. *Ciano Diaries*, March 12, 1939, 263.

41. Kennedy Papers, 8.2.2. Ambassador Correspondence, Subject File: Pope Pius XII—Coronation, Box 130, entry for Monday, March 13, 1939.

42. For a sense of what American intelligence circles and the State Department knew of Galeazzi and his American connections, see a detailed but inaccurate OSS Report from CB-301 to C.O., x-2, OSS, AFHQ, A.P.O. 512; no date. Report #162, in RG 226, Entry A1–210, Box #218, File WN 9765, 9767.

43. J. P. Kennedy to Jay Pierrepont Moffat, Chief, Division of European Affairs, Department of State, Washington, from London, March 17, 1939, in Kennedy Papers, 8.2.2 Ambassador Correspondence. Subject File: Pope Pius XII—Coronation, Box 130.

44. J. P. Kennedy to Sumner Welles, Under-Secretary of State, from London, April 5,

1939, in Kennedy Papers, 8.2.2 Ambassador Correspondence, Subject File: Pope Pius XII—Coronation, Box 130.

45. As discussed in Andrea Riccardi, *Il Potere del Papa da Pio XII a Giovanni Paolo II* (Rome-Bari: Laterza, 1993), 31. See also Charles-Roux's *Huit Ans au Vatican, 1932–1940* (Paris: Flammarion, 1947), 72.

46. Quoted by Riccardi, *Il Potere del Papa*, 32; see Engel-Janosi, *Il Vaticano fra fascismo e nazismo* (Florence: F. Le Monnier, 1973), 138.

47. See *Ciano Diaries, 1939*, 104. See also Riccardi, *Il Potere del Papa*, 32.

48. *Ciano Diaries*, March 2 and 3, 1939, 259.

49. See Giuseppe Bottai, *Diario, 1934–1945*, ed. G. B. Guerri (Milan: Rizzoli, 1982), 148, quoted by Riccardi, *Potere del Papa*, 32.

50. William R. Castle Diaries, February 14, 1939, in vol. 37, Jan. 2–June 28, 1939, at Harvard University—Houghton Library. I am very grateful to Charles Gallagher, S.J., for his generous collegiality in sharing his insights into the Castle Diaries.

51. "Roosevelt Sends Pope Message of Felicitation," *New York Times*, March 4, 1939, 3.

52. "Progressive Aims of the Pope Praised," *New York Times*, March 5, 1939, 41; "Laymen Here Laud Choice of Pacelli," *New York Times*, March 3, 1939, 5.

53. Castle Diaries, March 3, 1939, vol. 37, 111.

54. Edwin L. James, "Pius XII Not the Pope Totalitarians Desired," *New York Times*, March 5, 1939, E3.

55. The reaction of various British newspapers was summarized in Ferdinand Kuhn, Jr., "British View the Election as Sign of Continued Resistance to Totalitarianism," *New York Times*, March 3, 1939, 5.

56. "Name," *Time*, March 13, 1939, 19.

57. Guido Enderis, "Reich Is Reserved over New Pontiff," *New York Times*, March 3, 1939, 1.

58. In his diaries, Ciano reveals that in his first meetings with Pius XII as pope, and with Cardinal Maglione his secretary of state, Pacelli and Maglione both underscored their concern about Germany and its aggressive aims. *Ciano Diaries*, March 18, 1939, 268.

59. Guido Enderis, "Germany Holds Judgment," *New York Times*, March 5, 1939, E4.

60. Minutes of the meeting between Pius XII and German cardinals is in the ADSS, 2, Lettres de Pie XII, Appendix, 407–420, here at 419.

61. Camille Cianfarra, "Reporters Banned from the Vatican," *New York Times*, March 8, 1939, 9; and Cianfarra, "Pope Pius Confers with Reich Envoy," *New York Times*, March 9, 1939, 1.

62. In addition to the minutes of the meetings, which can be found in the ADSS, 2, Appendix, 407–420, see Angelo Martini, "Pio XII e Hitler," *La Civiltà Cattolica* 1

(1965): 342–354, for one of the first systematic analyses of these two crucial meetings.

63. Faulhaber memo in the Appendix to *Lettres de Pie XII aux eveques allemands, 1939–1944*, ADSS, vol. 2, 22; see Appendix to vol. 2 at 413. Bertram's memo is at 395–404.

64. Regarding minutes of the second meeting, see the Appendix to *Lettres de Pie XII aux eveques allemands*, 423–235.

65. Minutes of the meeting between Pius XII and German cardinals in ADSS, vol. 2, *Lettres de Pie XII*, Appendix, 407–420; see also Appendix to the *Lettres de Pie XII aux eveques allemands*, 22.

66. In addition to the memoranda produced by Bertram and Faulhaber for March 1939 meetings, see the long aide-mémoire that the Vatican sent to the Nazi government in July 1939, with an exhaustive account of the general and specific instances of Nazi persecution of the church. This is reproduced in *Aide-Memoire des Päpstl. Staatssekretariats an die Deutsche Botschaft beim Heilige Stuhl, Vatican, 10 July 1939*, in *Der Notenwechsel*, n. 27, 85–94.

67. Le secretaire de la National Catholic Welfare Conference, Ready, au delegue apostolique a Washington Cicognani, April 15, 1939, ADSS, vol. 1, no. 9, 111. For text of FDR's message to Hitler and Mussolini, see FRUS, 1939, I, 130–133.

68. Le cardinal Maglione au delegue apostolique a Washington, April 18, 1939, ADSS, vol. 1, no. 13, 114.

69. Le sous-secretaire d'Etat American Welles au Secretaire de la NCWC, Ready, Washington, April 20, 1939, ADSS, vol. 1, no. 14, 115.

70. The Easter homily is reprinted in "Pie XII au monde catholique Homelie pascale," ADSS, vol. 1, no. 7, 104–110. The Vatican heard from its nuncio in Berne, Switzerland (Bernardini), that both Catholics and Protestants in Switzerland were especially distressed that the Fascist invasion of Albania happened on Good Friday. See Bernardini to Maglione, April 16, 1939, ADSS, vol. 1, no. 11, 112–114.

71. E. Mounier, "En Interrogeant les Silences de Pie XII," in "Mounier Journaliste. Articles de 1938 et 1939," *Bulletin des Amis d'E. Mounier*, n. 23–24 (Seine: Association des Amis d'Emmanuel Mounier) (December 1964): 28–33, here 30.

72. Ibid., 29–30, here at 33. For some commentary, see Gian Maria Vian, "The Silence of Pius XII: The Origins of the Black Legend," published online at Sandro Magister's www.chiesaonline.it.

73. Mounier, "En Interrogeant les Silences de Pie XII," 31.

74. "Pie XII au Sacré College," Vatican, June 2, 1939, ADSS, vol. 1, no. 54, 161–165.

75. Notes du cardinal Maglione, Vatican, May 20, 1939, ADSS, vol. 1, no. 50, 154–158, here at 156.

76. Le nonce a Paris Valeri au cardinal Maglione, Paris, June 20, 1939, ADSS, vol. 1, no. 66, 179–180.

77. Le nonce a Paris Valeri au cardinal Maglione, Paris, June 21, 1939, ADSS, vol. 1, no. 68, 182–183.

78. Le P. Gillet, O.P., au Pape Pie XII, Paris, June 26, 1939, ADSS, vol. 1, no. 73, 187–188.

79. L'ambassadeur de France Charles-Roux a Mgr Tardini, Rome, August 20, 1939, ADSS, vol. 1, no. 106, 224–225.

80. Le ministre de Grande Bretagne Osborne a Mgr Tardini, Rome, August 23, 1939, ADSS, vol. 1, no. 111, 229–230.

81. Radio message du Pape Pie XII, ADSS, vol. 1, no. 113, 230–238.

82. Notes de Mgr Tardini, Vatican, August 24, 1939, ADSS, vol. 1, no. 116, 239–240. Papée was there again a couple of days later, as Tardini recounts in his notes; see Notes de Mgr Tardini, Vatican, August 26, 1939, ADSS, vol. 1, no. 132, 249.

83. Le nonce a Berlin Orsenigo au Cardinal Maglione, Berlin, August 25, 1939, ADSS, vol. 1, no. 123, 244. See also Notes de Mgr Tardini, ADSS, vol. 1, no. 127, and no. 128, 247–248; Le Cardinal Maglione au nonce a Varsovie Cortesi, Vatican, August 30, 1939, ADSS, vol. 1, no. 153, 263–264; Mgr Tardini au cardinal Maglione, August 30, 1939, ADSS, vol. 1, no. 152, 262–263.

84. Notes du cardinal Maglione, Vatican, September 1, 1939, ADSS, vol. 1, no. 171, 277; Charles-Roux to Tardini, Rome, September 11, 1939, ADSS, vol. 1, no. 198, 300–301. See also Charles-Roux, *Huits Ans au Vatican*, 334.

85. So said Maglione to Charles-Roux at the start of September 1939. See Notes du cardinal Maglione, Vatican, September 1, 1939, ADSS, vol. 1, no. 171, 277; and also Charles-Roux, *Huit Ans au Vatican*, 334.

86. See Le pape Pie XII à l'ambassadeur de Belgique, ADSS, vol. 1, no. 202, 304–306.

87. Pius XII, *Summi Pontificatus*, October 20, 1939, no. 106.

88. "Text of Pope's Address to College of Cardinals on Bases for Peace," unofficial translation in *New York Times*, December 25, 1939, 2. See the *Acta Apostolicae Sedis* for an official version, in AAS, 32 (1940), ser. II, vol. VII, num. 1 (January 22, 1940); see "Sermo," December 24, 1939.

89. Pius XII, *Summi Pontificatus*, October 20, 1939, nos. 7, 35, 51.

90. See Osborne's Political Review for 1939 in Hachey, *Anglo-Vatican Relations*, 397–403, dispatch no. 254, December 31, 1939.

91. The *New York Times* saw the pope's Christmas address as an unmistakable attack on the Soviet invasion of Finland. See "Uniting the Peace Seekers," *New York Times*, December 25, 1939, 22.

92. Notes de Mgr Tardini, Vatican, March 11, 1940, ADSS, vol. 1, no. 257, 384–387.

93. Message de Noël du pape Pie XII, ADSS, vol. 1, no. 235, 358.

94. An account of the pope's meeting with Ribbentrop can be found in various diplomatic sources, starting with Notes de Mgr Tardini, Vatican, March 11, 1940, ADSS,

vol. 1, no. 257, 384–387. The pope's version of the meeting as he told it to the Italian ambassador to the Holy See, Alfieri, is in the DDI, ser. 9, vol. 3, n. 536, 466–468. The German version, most likely recounted by Ribbentrop, is in *Akten* D, VIII, nr. 668, 704–706, while the pope's account of the meeting to Sumner Welles is in FRUS, 1940, vol. 1, 107–108.

95. Le chargé d'affaires á Angers Pacini au cardinal Maglione, Paris, March 13, 1940, ADSS, vol. 1, no. 262, 396; Le cardinal Maglione au chargé d'affaires á Angers Pacini, Vatican, March 22, 1940, ADSS, vol. 1, no. 273, 411; Pacini to Maglione, Angers, April 2, 1940, ADSS, vol. 1, no. 275, 413–415.

96. See "Pope Pius Denies Criticizing the Allies," *New York Times*, January 17, 1940, 5.

97. Notes de Mgr Tardini, Vatican, March 11, 1940, ADSS, vol. 1, no. 257, 384–387; Notes du cardinal Maglione, ADSS, vol. 1, no. 268, 404–406, which recounts Pius XII's meeting with Sumner Welles on March 18, 1940, in FRUS, 1940, vol. 1, 106–110.

98. Spellman to Maglione, New York, October 25, 1939, ADSS, vol. 1, no. 214, 323–324.

99. FDR to Pius XII, ADSS, vol. 1, no. 233, 348–350, and published also in FRUS, 1939, vol. 1, 871. On Pius XII's response to the presentation of Myron C. Taylor in March 1940, see Sumner Welles's summary in FRUS, 1940, vol. 1, 106–110.

100. FRUS, 1940, vol. 1, 106–110. Pius XII's message to Mussolini, April 24, 1940, Le pape Pie XII a Mussolini, ADSS, vol. 1, no. 284, 425–426.

101. In addition to the pope's letter to Mussolini, see FDR's appeal, printed in FRUS, 1940, vol. 2, 691–693. Mussolini's response to the pope is reprinted in ADSS, vol. 1, no. 290, 432–433.

102. Maglione to Micara, nuncio in Brussels, Vatican, May 3, 1940, ADSS, vol. 1, no. 293, 436. For an excellent summary of Müller and his relationship with Pius XII and his entourage, see Alvarez and Graham, *Nothing Sacred*.

103. Müller, *Positio Summ.*, 752.

104. Micara to Maglione, Brussels, May 4, 1940, ADSS, vol. 1, no. 294, 437. Charles-Roux's recollection of his meeting with the pope is recounted in Pierre Blet, *Pius XII and the Second World War, according to the Archives of the Vatican*, trans. Lawrence J. Johnson (New York: Paulist Press, 1999), 41–42, as Osborne's message to the FO.

105. Notes de Mgr Tardini, Vatican, May 10, 1940, ADSS, vol. 1, no. 298, 441; and Appendix to no. 298, dated from Paris, May 10, 1940, ADSS, vol. 1, no. 298, 442.

106. Lord Halifax's appeal to Pius XII was passed to the Vatican by Osborne. See Osborne to Maglione, Rome, May 10, 1940, ADSS, vol. 1, no. 300, 443–444.

107. The pope's telegrams dated May 10, 1940, are in ADSS, vol. 1, no. 301, 302, and 303, 444–445; Tardini's draft is in ADSS, vol. 1, Annex B to no. 304, 446–447. See also Blet, *Pius XII and the Second World War*, 43–44, who argues that Pius XII's condem-

nation of the invasions was clear, if implicit. One would have to "close one's eyes," he wrote, "not to see there . . . a formal condemnation" of the Nazi invasion of neutral countries.

108. Blet, *Pius XII and the Second World War*, 44. The American bishops' conference, the NCWC, issued a public repudiation of the attacks in a radio announcement dated November 23, 1942, in ACUA, NCWC Papers, Box 11.

109. Osborne's official memo to the Foreign Office was eventually redacted to soften some of the sharper edges of his criticism of papal responses to the Italian declaration of war on the side of Nazi Germany, but the revealing original can be read in its entirety at FO 371/24964, Osborne to Nicholas, dated June 22, 1940, and received/filed in the FO on August 24, 1940.

110. Notes de Mgr Tardini, Vatican, May 13, 1940, ADSS, vol. 1, no. 312, 453.

111. The pope's meeting with Alfieri was recorded by Montini; see Notes de Mgr Montini, Vatican, May 13, 1940, ADSS, vol. 1, no. 313, 453–455.

112. This account of what has been called the "Roman conversations" is drawn from various primary and secondary sources, including Josef Müller's deposition in the *Positio Summ.*, Pars II, 752. See also Alvarez and Graham, *Nothing Sacred*, 25; Harold C. Deutsch, *The Conspiracy against Hitler in the Twilight War* (Minneapolis: University of Minnesota Press, 1968); Chadwick, *Britain and the Vatican*, 86–100; and Klemens von Klemperer, *German Resistance against Hitler: The Search for Allies Abroad, 1938–1945* (Oxford: Oxford University Press, 1992).

113. Colonel Hans Oster, chief of Abwehr's Central Division and Major Hans Dohnanyi, political director of political affairs in Abwehr's Central Division.

114. See Robert Leiber, S.J., "Pius XII," *Stimmen der Zeit* 163 (1958), 98–99.

115. Müller, *Positio Summ.*, 755.

116. ADSS, vol. 1, 92–93.

117. Alvarez and Graham, *Nothing Sacred*, 27.

118. See ADSS, vol. 2, Introduction. This volume is dedicated entirely to Pius XII's correspondence with the German bishops, from 1939 to 1944. See also Blet, *Pius XII and the Second World War*, 55–56.

119. Pius XII to Cardinal Archbishop of Breslau, Betram, Vatican, December 8, 1940, ADSS, vol. 2, no. 57, 175–180.

120. Quoted by Blet, *Pius XII and the Second World War*, 65.

121. Blet, *Pius XII and the Second World War*, 67. The full original is Pius XII to Preysing, Vatican, September 30, 1941, ADSS, vol. 2, no. 76, 229–232.

122. Pius XII to Preysing, Vatican, April 22, 1940, ADSS, vol. 2, no. 45, 138–142, as translated in Blet, *Pius XII and the Second World War*, 61–62.

123. Harold H. Tittmann, *Inside the Vatican of Pius XII: The Memoir of an American Diplomat during World War Two* (New York: Doubleday, 2004), 40–42.

124. OSS, Spec. Det. G-2, Headquarters, Fifth Army, February 21, 1944, "The Military

Significance of Political Conditions in ROME," in RG 226, Entry 210, Box 327 (new box 313), Location 250/64/27/07.

125. Pius XII to the Bishop of Berlin (Preysing), Vatican, May 7, 1939, ADSS, vol. 2, no. 6, 70–72; Pius XII to Bishop Preysing, Vatican, April 22, 1940, ADSS, vol. 2, no. 45, 138–142, as translated in Blet, *Pius XII and the Second World War,* 61–62.

126. Notes de Mgr Tardini, Vatican, June 29, 1940, ADSS, vol. 1, no. 363, 499–500.

5. War and Holocaust

1. See Susan Zucotti, *Under His Very Windows: The Vatican and the Holocaust in Italy* (New Haven: Yale University Press, 2000), ch. 11.

2. Pius XII to Bishop Preysing, Vatican, April 30, 1943, ADSS, vol. 2, no. 105, 318–327.

3. Pius XII to Bishop of Limbourg, Vatican, February 20, 1941, ADSS, vol. 2, no. 65, 198–200.

4. "Le Saint Siège et la situation religieuse en Pologne et dans les pays baltes, 1939–1945," ADSS, vol. 3, part 1, 3.

5. See Le cardinal Maglione au ministre des Affaires Etrangères du Reich von Ribbentrop, Vatican, March 2, 1943, ADSS, vol. 3, part 2, no. 480, 742–752. Maglione's letter to the German foreign minister was arguably the most exhaustive and strongest Vatican denunciation of Nazi occupation policies, detailing among other things the persecution of the clergy and the church writ large everywhere in occupied Poland but especially in the Warthegau. The Jesuit historian Robert Graham described Maglione's letter as so serious and so "factual" as to be "devastating," so much so that, according to Graham, Pius XII "could well have expected a rupture of relations." See Robert A. Graham, S.J., *The Vatican and Communism during World War II: What Really Happened* (San Francisco: Ignatius Press, 1996), 155. In fact, the Holy See wanted very much to continue pursuing the path of diplomatic engagement with the Hitler regime, as evidenced by Maglione's covering letter, addressed to nuncio Orsenigo, which explained the origins and motives of such a detailed complaint about the so-called religious situation in the Warthegau. See Le cardinal Maglione au nonce à Berlin Orsenigo, Vatican, March 2, 1943, ADSS, vol. 3, no. 481, 753–754.

6. See Cardinal Hlond's reports to Pius XII, including this one from April 1940, collected in August Hlond, *The Persecution of the Catholic Church in German-Occupied Poland: Reports* (New York: Longmans Green, 1991), 79–86.

7. The relevant archival documentation from the Vatican's files detailing news of Soviet occupation practices can be found in various volumes of ADSS, but especially in vol. 3, part 1 (1939–1941) and part 2 (1942–1945) (Vatican City: Libreria Editrice Vaticana, 1967). See also Pierre Blet, *Pius XII and the Second World War, according to the Archives of the Vatican,* trans. Lawrence J. Johnson (New York: Paulist

Press, 1999), 76. For an excellent recent survey of Soviet occupation policies and practices in parts of Central Europe, see Alexander Statiev, *The Soviet Counterinsurgency in the Western Borderlands* (Cambridge: Cambridge University Press, 2010).

8. Archbishop Szeptyckyj (Léopol des Ruthènes or Lviv) to Cardinal Eugène Tisserant, Léopol, December 26, 1939, ADSS, vol. 3, no. 79, 168–173; and Archbishop Svireckas of Kaunas in the Baltics to Pius XII, Kaunas, October 10, 1941, ADSS, vol. 3, no. 316, 480–482; and also the letter from Bishop Grégoire Chomyszyn of Stanislaviv (Ukraine) to Angelo Rotta in Budapest, August 6, 1941, ADSS, vol. 3, 423–425. These are a few representative samples.

9. Metropolitan Szeptyckyj to Pius XII, Léopol (Lviv), August 29–31, 1942, ADSS, vol. 3, no. 406, 625–629, 29–31.

10. Preliminary Report of the International Catholic-Jewish Historical Commission (October 2000).

11. See Microfilm Copies of Foreign Records—Italian Military Documents, NARA, Archives II, RG T-821, Microfilm Roll 64, slides 0331–0335 and 0336–0337, documents dated June 13, 1942, and June 17, 1942. See, e.g., the correspondence between Antonio Santin, then bishop of Trieste, and Italian General Mario Roatta in T-821, Microfilm Roll 402, slides 1018–1024, dates August 15, 1942, and August 30, 1942.

12. Hlond to Maglione, Rome, December 21, 1939, ADSS, vol. 3, no. 74, 162; Orsenigo to Maglione, Berlin, December 23, 1939, ADSS, vol. 3, no. 77, 165–166.

13. In January 1940, for instance, Vatican Radio singled out German-occupied Poland as "a state of terror, of degradation . . . of barbarism, much akin to what the communists imposed on Spain in 1936. . . . The Germans employ the same methods, perhaps even worse, as those used by the Soviets," quoted in Blet, *Pius XII and the Second World War*, 75. See too Pius XII's decision to use Vatican Radio, as noted in Notes de Mgr. Tardini, Vatican, January 19, 1940, ADSS, vol. 3, no. 102, 204. This particular radio address was broadcast in German on January 21, 1940.

14. Notes by Mgr. Montini, January 27, 1940, ADSS, vol. 3, no. 108, 208–209.

15. It was Ambassador Bergen who wrote to Berlin on June 6, 1940, recounting details of a meeting between Secretary Gian Vincenzo Soro, formerly of the Italian Embassy in Warsaw, who met with the pope privately in early June to address the pope's questions about rumors of especially harsh, violent treatment of Polish women. Robert Leiber's response to the Bergen telegram, as reported in *Look* magazine, suggests that the pope believed sincerely that such tales of German treatment of Polish women were not true, at least not "the way it had been reported." Leiber concluded in his interview, "There was no raping of girls in that form. War rumors and truth were mixed up." See "Pius XII and the Third Reich," *Look*, May 17, 1966, 38.

16. See Hlond to Maglione, Lourdes, August 2, 1941, ADSS, vol. 3, no. 287, 418–422.

17. Le primat de Pologne cardinal Hlond au pape Pie XII, London, December 8, 1941, ADSS, vol. 3, no. 338, 507–508.

18. Radonski to Maglione, London, September 14, 1942, ADSS, vol. 3, no. 410, 633–636, as translated from the Latin in Blet, *Pius XII and the Second World War,* 82.

19. Sapieha, February 28, 1942, ADSS, vol. 3, no. 357, 539–541, as translated from the Latin in Blet, *Pius XII and the Second World War,* 81. See also Archbishop Sapieha to Maglione, Krakow, November 3, 1941, ADSS, vol. 3, no. 323, 489–491.

20. Hlond to Maglione, Lourdes, August 2, 1941, ADSS, vol. 3, no. 287, 418–422.

21. Harold H. Tittmann, assistant to Myron C. Taylor, in a report sent from the Minister in Switzerland (Harrison) to the secretary of state, July 30, 1942, FRUS, 1942, 3, 772–773.

22. Blet, *Pius XII and the Second World War,* 79.

23. Raczkiewicz's letter of January 2, 1943, in *Look* magazine's interview with Father Robert Leiber, "Pius XII and the Third Reich," 46.

24. Special Report IDS, no. 33, August 1942, RG 226, Entry 16, Box 139, Regular Report, 20315C. On Papée's recollections, see Gitta Sereny, *Into That Darkness: From Mercy Killing to Mass Murder* (New York: McGraw-Hill, 1974), 332.

25. Maglione to Radonski, Vatican, January 9, 1943, ADSS, vol. 3, no. 460, 713–717.

26. ADSS, vol. 3, no. 477, Radonski to Maglione, London, February 15, 1943 (received March 17, 1943), ADSS, vol. 3, no. 477, 736–737, as translated by Blet, *Pius XII and the Second World War,* 85.

27. Notes de Mgr. Tardini, Vatican, May 18, 1942, ADSS, vol. 3, no. 378, 569–571.

28. Oliver Logan, "Catholicism and Anti-Semitism," book review of Renato Moro, *La Chiesa e lo sterminio degli ebrei* (Bologna: Il Mulino, 2002), and Catherine Brice and Giovanni Miccoli, eds., *Les raciness chretiennes del'antisemitisme politique (fin XIXe–Xxe siecles)* (Rome: Collection de l'Ecole Francaise de Rome, 2003), *Modern Italy* 9 (May 2004): 101–105. See also Paul O'Shea, *A Cross Too Heavy: Pope Pius XII and the Jews of Europe* (New York: Palgrave Macmillan, 2011).

29. An undated telegram cable addressed to Cardinal Pacelli, probably from late 1938 or early 1939, a copy of which is in the Israeli State Archives, 72/4247/16.

30. A copy of Rabbi Herzog's telegram is in the Israeli State Archives, 72/4247/16, n.d.

31. See Osborne's Political Review for 1939, dated December 31, 1939, in Thomas E. Hachey, ed., *Anglo-Vatican Relations, 1914–1939: Confidential Annual Reports of the British Ministers to the Holy See* (Boston: G. K. Hall, 1972), 397–403.

32. For a survey of the range of clerical responses to Nazi policies, be it against German Jews or German Catholics, see Guenter Lewy, *The Catholic Church and Nazi Germany* (New York: McGraw-Hill, 1964); Kevin P. Spicer, *Resisting the Third Reich: The Catholic Clergy in Hitler's Berlin* (De Kalb: Northern Illinois University Press, 2004); Beth Griech-Polelle, "Image of a Churchman-Resister: Bishop von Galen,

the Euthanasia Project and the Sermons of Summer 1941," *Journal of Contemporary History* 36, no. 1 (2001): 41–57.

33. Pacelli to Orsenigo, April 4, 1933, ASV, AES, Germania, 1933–1934, Pos. 643, Fasc. 158, N. 915/33.

34. See detailed report from Orsenigo to Maglione, "Immigration of Jewish-Catholic Families to Brazil," September 11, 1939, ASV, AES, fasc. 606f, n. 162, prot. 8346/39. For a general survey, see Jeffrey Lesser, *Welcoming the Undesirables: Brazil and the Jewish Question* (Berkeley: University of California Press, 1995).

35. Blet, *Pius XII and the Second World War*, 142.

36. There are a number of revealing documents on the Brazil scheme in ADSS. See, for instance, Cardinal Innitzer to Pius XII, Vienna, January 20, 1941, ADSS, vol. 8, no. 5, 78–79; Cicognani to Maglione, Madrid, January 20, 1941, no. 6, 80; Maglione to Innitzer, Vatican, February 6, 1941, no. 15.

37. This money came from the United Jewish Appeal, donated to the Vatican in the memory of Pius XI. See Maglione's letter to the auxiliary bishop of Chicago, Sheil, dated December 31, 1939, in ADSS, vol. 6, no. 125, 211–212, note 2. It was in the amount of $125,000 for Jewish refugees, given to the pope to be distributed by Christian organizations to all Jewish refugees, converts or not. The Vatican instructed that $50,000 be given to the NCWC's Committee for Refugees and a committee devoted to German Catholic political refugees, headed by Mons. Rummel, archbishop of New Orleans. The remaining $75,000 was given to European aid organizations, principally the St. Raphael Society. See Notes de la Secretaire d'Etat, Vatican, January 4, 1940, ADSS, vol. 6, no. 126, 213–214.

38. See letter from Secretary General of the St. Raphael Society, Menningen, to Cardinal Maglione on December 27, 1940, ADSS, vol. 6, no. 419, 524. Definitive word from Brazilian authorities that they would not be easing immigration or refugee quotas to deal with the European crisis reached the Vatican in mid-1942. See a short note from the Brazilian Embassy to the Secretariat of State, July 15, 1942, ADSS vol. 8, no. 492, 600.

39. Innitzer to Pius XII, Vienna, January 20, 1941, ADSS, vol. 8, no. 5, 78–79.

40. Innitzer to Pius XII, Vienna, February 4, 1941, ADSS, vol. 8, no. 14, 90–92; Innitzer to Pius XII, Vienna, February 28, 1941, no. 33, 116–119.

41. There is a full-length biography of Scavizzi in Italian by Michele Manzo, *Don Pirro Scavizzi: Prete Romano, 1884–1964* (Casale Monferrato: Piemme, 1997).

42. Part of this letter is reproduced in Scavizzi to Maglione, ADSS, vol. 8, no. 206, 352, n. 2. For more on Scavizzi, see ADSS, vol. 8, no. 496, 669–670, n. 4.

43. On Taylor's letter to the pope, see Notes de Mgr. Montini, Vatican, September 27, 1942, ADSS, vol. 8, no. 493, 65. See also FRUS, 1942, vol. 3, 775. Scavizzi's report can be found in Notes de Mgr Montini, ADSS, vol. 8, no. 496, 669–670, n. 4.

44. P. Scavizzi to Pius XII, May 12, 1942, ADSS, vol. 8, no. 374, 534.

45. Notes de Mgr Montini, Vatican, September 27, 1942, ADSS, vol. 8, no. 493, 665–666, n. 2.

46. Notes de Mgr Montini, October 1, 1942, ADSS, vol. 8, no. 496, 669–670.

47. Scavizzi's recollection that Pius XII "wept like a child" has been cited in various sources, although the original source is difficult to verify. Accordingly, the evidence has to be read with a properly critical eye. This is drawn from what appears to be part of the material gathered for Scavizzi's beatification, in the section titled *Summarium Documentorum, Num. VI—Articoli, testimonianze, e scritti apparsi dopo la morte del Servo di Dio*, 557–561. Scavizzi was quoted in the press about this as early as the 1960s. See "Nazi Reprisal against Jews Held Fear of Pope Pius XII," *Religious News Service*, May 20, 1964. Scavizzi is also discussed in Carlo Falconi, *The Silence of Pius XII* (Boston: Little, Brown, 1970), 150–151 and 238, which in turns draws on recollections Scavizzi gave in *La Parrocchia*, May 1964.

48. Preysing to Pius XII, from Berlin, January 23, 1943, ADSS, vol. 9, no. 26, 93–94. From Orsenigo, see, for instance, Orsenigo to Maglione, Berlin, July 24, 1942, ADSS, vol. 8, no. 436, 605–606; and Orsenigo to Maglione, Berlin, October 19, 1942, ADSS, vol. 8, no. 520, 677.

49. Notes de la Secretaire d'Etat, Vatican, May 5, 1943, ADSS, vol. 9, no. 174, 274. I have used here the reliable translation in Blet, *Pius XII and the Second World War*, 164.

50. This is the text that appeared in "Text of Pope Pius XII's Christmas Message Broadcast from Vatican to the World," *New York Times*, December 25, 1942, 10. It is instructive to read the original, which was published officially in AAS, 35 (1943), 9–24.

51. See "Pope Assails Peril of 'Godless State,'" *New York Times*, December 25, 1942.

52. Father Leiber confirmed the gist of Tittmann's cable as well as the pope's response, including Pius XII's conviction that his Christmas message had made it clear "to the world" that he was referring to atrocities committed against Poles and Jews. See the interview "Pius XII and the Third Reich," *Look*, April 17, 1966, 46.

53. See RG 226, Records of the Office of Strategic Services, Reports ("Regular Series"), 1941–45, Entry 16, Box 251, Special Report IDS #116. The original date would seem to be January 4, 1943, though there is a hand-written correction that makes it appear the report was from a later date, possibly even after the war. The content of the report suggests the 1943 date as the most plausible.

54. Leiber, in "Pius XII and the Third Reich," 46.

55. So claimed Leiber in "Pius XII and the Third Reich," 48.

56. For biographical information on Father de Witte, see Lutz-Eugen Reutter, *Katholische Kirche als Fluchthelfer im Dritten Reich: die Betreuung von Auswanderern durch den St. Rapahels-Verein* (Freiburg: Paulus Verlag, 1971).

57. For a brief report on the Dutch situation, including Nazi reprisals against Dutch bishops' defense of Jews, see an OSS Report dated October 20, 1942, Pro-Deo Report #62 in RG 226, Entry 16, Box 188, Regular Report 22960C.

58. De Witte to Pius XII, Amsterdam, May 10, 1943, ADSS, vol. 9, no. 183, 287–291.

59. See, for instance, the case of a small number of Jews in Greece who in May and June 1944 were asking to be allowed to enter Spain and Portugal; documentation pertaining to these cases can be found in the Taylor mission papers of RG 59, Entry 1068, especially in Box 4. The Taylor mission papers also contain brief allusion to the Vatican's apparent success in getting the Cuban government to agree to admit an unspecified number of European Jews carrying passports/entrance visas issued by South American governments. It is not clear whether anything came of this initiative. See RG 59, Myron Taylor File, Box 4, unsigned and undated memo, c. 1944.

60. Le père De Witte au pape Pie XII, Amsterdam, May 10, 1943, and Annexe. Notes de la Secrétaire d'Etat, Vatican, May 28, 1943, ADSS, vol. 9, no. 183, 287–291.

61. Respighi to Maglione, Vatican, May 10, 1943, ADSS, vol. 9, no. 184, 291–292.

62. James Hennesey, S.J., "American Jesuit in Wartime Rome: The Diary of Vincent A. McCormick, S.J., 1942–1945," *Mid-America* 56 (January 1974): 32–55, here at 35.

63. Ibid., 36.

64. Ibid., 41.

65. See Harold H. Tittmann, *Inside the Vatican of Pius XII: The Memoir of an American Diplomat during World War II* (New York: Image Books/Doubleday, 2004), 133, 167; see also Blet, *Pius XII and the Second World War,* 202.

66. See Hennesey, "American Jesuit in Wartime Rome," 44.

67. So argues Blet, *Pius XII and the Second World War,* 208.

68. Tittmann, *Inside the Vatican,* 165.

69. Tittmann estimates 700. See ibid., 165. Blet estimates 1,500 dead in *Pius XII and the Second World War,* 208.

70. Tittmann, *Inside the Vatican,* 166.

71. Ibid., 167.

72. Ibid., 169.

73. This is from a cover letter from Osborne to Eden; Osborne was passing along a summary report by Mr. Hugh Montgomery of the British delegation to the Vatican; Osborne's cover was dated May 31, 1945; see NARA, RG 59, Taylor Papers, Entry 1068, Box 7.

74. Notes de la Secrétaire d'Etat, Vatican, August 31, 1943, ADSS vol. 9, no. 319, 464–465, for an internal memorandum on reports of a rumored plot to kidnap the pope. For an authoritative summary of the story about the alleged plot to kidnap the pope, see David Alvarez and Robert Graham, S.J., *Nothing Sacred: Nazi Espionage against the Vatican, 1939–1945* (London: F. Cass, 1997), 85.

75. See Alvarez and Graham, *Nothing Sacred*, 85. See also Walter Schellenberg, *The Labyrinth, Memoirs* (New York: Harper, 1956); *The Goebbels Diaries, 1942–1943*, ed. Louis Paul Lochner (Garden City, NY: Doubleday, 1948), 409; and Richard Lamb, *War in Italy, 1943–1945* (New York: St. Martin's Press, 1994), 45–46.

76. Wolff, *Positio Summ.*, Pars II, 837.

77. Ibid., 836–837.

78. See Alvarez and Graham, *Nothing Sacred*, 86–87; and *The Goebbels Diaries*, entry for July 27, 1943, 416.

79. We know that Maglione and the staff in the Secretariat of State saw the threat as credible. See Notes de la Secretaire d'Etat, Vatican, October 1, 1943, ADSS, vol. 9, no. 355, 495–496.

80. Notes de la Secretaire d'Etat, Vatican, September 17, 1943, ADSS, vol. 9, no. 336, 480–481.

81. A copy of the Herzog telegram to de Valera, dated July 7, 1943, is in the Herzog papers at the Israeli State Archives, 72/4247/16.

82. Notes de la Secretaire d'Etat, Vatican, September 27, 1943, ADSS, vol. 9, no. 349, 491; and September 29, 1943, no. 353, 494.

83. See Blet, *Pius XII and the Second World War*, 217–218. Among the more balanced and historically informed treatments of the subject is Andrea Riccardi, *L'inverno più lungo. 1943–44: Pio XII, gli ebrei e i nazisti a Roma* (Bari-Rome: Laterza, 2008); and Zuccotti, *Under His Very Window*. The most forceful—if unconvincing—exponent of the thesis which posits Pius XII as a rescuer of thousands of Jews is Pinchas Lapide, a Jewish scholar and future Israeli diplomat, who emerged around the same time as Hochhuth's *The Deputy* as an ardent Jewish defender of the pope's wartime record. Lapide wrote forcefully and widely about the pope's many efforts on behalf of persecuted Jews and speaks specifically about the refuge provided by religious orders in Rome during the period of Nazi occupation, with the pope's knowledge and approval, says Lapide. See his *Three Popes and the Jews* (New York: Hawthorn Books, 1967), as well as various articles such as "Pius XII and the Jews," which was published in 1964 in a Viennese periodical precisely to address what he says was Hochhuth's "great injustice" to the memory of Pope Pius XII. A copy of this article is in the CZA, C2/1976.

84. Notes de Mgr. Montini, Vatican, October 1, 1943, ADSS, vol. 9, no. 356, 496; and Notes de la Secretariat d'Etat, Vatican, October 23, 1943, no. 382, 518. See also Blet, *Pius XII and the Second World War*, 215.

85. See Saperstein's recollections in Harold I. Saperstein, *Witness from the Pulpit: Topical Sermons, 1933–1980*, ed. Marc Saperstein (Lanham, MD: Lexington Books, 2000). See in particular "The Deputy: Where Does the Guilt Lie," 230–237. Saperstein first told of Vicar Andre in "200 Jews Owe Life to Belgian Priest," *New York Times*, December 28, 1945, 10.

86. Lively accounts of Father Marie-Benoît's work can be found in a few different sources, starting with his own recollections, P. Marie-Benoît, "Résumé de mon activité en faveur des Juifs persecutes (1940–1944)," in *Livre d'or des congrégations françaises* (Paris: DRAC, 1948), 305–331. Another eyewitness version is from Fernande Leboucher, *The Incredible Mission of Father Benoît*, trans. J. F. Benard (New York: Doubleday, 1969). Leboucher worked closely with Father Benoît in his rescue and relief efforts. For a brief account of her work, see "Grateful Jews Help Care for a Holocaust 'Guardian Angel,'" *New York Times*, September 9, 2001, 8–14. Primary documentation pertaining to Father Benoît's relief and rescue efforts can be found in the Vatican's ADSS, confirming papal knowledge of and limited support for the Capuchin's work. See especially ADSS, vol. 9, 393–397, 401–402, 447–449, 465–467, 544–545. Invaluable primary documentation detailing Benoît's work is at the CDJC. For a more comprehensive look at his life, see the recent biography by Gérard Cholvy, *Marie-Benoît de Bourg d'Iré (1895–1990): Itinéraire d'un fils de Saint François Juste des Nations* (Paris: Les Éditions du Cerf, 2010).

87. See Father Benoît's report of DELASEM's activity, dated July 20, 1944, and reprinted in Renzo De Felice with Robert L. Miller, *The Jews in Fascist Italy: A History* (New York: Enigma Books, 2001), 756–758; James Rorty, "Father Benoît: Ambassador of the Jews," *Commentary*, December 1946, 507–513.

88. When Benoît met with Pius XII in July 1943, he confirmed the approval of the superior-general of the Capuchins, Father Donato Wynant a Welle (1890–1972), a Belgian who was head of the order between 1938 and 1946.

89. This according to the *Livre d'or*, 306.

90. For a brief history of DELASEM, see Sandro Antonini, *Delasem: storia della più grande organizzazione ebraica italiana di soccorso durante la seconda guerra mondiale*, intro. by Alberto Cavaglion (Genoa: De Ferrari, 2000).

91. Leboucher, *Incredible Mission*, 167–168. She cites the figure of four million dollars, presumably as the dollar figure equivalency at the time she wrote the memoir.

92. See Father Benoît's July 20, 1944, report on DELASEM's activity, reprinted in De Felice, *Jews in Fascist Italy*, 757–758.

93. Two primary accounts of Father Benoît's meeting with the pope and subsequent discussions are in the *Livre d'or* and in ADSS, vol. 9, starting at page 393. An abbreviated version is an interview Father Benoît gave to the Italian journalist Nicola Caracciolo. See Caracciolo, *Uncertain Refuge: Italy and the Jews during the Holocaust*, trans. and ed. Florette Rechnitz Koffler and Richard Koffler (Urbana: University of Illinois Press, 1995), 37–39. For general accounts of the situation of Jews under Italian occupation see, generally, L. Poliakov and J. Sabille, *Jews under the Italian Occupation* (Paris: Centre de Documentation Juive Contemporaine, 1954); Susan Zuccotti, *The Italians and the Holocaust: Persecution, Rescue, Survival* (New York:

Basic Books, 1987); Ivo Herzer, *The Italian Refuge: Rescue of Jews during the Holocaust* (Washington, DC: Catholic University of America Press, 1989).

94. As Father Benoît recalled it, the pope's exact words were "On n'aurait pas cru cela de la part de la France," as cited in *Livre d'or*, 309–311.

95. All of this is recounted in the *Livre d'or*, 309–311, while corroborating official Vatican documentation is in ADSS, vol. 9, 393–397.

96. Le nonce a Madrid Cicognani au cardinal Maglione, Madrid, August 24, 1943, ADSS, vol. 9, no. 311, 447–449; Father Marie Benoît, *Livre d'or*, 311.

97. Notes du père Marie-Benoît, Rome, July 16, 1943, ADSS, vol. 9, no. 267, 401–402.

98. Notes du père Marie-Benoît, Rome, September 1943, ADSS, vol. 9, no. 321, 465–467.

99. So says Father Benoît in his recollections as recorded in the *Livre d'or*, 314. The Italian rescuer Angelo Donati also blamed the Allies and especially General Eisenhower's announcement of the Armistice, while continuing to praise Pius XII and the Vatican for its efforts on behalf of Jews. See Donati as cited in L. Poliakov, *La condition des Juifs en France sous l'occupation italienne* (Paris, 1946), 40.

100. Zuccotti, *Under His Very Windows*, 155–156; Lilliana Picciotto Fargion, *Il Libro della Memoria: Gli Ebrei Deportati dall'Italia (1943–1945)* (Milan: Mursia, 1991), 42.

101. Notes de la Secretaire d'Etat, Vatican, October 17, 1943, ADSS, vol. 9, no. 374, 511.

102. Mme. X to Maglione, Rome, October 17, 1943, ADSS, vol. 9, no. 375, 512. See also the case of another "Mme. X," who wrote to the pope in November 1943; see Mme. X to Pius XII, Rome, November 20, 1943, ADSS, vol. 9, no. 434, 570–571.

103. The most authoritative discussion of Pignatelli's account is Robert A. Graham, "La Strana condotta di Ernst von Weizsäcker ambasciatore del Reich in Vaticano," *La Civiltà Cattolica*, anno 121, quaderno 2879 (June 6, 1970): 455–471; Graham heard this account directly from Pignatelli and then received written confirmation from one Karl Gustav Wollenweber, who was a staff member in Weizsäcker's office and apparently drove Pignatelli to meet with the pope the morning of October 16, 1943. For further commentary, see Zuccotti, *Under His Very Windows*, 158–159.

104. The Vatican account of this meeting is in Cardinal Maglione's notes from October 16, 1943, ADSS, vol. 9, no. 368, 505–506.

105. Zuccotti, *Under His Very Windows*, 159.

106. Ibid., 178.

107. Robert Leiber, "Pius XII +," *Stimmen der Zeit* 163 (1958–1959): 81–100; and "Pius XII und die Juden in Rom," 167 (1960–1961): 428–436. An announcement of the Leiber story carried by the NCWC News Service, dated November 12, 1964, in ACUA, Muench Papers, Series 13: Biography, Box 60, Folder 1; Lehnert, *Positio Summ.*, PARS I, 85, 103.

108. Leiber, "Pius XII and the Third Reich," 50.

109. Hudl to Stahel, ADSS, vol. 9, no. 373, 509–510.

110. Zuccotti, *Under His Very Windows*, 162; Graham, "La strana condotta," 470, n. 22. See also Carlo Pacelli's deposition *Positio Summ.*, 212–233, which makes no mention of his meeting with Hudal; Domenico Tardini, *Pio XII* (Vatican City: Tipografia Poliglotta Vaticana, 1960), 50. Tardini's memoirs of Pius XII are also available in English translation as *Memories of Pius XI*, trans. Rosemary Goldie (Westminster, MD: Newman Press, 1961). For other theories about the letter, see Chadwick, "Weizsäcker, the Vatican and the Jews of Rome," *Journal of Ecclesiastical History* 28, no. 2 (April 1977): 179–199; and Leonidas E. Hill, "The Vatican Embassy of Ernst von Weizsäcker, 1943–1945," *Journal of Modern History* 39, no. 1, (March 1967): 138–159.

111. Quoted by Zuccotti, *Under His Very Windows*, 162, which in turn draws from Saul Friedländer, *Pius XII and the Third Reich: A Documentation*, trans. Charles Fullman (New York: Knopf, 1996), 205–206. Note that Hudal sent a copy to the Vatican and is printed in Hudal to Stahel, October 16, 1943, ADSS, vol. 9, no. 373, 509–510.

112. Zuccotti, *Under His Very Windows*, 162–163. See also Friedländer, *Pius XII and the Third Reich*, 206–207, which draws on original documentation from German Foreign Ministry archives.

113. Blet, *Pius XII and the Second World War*, 216–217. Hudal maintained that General Stahel told him on October 17 that Himmler had ordered a stop to the sweep of arrests and deportations after hearing of a possible papal protest. See ADSS, vol. 9, no. 373, n. 4, 510. It is problematic that Blet accepts Hudal's version uncritically in Blet, *Pius XII and the Second World War*, 216.

114. See in particular Weizsäcker's report to the Foreign Ministry near the end of October 1943, quoted by Friedländer, *Pius XII and the Third Reich*, 207–208.

115. See Graham, "La Strana condotta," 456.

116. I agree here with Zuccotti that Graham's criticism of Weizsäcker on this count is "unfair." See Zuccotti, *Under His Very Windows*, 165.

117. Frauke Wildvang suggests that rounding up and deporting the remaining Jews in Rome was "no central concern" of the Nazi occupiers, a view British intelligence reports seem to have supported when reviewing the occupation of Rome at war's end. At the very least, it would appear that the Gestapo's work in Rome was "sporadic" and uncoordinated, perhaps due to the logistical challenge of identifying and finding the thousands of surviving Jews who had gone into hiding throughout the city. See Wildvang, "The Enemy Next Door: Italian Collaboration in Deporting Jews during the German Occupation of Rome," *Modern Italy* 12, no. 2 (June 2007): 189–204, here at 190–191.

118. Zuccotti, *Under His Very Windows*, 169–170.

119. The ADSS documentation does not appear to speak to any Vatican reaction

to the Ardeatine Cave Massacres. See Blet, *Pius XII and the Second World War,* 221–222.

120. See Montini, "Pius XII and the Jews," letter to the British periodical *The Tablet,* reproduced in Eric Bentley, *Storm Over "The Deputy,"* 67–68; Robert Leiber in "Pius XII and the Third Reich," 50.

121. See reports from nuncio Giuseppe Burzio, including to Maglione, Burzio to Maglione, Bratislava, September 18, 1941, in ADSS, vol. 8, no. 153, 279–285.

122. Maglione to Sidor, Vatican, November 12, 1941, ADSS, vol. 8, no. 199, 345–347.

123. Burzio to Maglione, May 23, 1942, ADSS, vol. 8, no. 298, 453.

124. See Bernardini in Berne to Vatican, May 24, 1942, ADSS, vol. 8, no. 300, 455. See also Rotta to Maglione, Budapest, March 13, 1943, ADSS vol. 8, no. 303, 457–459, in particular the Annexe to this document, which is the open letter from the Jews of Bratislava to the pope.

125. Vatican Sec. of State to Slovakian Delegation, Vatican, March 14, 1942, ADSS, vol. 8, no. 305, 459–460.

126. See various reports in ADSS, including Burzio to Maglione, Bratislava, March 31, 1942, ADSS, vol. 8, no. 334, 486–489; and Burzio to Maglione, no. 343, 501–502, n. 2; for Maglione's meeting with Sidor, see Notes du cardinal Maglione, Vatican, April 11, 1942, ADSS, vol. 8, no. 346, 504.

127. John Conway, "The Churches, the Slovak State and the Jews 1939–1945," *Slavonic and East European Review* 52, no. 126 (January 1974): 85–112, here at 106.

128. Tardini's comments about the two "lunatics" appear in a note appended to nuncio Burzio's letter to Maglione. See Le chargé d'affaires à Presbourg Burzio au cardinal Maglione, Presbourg, March 25, 1942, ADSS, vol. 8, no. 326, 479; for Tardini's comment about the Vatican's inability to stop a priest like Tiso, see Notes de Mgr. Tardini, Vatican, July 13, 1943, ADSS, vol. 8, no. 426, 597–598.

129. See, for instance, Notes of the Secretariat of State, reporting on a meeting with the secretariat staff and Sister Margherita Slachta (1884–1973), one of the founders of the Congregation of Social Missions, who wanted to warn the Holy See about the imminent deportation of Jews in Slovakia, and to ask that something be done to stop it. Notes de la Secretaire d'Etat, Vatican, March 8, 1943, ADSS, vol. 9, no. 86, 178–179. Slachta even received an audience with Pius XII on May 11, 1943, and followed this up with a letter to the pope warning him about the grave dangers faced by Jews in Hungary. See Sister Slachta to Pope Pius XII, Budapest, May 15, 1943, ADSS, vol. 9, no. 190, 299–300.

130. Maglione to Burzio, Vatican, March 9, 1943, ADSS, vol. 9, no. 87, 179–180; Burzio to Maglione, Presbourg, March 11, 1943, no. 89, 181.

131. The pastoral letter was issued on March 21, 1943. Burzio reported on it to Cardinal Maglione in a letter sent on April 10, 1943, ADSS, vol. 9, no. 147, 245–251. For commentary, see Conway, "The Churches, the Slovak State and the Jews," 106.

132. Burzio to Maglione, Bratislava/Presbourg, April 10, 1943, ADSS, vol. 9, no. 147, 245–251.

133. La Secretaire d'Etat à la Légation de Slovaquie," Vatican, May 5, 1943, ADSS, vol. 9, no. 176, 275–277.

134. Conway, "The Churches, the Slovak State and the Jews," 108–109. For a sample of continued Vatican entreaties to Slovak officials, see ADSS, vol. 10, no. 324, 418–419; no. 329, 422–423; nos. 340 and 341, 432–433; and nos. 377 and 378, 461–462.

135. Notes de Mgr. Tardini, Vatican, October 28, 1941, ADSS, vol. 10, no. 378, 461–462. See in particular the "Annexe," which is a note from Tardini to the nuncio Bernardini in Berne, who was being asked to pass along the note of papal disapproval to the nunciature in Slovakia.

136. See Lapide, *Three Popes and the Jews*, 149; and Conway, "The Churches, the Slovak State, and the Jews," 110.

137. An indication of the limits of papal influence over Tiso and Slovak officials is revealed in the president's letter to Pius XII, in which Tiso tried to justify his government's measure, Tiso to Pius XII, Presbourg, November 8, 1944, ADSS, vol. 10, no. 389, 475–478.

138. See a report from German official von Thadden, dated May 25, 1944, in the Nuremberg Documents cited by Friedländer, *Pie XII et le IIIe Reich*, Nouvelle Edition (Paris: Seuil, 2010), 258, n. 1.

139. For a sample of the appeals reaching the Vatican, see ADSS, vol. 10, no. 127, 198; no. 249, 335; no. 253, 341; no. 254, 342; no. 260, 347; no. 270, 357.

140. Aryeh L. Kubovy (Leon Kubowitzki), "The Silence of Pope Pius XII and the Beginnings of the 'Jewish Document,'" *Yad Vashem Studies* 6 (1967): 7–25, here at 14–15. For more on Father Morlion, see David Alvarez, *Spies in the Vatican: Espionage and Intrigue from Napoleon to the Holocaust* (Lawrence, Kan.: University Press of Kansas, 2002), 253–257.

141. See Rotta to Maglione, Budapest, April 28, 1944, ADSS, vol. 10, no. 172, 247–249.

142. Rotta to Maglione, Budapest, May 23, 1944, ADSS, vol. 10, no. 207, 283–288. The protest notes to the Foreign Ministry and the prime minister's office are in Annexe I and II respectively and are attached to Rotta's note to Maglione.

143. Pius XII to Regent of Hungary Horthy, Vatican, June 25, 1944, ADSS, vol. 10, no. 243, 328.

144. See, for instance, a lengthy memorandum of a conversation between Mons. Hughes, papal delegate for Egypt and Palestine, and the grand rabbi of Jerusalem, Herzog, in Cairo, September 5, 1944. It is reproduced at length in Friedländer's *Pie XII et le IIIe Reich*, 268–277, but a copy of the original is in CZA. Herzog here acknowledges and expresses gratitude for the pope's efforts. I would like to thank Sara Palmor in Israel for her diligent research assistance in the CZA and Israeli State Archives. See also part of a report sent by Myron Taylor to the Sec-

retariat of State, October 31, 1944, ADSS, vol. 10, no. 357, 446, n. 4, from the Washington-based Committee for Refugees which names Pius XII directly, as well as Archbishop Spellman, for their repeated efforts on behalf of "refugees in danger."

145. Aryeh L. Kubovy, "The Silence of Pope Pius XII," 16.

146. See Settinius to Taylor, Washington, October 25, 1944, in RG 59, Taylor Mission, Entry 1068, Box 4.

147. Le president du Conseil de Hongrie Kallay au pape Pie XII, Budapest, February 24, 1943, ADSS, vol. 7, no. 126, 241–248; the pope's response was recorded by Maglione in Notes du cardinal Maglione, Vatican, March 7, 1943, ADSS, vol. 7, no. 137, 262.

148. A. G. Cicognani, Apostolic Delegate, Washington, DC, to Leon Kubowitzki, World Jewish Congress, September 27, 1944, CZA, Jerusalem, C2/1976 (Records of the Office of the World Jewish Congress in Geneva).

149. See letter from Franklin Gowen to Taylor, November 7, 1944, in RG 59, Taylor Mission, Entry 1068, Box 4.

150. See OSS Report dated November 3, 1944, Distributed December 5, 1944, Subject: Tension between Vatican and German Government, in RG 226, Entry 16 (Box NA), doc. #105152.

6. A New World Order

1. This was reported in "Pope Sees Danger of a New Tyranny in Europe's Chaos," *New York Times,* June 3, 1945, 1 and 22. Note that in the part of the speech reproduced in ADSS, there is no mention of the pope's referring to German youth. See the official version of the speech printed in AAS 37 (1945): 163–165.

2. See Luigi Sturzo, "The Vatican's Position in Europe," *Foreign Affairs* 23 (January 1945): 211–221, here at 220.

3. See *Le Monde,* October 10, 1958, quoted by Philippe Chenaux, *Pie XII: diplomate e pasteur* (Paris: Cerf, 2003), 341.

4. See RG 59, Taylor File, Entry 1068, Box 14.

5. "Pope Sees Danger of a New Tyranny," 22.

6. The role of Catholic religious houses in the rescue of Jewish children, especially female religious orders in France and Poland, for instance, is studied in Madeleine Comte, *Sauvetages et baptêmes: Les religieuses de Notre-Dame de Sion face à la persecution des juifs en France (1940–1944)* (Paris: Harmattan, 2001); and Nahum Bogner, "The Convent Children: The Rescue of Jewish Children in Polish Convents During the Holocaust," *Yad Vashem Studies* 27 (1999): 235–285.

7. Estimates gathered at the time by organizations such as the World Jewish Congress estimated that between 200,000 and 300,000 Jewish children had survived

the Holocaust, and that at least 75,000 of them were left orphaned at war's end. For an excellent, concise summary of the issue, see Michael R. Marrus, "The Vatican and the Custody of Jewish Child Survivors after the Holocaust," *Holocaust and Genocide Studies* 21, no. 3 (Winter 2007): 378–403, here at 382. Indispensable firsthand insights are provided by Gerhart M. Riegner, then director of the World Jewish Congress's Geneva office and one of the central figures of the postwar relief effort. See his memoirs, *Never Despair: Sixty Years in the Service of the Jewish People and the Cause of Human Rights* (Chicago: Ivan R. Dee, 2006, in association with the United States Holocaust Memorial Museum).

8. There are several useful studies of the postwar custody issue, starting with Katy Hazan, "Recuperer les enfants cachés: Un imperative des oeuvres juives dans l'apres guerre," *Archives juives* 37, no. 2 (2004): 16–31. On Belgium, see Luc Dequeker, "Baptism and Conversion of Jews in Belgium, 1939–1945," in *Belgium and the Holocaust: Jews, Belgians, Germans,* ed. Dan Michman (Jerusalem: Yad Vashem, 1998). On the Netherlands, see Deborah Dwork, "Custody and Care of Jewish Children in the Postwar Netherlands: Ethnic Identity and Cultural Hegemony," in *Lessons and Legacies III: Memory, Memorialization, and Denial,* ed. Peter Hayes (Evanston, IL: Northwestern University Press, 1991), 119–130.

9. Marrus, "The Vatican and the Custody of Jewish Child Survivors," 383. Some valuable primary documentation on the efforts to locate Jewish child survivors, especially those who were in gentile homes, can be found in the CZA, S26/1402. My thanks to Sara Palmor in Jerusalem for her diligent research assistance in locating some of this material.

10. See Leon Kubowitzki's recollections in Aryey L. Kubovy (Leon Kubowitzki), "The Silence of Pope Pius XII and the Beginnings of the 'Jewish Document,'" *Yad Vashem Studies* 6 (1967), 7–25. Kubowitzki also generated a report of the meeting which can be found in the CZA, C2/1931. Many thanks to Sara Palmor for her assistance in identifying and providing copies of the originals from Israeli archives.

11. Kubowitzki, "The Silence of Pope Pius XII," 21.

12. Ibid., 22.

13. As Michael Marrus notes, this part of Kubowitzki's account was omitted from the 1967 account published in Yad Vashem, but is clearly legible in an earlier account found in CZA, C2/1931; Marrus, "The Vatican and the Custody of Jewish Child Survivors," 388.

14. Jewish authorities involved in rescue and relief activities after the war readily acknowledged the lack of "exact data" on the numbers of Jewish children who were in the custody of non-Jewish families. See, for instance, correspondence in 1947 between the Rescue Committee of the Jewish Agency and the World Jewish Congress, located in CZA, S26/1402.

15. Kubowitzki, "The Silence of Pope Pius XII," 23.

16. Riegner, *Never Despair*, 120–121.

17. Ibid., 122.

18. Ibid.

19. Quoted by Marrus, "The Vatican and the Custody of Jewish Child Survivors," 391–392. Original documentation comes from a report that was submitted to the Executive of the General Council of the Jews in Palestine, October 3, 1946, CZA, Ji/7264 (Hebrew). Kubowitzki's account of his meeting with the pope is recounted in "At the Opening of the Rescue Campaign" (Hebrew), in Yitzhak Goldshlag, ed., *Masa ha-hatsalah: Shevat 5706–Tishre 5707* (Jerusalem: n.p., 1947), 6–7.

20. Marrus, "The Vatican and the Custody of Jewish Child Survivors," 393.

21. See www.vaticanfiles.net/PTWF for copies of the documents in question. Marrus does a good job of explaining the media controversy generated by the discovery of the directives in French diocesan archives in 2004. See Marrus, "The Vatican and the Custody of Jewish Child Survivors."

22. The controversy began when the Italian historian Alberto Melloni published excerpts of and commentary on the directives. See his "Pio XII a Roncalli: Non restituite i bimbi ebrei," *Corriere della Sera*, December 28, 2004.

23. See Maritain's "A Propos de la Question Juive," in *Oeuvres Completes*, vol. 2, 1196–1203.

24. See *Cahiers Jacques Maritain*, 4, no. 2, "L'Ambassade au Vatican" (June 1982), 91–96.

25. Maritain's letter to Montini, dated July 12, 1946, has been published and widely circulated. See *Cahiers Jacques Maritain*, "Note Addressée à Monseigneur Montini (1946)," 23 (October 1991): 31–32. The most succinct and instructive analysis of the Maritain-Montini exchange is Michael R. Marrus, "A Plea Unanswered: Jacques Maritain, Pope Pius XII and the Holocaust," in *Jews, Catholics and the Burden of History*, ed. Eli Lederhendler (New York: Oxford University Press, 2005), 3–11. A briefer analysis can be found in Marrus, "The Ambassador and the Pope: Pius XII, Jacques Maritain and the Jews," *Commonweal*, October 22, 2004, 14–19.

26. Marrus, "The Ambassador and the Pope," 17.

27. W. H. Lawrence, "Poles Declare Two Hoaxes Caused High Toll in Pogrom," *New York Times*, July 6, 1946, 1–2.

28. Marrus, "The Ambassador and the Pope," 18.

29. Kubowitzki, "The Silence of Pope Pius XII," 24.

30. The claim was from Tardini and passed along to the Taylor mission in March 1945. See Taylor to the Secretary of State, "Asylum Given to Jews by the Catholic Clergy during the German occupation of Rome," March 26, 1945, RG 59, Taylor file, Entry 1068, Box 9.

31. The official text of the pope's message to the Arab delegation was published in AAS—Commentarium Officiale, 1946, Series 2, vol. 8, 322–323.

32. Cited by David Dalin, "Pius XII and the Jews," in *The Pius War: Responses to the*

Critics of Pius XII, ed. J. Bottum and David G. Dalin (Lanham, MD: Lexington Books, 2004), 22.

33. See Zolli's memoir, *Before the Dawn: Autobiographical Reflections* (New York: Sheed and Ward, 1954).

34. Quoted by Friedländer in *Pius XII and the Third Reich,* and reproduced here from the interview with Leiber for *Look* magazine, April 17, 1966, 46. A copy of the original is in Pius XII to Bishop Preysing, Vatican, April 30, 1943, ADSS, vol. 2, no. 105, 318–327.

35. A part of the pope's address was translated by Harold Tittmann, Taylor's assistant, who reported to the State Department about the pope's meeting with this and other Jewish delegations in the fall of 1945. See Tittmann to Secretary of State, Vatican City, November 30, 1945, RG 59, Taylor File, Entry 1068, Box 9. See Pius XII's encyclicals on the situation in Palestine, especially *In Multiplicibus Curis,* "On Prayers for Peace in Palestine," October 24, 1948, and *Redemptoris Nostri Cruciatus,* "On the Holy Places in Palestine," April 15, 1949.

36. For Roncalli diary entry, dated October 10, 1941, see Alberto Melloni, *Fra Istanbul, Atene e la guerra. La missione di A. G. Roncalli (1935–1944)* (Genova: Marietti, 1993), 240; on Frings, see ADSS, vol. 2, no. 119, 365. Frings also provided some insightful testimony in the deposition for Pacelli's canonization cause.

37. Meir Michaelis, "Christians and Jews in Fascist Italy," in *Judaism and Christianity under the Impact of National Socialism,* ed. Otto Dov Kulka and Paul R. Mendes-Flohr (Jerusalem: Historical Society of Israel and Zalmn Shazar Center for Jewish History, 1987), 271–298.

38. The Harvey-Osborne exchange is part of a thin but revealing file in "Pope's attitude towards Nazism and Fascism," March 25, 1947, FO 371/67917C, Z3056/199/57; Harvey's letter was dated March 4, 1947, also in FO, 371/67917C.

39. D. G. Osborne, "Holy See Personalities Report," July 1945, in FO 371/50092.

40. D. G. Osborne, March 1947, in FO 371/67917C. Osborne's letter to the editor of *The Times* was published under the title "Pope Pius XII and Germany," on May 20, 1963, 7.

41. See De Gaulle, *War Memories: Unity, 1942–1944* (London: Wiedenfeld and Nicolson, 1956). This excerpt is translated in Blet, *Pius XII and the Second World War,* 247–248.

42. Chenaux, *Pie XII,* 342. For more general considerations, see Chenaux, *Une Europe vaticane? Entre le Plan Marshall et les Traités de Rome* (Brussels: Editions Ciaco, 1990).

43. See Franklin C. Gowen report to Secretary of State, January 21, 1946, reporting on newspaper accounts related to the relationship between the Vatican, the American hierarchy, and the United States, in RG 59, Taylor File, Entry 1068, Box 13.

44. Some interesting reports were produced for the OSS on the basis of intelligence information gathered by sometimes dubious informants who claimed a privileged access to the Vatican. As a result, most of the OSS reports have to be taken with a grain of salt, although these assessments of the pope's inner circle and the workings of his office can generally be corroborated by other reliable sources. See, for instance, an OSS report produced in October–November 1944, from Rome, dated November 22, 1944, subject title "Opinions and Activities at the Vatican," in RG 226, Series 16, Box n/a; and a report from Vincent J. Scamporino, Chief, Italian Division, SI, MEDTO, to Whitney H. Shepardson, Chief, SI, Washington, and Earl Brennan, Chief, Italian Section, SI, February 9, 1945, RG 226, Entry 190, Box 163, File No. 1165. Scamporino's report seems, in the main, reliable and consistent with corroborating documentary evidence.

45. The British representative to the Holy See in the mid-1950s, Sir Douglas Howard, recalled how the absence of a secretary of state "contributed to a certain sense of isolation and frustration" among the foreign diplomatic corps at the Vatican. The French ambassador d'Ormesson complained that the absence of even a nominal secretary of state meant reduced access to the pope's inner circle. D'Ormesson and Howard are quoted by Anthony Rhodes, *The Vatican in the Age of the Cold War, 1945–1980* (Norwich: M. Russell, 1992), 230–231; d'Ormesson's note to AMAE is cited in Chenaux, *Pie XII*, 407 (see n. 5), while the original memo is in AMAE, Europe, Saint-Siège, serie 26, dated February 12, 1954.

46. See Mons. Ambrogio Marchioni in *Positio Summ.*, Pars I, 504–507.

47. These claims are made in Rhodes, *The Vatican in the Age of the Cold War*, 231. See also Mons. Ambrogio Marchioni in *Positio Summ.*, Pars I, 504–507. On Father Leiber's recollections, see Pierre Blet's deposition to the *Positio Summ.*, Pars I, 502–503.

48. So said Van Hoek in Kees Van Hoek, *Pope Pius XII—Priest and Statesman* (New York: Philosophical Library, 1944), part of which was published in the *Washington Post*, April 10, 1950, 9B.

49. Leiber interview with Father Colman Barry, O.S.B., biographer of Cardinal Muench, recorded in Rome, November 18, 1963, in ACUA, Muench Papers, Series 13: Biography, Box 60, Folder 4, 10.

50. "Religion: The Supreme Realist," *Time*, July 6, 1962.

51. The conspicuous German influence over Pius XII was the subject of commentary in the Italian press and subsequently by American officials at the Taylor mission. See a report by J. Graham Parsons, Foreign Service Office at the Taylor mission, commenting on an article that appeared in a Left-leaning Italian newspaper on August 6, 1947, under the title "Too Many Germans around the Pope—Pasqualina, Liebner [*sic*], Bea." In report from Parsons to the Secretary of State, dated August 13, 1947, RG 59, Entry 1068, Box 17.

52. Vincent J. Scamporino, Chief, Italian Division, SI, MEDTO, to Whitney H. Shepardson, Chief, SI, Washington, and Earl Brennan, Chief, Italian Section, SI, February 9, 1945, RG 226, Entry 190, Box 163, File No. 1165, p. 3.

53. So recorded Lombardi in his diary entry dated April 19, 1952, reproduced in Andrea Riccardi, *Pio XII e Alcide De Gasperi: una storia segreta* (Rome: Laterza, 2003), 95.

54. The account of this stormy meeting, which is well known to students of postwar Italian history, is recounted in various sources, including in primary documents such as Lombardi's diaries and the memoirs of De Gasperi family members. See Giancarlo Zizola, *Il microfono di Dio: Pio XII, padre Lombardi e i cattolici italiani* (Milan: Mondadori, 1990), 95, 300–305; and Maria Romana Catti De Gasperi, *De Gasperi, uomo solo* (Milan: Mondadori, 1964), 327–328.

55. Suzanne Brown-Fleming, *The Holocaust and Catholic Conscience: Cardinal Aloisius Meunch and the Guilt Question in Germany* (Notre Dame, IN: University of Notre Dame Press, 2006), 21.

56. Leiber interview with Father Barry Colman, ACUA—Muench Papers, Series 13, Box 60, Folder 4.

57. ACUA, Muench Papers, Series 13: Biography, Box 60, Folder 2. The folder includes a letter from Mother Pascalina to Muench, dated April 10, 1949, which speaks to the nature of Lehnert's practical influence over the distribution of material aid.

58. ACUA, Muench Papers, Series 1, Papers, Diaries, Reminiscences, and Notebooks. Diary, vol. 21, 1955–1957, Box 1, Folder 1, 9.

59. Pius XII was saying as much even before the war was over. See for instance his Christmas Eve sermon from December 24, 1945, in AAS, no. 1 (January 23, 1946): 15–25.

60. ACUA, Muench Papers, Series 1, Papers, Diaries, Reminiscences, and Notebooks. Diary, vol. 4, 06/19/1946 to 10/23/1946, Entry for July 12, 1946.

61. Brown-Fleming, *Holocaust and Catholic Conscience*, 21. Colman Barry's biography of Muench was published as *American Nuncio: Cardinal Aloisius Muench* (Collegeville, MN: Saint John's University Press, 1969).

62. ACUA, Muench Papers, Series 1, Papers, Diaries, Reminiscences, and Notebooks. Diary, vol. 4, 06/19/1946 to 10/23/1946, Entry for July 12, 1946.

63. Muench Diary, vol. 11: 10/9/1948 to 05/16/1948, Entry for October 25, 1948.

64. Muench Diary, vol. 11, Entry for November 7, 1948.

65. Quoted in Andrea Riccardi, *Il Potere del Papa da Pio XII a Giovanni Paolo II* (Rome: Laterza, 1993), 89.

66. Some useful insights into Pius XII's anxiety over possible Communist electoral inroads in Italy are provided by Luigi Gedda's unedited memoirs, *18 aprile 1948: Memorie inedited dell'artefice della sconfitta del Fronte popolare* (Milan: Mondadori, 1998), especially ch. 16.

67. See the deposition given by Giulio Pacelli, recounting this story, at T. XXXVIII, *Positio Summ.*, Pars I, 412.

68. See Robert A. Ventresca, *From Fascism to Democracy: Culture and Politics in the Italian Election of 1948* (Toronto: University of Toronto Press, 2004), 179–180. Secret memo from Griffis to State Department and AMVAT, dated July 31, 1947, in RG 59 Taylor Papers, Entry 1068, Box 17. The Taylor file at NARA contains a number of documents pertaining to Vatican communication with U.S. officials over allegations of persecution of Catholics in places like Albania and Yugoslavia. See, for instance, Franklin C. Gowen's report filed with the State Department, describing an oral report he received from Tardini, dated January 9, 1947, in RG 59, Entry 1068, Box 17.

69. The pope's speech has been widely quoted, including by Angelo Ventrone, *La cittadinanza repubblicana: Forma-partito e identità nazionale alle origini della democrazia italiana, 1943–1948* (Bologna: Il Mulino, 1996), 267.

70. This is quoted in Peter C. Kent, *The Lonely Cold War of Pope Pius XII: The Roman Catholic Church and the Division of Europe, 1943–1950* (Montreal: McGill-Queen's University Press, 2002), 238–239. The original is at the U.S. National Archives, RG 59, File 866A.001/2–2849, Dunn (Holy See), February 28, 1949.

71. For the official text, see AAS, 41 (1949), 334; cf. the *Documents Pontificaux*, 1949, 249–250.

72. Arguably the most useful analysis to date of the so-called Roman party is Andrea Riccardi, *Il "Partito Romano" nel secondo dopoguerra (1945–1954)* (Brescia: Morcelliana, 1983).

73. For further context on Pius XII's relationship with the so-called *partito romano*, see, among others, Ventresca, *From Fascism to Democracy*, 180; Chenaux, *Pie XII*, 345; Riccardi, *Il Potere del Papa*, 66. For a useful general survey of Vatican-Italian dynamics in the early Cold War, see John Pollard, "The Vatican, Italy and the Cold War," in *Religion and the Cold War*, ed. Diane Kirby, 103–117 (Houndsmill, UK: Palgrave Macmillan, 2003). For an interesting analysis of President Truman's use of religion in his "Cold War campaign" to get Americans out of isolationism at a delicate moment in the postwar era, see Diane Kirby, "Harry Truman's Religious Legacy: The Holy Alliance, Containment and the Cold War," in Kirby, ed., *Religion and the Cold War*, 77–102.

74. So says Francesco Malgeri in his Introduction to the correspondence between De Gasperi and Luigi Sturzo: *Luigi Sturzo–Alcide De Gasperi, Carteggio (1920–1953)*, ed. Francesco Malgeri (Soveria Mannelli, Italy: Rubbettino, 2006), xx–xxi, and see letters nos. 73 and 115.

75. See Ventresca, *Fascism to Democracy*, 184, n. 22.

76. See *Luigi Sturzo-Alcide De Gasperi*, xxvi–xxvii; and letter no. 128, De Gasperi to Sturzo, October 26, 1945; and no. 130, Sturzo to De Gasperi, December 3, 1945.

77. See Luigi Sturzo, "The Vatican's Position in Europe," *Foreign Affairs* 23 (January 1945): 211–221.

78. So argues Riccardi, *Pio XII e Alcide De Gasperi*, 21–22.

79. See the conversation between Mario Cingolani, a former member of the Italian Popular Party and later Christian Democratic parliamentarian, and Pius XII, October 17, 1951; notes in the De Gasperi papers and printed in Augusto D'Angelo, *De Gasperi, le destre e l'operazione Sturzo'. Voto amministrativo del 1952 e progetti di riforma elettorale* (Rome, 2002), 20–21. The exchange is discussed also in Andrea Riccardi's small but revealing book *Pio XII e Alcide De Gasperi*, 8–9.

80. The conversation is recounted in Riccardi, *Pio XII e Alcide De Gasperi*, 20, who in turn draws on Giancarlo Zizola's study of Lombardi, *Il microfono di Dio. Pio XII, padre Lombardi e I cattolici italiani* (Milan, 1990), 271. Parts of Lombardi's diary have been reprinted in Riccardi, *Pio XII e Alcide De Gasperi*, 93–98.

81. See Riccardi, *Pio XII e Alcide De Gasperi*, 26.

82. Ibid., 29–30.

83. Pavan's meetings with De Gasperi were reported on by officials at the Vatican's Secretariat of State. The originals remain closed within the Vatican Secret Archives, but copies were made available to the Italian historian Andrea Riccardi and reproduced in full in the appendix to *Pio XII e Alcide De Gasperi*, 71–98.

84. Colloquio Con Alcide De Gasperi Su Mandato di Sua Eccellenza Tardini a Nome del Santo Padre, 5 dicembre 1951, in Riccardi, *Pio XII e Alcide De Gasperi*, 72–73.

85. Riccardi, *Pio XII e Alcide De Gasperi*, 78.

86. See Giulio Andreotti's version of events, in which the pope was persuaded by Andreotti and other Christian Democrats that talk of an alliance with the parties of the Right or a Catholic bloc as alternative to the Christian Democrats was dangerous, in Andreotti, *A ogni morte di papa. I papi che ho conosciuto* (Milan: Rizzoli, 1980), 44–47; see also Giulio Andreotti, "Nell'anniversario di De Gasperi. Note sulla Operazione Sturzo," in *Concretezza*, August 16, 1965. A useful summary of all this is in Riccardi, *Pio XII e Alcide De Gasperi*, 25–29.

87. The episode is recounted in many different sources, including in the book by De Gasperi's daughter Maria Romana Catti De Gasperi, *De Gasperi: un uomo solo;* see also Riccardi, *Pio XII e Alcide De Gasperi*, 60–62. This quote is translated from "Pio XII contro De Gasperi," *La Repubblica*, December 28, 2005, 41.

88. Quoted in Riccardi, *Pio XII e Alcide De Gasperi*, 86–87. The dossier detailing this second meeting was titled "Conversazione Alcide De Gasperi—Mons. Pavan," at Villetta De Gasperi—Borgo di Valsugana, August 13, 1952, in *Pio XII e Alcide De Gasperi*, 81–87.

89. See NARA—RG 59, Taylor file for Parsons memo of a conversation with Montini, November 7, 1947, in Entry 1068, Box 15, loc. 250/48/29/01–05.

90. Writing to Truman in August 1947, the pope praised the great generosity and

charity of the American people toward "the suffering and the oppressed around the world." Pius XII saw in this generosity a testament to America's "Christian traditions and its commitment to universal peace and prosperity." Pius XII to Harry S Truman, August 26, 1947, in *Atti e discorsi di Pio XII* (Roma: Edizioni Paoline, 1942–1958), vol. 9, 235–238.

91. Sturzo, "The Vatican's Position in Europe," *Foreign Affairs* 23 (January 1945): 211–221.

92. See also Chenaux, *Pie XII,* 345. See also Ennio Di Nolfo, "Le Vatican, Les Etats-Unis et les debuts de la guerre froide," *Relations internationals* 28 (Summer 1981): 395–412; A. Acerbi, "Pio XII e l'ideologia dell'Occidente," in *Pio XII,* ed. Riccardi, 149–178 (Rome: Laterza, 1985). Arguably the best overview of the Vatican's policies vis-à-vis Eastern and Central Europe is Hansjakob Stehle, *Eastern Politics of the Vatican, 1917–1979* (Athens: Ohio University Press, 1981); see also Riccardi, *Il Vaticano e Mosca (1940–1990)* (Rome: Laterza, 1992).

93. See "Text of the Pope's Christmas Address on Attaining Real Peace," *New York Times,* December 25, 1951, 4.

94. So argues Peter C. Kent, "The Lonely Cold War of Pius XII," in Kirby, ed., *Religion and the Cold War,* 67–76, here at 71. A fuller and authoritative treatment is offered in Kent, *The Lonely Cold War of Pope Pius XII,* where he talks about the "impossibility" of Vatican neutrality. See ch. 15.

95. Kent, *The Lonely Cold War of Pope Pius XII,* 220.

96. A useful, concise summary is provided in Kent, *The Lonely Cold War of Pope Pius XII,* ch. 18. See, too, Andrea Riccardi, *Il Vaticano e Mosca,* especially chaps. 3 and 4.

97. Kent, *The Lonely Cold War of Pope Pius XII.*

98. Wyszynski testimony is in *Positio Summ.,* Pars II, 580–583. Even though he is critical of Pius XII's hard-line stance, Peter Kent acknowledges that by the second half of 1948, the pope's stance and that of the bishops "enhanced the stature of the pope and the east European hierarchy as they struggled alone against determined opponents." See Kent, *The Lonely Cold War of Pius XII,* 220.

99. Kent, *The Lonely Cold War of Pius XII,* 250.

100. See Wyszynski's testimony in *Positio Summ.,* Pars II, 580–583. See also Chenaux, *Pie XII,* 372, n. 1.

101. Wyszynski in *Positio Summ.,* Pars II, 574–577.

102. Pius XII, Apostolic Letter, *Cupimus Imprimis,* "On the Catholic Church in China," January 18, 1952. Chenaux sees the address to the Russian people in similar terms as discussed in Chenaux, *Pie XII,* 368.

103. So claimed the controversial and dubious Galeazzi-Lisi in his memoirs, *Dans L'Ombre et dans La Lumière de Pie XII* (Paris: Flammarion, Éditeur, 1960), 85.

104. The full story of the Holy See's massive relief and reconstruction efforts has yet to be told. The Vatican has published the bulk of its archives related to the

Vatican's Information Office for Prisoners-of-War, which is an important starting point. See *Inter Arma Caritas: L'Ufficio Informazioni Vaticano Per I Prigionieri di Guerra Istituto da Pio XII (1939–1947)*, 2 vols. (Vatican City: Vatican Secret Archives, 2004).

105. For some context, see Gerald Steinacher, "'The Cape of Last Hope': The Postwar Flight of Nazi War Criminals through South Tyrol/Italy to South America," in *Transatlantic Relations: Austria and Latin America in the 19th and 20th Centuries*, ed. Klaus Eisterer and Günter Bischof (Innsbruck: StudienVerlag, 2006), 204–224. A fuller treatment is provided in Steinacher, *Nazis on the Run: How Hitler's Henchmen Fled Justice* (Oxford: Oxford University Press, 2011).

106. That the Vatican ratlines were among the most important is an argument advanced in Christopher Simpson, *Blowback: The First Full Account of America's Recruitment of Nazis and Its Disastrous Effect on Our Domestic and Foreign Policy* (New York: Wiedenfeld and Nicolson, 1988), 176.

107. This is from the much-discussed "La Vista Report," prepared by Vincent La Vista to Herbert J. Cummings, filed May 15, 1947, in RG 59, Box 4080, located 250/36/29/02.

108. See Parsons to Dowling, August 13, 1947, RG 59, Box 59 [250/48/29/01–05]; quoted in Michael Phayer, *Pius XII, the Holocaust and the Cold War* (Bloomington: Indiana University Press, 2008), 243.

109. Osborne writing to Ernest Bevin, January 31, 1947, in FO 67371/R1768; part of the FO Yugoslavia File, No. 97, 1540–2394.

110. See the text of an oral message Parsons delivered to Monsignor Walter Carroll of the Vatican's Secretariat of State, with a cover letter to Walter C. Dowling dated August 29, 1947. This document was published by the Weisenthal Report on ratlines, taken from what appears to be RG 59, file 800—Emigration, Illegal into Italy. See also Osborne's report to Ernest Bevin on January 31, 1947, in FO 67371/R1768, part of the PRO-FO Yugoslavia File, No. 97, 1540–2394, where the British representative to the Holy See reports on his discussions with Monsignor Carroll, who was closely involved in the Vatican's many relief activities.

111. See Parsons's cover letter to Dowling, August 29, 1947.

112. For a sense of decisive American aid to the work of the PCA, see A. Giovagnoli, "La Pontificia Commissione d'Assistenza e gli aiuti americani (1945–1948)," *Storia Contemporanea* 9 (1978): 1081–1111.

113. Graham was interviewed and quoted by Mark Aarons and John Loftus in their highly entertaining if at times questionable book *Ratlines: How the Vatican's Nazi Networks Betrayed Western Intelligence to the Soviets* (London: Heinemann, 1991), 89.

114. Muench diary, ACUA, vol. 6, Entry for September 11, 1947.

115. For Phayer's claims, see his *Pius XII, the Holocaust and the Cold War*, 153–154. Here, again, Phayer draws heavily on a few intelligence reports—without apparently

questioning their veracity or reliability—which included an apparent meeting in 1944 between Pius XII and Prince Ruprecht of the deposed Bavarian Wittelsbach dynasty. See OSS reports from December 7, 1944, RG 226, Entry 210, Box 369 [250/64/28/06], for example.

116. Sturzo, "The Vatican's Position in Europe," *Foreign Affairs,* 211–221, here at 216–217.

117. On Eichmann's escape from Europe via Italy, with the perhaps unwitting assistance of Father Anton Weber and the Saint Raphael Society—an organization intended to facilitate the migration of Jewish converts to Catholicism since the 1930s—see David Cesarini, *Becoming Eichmann: Rethinking the Life, Crimes, and Trial of a "Desk Murder"* (Essex, UK: Da Capo Press, 2004), 207–209.

118. For a detailed description of Draganović's role in the so-called Italian ratline, see a 1950 report from Paul E. Lyon, IB Operations Officer, titled "History of the Italian Ratline," April 10, 1950. Discussion of the contents and significance of the Lyon report can be found in Allan A. Ryan Jr., Special Assistant to the Attorney General, Criminal Division, U.S. Department of Justice, *Klaus Barbie and the United States Government: A Report to the Attorney General of the United States,* August 1983. See also Phayer, *Pius XII, the Holocaust and the Cold War,* 220–221. On Draganović's being asked to leave St. Jerome, see Information Report, Subject: "The Priest Krunoslav Draganovic being asked to leave the College of St. Jerome of the Illirici," CIA Operational Files, December 11, 1958. For an early American intelligence assessment of Draganović, see RG 226 Intelligence Report, May 10, 1945, Entry A1–86, Box 12. Also, for more general background information on Draganović, see Norman J. W. Goda, "The Ustasa: Murder and Espionage," in *U.S. Intelligence and the Nazis,* ed. Richard Breitman, Norman J. W. Goda, Timothy Naftali, and Robert Wolfe (Cambridge University Press, 2005).

119. Phayer, *Pius XII, the Holocaust and the Cold War,* 231.

120. Uki Goni, *The Real Odessa: Smuggling the Nazis to Perón's Argentina* (London: Granta, 2002), 328.

121. See Report of Special Agent Robert C. Mudd, September 5, 1947, Entry 134B, RG 319; and Special Report of Special Agent Robert C. Mudd, n. d. entry A1–86, Box 12, RG 262.

122. FO 371/59423, R 17406/58/92, December 2, 1946. The advisor's letter, which is contained in the general file, was dated November 21, 1946.

123. Byrnes to Murphy, January 2, 1946, in *FRUS,* 1946, 5:794.

124. See ACUA, Muench Papers, Series 7, Liaison Consultant OMGUS, 1946–1959, Box 40, Folder 33, for a petition related to Weizsäcker's case.

125. Tittmann to Ambassador Robert D. Murphy, U.S. Political Advisor for Germany, July 21, 1945 and July 26, 1945, in RG 59, Taylor Papers, Entry 1068, Box 7, Folder 711, "German Diplomats in V.C."

126. See Dunn's report to Secretary of State Marshall, as cited by Phayer, *Pius XII, the*

Holocaust and the Cold War, 162; see Dunn to Marshall, October 29, 1948, RG 59, Entry 1071, Box 30 [250/48/29/01–05].

127. Tittmann acted as intermediary to have Dostler's plea for clemency delivered to the pope and then to transmit the pope's request to the State Department. See Tittmann's memo from Vatican City, December 3, 1945, in RG 59, Myron Taylor File, Entry 1068, Box 8. For a text of the trial transcript, see *Law Reports of Trials of War Criminals, the U.N. War Crimes Commission,* vol. 1 (London: HMSO, 1949); available online at www.ess.uwe.ac.uk/wcc/dostler.htm. For the pope's appeals to the Italian government on behalf of former Fascists facing death sentences from Italian tribunals, see Gowen to Sec. State James F. Byrnes, Vatican, January 9, 1946, RG 59, Myron Taylor File, Entry 1068, Box 13. For an appeal on behalf of the Italian General Umberto Presti, Commanding Officer of the Corpo di Polizia dell'Africa Italiana, see RG 59, Myron Taylor File, Entry 1068, Box 7. The relevant documentation is from September to November 1944. For an appeal on behalf of four Italian nationals condemned by U.S. military tribunals, see RG 59, Myron Taylor File, Entry 1068, Box 26, folder 321.6, "Appeal of Holy See in Behalf of War Criminals."

128. Phayer points out that the pope issued a call for "blanket clemency" for prisoners in Landsberg prison. This would have included men like Oswald Pohl, who, Phayer notes, was involved in the organization and operation of death camps, and Otto Ohlendorf, implicated in one of the SS *Einszatgruppen,* and Dr. Hans Eisele, responsible for the deaths of some 1,000 people. See Phayer, *Pius XII, the Holocaust and the Cold War,* 161–163. According to Suzanne Brown-Fleming, Muench counseled the Vatican against intervening on behalf of Ohlendorf, despite earlier interventions by the Holy See on behalf of men imprisoned at Landsberg. See Brown-Fleming, *The Holocaust and Catholic Conscience,* 95–98. The Muench Papers at ACUA contain several files related to the issue of war criminals and POWs and clemency appeals.

129. Quoted by Phayer, *Pius XII, the Holocaust and the Cold War,* 152; see original at NARA, Taylor to U.S. State Department, June 30, 1948, RG 59, Box 4012.

130. See Mark Mazower, *Hitler's Empire: How the Nazis Ruled Europe* (New York: Penguin Press, 2008), 346–347.

131. For primary documentation relating to the Croatian case, see ADSS, vol. 9, starting with a useful summary in the Introduction section of the volume at pages 32–34, with representative documentation at nos. 62, 98, 123, 126, 198, and 211.

132. On the Nedic suicide, see FO 371/59401, R2154/58/92, February 11, 1946. Allied authorities began to look seriously into Pavelić's whereabouts in early 1946, in response to Yugoslav demands that he be arrested and returned immediately to Yugoslav hands. Yugoslavian authorities initially believed that Pavelić was in British custody—imprisoned at Klagenfurt, Austria, which was in the British occupa-

tion authorities. At the time, the British Foreign Office did not know for certain whether this was true. See FO 371/59401, R2060/58/92, and R2096/58/92 for preliminary inquiries. Prompt denials that Pavelić was in British custody came quickly, as evident in the files contained in FO 371/59401, R 2234/58/92. The search for Pavelić even emerged publicly, in parliamentary question periods, for instance, in early 1946, which left British authorities to confess that they did not know where Pavelić was, but that they were making every effort to apprehend him.

133. By December 1946, the Holy See was also pleading the case of Archbishop Ivan Saric of Sarajevo. See Letter from the Vatican's Secretariat of State to Osborne, December 5, 1946, FO 371/59423, R18179/58/92.

134. FO 371/59401, R3014/58/92, February 25, 1946, and R3248/58/92, February 28, 1946. The American position on Rozman was communicated to the Foreign Office on February 28, 1946. See FO 371/59401, R3250/58/92, February 28, 1946.

135. FO 371/59401, R3385/58/42, March 4, 1946.

136. FO 371/59423, R17556/58/92, January 3, 1947. The men identified by Yugoslavia were Vladimir Velmar Jankovic, Dr. Milorad Redeljkovic, the engineer Miloslav Vasiljevic, Marisav Petrovic, and Dr. Ilya Vujovic. Yugoslav officials had compiled a lengthy list of "traitors and quislings," many of whom were in Italy in Allied military camps, principally at Eboli. See FO 371/59423, R18243/58/92, sent by the Yugoslavian Embassy in London to the Foreign Office around December 17, 1946. It is interesting to note that a few of the men on the longer list were believed to be in Rome and living on the Via della Conciliazione, in other words, very near the Vatican and presumably in Vatican properties. It is not clear why the five men believed to be at Saint Jerome College (described at times in this documentation as the *Collegio orientale,* or eastern College) were singled out for particular attention other than that Allied authorities realized that, if the men were in Vatican properties, there was little they could to secure their extradition to Yugoslavia for trial.

137. See reports of Yugoslav government's note to the Holy See, from early February 1947, asking about the whereabouts of the five so-called quislings presumed to be somewhere in Vatican territory, as well as about the work of the Pontifical Aid Commission and apparent assistance being procured for wanted war criminals, in FO 371/67371, R 1939/97/92, February 12, 1947.

138. FO 371/67370, R 166/97/92, January 27, 1947.

139. In addition, the institute where the former Ustaša were said to be staying was a Vatican property, not Vatican territory, so by virtue of the 1929 Lateran Accord (Annex 3), the property enjoyed certain privileges related to tax exemptions, but it did not enjoy the privilege of extraterritoriality; in short, this meant that it was conceivable that Allied authorities could forcibly search the property and arrest

the men in question. Osborne thought doing so would create "a most unfortunate impression" and so counseled from the start that the Yugoslav government be instructed to deal directly with the Vatican on the particular matter of these five men. See Dispatch from Osborne at Holy See to Foreign Office, October 16, 1946, FO 371/59420, R15293.

140. For primary documentation on the Stepinac trial, as seen through the lens of the Taylor mission, see RG 59, Myron Taylor papers, box 34, "Stepinac Case—1946," U.S. National Archives. For a succinct, excellent summary of Vatican-Yugoslavian relations in the immediate postwar period, and the role of the United States therein, see Charles R. Gallagher, "The United States and the Vatican in Yugoslavia, 1945–1950," in Kirby, ed., *Religion and the Cold War*, 118–144. Also indispensable to understanding the nature of Vatican-U.S. relations vis-à-vis Yugoslavia and the early Cold War is Gallagher, *Vatican Secret Diplomacy: Joseph P. Hurley and Pope Pius XII* (New Haven: Yale University Press, 2008).

141. FO 371/59423, R17586/58/92. Osborne's letter to the Foreign Office was dated November 28, 1946; M. S. Williams's response on behalf of the Foreign Office was dated January 3, 1947.

142. See FO, Aide-Mémoire, January 13, 1947, and Osborne to FO, January 16, 1947, in FO 371/67370 R1166.

143. Note the lawsuit filed against the Vatican bank and the Franciscan Order on assumption that Ustaša who hid at Saint Jerome College had with them looted gold, which they eventually funneled through the Vatican bank. See *Alperin v. Vatican Bank*, 2006 U.S. Dist. LEXIS 42902 (N.D. Cal., June 15, 2006); Reuben Hart (2006), "Property, War Objectives and Slave Labor Claims: The Ninth Circuit's Political Question Analysis in *Alperin v. Vatican Bank*, 36 Golden Gate U. L. Rev. 19; see *Orders of Friars Minor v. Alperin*, 126, S. Ct. 1141, 163, L. Ed., 2d 1000, 2006, U.S. Lexis, 774 (U.S. 2006); and *Istituto per le Opere di Religione v. Alperin*, 126 S. Ct. 1160, 163 L. Ed. 2d 1000, 2006 U.S. LEXIS 775 (U.S., 2006). For a more general consideration, see S. E. Eizenstat and W. Z. Slany, *Supplement to Preliminary Study on US and Allied Efforts to Recover and Restore Gold and Other Assets Stolen during World War II* (Washington, DC: Department of State, Bureau of Public Affairs, Office of the Historian, 1998).

144. FO 371/59423, R18024/58/92, which dealt with "Yugoslav quislings: search for Pavelić," December 18, 1946.

145. FO 371/67371, R1769/97/92, February 10, 1947, "Five Yugoslavs on Vatican Property: Exodus of Yugoslav War Criminals to S. America." Osborne's letter in this instance is addressed to Ernest Bevin, dated February 4, 1947.

146. These were the words of J. R. Colville writing in February 1947. See PRO FO 371/67371 R1769, February 10, 1947.

147. FO 371/67370, R1200/97/92, January 28, 1947.

148. See the correspondence between Victor Perowne—an expert on Argentina at the

British Foreign Office and eventual British representative to the Holy See—and the Foreign Office, FO, Perowne to Wallinger, November 18, 1947; Wallinger to Perowne, December 5, 1947, both in PRO-FO, 371/67401 R15533. The Dowling-Parsons exchange is dated May 22, 1947, in RG 59, Taylor Papers, Entry 1068, Box 17.

149. See John Moors Cabot to U.S. State Department, June 11, 1947, RG 59, Box 3623 [250/36/10/6], quoted by Phayer, *Pius XII, the Holocaust and the Cold War*, 237–238.

150. See Gowen's report to CIC HQ in Rome, September 12, 1947, in RG 319, Box 173, File IRR XE001109, Pavelić; quoted by Phayer, *Pius XII, the Holocaust and the Cold War*, 228.

151. David Alvarez, *Spies in the Vatican: Espionage and Intrigue from Napoleon to the Holocaust* (Lawrence: University Press of Kansas, 2002), 294–296.

152. Parsons to Dowling, July 26, 1947, in RG 59, Taylor Papers, Entry 1068, Box 17.

153. See Bernard J. Grennan, Special Counter Intelligence Corps Agent, Mediterranean Theater Chief of Operations to Supervising Intelligence Corp Agent of Zone 5, undated memorandum, Box 173, File IRR XE001109, Pavelić in RG 319 [270/84/1/4], as discussed in Phayer, *Pius XII, the Holocaust and the Cold War*, 228.

154. Phayer, *Pius XII, the Holocaust and the Cold War*, 227.

155. See the reports produced by CIC agent Paul E. Lyon and Charles Crawford in the late 1940s and 1950s, detailing the history of the Italian and Austrian ratlines. There is the Lyon-Crawford report from 430th CIC Detachment in Vienna, dated July 12, 1948, "Rat Line from Austria to South America"; and the more comprehensive report from Paul Lyon dated April 10, 1950, "History of the Italian Rat Line." These reports were declassified in the early 1980s and have been widely publicized and utilized; copies can be found in Klaus Barbie and U.S. Government and Exhibits, Appendix to the 1983 Report.

156. David Alvarez notes that just after World War II, the U.S. State Department prepared a detailed report on the Secretariat of State which concluded that, other than that of the USSR, no diplomatic service was as tightly controlled or as secretive as the Vatican's. See Alvarez, *Spies in the Vatican*, 295. The original is at the National Archives in College Park, MD, Memorandum by McFadden, December 5, 1947, box 17, Political-General, Record Group 59: State Department Records: Records of the Personal Representative of the President to Pope Pius XII; see also the memorandum by Parsons, May 22, 1948, box 19, Memoranda-Confidential also in the Taylor mission papers.

7. The Universal Pope

1. Jacques Maritain, "Impressions d'ensemble," in "L'Ambassade au Vatican, 1945–1948," *Cahiers Jacques Maritain*, 4, no. 2, June 1982, 91–96, here at 91.

2. Maritain, "Impressions d'ensemble," 94.

3. Pius XII, *Humani Generis*, "Concerning Some False Opinions Threatening to Undermine the Foundations of Catholic Doctrine," August 12, 1950, nos. 2–7.

4. Joseph A. Komonchak, "Theology and Culture at Mid-Century: The Example of Henri De Lubac," *Theological Studies* 51 (1990): 579–602.

5. Pius XII, *Humani Generis*, nos. 19–20.

6. Pius XII, *Humani Generis*, nos. 38–39. For an authoritative and revealing commentary on the implications of *Humani Generis* for biblical scholarship, see Augustin Bea, "L'Enciclica 'Humani Generis' e gli Studi Biblici," in *La Civiltà Cattolica*, 4, no. 2410 (November 11, 1950): 417–430.

7. This may explain why Jacques Maritain, then French ambassador at the Holy See, urged de Lubac to try to see Montini and Pius XII directly. There was reason to believe that the pope himself was not nearly as worried about the work of the French Jesuits as others in curial circles were. Regarding Maritain's advice, see the appendix to Henri de Lubac, *At the Service of the Church: Henri de Lubac Reflects on the Circumstances That Occasioned His Writings* (San Francisco: Communio Books, 1989), 251–252.

8. As quoted by John McGreevy, *Catholicism and American Freedom: A History* (New York: W. W. Norton, 2003), 207; Yves Congar, O.P., *Dialogue between Christians: Catholic Contributions to Ecumenicism*, trans. Philip Lortez, S.J. (Westminster, MD: Newman Press, 1966), 34.

9. So says McGreevy in *Catholicism and American Freedom*, 207, drawing on Etienne Fouillox, "Du role des theolgiens au debut de Vatican II: Un Point de vue romain," in *Cristianesimo nella storia: Saggi in onore di Giuseppe Alberigo*, ed. Alberto Melloni et al. (Bologna: Il Mulino, 1996), 289–290. For a more detailed analysis of the Courtney Murray case of the mid-1950s, see Joseph A. Komonchak, "Catholic Principle and the American Experiment: The Silencing of John Courtney Murray," *U.S. Catholic Historian* 17, no. 1 (Winter 1999): 28–44. John XXIII's reaction is described here by de Lubac, *At the Service of the Church*, 116–117.

10. Fergus Kerr, *Twentieth Century Catholic Theologians* (Malden, MA: Blackwell, 2007), chapter 5, which is devoted to Henri de Lubac. Fascinating insights are provided in de Lubac's own account of this period, including his dealings with Pius XII, in de Lubac, *At the Service of the Church*.

11. The Bea letter is cited in de Lubac, *At the Service of the Church*, 89–90.

12. Quoted by Rino Fisichella, "Di Fronte alla Modernità," in *In difesa di Pio XII: Le ragioni della storia*, a cura di Giovanni Maria Vian (Venice: Marsilio Editori, 2009), 94–95, here at 93.

13. Quoted by Schmidt, *Augustin Bea, the Cardinal of Unity* (New Rochelle, N.Y.: New City Press, 1992), 171, n. 57; original is reproduced in Pope Paul VI, *Insegnamenti di Paolo VI*, XIII (1975), 216.

14. Quoted by Fisichella, "Di Fronte alla Modernità," 94–95. For a more detailed

NOTES TO PAGES 275–278

summation of Montini's assessments of Pius XII's legacy, see Giovanni Battista Montini, "Su Pio XII," *Notiziario Istituto Paolo VI*, 17 (November 1998): 21–76. It is composed of various speeches, interviews, and other unedited documentation from Montini/Paul VI, essentially a measured *apologia* for Pius XII's pontificate.

15. Bea was made a cardinal by John XXIII the year after Pacelli died, and then in 1960 was appointed president of the newly established Secretariat for Promoting Christian Unity. Of special importance were Bea's contributions to the council's eventual declaration on Jews and Judaism, expressed authoritatively in the Nostra Aetate. See Augustin Bea, *The Church and the Jewish People* (New York: Harper and Row, 1966). For brief but insightful biographical descriptions of Bea's life and work, see L. K. Grimely's entry on Bea in *Twentieth Century Dictionary of Christian Biography*, ed. J. D. Douglas (Grand Rapids, MI: Baker Books; and Carlisle, Cumbria: Pater Noster Press, 1995), 48. See also Michael A. Fahey's entry on Bea in *Biographical Dictionary of Christian Theologians*, ed. Patrick W. Carey and Joseph T. Lienard (Westport, CT: Greenwood Press, 2000), 60. For a fuller explanation of Bea's assessment of Pius XII, culled largely from the cardinal's private papers, see Schmidt's biography *Augustin Bea*, here at 178–179, for Bea's commentary on Pius XII's legacy.

16. So wrote Bea in *The Unity of Christians* (New York: Herder and Herder, 1963), 206–207, quoted here by Schmidt, *Augustin Bea*, 171.

17. For a general survey of these encyclicals and their impact, see Eamon Duffy, *Saints and Sinners: A History of the Popes*, 3rd ed. (New Haven: Yale University Press, 2006), 350–351.

18. See Thomas A. Collins and Raymond E. Brown, "Church Pronouncements," in *The Jerome Biblical Commentary*, ed. Raymond E. Brown, Joseph P. Fitzmyer, and Roland O. Murphy (Englewood Cliffs: Prentice Hall, 1968), 625; an excellent review of the impact of the DAS can be found in Robert Bruce Robinson, *Roman Catholic Exegesis since Divino Afflante Spiritu: Hermeneutical Interpretations* (Atlanta: Scholars Press, 1988), see especially chapter 1.

19. J. F. Whealon, "Divino Afflante Spiritu," *New Catholic Encyclopedia*, vol. 4 (Washington, DC: Catholic University of America, 1967; reprinted 1971), 925–926.

20. Robinson, *Roman Catholic Exegesis*, 19. See also Keith D. Stephenson, "Roman Catholic Biblical Scholarship: Its Ecclesiastical Context in the Past Hundred Years," *Encounter* 33/34 (1972): 317–318. For original commentary by Bea, arguably the most important contributor to the DAS, see Bea, "Divino Afflante Spiritu," *Biblica* 24 (1943): 313–322.

21. In the words of the Polish-born French chemist Bernard Pullman, Pius XII realized that the church could not remain "indifferent," let alone passive, to the pioneering advances in physics of the day. Bernard Pullman, *The Atom in the History of Human Thought* (Oxford University Press, 2001), 317–321.

22. Pius XII, "Discorso di Sua Santità Pio XII Per L'Inaugurazione del VII Anno della Pontificia Accademia delle Scienze," February 21, 1943. Available at http://www .vatican.va/holy_father/pius_xii/speeches/1943/documents/hf_p-xii_spe_1943 0221_accademia-scienze_it.html. See the pope's Christmas 1955 message and the 1956 Easter message broadcast, excerpts of which are reprinted in Maurice Quinlan, ed., *Guide for Living: An Approved Selection of Letters and Addresses of His Holiness Pope Pius XII* (London: Evans Brothers, 1958).

23. See Tardini, *Pio XII* (Vatican City: Tipografia Poliglotta Vaticana, 1960), 60–61. See too the interesting and informative recollections of D. J. K. O'Connell, Director of the Vatican Observatory during Pius XII's time. O'Connell confirms Tardini's testimony here, insofar as he reiterates Pius XII's desire to achieve an above-average mastery of technical subjects but also the pope's conscientiousness in not posing as an authority. D. J. K. O'Connell, "Pius XII: Recollections and Impressions," *Studies: An Irish Quarterly Review* 47, no. 188 (Winter 1958): 361–368, here at 362.

24. Quoted in O'Connell, "Pius XII: Recollections and Impressions," 363 and 365. The first is from Pius XII's last address on the subject of astronomy, delivered May 20, 1957, at the opening of a conference on Stellar Populations sponsored by the Pontifical Academy of Sciences and the Vatican Observatory. The second statement was made in 1954 to the 10th General Assembly of the International Union of Geodesy and Geophysics in Rome.

25. Pius XII, "Alle Associazioni delle Famiglie numerose," November 26, 1951, Castel Gandolfo, Convegno del "Fronte della Famiglia" e "Associazione delle Famiglie Numerose," in *Pio XII: Discorsi ai Medici*, ed. S. E. Mons. Fiorenzo Angelini (Edizioni "Orizzonte Medico," 1959), 175–180.

26. Pius XII, "Alle Congressiste dell'Unione Cattolica Italiana Ostetriche," in Mons, ed., *Pio XII: Discorsi ai Medici*, 155–172, here at 162–163.

27. Ibid., 163.

28. Wenger's interview with Pius XII is recounted in Philippe Chenaux, *Pie XII: diplomate et Pasteur* (Paris: Cerf, 2003), 379.

29. The pope's inner circle, like Pius XII himself, was well aware of the criticism, as is evident in recollections by Bea, Tardini, and Leiber. For instance, see Schmidt, *Augustin Bea*, 172–173; O'Connell, "Pius XII: Recollections and Impressions," 362; and Tardini, *Pius XII*, 61–62.

30. See the encyclical *Orientales Ecclesias*, "On the Persecuted Eastern Church," December 15, 1952; the apostolic letter *Cupimus Imprimis*, "On the Catholic Church in China," January 18, 1952; and the encyclical *Ad Sinarum Gentum*, "On the Supranationality of the Church," October 7, 1952, which was addressed to the bishops, clergy, and people of China; see also the apostolic letter *Dum Maerenti Animo*, June 29, 1956, to Mindzenty, Stepinac, Wyszynski, and the hierarchy in Albania,

Bulgaria, Czechoslovakia, Hungary, Yugoslavia, Poland, Romania, "Eastern Germany," and other peoples of Europe "who enjoy peace and union with the Apostolic See," available in Latin at http://www.vatican.va/holy_father/pius_xii/apost_letters/documents/hf_p-xii_apl_19560629_dum-maerenti-animo_lt .html. A very useful collection containing English translations of select encyclicals, speeches, and letters from Pius XII is Quinlan, ed., *Guide for Living*.

31. John Courtney Murray, *The Problem of Religious Freedom* (Westminster, MD: Newman Press, 1965).

32. Pius XII issued several encyclicals pertaining to the situation in the Middle East, including *In Multiplicibus Curis*, "On Prayers for Peace in Palestine," October 24, 1948, and *Redemptoris Nostri Cruciatus*, "On the Holy Places in Palestine," April 15, 1949.

33. Pius XII, *Fidei Donum*, "On the Present Condition of the Catholic Missions, Especially in Africa," April 21, 1957; "The Universal Pope," *Life*, October 20, 1958, 34.

34. "The Pope on Colonialism," *America*, January 7, 1956, 390–391; *Ad Apostolorum Principis*, "On Communism and the Church in China," June 29, 1958, no. 6.

35. See, among Pius XII's many statements on these themes, his address to workers in Madrid and elsewhere in Spain, titled "Peace in Industry," March 11, 1951; to delegates of the International Labor Organization at Castel Gandolfo on November 20, 1954; and to some 30,000 delegates of the Young Christian Workers gathered in Rome on September 25, 1957, reproduced in Quinlan, ed., *Guide for Living*.

36. See Vesna Drapac, *War and Religion: Catholics in the Churches of Occupied Paris* (Washington, DC: Catholic University of America Press, 1998), 54. The original was published by the Saint-Philippe du Roule (VIII) parish in Paris, February 1940. As Drapac notes, a similar response can be found in other parish papers. For a small sample of contemporary commentary in the Catholic press on Pius XII's historic appointments, both international and at a local level, see "The Pope Consecrates 12 Bishops," *Commonweal*, November 10, 1939, 65; and "Pope Consecrates Twelve Mission Bishops," *Catholic Record* (London, Ontario, Canada), November 11, 1939.

37. "The Universal Pope," *Life*, October 20, 1958, 34.

38. "Religion: On the Roads to Rome," *Time*, February 18, 1946.

39. The full text of the speech, in Italian, is in the AAS, XXXVIII (1946), Series II, Vol. XIII, Num. 5 (April 1, 1946). See Allocutiones, "Saluto Ai Nuovi Cardinali," February 20, 1946, 141–151.

40. "The Universal Pope," *Life*, October 20, 1958, 34. For the text of Pius XII's address to Christians in India, which was delivered by radio in English on December 31, 1952, see AAS, XXXXV (1953), Series II, Vol. XII, Num. 2 (February 16, 1953), 96–99.

41. Ibid., 146–147.

42. Pascalina Lehnert, *Positio Summ.*, 90–91. Interestingly, the News Service of the National Catholic Welfare Conference of U.S. Catholic Bishops in Washington reported on comments made by Cardinal Tedeschini at Fatima, Portugal, to the effect that Pius XII had in 1950 seen the same "miracle of the sun" that thousands had claimed to see at Fatima decades before. The NCWC News Service tried to spin the story so as to qualify and minimize what Tedeschini reportedly said, while noting the Vatican's silence on the matter. See ACUA, NWCW, Office of the General Secretary, Box 22: Church: Vatican: Holy Father, Folder 9. For an insightful discussion of how Augustin Bea, the pope's confessor, reacted to the pope's visions, see Schmidt, *Augustin Bea,* 180–184.

43. Arnaldo Cortesi, "As the Catholic Church Prepares to Choose a New Leader," *New York Times,* October 12, 1958, E6; see also the unsigned "Pius Assigned Many Americans to Posts of Authority in Church," *New York Times,* October 9, 1958, 22.

44. Muench Diary, vol. 18: 05/23/1953 to 10/01/1953 at ACUA, entry for July 24, 1953.

45. Bea's correspondence is in his personal papers, N 1956/22 and N 1955/143, quoted by Schmidt, *Augustin Bea,* 168.

46. Muench Diary, vol. 19: 10/02/1953 to 02/23/1954, entry for October 19, 1953.

47. Muench Diary, vol. 20: 1954–1955, entry for February 24–28, 1954.

48. Muench diary, vol. 20: 1954–1955, entries for December 3 and 16, 1954.

49. Father Virginio Rotondo, S.J., *Positio Summ.,* 237.

50. Wilhelm Hentrich, *Positio Summ.,* 41.

51. "Pope's Survival Called Disappointment to Him," *New York Times,* December 25, 1955, 40.

52. Lehnert, *Positio Summ.,* 89.

53. Hentrich, *Positio Summ.,* 22.

54. Cardinal Nasalli Rocca, *Positio Summ.,* 472–477.

55. Hentrich, *Positio Summ.,* 19–27.

56. Cardinal Nasalli Rocca, *Positio Summ.,* 472–477; Cesidio Lolli, *Positio Summ.,* 276–278; Hentrich , *Positio Summ.,* 22.

57. "Vision Publicity Displeases Pope," *New York Times,* December 11, 1955, 34.

58. See Father Rotondi's version of events in *Positio Summ.,* 238–239. Father Rotondi eventually passed the story on to the Italian magazine *Oggi,* which published the account a year later, prompting news services around the world to report on the pope's alleged visions. The Vatican was compelled to respond publicly through its newspaper *L'Osservatore Romano* in December 1955. For a concise contemporary summary of the episode, see "The Pope's Vision," *The Tablet,* 206 (December 17, 1955), 617. According to the Muench diaries, it was Mother Pascalina who told a "Jesuit priest"—presumably Rotondi—about the visions, which were indeed to be kept secret. See Muench diary, vol. 20, entry for March 23, 1956.

59. See Tardini, *Pius XII,* 100–101.

60. Bea, quoted by Schmidt, *Augustin Bea*, 181; original is from Bea's correspondence, Nm. 3 (1955).

61. Quoted by Schmidt, *Augustin Bea*, 181; original is in Bea, N 1956/13.

62. Muench diary, vol. 21, entry for May 13, 1957.

63. See the report prepared by the NCWC News Service, "Step by Step Account of Pope's Final Days," *The New World*, October 17, 1958, 10, in ACUA, NCWC General Reference File: Hierarchy and Clergy; Pius XII.

64. "Plastic Surgeons Get Warning from Pope," *New York Times*, October 7, 1958, 6.

65. Galeazzi-Lisi was known as the "archiater"—which meant the first or chief physician; in this instance it was understood to mean that Galeazzi-Lisi was the pope's personal physician. See "Pope, Press and Archiater," in *Time*, November 3, 1958.

66. So surmised Carlo Pacelli in his testimonial for the beatification cause. See *Positio Summ.*, 227. See "Doctor Describes Illness of Pope," *New York Times*, October 12, 1958, 4.

67. "Rome's Catholics Pray for Pontiff," *New York Times*, October 7, 1958, 8; "Secret Proposal on Curia Reported Left by Pius XII," *New York Times*, October 17, 1958, 1, 5; "Cardinal Camerlengo: Benedetto Aloisi Masella," *New York Times*, October 10, 1958, 13.

68. See the special report from Rome by Arnaldo Cortesi, *New York Times*, October 8, 1958, 1, 3.

69. Carlo Pacelli, *Positio Summ.*, 232.

70. Paul Hofmann, "Rome Hears Toll of Bells for Pius," *New York Times*, October 9, 1958, 1.

71. So recalled Carlo Pacelli in *Positio Summ.*, 233.

72. Hofmann, "Rome Hears Toll of Bells for Pius," 1.

73. So reported Arnaldo Cortesi, "Pontiff 19 Years," *New York Times*, October 9, 1958, 1.

74. Paul Hofmann, "Curia Cardinals Rule Informally," *New York Times*, October 8, 1958, 3.

75. Hentrich, *Positio Summ.*, 44.

76. As reported in *Time*, "Pius XII, 1876–1958," October 20, 1958; and "Nun Takes Away Pope's Pet Birds," *New York Times*, October 11, 1958, 5.

77. Lehnert, *Positio Summ.*, 129.

78. See ibid., 128–129. The details regarding the last will and testament are confirmed by Carlo Pacelli's testimonial. See also reports of Cardinal Tisserant's role in "Will of Pope Asks Forgiveness of Any He May Have Hurt," *New York Times*, October 11, 1958, 1.

79. "Papers of Pius XII Discussed in Rome," *New York Times*, October 23, 1958, 8.

80. Arnaldo Cortesi, "Pius XII Is Borne to Vatican Bier; Crowds Line Way," *New York Times*, October 10, 1958, 1, 3; "Pius XII, 1876–1958," *Time*, October 28, 1958.

81. Paul Hofmann, "Mourners Visit Bier of Pius XII," *New York Times*, October 10,

1958, 1, 12; "Spellman Quits Ship and Flies to Rome to Pay His Homage," *New York Times,* October 10, 1958, 1, 12.

82. This according to Peter Hebblethwaite, *John XXIII: Pope of the Century* (London: Continuum, 1994), 132, on the basis of Roncalli's diary entry for October 11, 1958.

83. Carlo Pacelli, *Positio Summ.,* 233.

84. "Old Method Used to Embalm Pope," *New York Times,* October 14, 1958, 3.

85. From Milan's daily *Il Giorno,* quoted in "The Press: Pope, Press and Archiater," *Time,* November 3, 1958.

86. See the account of one eyewitness/participant, Giulio Bartoloni, as told to the Italian journalist and Pacelli biographer Andrea Tornielli, in "La tenda si mosse e il papa morì due volte," *Il Giornale,* November 14, 2001, and re-told in Tornielli, *Pio XII: Eugenio Pacelli: un uomo sul trono di Pietro* (Milan: Mondadori, 2007), 565– 567. See also "Pope, Press and Archiater," *Time,* November 3, 1958.

87. Various insiders claimed that Galeazzi-Lisi was responsible for the pictures. See, for instance, the testimonial of Monsignor Quirino Paganuzzi, *Positio Summ.,* 342.

88. See reports in the Roman daily *Il Tempo,* October 18 and 19, 1958; and Turin-based *La Stampa;* cross-reference reports in the American media, including detailed accounts by Paul Hofmann, "Vatican Rebukes Pope's Doctor for Selling Diary of Last Days," *New York Times,* October 19, 1958, 1; and "Pope, Press and Archiater," *Time,* November 3, 1958.

89. Paul Hofmann, "Pius XII's Doctor Resigns His Post," *New York Times,* October 21, 1958, 7; "Italy Investigates Pontiff's Physician," *New York Times,* October 20, 1958, 3; "Pius' Doctor is Barred from Practice in Italy," *New York Times,* December 13, 1958, B2.

Epilogue

1. "The Universal Pope," *Life,* October 20, 1958, 34.

2. "Pope Pius XII," *Wall Street Journal,* October 10, 1958, 10; "Pius XII," *New York Times,* October 9, 1958, 36; "Wyszynski Hails Pope as Anti-Totalitarian," *New York Times,* October 13, 1958, 3.

3. See the extensive coverage from the NCWC News Service, "U.S., Canadian Church Leaders Mourn Supreme Pontiff," *The New World,* October 17, 1958, 12.

4. See *Christian News from Israel* 9, no. 34, December 1958, quoted in Andrea Tornielli, *Pio XII: Il Papa degli Ebrei* (Edizioni Piemme, 2001), 29.

5. See Pinchas Lapide, *Roma e gli ebrei. L'azione del Vaticano a favore delle vittime del nazismo* (Milan: Mondadori, 1967), especially 304–305, for Jewish community praise of Pius XII; Toaff is quoted in the NCWC News Service report, "U.S., Canadian Church Leaders Mourn Supreme Pontiff," *The New World,* October 17, 1958, 12; see also Tornielli, *Pio XII: Il Papa degli Ebrei,* 28–31.

6. On prudence in the Aristotelian-Thomistic tradition, see Josef Pieper, *The Four Cardinal Virtues* (South Bend, IN: University of Notre Dame Press, 1990; orig. pub. 1966).

7. Ibid., 3–5.

8. As discussed in Chapter 6, the claim was made by Tardini and conveyed to the Taylor mission in March 1945; see Taylor to the Secretary of State, "Asylum Given to Jews by the Catholic Clergy during the German Occupation of Rome," March 26, 1945, RG 59, Taylor file, Entry 1068, Box 9.

9. Renzo De Felice, "Foreword" to Nicola Caracciolo, *Uncertain Refuge: Italy and the Jews during the Holocaust,* trans. and ed. Florette Rechnitz Koffler and Richard Koffler (Urbana: University of Illinois Press, 1995), xx; Mier Michaelis, *Mussolini and the Jews: German-Italian Relations and the Jewish Question in Italy, 1922–1945* (Oxford: Clarendon Press, 1978); Susan Zuccotti, *The Italians and the Holocaust: Persecution, Rescue, Survival* (New York: Basic Books, 1987); Martin Gilbert, *The Holocaust: A History of the Jews of Europe during the Second World War* (New York: Holt Paperbacks, 1987); and Gilbert, *The Righteous: The Unsung Heroes of the Holocaust* (New York: Holt Paperbacks, 2004), especially ch. 15, which deals with the Vatican and Italy; L. Picciotto, *L'occupazione tedesca e gli ebrei di Roma* (Rome: Carocci, 1979); and Piccotto, "The Shoah in Italy: Its History and Characteristics," in *Jews in Italy under Fascist and Nazi Rule, 1922–1945,* ed. J. D. Zimmerman (Cambridge: Cambridge University Press, 2005), 209–233.

10. A highly readable, comprehensive survey of the papacy is Eamon Duffy, *Saints and Sinners: A History of the Popes,* 3rd ed. (New Haven: Yale University Press, 2006).

11. The best study to date of Vatican finances, including the so-called American connection, is John F. Pollard, *Money and the Rise of the Modern Papacy: Financing the Vatican, 1850–1950* (Cambridge: Cambridge University Press, 2005).

12. "The Life of Pope Pius XII: Tradition and Modernity in the Vatican," *The Times,* October 10, 1958, 16.

13. John 10:16.

14. Jacques Maritain, "Impressions d'ensemble," in "L'Ambassade au Vatican, 1945–1948," *Cahiers Jacques Maritain,* 4, no. 2, June 1982, 91–96, here at 96.

15. Quoted in Stjepan Schmidt, *Augustin Bea: The Cardinal of Unity* (New Rochelle, NY: New City Press, 1992), 184–185. Original is in Bea's papers at the Jesuit headquarters in Munich, R 1959/60, 8, 5.

16. Schmidt, *Augustin Bea,* 185. Original is in Bea's correspondence, N 1959/79.

17. The remark may be apocryphal, but there are some credible sources to suggest it is accurate. See John Jay Hughes, review of *Bishop von Galen: German Catholicism and National Socialism* by Beth A. Griech-Polelle, *Catholic Historical Review* 89, no. 2 (April 2003): 321–325.

Acknowledgments

I would like to acknowledge a number of individuals and institutions whose assistance and encouragement helped me to complete this project. Like any historian, I am deeply indebted to numerous scholars whose work has informed and challenged my thinking. An equally profound debt is owed to the many archivists and librarians who facilitated access to the documentary record that is the stuff of historical research and writing. I want to thank in particular the staff of the Cardinal Carter Library at my home institution, King's University College at the University of Western Ontario, for their kindness and ingenuity in tracking down even the most obscure sources. Research funding, which made it possible to consult a wide array of foreign archives, was provided in part by grants from the Social Sciences and Humanities Research Council of Canada and from King's University College at the University of Western Ontario. My thanks to Phyllis Fidler, manager of general accounting at King's University College, for her diligent management of the grants, and for her time and assistance in helping to facilitate various aspects of this project.

I was fortunate to have a team of dedicated research assistants: Adriano Ciani, Cindy Brown, Sara Palmor, Nicolas Virtue, and Ashleigh Ross. A special word of gratitude goes to Carlotta Lemieux, who lent her vast knowledge and experience to offer a close, critical, and conscientious reading of an early draft of the manuscript. I also want to thank the anonymous readers of the manuscript for their many expert suggestions. In some instances, they have kept me from making embarrassing mistakes, but even more, their sage, collegial advice lent depth, breadth, and greater interpretive clarity to the project.

I cannot say enough about the invaluable work of my editors at Harvard University Press. From our earliest conversations about the idea to write a biography of Pius XII, Kathleen McDermott has been what every author hopes for in an editor—someone with creative vision as well as sound practical judgment, not to mention sensitivity to both the author's voice and the reader's ear. Christine Thorsteinsson's expert editing of the manuscript served as a humbling reminder of how much I have to learn about writing well. It is no mere cliché to say that Christine's careful work helped to make this a much better book. In short, I have learned a great deal from my editors about what makes for a good story and what constitutes good, accessible historical writing. Any failings on either count are entirely my own responsibility.

I have been fortunate to draw upon several sources not readily accessible to researchers. Notable in this regard is the *Position* (*Positio*) assembled under the auspices of the Vatican's Congregation for the Causes of the Saints to examine the cause to declare Eugenio Pacelli a saint. It consists of a multivolume collection of testimonials and other primary documentation related to Pacelli's life. Begun in the late 1960s, the *Position* was completed in 2004—the culmination of almost forty years of research and analysis. I traveled to Rome on several occasions beginning in 2007 to view these documents at the invitation of Father Peter Gumpel, S.J., the relator of the cause and, as such, one of the primary editors of the *Position*. I am grateful to Father Gumpel and Father Paolo Molinari, S.J., for their generosity in facilitating my independent study of these papers.

This book likely would never have been written without the decisive intervention of my colleague and good friend Rande Kostal. I owe Rande a special debt of gratitude for having the foresight to see merit in this project when other voices were urging different choices. Besides that, he is a scholar who leads by example and practices our craft to exacting standards: were it that we could all be like him. In a similar vein, I want to thank another fellow traveler, Peter Neary—a gentleman and a scholar, if ever there was one. Peter has been an enthusiastic promoter of this project from the start, a constant stimulus whenever inertia, exhaustion, or distraction appeared to tempt me. For his reading of very early drafts of the manuscript, for his many constructive suggestions, and for the warm hospitality over tea that Peter and his wife, Hilary, have shown me time and again, I am eternally grateful. In Rome, my cousin and dear friend Guglielmo Antonio Sciarra was a constant source of support and good company as I learned to survive the chaos and revel in the unique charm of the Eternal City. Numerous other colleagues and close friends have sustained me over the years through good conversation and great meals: Albert La France and Renée Soulodre-La France; Claudia Clausius, Murray Watson, and Graham Broad. To my in-laws, the Hamzo family of London, Ontario, a special word of thanks for your moral support and for helping to manage the home base during my frequent trips abroad, especially during the record snowfall of December 2010.

Finally, and above all, I thank my siblings—Annie, Carm, and Krista. Having gone through life enjoying an abundance of blessings, we have faced our share of hardships and losses these past few years. They have each in their own way inspired me with their strength and perseverance. As always, we are sustained by the resilience, sensibility, and devotion of our mother, Rita, who, along with the memory of our father, Domenico, keeps us together—and laughing. Now with little Nico around, these are better days.

No one deserves more credit than my wife, Yola. Without her support this book could never have been written. She has lived with Pius almost as long as I have. Doubtless, she felt at times that three really was a crowd; in fact, we often laughed about it. Her good humor, patience, and understanding—especially while I was abroad chasing archival ghosts—made it all possible, and bearable. This book, with much love, is for her.

Index